MW00679187

Fodor's

SHANGHAI

1st Edition

Where to Stay and Eat for All Budgets

Must-See Sights and Local Secrets

Ratings You Can Trust

Fodor's Travel Publications New York, Toronto, London, Sydney, Auckland
www.fodors.com

FODOR'S SHANGHAI
Editor: Felice Aarons, Shannon Kelly

Editorial Production: Bethany Cassin Beckerlegge
Editorial Contributors: Emmanuelle Alspaugh, Rachel King Berlin, Chris Horton, Heidi Johansen, Margaret Kelly, Lisa Movius, Elyse Singleton, David Taylor, Ada Yuan
Maps and Illustrations: Henry Columb and Mark Stroud, Moon Street Cartography; David Lindroth, Inc.; William Wu; Bob Blake and Rebecca Baer, *map editors*
Design: Fabrizio La Rocca, *creative director;* Guido Caroti, *art director;* Tina Malaney, Chie Ushio, *designers*; Melanie Marin, *senior picture editor*
Production/Manufacturing: Colleen Ziemba
Cover Photo (Nanjing Street): Alex Mares-Manton/Asia Images/Getty Images

First Edition

ISBN 978-1-4000-1745-4

ISSN 1934-5526

SPECIAL SALES
This book is available for special discounts for bulk purchases for sales promotions or premiums. Special editions, including personalized covers, excerpts of existing books, and corporate imprints, can be created in large quantities for special needs. For more information, write to Special Markets/ Premium Sales, 1745 Broadway, MD 6-2, New York, New York 10019 or e-mail specialmarkets@randomhouse.com.

AN IMPORTANT TIP & AN INVITATION
Although all prices, opening times, and other details in this book are based on information supplied to us at press time, changes occur all the time in the travel world, and Fodor's cannot accept responsibility for facts that become outdated or for inadvertent errors or omissions. So **always confirm information when it matters,** especially if you're making a detour to visit a specific place. Your experiences—positive and negative—matter to us. If we have missed or misstated something, **please write to us.** We follow up on all suggestions. Contact the Shanghai editor at editors@fodors.com or c/o Fodor's at 1745 Broadway, New York, New York 10019.

PRINTED IN THE UNITED STATES OF AMERICA

10 9 8 7 6 5 4 3 2 1

Be a Fodor's Correspondent

Your opinion matters. It matters to us. It matters to your fellow Fodor's travelers, too. And we'd like to hear it. In fact, we *need* to hear it.

When you share your experiences and opinions, you become an active member of the Fodor's community. That means we'll not only use your feedback to make our books better, but we'll publish your names and comments whenever possible. Throughout our guides, look for "Word of Mouth," excerpts of your feedback.

Here's how you can help improve Fodor's for all of us.

Tell us when we're right. We rely on local writers to give you an insider's perspective. But our writers and staff editors—who are the best in the business—depend on you. Your positive feedback is a vote to renew our recommendations for the next edition.

Tell us when we're wrong. We're proud that we update most of our guides every year. But we're not perfect. Things change. Hotels cut services. Museums change hours. Charming cafés lose charm. If our writer didn't quite capture the essence of a place, tell us how you'd do it differently. If any of our descriptions are inaccurate or inadequate, we'll incorporate your changes in the next edition and will correct factual errors at fodors.com *immediately.*

Tell us what to include. You probably have had fantastic travel experiences that aren't yet in Fodor's. Why not share them with a community of like-minded travelers? Maybe you chanced upon a restaurant or neighborhood that you don't want to keep to yourself. Tell us why we should include it. And share your discoveries and experiences with everyone directly at fodors.com. Your input may lead us to add a new listing or highlight a place we cover with a "Highly Recommended" star or with our highest rating, "Fodor's Choice."

Give us your opinion instantly at our feedback center at www.fodors.com/feedback. You may also e-mail editors@fodors.com with the subject line "Shanghai Editor." Or send your nominations, comments, and complaints by mail to Shanghai Editor, Fodor's, 1745 Broadway, New York, NY 10019.

You and travelers like you are the heart of the Fodor's community. Make our community richer by sharing your experiences. Be a Fodor's correspondent.

Bon voyage!

Tim Jarrell, Publisher

CONTENTS

CLOSEUPS

SHANGHAI IN FOCUS

China
RUSSIA
KAZAKHSTAN
Ozero Balkash
Uliastay
BISHKEK
Almaty
Yining
JUNGGAR PENDI
KYRGYZSTAN
Urümqi
Turpan
TIEN SHAN
Kashgar
GOBI
Dunhuang
TAKLIMAKAN PENDI
ALTUN SHAN
QILIAN SHAN
KARAKORAM
KUNLUN SHAN
QAIDAM PENDI
Qinghai Hu
Xining
KASHMIR
HIMALAYAS
NEW DELHI
Lancang
Yangzi
Nu
Lhasa
Shigates
Shegar
Gyantse
NEPAL
KATHMANDU
THIMBU
BHUTAN
Tiger Leaping George
Lijiang
Benares
Ganges
INDIA
BANGLADESH
Dali
INDIA
Ruili
Kunming
Calcutta
DHAKA
MYANMAR
Jinghong
Mandalay
Bay of Bengal
Irrawaddy
0
300 mi
0
300 km
LAOS
THAILAND

RUSSIA
Irkutsk
Ozero Baykal
Habarovsk
Chatanga
Hailar
Hulun Hu
DA HINGGAN LING
MANCHURIA
Qiqihar
ULAANBAATAR
Harbin
MONGOLIA
Vladivostok
Jilin
Changchun
CHANGBAI SHAN
Sea of Japan
DESERT
Shenyang
Fushun
NORTH KOREA
Anshan
Great Wall
Jining
Chengde
Hohhot
PYONGYANG
Baotou
Beidaihe
Shanhaiguan
Yellow
BEIJING
Tangshan
Dalian
Korea Bay
Tianjin
SEOUL
Bo Hai
Shijiazhuang
Yantai
Yinchuan
SOUTH KOREA
Taegu
Taiyuan
Zibo
Great Wall
Jinan
Pusan
Mt. Tai
Qingdao
River
Lanzhou
Qufo
Yellow Sea
Nagasaki
Zhengzhou
Xi'an
Luoyang
JAPAN
Nanjing
Yangzhou
Shanghai
Hefei
Suzhou
Songpan
Chengdu
THREE GORGES
Wuhan
River
Hangzhou
Yichang
Jiangling
Emeishan
East China Sea
Leshan
Chongqing
Nanchang
Luzhou
Changsha
QIULING
Longshen
Kaili
Fuzhou
Guiyang
DONGAN
Guilin
Taipei
Xiamen
Yangshuo
TAIWAN
Guangzhou
Shenzhen
Kaohsiung
Nanning
Hong Kong
VIETNAM
Beihai
Macau
South China Sea
Zhanjiang
HANOI
Haikou
Gulf of Tonkin
Hainan Island
PHILIPPINES

ABOUT THIS BOOK

Our Ratings

Sometimes you find terrific travel experiences and sometimes they just find you. But usually the burden is on you to select the right combination of experiences. That's where our ratings come in.

As travelers we've all discovered a place so wonderful that its worthiness is obvious. And sometimes that place is so unique that superlatives don't do it justice: you just have to be there to know. These sights, properties, and experiences get our highest rating, **Fodor's Choice,** indicated by orange stars throughout this book.

Black stars highlight sights and properties we deem **Highly Recommended,** places that our writers, editors, and readers praise again and again for consistency and excellence.

By default, there's another category: any place we include in this book is by definition worth your time, unless we say otherwise. And we will.

Disagree with any of our choices? Care to nominate a place or suggest that we rate one more highly? Visit our feedback center at www.fodors.com/feedback.

Budget Well

Hotel and restaurant price categories from **¢** to **$$$$** are defined in the opening pages of each chapter. For attractions, we always give standard adult admission fees; reductions are usually available for children, students, and senior citizens. Want to pay with plastic? **AE, DC, MC, V** following restaurant and hotel listings indicate whether American Express, Diner's Club, MasterCard, and Visa are accepted. The Discover card is accepted almost nowhere in South America.

Restaurants

Unless we state otherwise, restaurants are open for lunch and dinner daily. We mention dress only when there's a specific requirement and reservations only when they're essential or not accepted—it's always best to book ahead.

Hotels

Hotels have private bath, phone, and TV and operate on the European Plan (aka EP, meaning without meals), unless we specify that they use the Continental Plan (CP, with a continental breakfast), Breakfast Plan (BP, with a full breakfast), or Modified American Plan (MAP, with breakfast and dinner) or are all-inclusive (including all meals and most activities). We always list facilities but not whether you'll be charged an extra fee to use them, so when pricing accommodations, find out what's included.

Many Listings

- ★ Fodor's Choice
- ★ Highly recommended
- Physical address
- Directions
- Mailing address
- Telephone
- Fax
- On the Web
- E-mail
- Admission fee
- Open/closed times
- Start of walk/itinerary
- Metro stations
- Credit cards

Hotels & Restaurants

- Hotel
- Number of rooms
- Facilities
- Meal plans
- Restaurant
- Reservations
- Dress code
- Smoking
- BYOB
- Hotel with restaurant that warrants a visit

Outdoors

- Golf
- Camping

Other

- Family-friendly
- Contact information
- See also
- Branch address
- Take note

Experience Shanghai

THE HEAD OF THE DRAGON

Tai Chi on the Bund

WORD OF MOUTH

"Shanghai grabbed me, and I'd go back anytime. You have a great chance to see a great country at a pivotal point in its history, and nowhere illustrates this more dramatically than Shanghai.

–Neil_Oz

www.fodors.com/forums

SHANGHAI PLANNER

City of the Future

As the most Westernized city in China after Hong Kong, Shanghai is on the cutting edge of China's race for modernization. It isn't an ancient Chinese city with loads of historic temples and ruins to visit. It's a young new city more akin to Hong Kong than Beijing. The street scene and on-the-go vibe reflect China's future more than its past. Almost a quarter of the world's construction cranes stand in this city of 15 million. On the other hand, architectural remnants of a strong colonial past survive along the charming, winding, bustling streets that make this city undeniably and intimately Chinese.

When to Go

The best time to visit Shanghai is early fall, when the weather is good and crowds diminish. Although temperatures are scorching and the humidity can be unbearable, summer is the peak tourist season, and hotels and transportation can get very crowded. If possible, book several months in advance for summer travel.

Avoid the three national holidays: Chinese New Year, which ranges from mid-January to mid-February; the Labor Day holiday during the first week of May; and the National Day holiday during the first week of October. Imagine 1.2 billion people on the move, and you'll understand why it isn't a good time to travel.

Navigating

Shanghai is divided into east and west sides by the Huangpu River. The metro area is huge, but the city center is a relatively small district in Puxi (west of the river). On the east side lies the district that many think is Shanghai's future—Pudong (east of the river). The city is loosely laid out on a grid and most neighborhoods are easily explored on foot. Massive construction makes pavements uneven and the air dusty but if you can put up with this, walking is the best way to really get a feel for the city and its people. Taxis are readily available and good for traveling longer distances.

Major east–west roads are named for Chinese cities and divide the city into *bei* (north), *zhong* (middle), and *nan* (south) sections. North–south roads divide the city into *dong* (east), *zhong* (middle), and *xi* (west) segments. The heart of the city is found on its chief east–west streets—Nanjing Lu, Huaihai Lu, and Yanan Lu.

■ TIP→ **Transport cards costing Y10 are available from the metro stations and can be charged with however much money you like. These can be used in taxis, on metros, and on some buses. They aren't discounted, but they'll save you time you would have spent joining queues and fumbling for cash.**

Navigating Vocabulary

Below are some terms you'll see over and over again. These words will appear on maps and street signs, and they are part of the name of just about every place you go:

Dong is east, **xi** is west, **nan** is south, **bei** is north, and **zhong** means middle. **Jie** and **lu** mean street and road respectively, and **da** means big.

Qiao, or bridge, is part of the place name at just about every entrance and exit on the ring roads.

Men, meaning door or gate, indicates a street that once passed through an entrance in the fortification wall that surrounded the city hundreds of years ago. The entrances to parks and some other places are also referred to as *men*.

1

Getting Around

By Taxi: Taxis are plentiful, cheap, and easy to spot. Your hotel concierge can call for one by phone or you can hail one on the street. Taxi stands are cropping up all over the city, but during peak hours or in rainy weather it's still every man for himself and fights for the free taxis can get physical. The available ones have a small lit-up sign on the passenger side. If you're choosing a cab from a line, peek at the driver's license on the dashboard. The lower the license number, the more experienced the driver. Drivers with a number below 200,000 can usually get you where you're going.

Most cab drivers don't speak English, so it's best to give them a piece of paper with your destination written in Chinese. (Keep a card with the name of your hotel on it handy for the return trip.) Hotel doormen can help you tell the driver where you're going. It's a good idea to study a map and have some idea of where you are, as some drivers will take you for a ride—a much longer one—if they think they can get away with it.

By Subway: The subway is a great way to get someplace fast without getting stuck in Shanghai's traffic-choked streets. As the subway is improved and extended, more English maps and exit signs are being included. The new electronic ticket machines have an English option that gives maps in English so you can pick your destination.

Stations are clean and glass walls are being installed to protect passenger safety. If you aren't sure which exit to take, take any and negotiate your way when above ground. In-car announcements for each station are given in both Chinese and English. Keep your ticket handy; you'll need to insert it into a second turnstile as you exit at your destination. Transport cards are swiped at entry and exit.

By Ferry: Ferries run around the clock every 10 minutes between the Bund and Pudong's terminal just south of the Riverside Promenade. The per-person fare is Y2 per person each way.

By Bus: Taking the bus is not recommended as they are often crowded, slow, and nearly impossible to negotiate without speaking Chinese.

Opening Hours

Almost all businesses close for Chinese New Year (sometime in mid-January to mid-February) and other major holidays.

Shops: Stores are generally open daily 9 to 7; some stores stay open as late as 10 PM especially in summer.

Temples & Museums: Most temples and parks are open daily 8 to 5. Museums and most other sights are generally open 9 to 5, six days a week, with Monday being the most common closed day.

Banks & Offices: Most banks and government offices are open weekdays 9 to 5, although some close for lunch (sometime between noon and 2). Bank branches and CITS tour desks in hotels often keep longer hours and are usually open Saturday morning. Many hotel currency-exchange desks stay open 24 hours.

Visitor Centers

China International Travel Service (CITS), an official government agency, maintains offices in many hotels and at some tourist venues. The Shanghai Tourism Administration maintains a 24-hour hotline for tourist inquiries and complaints, with operators fluent in English.

China International Travel Service (CITS) 1277 Beijing Xi Lu, Jing'an 021/6289-4510. **Shanghai Tourist Information Services** Yu Garden, 159 Jiujiaochang Lu, Huangpu 021/5355-5032 Hongqiao International Airport 021/6268-8899. **Tourist Hotline** 021/6439-0630 or 021/6439-8947.

TOP ATTRACTIONS

(A) Yu Garden

The Garden offers an atmosphere of peace and beauty amid the clamor of the city, with rocks, trees, and walls curved to resemble dragons, bridges, and pavilions.

(B) The Bund

Shanghai's famous waterfront boulevard is lined with art-deco buildings and souvenir stands. It's great for people-watching, being watched yourself, shopping for increasingly chic clothes, and sampling some of Shanghai's most famous restaurants. It's also where you'll get that postcard view of the futuristic skyline in Pudong.

(C) Shanghai Museum

China's best museum houses an incomparable collection of art and artifacts, including paintings, sculpture, ceramics, calligraphy, furniture, and fantastic bronzes.

(D) Shopping on Nanjing Dong Lu

People come from all over China to shop on what was once China's premier shopping street—and it sometimes feels as though they're all here at the same time. Although it's still a little tawdry, like a phoenix rising from the ashes, pedestrian-only Nanjing Dong Lu is undergoing a massive face-lift, and trendy designer boutiques are beginning to emerge alongside pre-1960s department stores and old-fashioned silk shops.

(E) Oriental Pearl Tower or Jinmao Tower

Choose between the 1960s *Jetsons* kitsch of the Pearl Tower or the pagoda-inspired Jin Mao. If you head to the top of either of these two Pudong skyscrapers you'll be in for a bird's-eye view of the city and its surroundings. Try to count the cranes working incessantly on restructuring the city's skyline. Cloud Nine is a bar at the

top of the Grand Hyatt in the Jin Mao, so you can sip a cocktail while looking out at the zillions of twinkling lights.

(F) The Former French Concession

Whether you're an architecture fanatic, a photographer, a romantic, or just plain curious, a wander through these streets is always a wonderful way to pass an afternoon. Fuxing Lu is a good long walk and the streets around Sinan Lu and Fuxing Park have some real architectural treats. Take your time and allow for breaks at cafés or in small boutiques.

(G) Dongtai Lu Antiques Market

This is an ideal spot for souvenir shopping, practicing your Chinese bargaining, and observing Shanghai life at its most charming. On any given day, you might be caught up in part of a wedding, see fat-cheeked babies, or watch old men bent over a game of chess.

(H) Xintiandi

Shopping, bars, restaurants, and museums mix together in restored traditional *shikumen*(stone gate) houses. Xintiandi is a popular location for hanging out and people-watching, and there are a few great boutiques. The small museums have interesting exhibits related to Shanghai's and the Communist Party's history.

CITY ITINERARIES

Shanghai is fast and tough, so bring good shoes and a lot of patience. Don't expect the grandeur of ancient sights, but rather relish the small details like exquisitely designed art-deco buildings or laid-back cafés. Shanghai hides her gems well, so it's important to be observant and look up and around. The crowds of people and the constant change can make travelers weary, so take advantage of the wide range of eateries and convenient benches.

Best of Shanghai

On Day 1, start at **Yu Garden,** and take a walk through the old city streets and markets surrounding it. Next, head to **the Bund** for a waterfront stroll and a look at some of Shanghai's grandest historic buildings. Segue down **Nanjing Lu,** Shanghai's busiest street, for a spot of shopping. For dinner, check out New Heights at Three on the Bund for its chic all-white interior and view of the Bund lit up at night.

Head to **People's Square** on Day 2 and make your way to the **Shanghai Museum.** If you aren't suffering museum fatigue, choose from the other worthy offerings in this area, such as the **Urban Planning Exhibition Centre.** In the afternoon take a cab north to **Jade Buddha Temple** and to **M50** on Moganshan Lu to check out China's art scene. That night you can take a relaxing cruise along the Huangpu River or go dancing. Cocktails at Face is a calmer choice for those with sore feet.

Make a trip to Pudong in the morning of Day 3, and go to the top of the **Oriental Pearl Tower** for a bird's-eye view of the city. Relax on the riverfront promenade, or take the kids to the **Shanghai Aquarium** or **Century Park.** After lunch, take the wacky **Bund Tourist Tunnel** back to Puxi. In the afternoon, spend some time walking around the **Former French Concession** for a view of old Shanghai and the city's new chic stores. After dinner at Xintiandi, catch a show of the Shanghai acrobats.

Retail Therapy

Shanghai has possibly the best shopping on the mainland, from designer pieces to knockoff items picked up at market stalls. The Bund and the glamorous Plaza 66 are the up and coming designer areas. If you want something more "Chinese," the boutiques in and around Xintiandi offer very stylish fusion pieces. For those on a smaller budget, the Dongtai Lu Antiques Market is near Xintiandi. Taikang Lu offers more funky merchandise, and the antiques market there is blissfully un-crowded, but you need to be ready to search. The Shanghai Museum shop is also great for browsing and always has some wonderful treasures to remind you of your trip.

For the History Buff

You won't find much ancient history here—go to Beijing for that—but from the art-deco architectural gems on the Bund to the closed-down brothels in the Former French Concession, there are many venues to visit if you want to find out why Shanghai was once called the Paris of the East. Although massively restored, Xintiandi is composed of Shanghai's traditional shikumen homes. Around the Former French Concession area, streets like Shaoxing Lu are still relatively untouched by development. Finally, take a long walk through Hongkou District, across the Garden bridge and down Sichuan Bei Lu where apartment blocks, bridges, and a huge post office still stand testimony to the past glory of the city.

SHANGHAI WITH KIDS

While in the past, there was little in the way of entertainment catered especially to children, today's little emperors have all sorts of fun options for activities. From parks and museums to restaurants that cater to kids, yours will be begging to stay.

Century Park. Run them ragged in this large green space with pedal cars, cycling, and boating. When they get tired, take a picnic in the designated areas. Alternatively, pack the rollerblades as the paths are perfect for cruising.

Aquaria 21. Kids can even go scuba diving in this huge underground theme park with an emphasis on sea life. There are also exotic exhibits such as whales and penguins.

Oriental Pearl Tower. It's appealingly space-age, and kids can survey the endless sprawl of Shanghai from the kitschy pink "pearls," and then check out the History Museum below. There's a restaurant at the top for lunch with a view.

Science and Technology Museum. Walk through an indoor rain forest and check out the IMAX cinemas along with a wide range of hands-on activities. There are also changing exhibitions that are often free of charge.

Shanghai Urban Planning Exhibition Centre. Marvel at the extensive models of Shanghai. Kids particularly love the IMAX virtual tour of the city. There are various, if somewhat tacky, multimedia displays and lots of maps and photos. In the basement is a street scene from Old Shanghai with shops and cafés.

Bund Tourist Tunnel. Take a psychedelic trip under the river in clear pods and see a light show that includes strobes, lasers, and tinsel. It isn't quite what one expects under a river, but it's good for a giggle.

Shanghai Acrobats. Children are usually delighted to watch the performers twist themselves into all sorts of challenging positions, squeeze into barrels, and spin plates on sticks. Just make sure they don't try this at home.

SuperBrand Mall Ice Rink. For the little Chen Lu, Shanghai's giant Super Brand Mall offers ice skating, cinema, and loads of restaurants. Even better is that parents can go shopping while their offspring spin around the ice.

Dining with Kids

Now that many expats are moving to Shanghai with their families, restaurants beyond the usual American fast food chains have cottoned on to the idea that they need to be child-friendly. Some now have playing areas or at least children's menus. Also, in many local restaurants, the wait staff is more than happy to play with kids. Just keep in mind that toilets might be a little dodgy. Blue Frog, Mesa, O'Malleys and Mimosa Supper Club are some of the city's most child-friendly restaurants.

Other Experiences Kids Love

- Take the 911 double-decker bus down Huaihai Lu for a bird's-eye view of the town
- Go fast on the Maglev from Pudong
- Fly a kite in People's Square
- Visit the fish and the birds at the Bird and Flower Market
- Cook your own food at a hotpot restaurant
- Buy new clothes and toys in the Puan Lu Children's Market

SIGHTSEEING TOURS

Getting around Shanghai independently is the best way to see the city, and an increasing number of travelers are doing just that. Organized tours are often rushed and on again and off again in style, which is a shame as Shanghai really is a great city to walk around. English is increasingly spoken, especially in tourist-frequented areas and restaurants. If you get lost, there's often a friendly local nearby to help you out. All the same, here are some day tour options that might help you get your bearings on that stressful first afternoon.

Boat Tours

A boat tour on the Huangpu River affords a great view of the Pudong skyline and the Bund, but after that it's mostly ports and cranes.

Huangpu River Cruises launches several small boats for one-hour daytime cruises as well as its unmistakable dragon boat for two-night cruises. The company also runs a 3½-hour trip up and down the Huangpu River between the Bund and Wusong, the point where the Huangpu meets the Yangzi River. You'll see barges, bridges, and factories, but not much scenery. All tours depart from the Bund at 239 Zhongshan Dong Lu. You can purchase all tickets at the dock or through CITS (⇨ *see* Visitor Information, *below*); prices range Y35 to Y90. *239 Zhongshan Dong Er Lu (the Bund), Huangpu District 021/6374–4461*

Shanghai Oriental Leisure Company runs 40-minute boat tours along the Bund from the Pearl Tower's cruise dock in Pudong. Daytime cruises cost Y40, nighttime Y50. Follow the brown signs from the Pearl Tower to the dock. *Oriental Pearl Cruise Dock, 1 Shiji Dadao, Pudong 021/5879–1888 Ext. 80435*

Shanghai Scenery Co., Ltd. This company owns three boats that run one-hour tours along the Huangpu River starting from Yangzijiang Doc. Day tours cost Y45 and at night, Y68. *108 Huangpu Rd., Huangpu District 021/6356–1932 www.shanghaiscenery.com*

Bus Tours

Grayline Tours has escorted half- and full-day coach tours of Shanghai as well as one-day trips to Suzhou, Hangzhou, and other nearby waterside towns. Prices range from Y289 to Y1,323. *2 Hengshan Lu, Xuhui District 135/1216–9650*

Jinjiang Tours runs a full-day bus tour of Shanghai that includes the French Concession, People's Square, Jade Buddha Temple, Yu Garden, the Bund, and Pudong. Tickets cost Y250 and include lunch. Small groups can arrange for a tour by car with an English-speaking guide. *161 Chang Le Lu, Luwan District 021/6415–1188*

The Shanghai Sightseeing Bus Center has more than 50 routes, including 10 tour routes that make a circuit of Shanghai's main tourist attractions. There are also one-stop itineraries and weekend overnight trips to sights in Zhejiang and Jiangsu provinces. One-day trips range from Y30 to Y200; overnight trips cost as much as Y400. You can buy tickets up to a week in advance. The main ticket office and station, beneath Staircase No. 5 at Shanghai Stadium, has plenty of English signage to help you through the ticketing process. *No. 5 Staircase, Gate 12, Shanghai Stadium, 666 Tianyaoqiao Lu, Xuhui District 021/6426–5555*

Heritage Tours

Shanghai Jews. This half-day tour is available daily and takes a minimum of four visitors to the sites related to Shanghai's Jewish history. Costs vary depending on the number of people in the group;Y320 for groups of over 12 and Y400 for groups less than 12. *021/6283–9235 www.shanghaijews.com*

WHEN IN SHANGHAI . . .

. . . do as the Shanghainese. Or at least try. You may find it a lot harder to adopt the social customs in China than in Rome. Here are a few ways you can show your hosts that you're doing your best to blend.

Indulge in a Steamed Pork Dumpling

You can pick up *xiao long bao* (steamed pork dumpling) on the street—look for the steam coming out from a store or the giant bamboo baskets or at many restaurants. Be careful when you bite into them not to get hot juice in your lap as you'll look like a novice.

Strike a Bargain

There's nothing quite like negotiating a purchase price in a Chinese market. You can learn this valued Chinese skill by bargaining for something inexpensive, so you won't mind if you spend a little too much. Remember that saving face is everything when communicating in China. Smile constantly and remain pleasant. Avoid getting angry and making direct criticisms. Acting noncommittal about the item you desperately want might increase your bargaining power.

Get a Little Bit Closer

Get ready to shove, push, squeeze, and cut in line. You may think that a bus or a subway has no room for you, but then someone else will jump in front of you and find an opening. The Chinese have a different idea of personal space than Westerners, so crowding, bumping, and jostling in public are common. You may be annoyed at first, but if you can think like the Chinese, you may make it onto that crowded ferry without having to wait for the next one.

Give a Gift, Pay a Compliment

Visiting someone you know in Shanghai? If you come bearing a gift, offer it up with both hands to show respect. Expect it to be refused as much as three or four times before finally being accepted. Be persistent in offering it. The receiver may not open it in front of you, so don't insist. If your host or hostess speaks even a little English, be sure to compliment his or her use of it. Your host will probably deny this so be ready to insist gently and repeat the compliment.

Slurp Your Noodles

Your mother would scold you for your bad manners, but China is the perfect place to liberate yourself from rigid table etiquette. Get your head into the bowl, use your chopsticks to bring the noodles into your mouth and then suck them up with noisy gusto. It makes eating so much more fun.

Stare

The smallest of incidents will draw a crowd in China, so if you see a bunch of people massing, typically with hands folded behind their backs, get in there and have a look for yourself. You may find that people also look you up and down in the street, so join in and don't hold back on unabashed people-watching.

Got Phlegm?

Feel free to spit it out on the sidewalk. Although there have been efforts since SARS to decrease spitting, it's still quite a common practice, as is blowing your nose on to the street by holding one nostril while voiding the other. Such displays are disappearing, but what is still de rigueur is spitting out bones when eating—either on the floor, your plate, or the table.

FREE THINGS TO DO

From free booze to free music and art, Shanghai has a lot to offer if you're a bit short on cash or just plain cheap.

Free Art

M50. The galleries at Moganshan Lu are all free, so you can browse to your heart's content. (Putuo District, North Shanghai).

Studio Rouge. This little gallery near the Bund always has a good representation of the latest in Chinese art. (Huangpu District, Bund and Nanjing Dong Lu).

Bund Museum. Check out photos that show the history of the Bund in this quirky little building. (Huangpu District, Bund and Nanjing Dong Lu).

Wenmiao. On Sunday it only costs Y1 to get into the book market and have a look at the temple. (Huangpu District, Old City).

■ TIP→ **No one will charge you for popping your head into buildings such as the Bank of China, Peace Hotel, and former Hong Kong and Shanghai Bank buildings on the Bund.**

Free Drinks

See Shanghai night owls at their wildest at ladies' nights all over town. Drinks for women are mostly free and unlimited (sorry, guys). The queen of them all is on Wednesday night at Zapata's on Hengshan Lu when dancing on the bar is almost compulsory and definitely seems like a good idea after a few free margaritas.

Free Shows

Free shows in Shanghai come and go. The best way to get information is to pick up a copy of one of the great (and also free) English-language magazines at bars, restaurants, shops, and cafés around Shanghai.

Shuffle Bar is a dark, bare bones kind of bar, but it's actually one of Shanghai's better music venues. You might have to pay a cover charge on some nights, but on others you can check out all kinds of music—from blues to punk—for absolutely nothing.

Tanghui has an open-mike night on Wednesday from 9 PM on where all kinds of music are welcome.

Free Quintessential Experiences

Set aside some time for random wandering. Shanghai is a great walking city because so many of its real treasures are un-touted: tiny alleyways barely visible on the map, garden squares, shop windows, sudden vistas of skyline or park. With comfortable shoes, walking might well become your favorite free activity here.

Slip into one of Shanghai's numerous parks or green spaces, such as Fuxing Park or Lu Xun Park, to check out the older generation enjoying their retirement.

Watch the gentle elegance of tai chi or the sweep of the brush as people practice their calligraphy on the sidewalk in water not ink.

Take your camera and head to the Bund to get your essential shots of that Pudong skyline with the over the top Oriental Pearl Tower sticking out there like a giant syringe. It's impressive during the day, but magical at night.

Get online at the increasing numbers of restaurants and cafés that offer free wireless, including many branches of Starbucks and Arch.

Get into the Chinese Festival spirit with various traditional activities such as seeing the bell ringing at Longhua Temple for New Year, enjoying the lights in the Yu Garden for Lantern Festival that occurs at the end of the Chinese New Year, or gazing at the huge harvest moon for Mid-Autumn Festival.

GET A MASSAGE

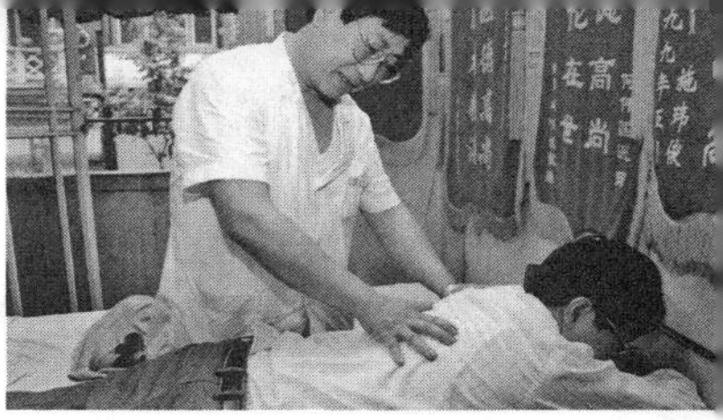

In China, a massage isn't an indulgence; it's what the doctor orders. According to the tenets of traditional Chinese medicine, massage can help the body's *qi*, or energy, flow freely and remain in balance.

Of course, where you choose to have your massage can tip the scale toward indulgence. Around Shanghai are hundreds of blind massage parlors, inexpensive no-frills salons whose blind masseurs are closely attuned to the body's soft and sore spots. At the other end of the spectrum lie the hotel spas, luxurious retreats where pampering is at a premium. Here are just a few of the massage outlets in Shanghai that can attend to your needs.

The **Banyan Tree Spa** Westin Shanghai, 88 Henan Zhong Lu, 3rd fl., Huangpu District 021/6335–1888, the first China outpost of this ultraluxurious spa chain, occupies the 3rd floor of the Westin Shanghai. The spa's 13 chambers as well as its treatments are designed to reflect *wu sing*, the five elemental energies of Chinese philosophy: earth, gold, water, wood, and fire. Relax and enjoy one of five different massages (Y780 plus service charge), facials, body scrubs, or indulgent packages that combine all three.

With instructions clearly spelled out in English, **Double Rainbow Massage House** 47 Yongjia Lu, Luwan District 021/6473–4000 provides a cheap (Y35–Y50), nonthreatening introduction to traditional Chinese massage. Choose a masseur, state your preference for soft, medium, or hard massage, then keep your clothes on for a 45- to 60-minute massage. There's no ambiance, just a clean room with nine massage tables.

Dragonfly 20 Donghu Lu, Xuhui District 021/5405–0008 is a therapeutic retreat center that has claimed the middle ground between expensive hotel spas and workmanlike blind-man massage parlors. Don the suede-soft treatment robes for traditional Chinese massage (Y120), or take them off for an aromatic oil massage (Y200).

The Three on the Bund complex includes the first **Evian Spa** Three on the Bund, Zhongshan Dong Yi Lu, Huangpu District 021/6321–6622 outside of France. Its 14 theme rooms offer treatments from head to toe and 9 different massages, including an Indian head massage (Y600) or a hot-stone aromatherapy massage (Y900).

With its exposed wood beams, unpolished bricks, and soothing fountains, the **Mandara Spa** 399 Nanjing Xi Lu, Huangpu District 021/5359–4969 in the JW Marriott resembles a traditional Chinese water town. Face, beauty, and body treatments include the spa's signature Mandara massage (Y960), a 90-minute treatment in which two therapists administer a blend of five massage styles: Shiatsu, Thai, Lomi Lomi, Swedish, and Balinese.

Ming Massage 298 Wulumuqi Nan Lu, Xuhui District 021/5465–2501 is a Japanese-style salon that caters to women, who receive a 20% discount daily from 11 to 2. Cross over the footbridge to one of five small treatment rooms for a foot, body, or combination "Ming" massage (Y178).

GOLF

With its own international tournament—the Volvo China Open—and several courses designed by prestigious names, Shanghai is making its mark on the golf scene. Approximately 20 clubs dot the countryside within a two-hour arc of downtown. All clubs and driving ranges run on a membership basis, but most allow nonmembers to play when accompanied by a member. A few even welcome the public. Most clubs are outside the city, in the suburbs and outlying counties of Shanghai.

Grand Shanghai International Golf and Country Club. This club has a Ronald Fream–designed 18-hole championship course and driving range. *18 Yangcheng Zhonglu, Yangcheng Lake Holiday Zone, Kunshan City, Jiangsu Province 0512/5789–1999*

Shanghai Binhai Golf Club. Peter Thomson designed the Scottish links–style, 27-hole course at this club in Pudong. Another 27 holes are on the books. *Binhai Resort, Baiyulan Dadao, Nanhui County, Pudong 021/5805–8888*

Shanghai International Golf and Country Club. This 18-hole course designed by Robert Trent Jones Jr. is Shanghai's most difficult. There are water hazards at almost every hole. *961 Yin Zhu Lu, Zhu Jia Jiao, Qingpu District 021/5972–8111*

Shanghai Links Golf and Country Club. This Jack Nicklaus–designed 18-hole course is about a 45-minute ride east of downtown. It's open to the public on Tuesday for Ladies' Day. *1600 Lingbai Lu, Tianxu Township, Pudong 021/5897–5899*

Shanghai Riviera Golf Resort. The late Bobby J. Martin designed this 18-hole course and driving range. *277 Yangtze Lu, Nanxiang Town, Jiading District 021/5912–6888*

Shanghai Silport Golf Club. This club hosts the Volvo China Open. Its 27-hole course on Dianshan Lake was designed by Bobby J. Martin; a new 9 holes designed by Roger Packard opened in 2004. *1 Xubao Lu, Dianshan Lake Town, Kunshan City, Jiangsu Province 0512/5748–1111*

Shanghai Sun Island International Club. You'll find a 27-hole course designed by Nelson & Haworth plus an excellent driving range at this club. *2588 Shantai Lu, Zhu Jia Jiao, Qingpu District 021/5983–0888 Ext. 8033*

Tianma Country Club. Tianma is the most accessible course to the public. Its 18 holes have lovely views of Sheshan Mountain. *3958 Zhaokun Lu, Tianma Town, Songjiang District 021/5766–1666*

Tomson Shanghai Pudong Golf Club. The closest course to the city center, Tomson has 18 holes and a driving range designed by Shunsuke Kato. Robert Trent Jones Jr. has inked a deal to develop the club's second course. *1 Longdong Dadao, Pudong 021/5833–8888*

QUIRKY SHANGHAI

Learn about China

Get hands on and dive into some Chinese culture lessons. Cook up a storm, learn to speak the lingo, or try a hand at calligraphy.

Chinese Cooking Workshop runs cooking workshops in making dim sum and also cooking with a wok. They offer both private and group cooking lessons, and special guest chefs sometimes make appearances. *1st fl., No.35, 865 Yu Yuan Rd. and Room 2103, Building 10, Lianyang Nianhua, La. 910, Dingxiang Rd., Mingsheng Rd., Pudong 021/5465–0730 www.chinesecookingworkshop.com*

Enjoy Mandarin offers a range of cultural encounters ranging from language to seal cutting, so you can even make your own souvenirs. Private classes cost Y120 per hour and classes lasting a few hours can be booked a day in advance. *Room 411, Qing Gong Building, 1576 Nan Jing Xi Rd., Jing'an District 021/6258–6885 www.enjoymandarin.com*

Artist **Chen Li Fan** holds calligraphy lessons in Da Marco, an Italian restaurant, every Friday morning from 9:30 to 11:30 for Y100, or in his studio on request. *103 Dongzhuanbang Lu, TKTK 021/6210—4495*

Go-Karting

Driving in Shanghai is pretty crazy, so it's best to leave it to the locals. However, the city does host the Grand Prix track, so live out your driving dreams with a go-kart. Checkered flag and Grand Prix babes optional.

DISC Kart. This is definitely not your father's go-kart. A lap on a 160cc cart around the tight indoor track can, at times, seem more like a demolition derby. *326 Aomen Lu, Jingan District 021/6277–5641*

Shanghai Hauge Racing Car Club. Races are a bit more civilized at this club. You are required to wear a helmet while racing its 50cc to 200cc go-karts around its large outdoor track. *880 Zhongshan Bei Yi Lu, Hongkou District 021/6531–6800*

Skiing

Shanghai isn't the first place one would expect to find skiing opportunities, especially since snow falls rarely. However, in the city that has everything, you can be a snow bunny too.

Shanghai Yin Qi Xing Indoor Skiing Site. This innovative indoor venue brings winter fun to Shanghai's tropical climes. The world's second largest indoor ski run, the gentle 4,100-foot (1,250 m) slope is good for beginners, who can take snowboarding or skiing lessons in Chinese or Japanese. *1835 Qixing Lu, Minhang District 021/6478–8666*

Chinese Opera

Popular with the older set, Chinese opera can be squeaky, discordant, and difficult to follow. However, it's an important part of Chinese culture and the costumes and makeup are fantastic. There are different forms of Chinese opera including Kunju, Yueju, and, probably the most well known, Peking (Bejing) Opera. In Shanghai, Yueju Opera is very popular. Classics include *Butterfly Lovers,* a Romeo and Juliet–style tale, and *A Dream of Red Mansions* based on the classic Qing Dynasty novel by Cao Xueqin about the fate of a feudal family. Join the weekend crowd at the **Yifu Theatre.** *701 Fuzhou Lu, Huangpu District 021/6351–4668*

SHANGHAI THEN & NOW

Shanghai, the most notorious of Chinese cities, once known as the Paris of the East, now calls itself the Pearl of the Orient. No other city can better capture the urgency and excitement of China's economic reform, understandably because Shanghai is at the center of it.

A port city, lying at the mouth of Asia's longest and most important river, Shanghai is famous as a place where internationalism has thrived. Opened to the world as a treaty port in 1842, Shanghai for decades was not one city but a divided territory. The British, French, and Americans each claimed their own concessions, neighborhoods where their laws and culture—rather than China's—were the rule.

By the 1920s and '30s, Shanghai was a place of sepia-lighted nightclubs, French villas, and opium dens. Here rich taipans walked the same streets as gamblers, prostitutes, and beggars, and Jews fleeing persecution in Russia lived alongside Chinese intellectuals and revolutionaries.

But now Shanghai draws more parallels to New York City than Paris. The Shanghainese have a reputation for being sharp, open-minded, glamorous, sophisticated, and business-oriented, and they're convinced they have the motivation and attitude to achieve their place as China's powerhouse. Far away from Beijing's watchful political eyes, yet supported by state officials who call Shanghai their hometown, the people have a freedom to grow that their counterparts in the capital don't enjoy. That ambition can be witnessed firsthand across Shanghai's Huangpu River, which joins the Yangzi at the northern outskirts of the city. Here lies Shanghai's most important building project—Pudong New Area, China's 21st-century financial, economic, and commercial center. Pudong, literally "the east side of the river," is home to Shanghai's stock-market building, the tallest hotel in the world, the city's international airport, and the world's first commercial "Maglev" (magnetic levitation) train. Rising from land that just a few years ago was dominated by farm fields is the city's pride and joy, the Oriental Pearl Tower—a gaudy, flashing, spaceshiplike pillar, the tallest in Asia. As Shanghai prepares to host the 2010 World Expo, Pudong is again immersed in a decade-long round of construction.

IMPORTANT DATES IN SHANGHAI'S HISTORY

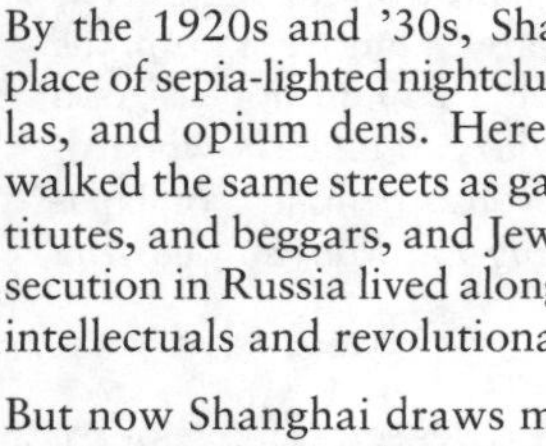

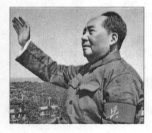

1842	Signing of the Treaty of Nanjing at the end of the First Opium War gives the British the right to settle in selected Chinese cities, including Shanghai
1895	After defeating the Chinese in the Sino-Japanese War, the Japanese gain the right to engage in trade and set up factories in Shanghai
1922	The first meeting of the Chinese Communist Party is held in Shanghai
1937	Shanghai is bombed by the Japanese amidst their growing control of China

Puxi, the west side of the river and the city center, has also gone through staggering change. Charming old houses are making way for shiny high-rises. The population is moving from alley housing in the city center to spanking-new apartments in the suburbs. Architecturally spectacular museums and theaters are catching the world's attention. Malls are popping up on every corner. In 1987 there were about 150 high-rise buildings in the city. Today there are more than 3,000, and the number continues to grow. Shanghai is reputed to be home to one-fifth of all the world's construction cranes.

Shanghai's open policy has also made the city a magnet for foreign investors. As millions of dollars pour in, especially to Pudong, Shanghai has again become home to tens of thousands of expatriates. Foreign influence has made today's Shanghai a consumer heaven. Domestic stores rub shoulders with the boutiques of Louis Vuitton, Christian Dior, and Ralph Lauren. Newly made businessmen battle rush-hour traffic in their Mercedes and Lexus cars. Young people keep the city up until the wee hours as they dance the night away in clubs blasting techno music. And everyone walks around with a cell phone. It's not surprising that the Shanghainese enjoy one of the highest living standards in China. Higher salaries and higher buildings, more business and more entertainment—they all define the fast-paced lives of China's most cosmopolitan and open people.

1941	The Japanese take the International Settlement and inter foreign residents in prison camps
1945	Japan surrenders and the American military occupies Shanghai
1949	The People's Republic of China is born and the Communist People's Liberation Army enters Shanghai
1976	The death of Chairman Mao and the arrest and trial of the Gang of Four lead to the end of the Cultural Revolution
1978	Deng Xiaoping starts the process of opening up and reforming China
1990	Shanghai is officially chosen to be China's main hope for its economic future
2002	Shanghai wins the bid for the World Expo 2010

HOLIDAYS AND FESTIVALS

Festivals in China are hard to pin down as the traditional ones are organized by the Chinese lunar calendar. This means they are often on different dates every year. For major holidays such as May Day and National Day, the government announces the official holiday period close to the event, which can be frustrating for those wishing to make travel plans. If you want to avoid traveling during major holiday times, remember to book well ahead and expect to pay a higher rate.

Chinese New Year: This is the biggest holiday of the year and usually occurs in January or February. Families get together to eat dumplings and children are given new clothes and red envelopes with money inside. Fireworks displays are put on by the city and you'll find traditional dance performances at the large temples. Things can get a little quiet commercially, however, as some businesses close during the week-long holiday.

Lantern Festival: This often falls soon after Chinese New Year. Lanterns in all shapes and sizes including rabbits and lotus flowers are lit. Special treats to eat include sweet dumplings called yuanxiao and tangyuan.

Qing Ming Festival: The tomb-sweeping festival takes place on the 4th or 5th of April each year. On this day, Chinese people are supposed to visit their ancestors' graves and do a bit of maintenance. There are no special organized events.

May Day: This is the Chinese form of Labor Day and takes place in the first week of May. Expect fireworks and massive crowds everywhere. Some businesses may also close as the owners take their own holiday.

Children's Day: It seems like every day is Children's Day for some of China's little emperors. However, they also get their own special day on June 1 with parties and special deals at various child-friendly establishments.

Dragon Boat Festival: Around 2000 years ago, a poet named Qu Yuan threw himself into the river in protest against the Emperor. To commemorate him, people now race dragon boats and eat *zongzi* (sticky rice dumplings). The date of this festival varies every year but is often in May or June.

Seven Sisters Festival: The Chinese equivalent of Valentine's Day usually occurs in July or August. It is celebrated with romantic gifts and dinners but is not as commercialized as February 14th.

Mid-Autumn Festival: Based on a legend of a woman in the moon called Chang'e, families reunite to eat mooncakes and gaze upon the full moon during this festival. It usually takes place in September or October.

National Day: On October 1, 1949, Mao Zedong stood on Tiananmen Square and proclaimed that the people of China had stood up. This was the birth of the People's Republic of China. It's commemorated each year with a week-long holiday. In Beijing, there are military parades in Tiananmen Square, but in Shanghai the action is limited to large crowds, a plethora of Chinese flags, and fireworks.

ON THE HORIZON

Shanghai changes almost daily. Go away for a holiday and your favorite café might have been completely renovated or your neighborhood convenience store torn down to accommodate yet more apartment blocks. The Pudong skyline was changed from rural to sci-fi in a mere decade. The future will bring even more developments and delights. So what's in the works now? Here's a taster:

The **Shanghai World Financial Center** being built in Pudong across the street from the Jinmao Tower is sent to be completed in 2007. Although it resembles a giant bottle opener in shape, at a planned 101 stories high, it's going to be one of, if not the tallest building in the world.

Rumors abound that Shanghai will get its own **Disneyland,** but this isn't due to happen until 2010. In the meantime, there's a brand-new **Universal Studios** to pave the way.

Shanghai's art scene is getting hotter and hotter with the renowned French modern art museum, the **Centre Pompidou,** being pegged to open up a temporary site in the Luwan district at the end of 2007, with a final site set to be completed in 2009.

Shanghai's transport will soon improve dramatically. Approval for a **Maglev** to run between Shanghai and Hangzhou was given in 2006, but talks between Germany and China regarding its construction are not progressing. If it ends up being built, everything should be finished by 2010. Construction on the Shanghai Metro continues to expand with a planned 11 lines to be built and in service by 2010.

On Chongming Island in the Yangtze, the **Dongtan Eco-City** and areas for ecological tourism are being developed. By 2010, Dongtan Eco-City is projected to have a population of 25,000 and be the world's first purpose-built ecologically sustainable city.

21ST
CENTURY
CHINA

Since the late 1970s, China and its billion-plus population have been moving from a centrally planned socialist economy to a market-oriented consumer society on a scale and at a speed unparalleled in history.

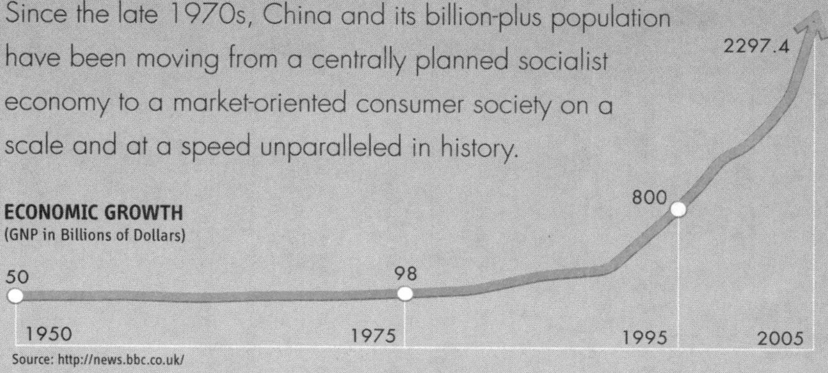

A Chinese Century?

The SARS hiccup aside, China's economy has been red hot since joining the World Trade Organization in 2001. One of the engines driving the global economy, it helped revive Japan's sagging economy and the slumping international shipping industry. Worldwide commodities markets have also been boosted by China's increasing hunger for everything from copper to coffee.

GDP-ANNUAL GROWTH RATE

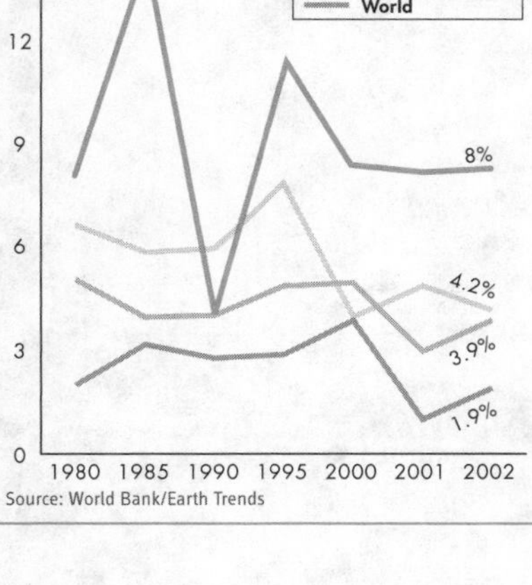

Source: World Bank/Earth Trends

The country that was long written off as just a cheap exporter is now a net importer. It's the fourth-largest economy in the world after the United States, Japan, and Germany, whose economies are growing at less than half the rate.

Such development is nothing short of remarkable, but national problems such as energy, the environment, and wealth inequality are threatening the country.

Internationally, it's how China and the United States cooperate on global issues, and how they manage their own complex relationship, that may have the greatest impact on the rest of the century. Since Nixon first opened the door in 1972, the two countries have managed to forge a working relationship. But Yuan revaluation, trade issues, energy supply (especially oil), and both countries' military role in the Asia-Pacific region are all issues that could sour this budding friendship.

(top) Architectural stars (or starchitects) like Rem Koolhaas, Li Hu, Paul Andreu, and Jacques Herzog and Pierre de Meuron (Olympic Stadium, above) are descending on Beijing for construction of state-of-the-art Olympic venues. (right) Hong Kong skyline.

Fueling the Chinese Dream

China is now the number two energy consumer in the world, after the United States. Its consumption has exploded by an average of 5% yearly since 1998. This thirst for fuel is evident on roads all over the country. The land of the bicycle is now car-crazy. Three million vehicles were recently sold, and higher sales are predicted in the coming years.

Back in 2005, the country consumed 320 million tons of crude oil, roughly one-third of which was imported. It's expecting to import 500 million tons by 2020, two-thirds of its projected total imports.

Where will China get this oil? Much comes from countries with troubled relations with the west such as Iran and Sudan, but it is also working on importing more from traditional U.S. suppliers such as Saudi Arabia.

There's also a growing demand for electricity, 75% of which comes from coal. In the coming 25 years, the greenhouse gases produced by China's coal burning will probably exceed that of all industrial nations combined. And the country will continue to rely on coal for electricity in the years to come, despite large hydropower projects and a plan to increase the number of nuclear power plants.

Aside from developing clean, renewable energy sources, China needs to improve its poor energy efficiency—it uses nine times the energy Japan does to produce one GDP unit. But plans are being made to improve energy efficiency by 20% from 2006 to 2010.

WORLD OIL CONSUMPTION

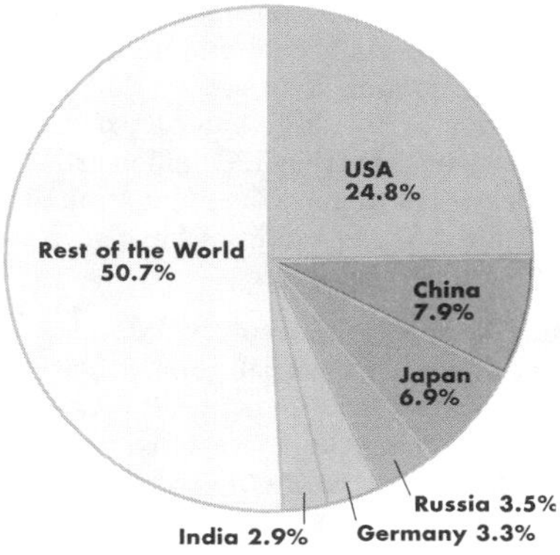

Source: http://www.nationmaster.com/

Can China go Green?

A devastated environment is a major result of China's economic transformation. For example, because of deforestation around the capital, Beijing is threatened by the encroaching Gobi Desert, which dumped 300,000 tons of sand on the city in one week in 2006. Industrial carelessness and lack of regulation result in accidents such as the 50-mile benzene spill in a river near Harbin in late 2005.

Cities have been smoggy for decades because of pollution from factories, vehicles, and especially coal. But air quality is now becoming obscured by water issues. In mid-2006, the Water Resources Ministry reported that 320 million urban residents—more than the population of the United States—did not have access to clean drinking water.

Much of this is the result of a development-at-any-cost mentality, particularly in the wake of economic reform. Companies and factories, many of which are foreign-owned, have only recently had to deal with environmental laws— "scoff laws"—that are often circumvented by bribing local officials. And average citizens don't have freedom of speech or access to political tools to fight environmentally damaging projects.

Is the central government waking up? In 2006, the vice-chairman of China's increasingly outspoken State Environmental Protection Agency put it bluntly: "We will face tremendous problems if we do not change our development patterns."

Mind the Gap

China has come a long way from the days when everyone had an "iron rice bowl," or a state-appointed job that was basically guaranteed regardless of one's abilities or work performance.

Since 1980, the country has quadrupled per capita income and raised more than 220 million of its citizens out of poverty. A belt of prosperity is emerging along the coast, but hundreds of millions still live on less than $1 per day.

(left) Owning a car is the new Chinese dream. (top right) The Three Gorges Dam will be the largest in the world, supplying the hydroelectric power of 18 nuclear plants. (bottom right) China's cities are some of the most polluted in the world.

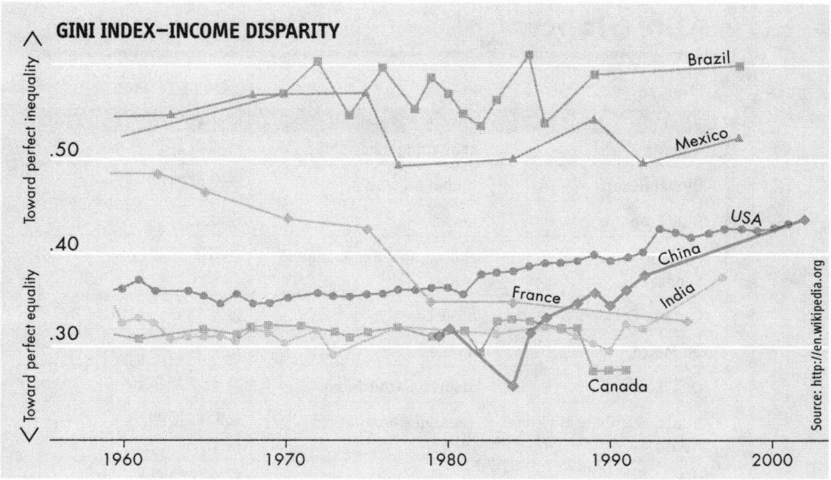

Economists use a statistical yardstick known as the Gini coefficient to measure wealth inequality in a society, with zero being perfect equality and one being perfect inequality. The World Bank estimates that China's national Gini coefficient rose from 0.30 to 0.45 from 1982, a 50% jump in two decades. In 2006, some academics estimated China's current Gini coefficient to be closer to, or even higher, than Latin America's 0.52.

As economic inequality has grown, so has discontent, particularly in rural areas. The country recorded 87,000 public protests in 2005, an increase of 11,000 over the year before.

Many of these protests are incited by the acts of local, particularly rural, officials whose corruption policies are sometimes beyond Beijing's sphere of influence.

Most protests are focused on specific incidents or officials rather than general dissent against the government, but the growing frequency of such events is not going unnoticed by the central government. In 2005, 8,400 officials were arrested on corruption-related charges.

CHINA IN NUMBERS

	CHINA	U.S.
Area in sq km:	9,560,960	9,631,420
Population	1.3 bil	300 mil
Men (15–64 yrs)	482 mil	100 mil
Women (15–64 yrs)	456 mil	101 mil
Population growth	0.59%	0.91%
Life expectancy: men	70.8	75
Life expectancy: women	74.6	80.8
GDP per head	$1,090	$37,240
Health spending, % GDP	5.8	14.6
Doctors per 1000 pop.	1.6	2.8
Hospital beds per 1000 pop.	1.6	3.0
Infant mortality rate per 1000 births	23.12	6.43
Education spending, % GDP	2.1	5.7
Adult literacy: men	95.1%	99%
Adult literacy: women	86.5%	99%
Internet users	111 mil	204 mil

At a Glance

ENGLISH	PINYIN	CHINESE CHARACTERS
POINTS OF INTEREST		
Aquaria 21	chángfēng hǎidǐ shìjiè	长风海底世界
Binhai Resort	bīnhǎi dùjiàqū	滨海度假区
Blue Frog	lánwā	蓝蛙
China International Travel Service	zhōngguó guójì lǚxíngshè	中国国际旅行社
Chinese Cooking Workshop	bōsàidùn	波塞顿
Da Marco	dàmǎkě	大马可
DISC Kart	dīshìkǎ sàichēchǎng	迪士卡赛车场
Double Rainbow Massage House	shuāngcǎihóng ànmó	双彩虹按摩
Dragonfly	yōutíng bǎojiàn huìsuǒ	悠亭保健会所
Enjoy Mandarin	hànxǐ	汉玺
Evian Spa	yīyún shuǐliáo	依云水疗
Grand Shanghai International Golf and Country Club	dàshànghǎi guójì gāoěrfū dùjiàcūn	大上海国际高尔夫度假村
Grayline Tours	huīxiàn lǚyóu	灰线旅游
Huangpu River Cruises	pǔjiāng yóulǎn	浦江游览
Jinjiang Tours	jǐnjiāng lǚyóu	锦江旅游
Mandara Spa	màndáměng shuǐliáo	蔓达梦水疗
Mesa	méisà	梅萨
Ming Massage	míngyī ànmó	明一按摩
Old China Hand Reading Room	hànyuán shūwū	汉源书屋
O'Malley's	ōumǎlì	欧玛莉
Partyworld	qiánguì	钱柜
Putuoshan	pǔtuóshān	普陀山
Shanghai Acrobats	shànghǎi zájìtuán	上海杂技团
Shanghai Binhai Golf Club	shànghǎi bīnhǎi gāoěrfū jùlèbù	上海滨海高尔夫俱乐部
Shanghai Hauge Racing Car Club	shànghǎi qǔyáng kǎdīngchē jùlèbù	上海曲阳卡顶车俱乐部
Shanghai International Golf and Country Club	shànghǎi guójì gāoěrfūqiú xiāngcūn jùlèbù	上海国际高尔夫球乡村俱乐部
Shanghai Jews	shànghǎi yóutàirén	上海犹太人

Shanghai Oriental Leisure Company	shànghǎi míngzhū shuǐshàng yúlè fāzhǎn yǒuxián gōngsī	上海明珠水上娱乐发展有限公司
Shanghai Riviera Golf Resort	shànghǎi dōngfāng bālí gāoěrfū xiāngcūn jùlèbù	上海东方巴黎高尔夫乡村俱乐部
Shanghai Scenery Co.	shànghǎi fēngcǎi	上海风采
Shanghai Sightseeing Bus Centre	shànghǎi lǚyóu jísàn zhōngxīn	上海旅游集散中心
Shanghai Silport Golf Club	shànghǎi xùbǎo gāoěrfū jùlèbù	上海旭宝高尔夫俱乐部
Shanghai Sun Island International Club	shànghǎi tàiyángdǎo gāoěrfū jùlèbù	上海太阳岛高尔夫俱乐部
Shanghai Tourist Information Services	shànghǎi lǚyóu zīxún fúwù zhōngxīn	上海旅游咨询服务中心
Shanghai Yin Qi Xing Indoor Skiing Site	shànghǎi yínqīxīng shìnèi huáxuěchǎng	上海银七星室内滑雪场
Starbucks	xīngbākè	星巴克
Super Brand Mall Ice Rink	sīkǎitè zhèngdà zhēnbīng liūbīngchǎng	司凯特正大真冰溜冰场
Tang Hui	tánghuì	堂会
Tianma Country Club	shànghǎi tiānmǎ gāoěrfū xiāngcūn jùlèbù	上海天马高尔夫乡村俱乐部
Tomson Shanghai Pudong Golf Club	tāngchén shànghǎi pǔdōng gāoěrfū qiúchǎng	汤臣上海浦东高尔夫球场
Tongli	tónglǐ	同里
Tourist Hotline	lǚyóu rèxiàn	旅游热线
Yangcheng Lake Holiday Zone	yángchénghú dùjiàqū	阳澄湖度假区
Yifu Theatre	yìfū wǔtái	逸夫舞台
Zapata's	zhápàtǎ	扎帕塔
DISTRICTS		
Changning District	chángníng qū	长宁区
Huangpu District	huángpǔ qū	黄浦区
Jing'an District	jìng'ān qū	静安区
Lujiazui	lùjiāzuǐ	陆家嘴
Luwan District	lúwān qū	卢湾区
Minhang District	mǐnháng qū	闵行区

Pudong	pŭdóng	浦东
Putuo District	pŭtuó qū	普陀区
Puxi	pŭxī	浦西
Xuhui District	xúhuì qū	徐汇区
Zhabei District	zhábĕi qū	闸北区
IMPORTANT STREETS		
Duolun Lu	duōlún lù	多伦路
Fangbang Lu	fāngbāng lù	方浜路
Fuzhou Lu	fúzhōu lù	福州路
Guangdong Lu	guăngdóng lù	广东路
Jinling Lu	jīnlíng lù	金陵路
Julu Lu	jùlù lù	巨鹿路
Maoming Lu	màomíng lù	茂名路
Moganshan Lu	mògānshān lù	莫干山路
Nanjing Dong Lu (Nanjing East)	nánjīng dōng lù	南京东路
Nanjing Xi Lu (Nanjing West)	nánjīng xī lù	南京西路
Renmin Dadao	rénmín dàdào	人民大道
Shaanxi Nan Lu (Shaanxi South)	shaănxī nán lù	陕西南路
Xintiandi	xīntiāndì	新天地
Zhongshang Dong Yi Lu (Zhongshan East No. 1 Road)	zhōngshān dōng yī lù	中山东一路
Zhongshang Xi Lu (Zhongshang West)	zhōngshān xī lù	中山西路

Neighborhoods

Yuyuan Garden

WORD OF MOUTH

"Shanghai is not [as much] about shopping as it is about experiencing a cosmopolitan China. Shanghai is like a woman or a man—whichever you prefer—a city that is alive and is waiting for you to get to know her."

–sbobao

Shanghai
KEY
Shanghai Metro
Bund — Station
Line 2
Line 1
Shanghai Railway Station
Shanghai Railway Station
Nade Buddha Temple
Hanzhong Rd.
Xinzha Rd.
JING'ANSI
Nanjing Dong Lu
Shimen No.1 Rd.
People's Square
People's Park
Jing'ansi
Jing'an Park
Changshou Park
Central Yan'an Rd.
Yan'an Rd. (W.)
Huangpi Rd. (S.)
Xiangyang Park
Shanxi Rd. (S.)
Changshu Rd.
Fuxing Park
Former Residence of Dr. Sun Yat-Sen
Former Residence of Zhou Enlai
Former Residence of Mme. Soong Qing Ling
Hengshan Rd.
DAPUQIAO
Aomen Rd.
Putuo Rd.
Changshou Rd.
Tianmu Rd. (W.)
Datong Rd.
New Gonghe Rd.
Wusong River
Xinhui Rd.
Anyuan Rd.
Haifang Rd.
Yuyao Rd.
Changping Rd.
Kangding Rd.
Wuding Rd.
Xinzha Rd.
Beijing Rd. (W.)
Fengyang Rd.
Guangfu Rd.
Suzhou Rd. (S.)
Wuzhen Rd.
Weihai Rd.
Wusheng Rd.
Dagu Rd.
Julu Rd.
Huangshan Rd.
Changle Rd.
Jinling Rd. (W.)
Central Huaihai Rd.
Taicang Rd.
Nanchang Rd.
Zizhong Rd.
Fuxing Rd. (W.)
Central Fuxing Rd.
Central Fuxing
Wanhangdu Rd.
Yuyuan Rd.
Wukang Rd.
Yongjia Rd.
Jianguo Rd. (E.)
Central Jianguo Rd.
Jianguo Rd. (W.)
Xujiahui Rd.
Zhaojiabang Rd.
Liyuan Rd.
Yixueyuan Rd.
Qingzhen Rd.
Xietu Rd.
Xietu Rd. (W)
Quxi Rd.
Zhongshan Nan
Shanxi Rd. (N.)
Xikang Rd.
Jiangning Rd.
Changhua Rd.
Hengfeng Rd.
Meiyuan Rd.
Chengdu Rd. (N.)
Xinchang Rd.
Dalian Rd.
Shimen No.2 Rd.
Taixing Rd.
Wuning Rd. (S.)
Yanping Rd.
Jiaozhou Rd.
Changde Rd.
Zhenning Rd.
Wulumuqi Rd. (N.)
Tongren Rd.
Maoming Rd. (N.)
Shimen No.1 Rd.
Changshu Rd.
Xiangyang Rd. (N.)
Central Wulumuqi Rd.
Maoming Rd. (S.)
Ruijing No.1 Rd.
Shanxi Rd. (S.)
Chongqing Rd. (S.)
Sinan Rd.
Danshui Rd.
Madang Rd.
Huangpi Rd. (S.)
Shunchang Rd.
Wanping Rd.
Hengshan Rd.
Gaoan Rd.
Wuxing Rd.
Wulumuqi Rd. (S.)
Yueyang Rd.
Taiyuan Rd.
Xiangyang Rd. (S.)
Jiashan Rd.
Luban Rd.
Mengzi Rd.
Jumen Rd.
Wanping Rd. (S.)
Dong'an Rd.
Fenglin Rd.
Xiaomuqiao Rd.
Ruijin Rd. (S.)
Dapu Rd.

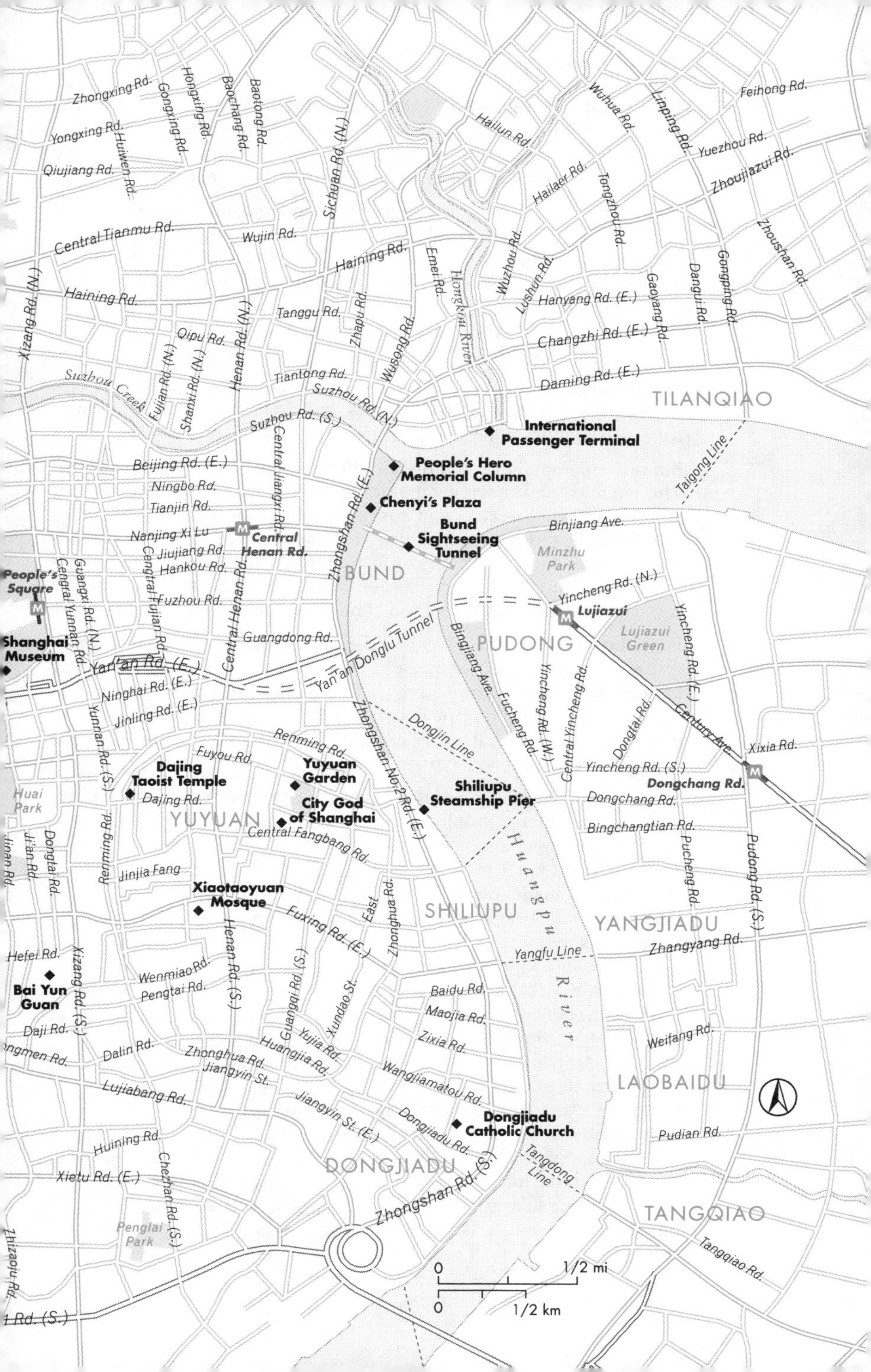

Zhongxing Rd.
Yongxing Rd.
Qiujiang Rd.
Huiwen Rd.
Hongxing Rd.
Gongxing Rd.
Baochang Rd.
Baotong Rd.
Sichuan Rd. (N.)
Hailun Rd.
Wuhua Rd.
Linping Rd.
Feihong Rd.
Yuezhou Rd.
Zhoujiazui Rd.
Hailaer Rd.
Tongzhou Rd.
Zhoushan Rd.
Central Tianmu Rd.
Wujin Rd.
Haining Rd.
Emei Rd.
Hongkou River
Wuzhou Rd.
Lushun Rd.
Gaoyang Rd.
Dangui Rd.
Gongping Rd.
Xizang Rd. (N.)
Haining Rd.
Henan Rd. (N.)
Tanggu Rd.
Zhapu Rd.
Wusong Rd.
Hanyang Rd. (E.)
Qipu Rd.
Changzhi Rd. (E.)
Fujian Rd. (N.)
Shanxi Rd. (N.)
Tiantong Rd.
Daming Rd. (E.)
Suzhou Creek
Suzhou Rd. (N.)
TILANQIAO
Suzhou Rd. (S.)
International Passenger Terminal
Beijing Rd. (E.)
Central Jiangxi Rd.
People's Hero Memorial Column
Ningbo Rd.
Taigong Line
Tianjin Rd.
Chenyi's Plaza
Zhongshan Rd. (E.)
Bund Sightseeing Tunnel
Binjiang Ave.
Nanjing Xi Lu
Central Henan Rd.
Minzhu Park
Jiujiang Rd.
Central Fujian Rd.
Hankou Rd.
BUND
People's Square
Guangxi Rd. (N.)
Central Yunnan Rd.
Yincheng Rd. (N.)
Fuzhou Rd.
Central Henan Rd.
Lujiazui
Yincheng Rd. (E.)
Bingjiang Ave.
Lujiazui Green
PUDONG
Guangdong Rd.
Shanghai Museum
Yan'an Donglu Tunnel
Yan'an Rd. (E.)
Ninghai Rd. (E.)
Yincheng Rd. (W.)
Central Yincheng Rd.
Jinling Rd. (E.)
Fucheng Rd.
Dongtai Rd.
Century Ave.
Zhongshan No.2 Rd. (E.)
Dongjin Line
Renming Rd.
Xixia Rd.
Fuyou Rd.
Yuyuan Garden
Yunnan Rd. (S.)
Dajing Taoist Temple
Yincheng Rd. (S.)
Shiliupu Steamship Pier
Dongchang Rd.
Dajing Rd.
Huai Park
City God of Shanghai
Dongchang Rd.
YUYUAN
Central Fangbang Rd.
Bingchangtian Rd.
Jinan Rd.
Ji'an Rd.
Dongtai Rd.
Renming Rd.
Huangpu River
Pucheng Rd.
Pudong Rd. (S.)
Jinjia Fang
Xiaotaoyuan Mosque
East Zhonghua Rd.
SHILIUPU
Fuxing Rd. (E.)
YANGJIADU
Hefei Rd.
Xizang Rd. (S.)
Guangqi Rd. (S.)
Yangfu Line
Zhangyang Rd.
Wenmiao Rd.
Henan Rd. (S.)
Bai Yun Guan
Pengtai Rd.
Xundao St.
Baidu Rd.
Maojia Rd.
Daji Rd.
Yujia Rd.
Zixia Rd.
Weifang Rd.
Dalin Rd.
Zhonghua Rd.
Huangjia Rd.
Jiangyin St.
Wangjiamatou Rd.
LAOBAIDU
Lujiabang Rd.
Jiangyin St. (E.)
Dongjiadu Rd.
Dongjiadu Catholic Church
Huining Rd.
Pudian Rd.
Tangdong Line
Xietu Rd. (E.)
Chezhan Rd. (S.)
DONGJIADU
Zhongshan Rd. (S.)
TANGQIAO
Penglai Park
Zhizaoju Rd.
Tangqiao Rd.
0
1/2 mi
0
1/2 km

SHANGHAI, THE MOST NOTORIOUS OF CHINESE CITIES, once known as the Paris of the East, now calls itself the Pearl of the Orient. No other city can better capture the urgency and excitement of China's economic reform, understandably because Shanghai is at the center of it.

A port city, lying at the mouth of Asia's longest and most important river, Shanghai is famous as a place where internationalism has thrived. Opened to the world as a treaty port in 1842, Shanghai for decades was not one city but a divided territory. The British, French, and Americans each claimed their own concessions, neighborhoods where their laws and culture—rather than China's—were the rule.

By the 1920s and '30s, Shanghai was a place of sepia-lighted nightclubs, French villas, and opium dens. Here rich taipans walked the same streets as gamblers, prostitutes, and beggars, and Jews fleeing persecution in Russia lived alongside Chinese intellectuals and revolutionaries.

But now Shanghai draws more parallels to New York City than Paris. The Shanghainese have a reputation for being sharp, open-minded, glamorous, sophisticated, and business-oriented, and they're convinced they have the motivation and attitude to achieve their place as China's powerhouse. That ambition can be witnessed firsthand in Shanghai's most important building project—Pudong New Area, China's 21st-century financial, economic, and commercial center.

Puxi, the west side of the river and the city center, has also gone through staggering change. Charming old houses are making way for shiny high-rises. The population is moving from alley housing in the city center to spanking-new apartments in the suburbs. Architecturally spectacular museums and theaters are catching the world's attention and malls are popping up on every corner.

Shanghai's open policy has also made the city a magnet for foreign investors. As millions of dollars pour in, especially to Pudong, Shanghai has again become home to tens of thousands of expatriates. Foreign influence has made today's Shanghai a consumer heaven. Domestic stores rub shoulders with the boutiques of Louis Vuitton, Christian Dior, and Ralph Lauren. Newly made businessmen battle rush-hour traffic in their Mercedes and Lexus cars. Young people keep the city up until the wee hours as they dance the night away in clubs blasting techno music. It's not surprising that the Shanghainese enjoy one of the highest living standards in China. Higher salaries and higher buildings, more business and more entertainment—they all define the fast-paced lives of China's most cosmopolitan and open people.

A NOTE ABOUT NEIGHBORHOODS & DISTRICTS

Shanghai is a large, sprawling city, and the size of its districts reflects that. We have simplified your experience by creating a series of smaller neighborhoods, centered around the attractions. However, because you may still need to know the official districts, we have listed them at the end of each entry in the dining, lodging, and shopping chpaters. They'll be useful in dealing with the local tourist resources, hotels, and taxi drivers.

OLD CITY

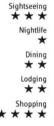

Sightseeing ★★★
Nightlife ★
Dining ★★
Lodging ★★
Shopping ★★★★

Tucked away in the east of Puxi are the remnants of Shanghai's Old City. Once encircled by a thick wall, a fragment of which still remains, the Old City has a sense of history among its fast disappearing old *shikumen* (stone gatehouses), temples, and markets. Delve into narrow alleyways where residents still hang their washing out on bamboo poles and chamber pots are still in use. Burn incense with the locals in small temples, sip tea in a teahouse, or get a taste of Chinese snacks and street food. This is the place to get a feeling for Shanghai's past, but you'd better get there soon, as the wrecker's ball knows no mercy.

What's Here

Wenmiao is a short cab ride (or a 30-minute walk) from the **Huangpi Nan Lu** metro station. You can see in the surrounding areas where whole blocks of Shanghai's architectural heritage have been razed down in the name of progress. **Wenmiao** is on a small street lined with trinket shops popular with students. The interior of the temple is cool and calm except during the Sunday book market. You can walk from here to the **Yu Garden** complex. The side streets are buzzing with life. Old people recline in chairs and fan themselves in the summer heat, and dogs and children play in the streets under haphazardly strung washing lines. Sadly, many of these buildings bear the character that indicates that they are soon to be demolished.

If you enter the **Yu Garden** area at **Dajing Lu**, you'll come across what is left of the **Old City Wall** that once encircled the city. Inside the **Yu Garden** complex itself are several sights, but be prepared for crowds, par-

GETTING ORIENTED

GETTING HERE

At press time, Shanghai's ever expanding metro system had not yet reached Old City. However, it's a short walk east from Henan Zhong Lu station on Line 2, and a slightly longer, but interesting walk south from Huangpi Nan Lu on Line 1. TIP→ **Be warned that taxis are nearly impossible to find in this area when you want to leave.**

TOP REASONS TO GO

- **Shanghai's backstreets:** step back in time by wandering through the narrow alleys before their imminent destruction.
- **Wenmiao:** Shanghai's only Confucian temple has a buzzing Sunday book market and great street food just outside.
- **Yu Garden:** get your souvenir shopping done at this hectic mix of souvenir shops, old buildings, and teahouses.
- **Huxingting teahouse:** choose from a wide selection of teas, listen to Chinese classical music, and watch the consumer madness below.
- **South Bund Soft Spinning Material Market:** drape yourself in silks and brocades and have a little something whipped up by a tailor.

QUICK BITES

The **Huxinting Teahouse** (✉ 257 Yuyuan Lu, Huangpu District ☎ 021/6373-6950 downstairs, 021/6355-8270 upstairs), Shanghai's oldest. Although tea is cheaper on the 1st floor, be sure to sit on the top floor by a window overlooking the lake. A traditional tea ceremony is performed every night from 8:30 PM to 10 PM.

On the west side of the central man-made lake in Yu Garden is **Nanxiang Steamed Bun Restaurant** (✉85 Yuyuan Lu, Huangpu District ☎021/6326-5265), a great dumpling house famed for its *xiao long bao* (steamed pork dumplings).

MAKING THE MOST OF YOUR TIME

This area could take a very long afternoon or morning as it's a good one to do on foot, especially if you're interested in photography. Browsing the shops in and around the Yu Garden might add a couple of hours, although a confirmed shopaholic could extend that time period indefinitely. If you take a cab between areas, half a day should be sufficient.

SAFETY

Pickpockets are the main problem in Old City. Keep your belongings close at hand and zip valuables away, especially in crowded areas.

NEAREST PUBLIC RESTROOMS

Although not exactly public, a visit to the Shanghai Classical Hotel's foyer toilets on Fuyou Lu and Lishui Lu is likely to go unchallenged by hotel staff. In the unlikely event that someone questions you, say you've come from the attached Starbucks. It's clean enough on a good day, but bring your own toilet paper.

A GOOD WALK

From the gate at Fangbang Lu and Henan Lu, turn left and head into the area there. You'll feel that you have momentarily left modern Shanghai. More a wander than a walk, it's well worthwhile to head into the backstreets around the Yu Garden to see life in the shikumen gatehouses.

A BRIEF HISTORY

This area of the city has been inhabited for over 2,000 years. It started out as a fishing town, but when Shanghai was carved up by foreign powers, one part of the central city remained under Chinese law and administration. Surrounded by the ring road of Renmin Lu/ Zhonghua Lu, these old winding back alleys eventually became notorious as gangster- and opium-filled slums until the Communists cleaned up the area. Today the vices have disappeared for the most part and only the narrow meandering lanes and a dwindling number of tiny, pre-1949 shikumen houses are still standing. Rapid development means that the Old City is fast losing its historical buildings and laneways to be replaced by shiny apartment blocks.

ticularly on the weekend when you can hardly move. The **Yu Garden** is worth a look, although to be honest, it's terribly crowded and not the finest example of a Chinese garden (the one in Suzhou is more interesting). Stop at the elegant **Huxinting Teahouse** for a rest from the madness and then wend your way around the shops to the **Cheng Huang Miao,** the larger of the two temples, and a Taoist one to boot. If you're lucky, you might catch a live performance of music or dance on your way.

You can do your souvenir shopping at the myriad of shops that surround the bazaar, but one of the best places to check out is the **Cang Bao Antiques Building** on **Fangbang Lu.** On the way, stop off at the tiny **Chen Xiangge Temple,** which is run by nuns. For modern items ranging from Hello Kitty slippers to rather large and sensible looking underwear, visit the large markets on **Fuyou Lu.**

If you have the energy, walk the **Renmin/Zhonghua** loop road around until you get to **Dongjiadu Lu** where you'll find **Dongjiadu Cathedral,** built in 1849. Finally, about 500 meters (1640 feet) south is the new **South Bund Soft-Spinning Material Market** where you can browse amongst bolts of silks and other fabrics and have clothes made.

What to See

Temple of the City God (Chenghuang Miao) lies at the southeast end of the bazaar. This Taoist Temple of the City God was built during the early part of the Ming Dynasty and later destroyed. The main hall was rebuilt in 1926 and has been renovated many times over the years. Inside are gleaming gold figures, and atop the roof you'll see statues of crusading warriors—flags raised, arrows drawn. ✉ *Xi Dajie Lu, Huangpu District* ☎ *021/6386–8649* 🎫 *Y5* ⏲ *Daily 8:30–5 (doors close at 4:30).*

Chen Xiangge Temple. If you find yourself passing by this tiny temple on your exploration of the Old City, you can make an offering to Buddha with the free incense sticks that accompany your admission. Built in 1600 by the same man who built Yu Garden, it was destroyed during the Cul-

> **WORD OF MOUTH**
>
> "The Yu Garden . . . is probably the best place for traditional Chinese gift items. Hint: bring your own shopping bags with cloth handles to make it easier to carry everything." –Lia

tural Revolution and rebuilt in the 1990s. The temple is now a nunnery, and you can often hear the women's chants rising from the halls beyond the main courtyard. ✉ *29 Chenxiangge Lu, Huangpu District* ☎ *021/6320–0400* *Y5* ⏲ *Daily 7–4.*

Old City Wall. The Old City used to be completely surrounded by a wall, built in 1553 as a defense against Japanese pirates. Most of it was torn down in 1912, except for one 50-yard-long (40 meter) piece that still stands at Dajing Lu and Renmin Lu. You can walk through the remnants and check out the rather simple museum nearby, which is dedicated to the history of Old City (the captions are in Chinese). Stroll through the tiny neighboring alley of Dajing Lu for a lively panorama of crowded market life in the Old City. ✉ *269 Dajing Lu, at Renmin Lu, Huangpu District* ☎ *021/6385–2443* *Y5* ⏲ *Daily 9–4.*

Fodor'sChoice ★ **Yu Garden.** Since the 18th century, this complex, with its traditional red walls and upturned tile roofs, has been a marketplace and social center where local residents gather, shop, and practice *qi gong* in the evenings. Although a bit overrun by tourists and not as impressive as the ancient palace gardens of Beijing, Yu Garden is a piece of Shanghai's past, and one of the few old sights left in the city.

To get to the garden itself, you must wind your way through the bazaar. The garden was commissioned by the Ming Dynasty official Pan Yunduan in 1559 and built by the renowned architect, Zhang Nanyang, over 19 years. When it was finally finished it won international praise as "the best garden in southeastern China." In the mid-1800s the Society of Small Swords used the garden as a gathering place for meetings. It was here that they planned their uprising with the Taiping rebels against the French colonists. The French destroyed the garden during the first Opium War, but the area was later rebuilt and renovated.

Winding walkways and corridors bring you over stone bridges and carp-filled ponds and through bamboo stands and rock gardens. Within the park are an **old opera stage,** a **museum** dedicated to the Society of Small Swords rebellion, and an **exhibition hall,** opened in 2003, of Chinese calligraphy and paintings. One caveat: the park is almost always thronged with Chinese tour groups, especially on weekends. As with most sights in Shanghai, don't expect a tranquil time alone. ✉ *218 Anren Lu, bordered by Fuyou Lu, Jiujiaochang Lu, Fangbang Lu, and Anren Lu, Huangpu District* ☎ *021/6326–0830 or 021/6328–3251* *Y30* ⏲ *Gardens, daily 8:30–5.*

XINTIANDI & THE CITY CENTER

Sightseeing ★★★★
Nightlife ★★★
Dining ★★★★
Lodging ★
Shopping ★★★★

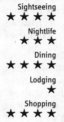

Xintiandi is Shanghai's showpiece restoration project. Reproduction shikumen houses contain expensive bars, restaurants, and chic boutiques. It's at its most magical on a warm night when locals, expats, and visitors alike pull up a chair at one of the outside seating areas and watch the world go by. Nearby, the area around People's Square has some magnificent examples of modern and historical architecture and a smattering of some of Shanghai's best museums. The adjoining People's Park is a pleasant green space where it's possible to escape the clamor of the city for a while.

What's Here

As you come out of **People's Square** metro station, look up at the varied skyline including the UFO-like **Radisson** building and the art-deco **Park Hotel.** You have to admit, Shanghai really knows how to do skyscrapers.

Once above ground, head for the **Shanghai Museum,** the city's largest. It's best explored when energy levels are still high. Wander amongst ancient bronzes and divine ceramics and pick up some gifts at the great museum store. After that, at the **Shanghai Urban Planning Center,** children will particularly enjoy the virtual tour of Shanghai and the master-plan model of the city is truly mind-boggling. As you go toward the art museum, gaze up at the **Grand Theatre,** which is particularly splendid when it's lit up at night. Head down **Huangpi Bei Lu** and then into **Nanjing Xi Lu.** Here you'll find the **Shanghai Art Museum** in what was once the main building at the racetrack. **Kathleen's 5** is a good place to stop for refreshment. After touring the art gallery, slip into **People's Park.** In

A BRIEF HISTORY

Shikumen (stone gatehouses) were terraced buildings in lanes built in the 1920s and 1930s and although few survive, they once used to be found all over Shanghai. **People's Square** was once the Shanghai racetrack, built in 1862 and after Japanese occupation in 1941 was a place where the Japanese kept foreigners interred. It was also used by the Red Guard during the Cultural Revolution as a site for struggle sessions where people deemed to be anti-revolutionary were forced to give self-criticisms and often subject to torture.

summer, a pond full of magnificent lotus blooms with the Moroccan-style building of **Barbarossa** behind. Keep this in mind for an afternoon beverage. Inside the park, you'll find peace and greenery, old people chatting, young couples, and the **Museum of Contemporary Art,** which has exhibitions of local and overseas artists.

Head down **Huangpi Bei/Nan Lu** to arrive at **Xintiandi.** If you want to shop for souvenirs, then **Dongtai Lu Antiques Market** is close by. Antiques might be a bit hard to find, but there are some great trinkets.

At **Xintiandi,** the **Shikumen Museum,** and the **Site of the First National Congress of the Communist Party** are both places that give interesting insights into Shanghai's history. Inside the **Shikumen Museum** you can see what the interiors of these traditional Shanghainese houses may have looked like in the 1920s and 1930s. If you fall in love with the furniture, which you will, you can always head out to one of the antiques showrooms in the Hongqiao and Gubei area to get something similar. The **Site of the First National Congress of the Communist Party** edges slightly toward propaganda at times, but is quite informative about the people and events that led to the forming of the Communist Party.

Xintiandi has some great shops including the lovely **Shanghai Trio** and **Shanghai Tang,** one of China's own designer brands. It's also a pleasant place for dinner with a varied selection of restaurants, so grab a chair and indulge in a bit of people-watching.

What to See

Fodor's Choice ★ **Dongtai Lu Antiques Market.** A few blocks east of Xintiandi, antiques dealers' stalls line the street. You'll find porcelain, Victrolas, jade, and anything else worth hawking or buying. The same bowls and vases pop up in multiple stalls, so if your first bargaining attempt isn't successful, you'll likely have another opportunity a few stores down. Prices have shot up over the years, and fakes abound, so be careful what you buy. ✉ *Off Xizang Lu, Huangpu District* ⏲ *Daily 9–dusk.*

Site of the First National Congress of the Communist Party. The secret meeting on July 31, 1921, that marked the first National Congress was held at the Bo Wen Girls' School, where 13 delegates from Marxist, Communist, and Socialist groups gathered from around the country. Today,

GETTING ORIENTED

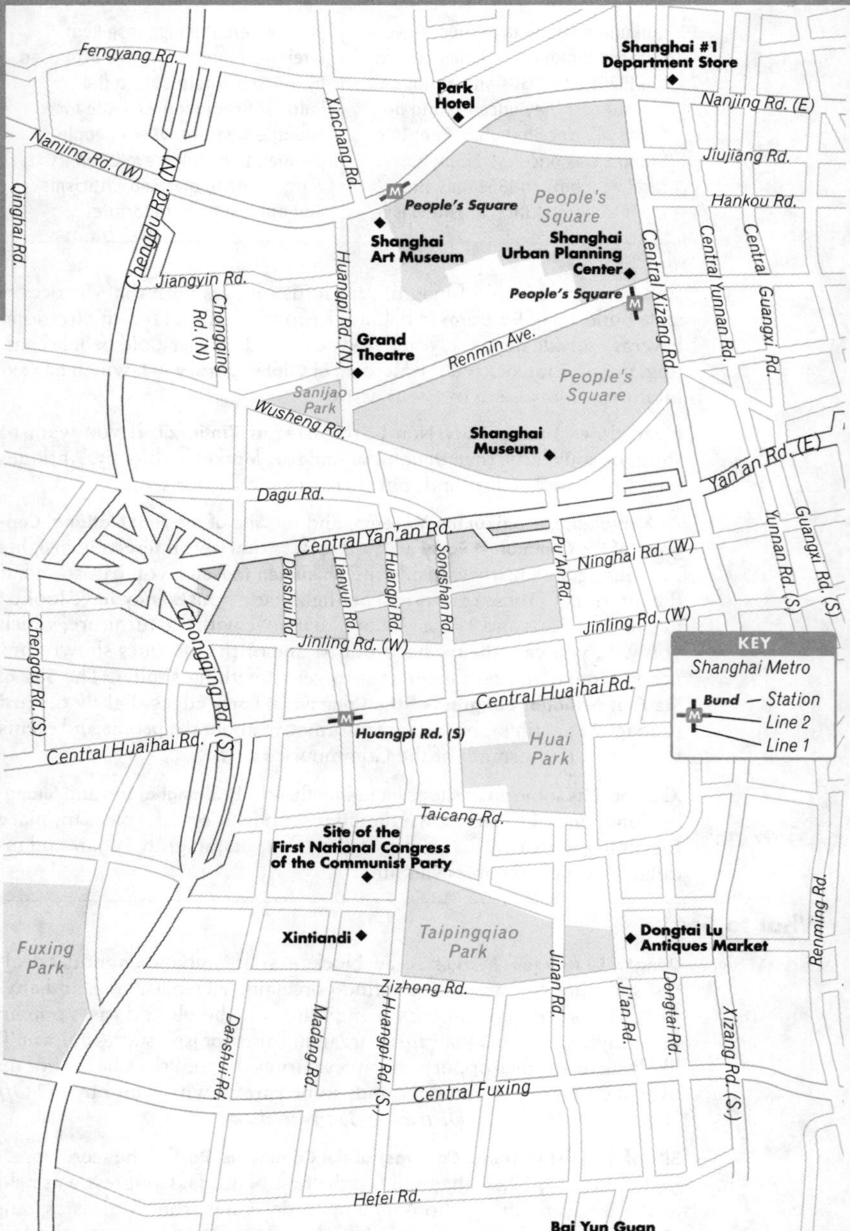
Fengyang Rd.
Shanghai #1 Department Store
Park Hotel
Nanjing Rd. (E)
Nanjing Rd. (W)
Xinchang Rd.
Jiujiang Rd.
Hankou Rd.
People's Square
People's Square
Shanghai Art Museum
Shanghai Urban Planning Center
Qinghai Rd.
Chengdu Rd. (N)
Jiangyin Rd.
Huangpi Rd. (N)
Central Xizang Rd.
Central Yunnan Rd.
Central Guangxi Rd.
People's Square
Chongqing Rd. (N)
Grand Theatre
Renmin Ave.
People's Square
Sanijao Park
Wusheng Rd.
Shanghai Museum
Yan'an Rd. (E)
Dagu Rd.
Central Yan'an Rd.
Danshui Rd.
Lianyun Rd.
Huangpi Rd.
Songshan Rd.
Pu'An Rd.
Ninghai Rd. (W)
Yunnan Rd. (S)
Guangxi Rd. (S)
Chengdu Rd. (S)
Chongqing Rd. (S)
Jinling Rd. (W)
Jinling Rd. (W)
KEY
Shanghai Metro
Bund — Station
Line 2
Line 1
Central Huaihai Rd.
Central Huaihai Rd.
Huangpi Rd. (S)
Huai Park
Taicang Rd.
Site of the First National Congress of the Communist Party
Fuxing Park
Xintiandi
Taipingqiao Park
Dongtai Lu Antiques Market
Renming Rd.
Zizhong Rd.
Danshui Rd.
Madang Rd.
Huangpi Rd. (S.)
Jinan Rd.
Ji'an Rd.
Dongtai Rd.
Xizang Rd. (S.)
Central Fuxing
Hefei Rd.
Bai Yun Guan

TOP REASONS TO GO

- **Shanghai Museum:** this well thought out, well labeled museum has a comprehensive selection of items from China's past and particularly impressive porcelain and bronze collections.
- **Xintiandi:** although pricey, this enclave is still worth a look for the reconstructed buildings, and it's also home to some great restaurants.
- **Shanghai Art Museum:** housed in the rather lovely old racetrack building, there's a good mix of local and international exhibitions here.
- **Shanghai Urban Planning Center:** get a fascinating look at the massive changes in Shanghai and the government's plans for its future.
- **Dongtai Lu Antiques Market:** often more peaceful than the Yu Garden, you'll find a good range of souvenir shopping amongst real old Shanghai houses.

QUICK BITES

Ye Shanghai's (✉ 338 Huangpi Nan Lu, Luwan District ☎ 021/6311-2323) Sunday dim-sum brunch is a good bet both for price and quality, and on other days, it's a stylish introduction to Shanghainese food.

Vegetarian Lifestyle (✉ 77 Songshan Lu, Luwan District ☎ 021/6384-8000) makes the list of Shanghai's best restaurants mainly for the lightness and creativity of its food.

Barbarossa (✉ 231 Nanjing Xi Lu [inside People's Park], Huangpu District ☎ 021/6318-0220) is a romantic place to view the sunset during its happy hour from 5-8 PM.

MAKING THE MOST OF YOUR TIME

The sights in this area are divided into two neat clusters—those around People's Square and those around Xintiandi. You can easily walk between the two in about 20 minutes. Visiting all the museums in the People's Square area could take a good half day. Xintiandi's sights don't take very long at all, so you could go before an early dinner, check out the museums, and then settle down for a pre-dinner drink and people-watch.

GETTING HERE

People's Square metro station is at present the main point of convergence for Shanghai's metro lines. The underground passageways can be confusing, so it's best to take the first exit and then find your way above ground. Xintiandi is a block or two south of Line 1's Huangpi Nan Lu metro station.

SAFETY

Be careful in the mad press of people and traffic when crossing the roads around People's Square. There are people employed to supervise the crossings, and if the police catch you jaywalking, you might get fined.

NEAREST PUBLIC RESTROOMS

Dotted around the outside of People's Square are rather grand looking and well-maintained public toilet buildings.

ironically, the site is surrounded by Xintiandi, Shanghai's center of conspicuous consumption. The upstairs of this restored shikumen is a well-curated museum explaining the rise of communism in China. Downstairs lies the very room where the first delegates worked. It remains frozen in time—the table set with matches and tea cups. ✉ *374 Huangpi Nan Lu, Luwan District* ☎ *021/5383–2171* 🎫 *Y3* ⏲ *Daily 9–5, last ticket sold at 4.*

Grand Theater. The spectacular front wall of glass shines as brightly as the star power in this magnificent theater. Its three stages host the best domestic and international performances, including the debut of *Les Misérables* in China in 2002 and *Cats* in 2003. The dramatic curved roof atop a square base is meant to invoke the Chinese traditional saying, "the earth is square and the sky is round." ■ TIP→ **See it at night.** ✉ *300 Renmin Dadao, Huangpu District* ☎ *021/6386–8686* 🎫 *Tour, Y40* ⏲ *Tours Mon. 9–11.*

Park Hotel. This art-deco structure overlooking People's Park was originally the tallest hotel in Shanghai. Completed in 1934, it had luxury rooms, a nightclub, and chic restaurants. Today it's more subdued, and the lobby is the most vivid reminder of its glorious past. It was also apparently an early inspiration for famous architect I. M. Pei (of the glass pyramids at the Louvre). ✉ *170 Nanjing Xi Lu, Huangpu District* ☎ *021/6327–5225.*

People's Park. In colonial days, this park was the northern half of the city's racetrack. Today the 30 acres of flower beds, lotus ponds, and trees are crisscrossed by a large number of paved paths. There's also an art gallery, the **Museum of Contemporary Art,** and a bar and restaurant, **Barbarossa,** inside. ✉ *231 Nanjing Xi Lu, Huangpu District* ☎ *021/6327–1333* 🎫 *Free* ⏲ *Daily 6–6 in winter and 5–7 in summer.*

Fodor's Choice ★ **People's Square.** Once the southern half of the city's racetrack, Shanghai's main square has become a social and cultural center. The Shanghai Museum, Municipal Offices, Grand Theater, and Shanghai Urban Planning Center surround it. During the day, visitors and residents stroll, fly kites, and take their children to feed the pigeons. In the evening, kids roller-skate, ballroom dancers hold group lessons, and families relax together. Weekends here are especially busy. ✉ *Bordered by Weihai Lu on south, Xizang Lu on east, Huangpi Bei Lu on west, and Fuzhou Lu on north, Huangpu District.*

Shanghai Art Museum. At the northwest corner of People's Park, the former site of the Shanghai Library was once a clubhouse for old Shanghai's sports groups, including the Shanghai Race Club. The building is now the home of the state-run Shanghai Art Museum. Its permanent collection includes paintings, calligraphy, and sculpture, but its rotating exhibitions have favored modern artwork. There's a museum store, café, and a rooftop restaurant. 325 Nanjing Xi Lu, at Huangpi Bei Lu, Huangpu District ☎ 021/6327–2829 🖷 021/6327–2425 🎫 Varies, depending on exhibition. Generally Y20 ⏲ Daily 9–5.

Fodor'sChoice ★ **Shanghai Museum.** Truly one of Shanghai's treasures, this museum has the country's premier collection of relics and artifacts. Eleven galleries exhibit Chinese artistry in all its forms: paintings, bronzes, sculpture, ceramics, calligraphy, jade, Ming and Qing Dynasty furniture, coins, seals, and art by indigenous populations. Its bronze collection is one of the best in the world, and its dress and costume gallery showcases intricate handiwork from several of China's 52 minority groups. If you opt not to rent the excellent acoustic guide, information is well presented in English. You can relax in the museum's pleasant tearoom or buy postcards, crafts, and reproductions of the artwork in the stellar bookshop. ✉ *201 Renmin Da Dao, Huangpu District* ☎ *021/6372–3500* 🌐 *www.shanghaimuseum.net* 🎟 *Y20, Y60 with acoustic guide* ⏲ *Daily 9–4.*

WORD OF MOUTH

"I must suggest the Shanghai Museum! That was one of the highlights of the trip. We could have stayed there for hours."
–Wandal

Shanghai Urban Planning Center. To understand the true scale of Shanghai and its ongoing building boom, visit the Master Plan Hall of this museum. Sprawled out on the 3rd floor is a 6,400-square-foot planning model of Shanghai—the largest model of its kind in the world—showing the metropolis as city planners expect it to look in 2020. You'll find familiar existing landmarks like the Pearl Tower and Shanghai Center as well as future sites like the so-called Flower Bridge, an esplanade over the Huangpu River to be built for Expo 2010. ✉ *100 Renmin Dadao, Huangpu District* ☎ *021/6372–2077* 🎟 *Y30 unless there is a special exhibition* ⏲ *Mon.–Thurs. 9–5, Fri.–Sun. 9–6, last ticket sold 1 hr before closing.*

Fodor'sChoice ★ **Xintiandi.** By WWII, around 70% of Shanghai's residents lived in shikumen or "stone gatehouses." Over the last two decades, most have been razed in the name of progress, but this 8-acre collection of stone gatehouses was renovated into an upscale shopping and dining complex and renamed Xintiandi, or "New Heaven on Earth." The restaurants are busy from lunchtime until past midnight, especially those with patios for watching the passing parade of shoppers. Just off the main thoroughfare is the visitor's center and the **Shikumen Museum** (✉ House 25, North Block, 123 Xingye Lu, Luwan District ☎ 021/3307–0337), a shikumen restored to 1920s style and filled with furniture and artifacts collected from nearby houses. Exhibits explain the European influence on shikumen design, the history of the Xintiandi renovation, as well as future plans for the entire 128-acre project. ✉ *181 Taicang Lu, Luwan District, bordered by Taicang Lu, Madang Lu, Zizhong Lu, and Huangpi Nan Lu* ☎ *021/6311–2288* 🌐 *www.xintiandi.com* 🎟 *Museum Y20* ⏲ *Museum, daily 10–10.*

THE BUND & NANJING DONG LU

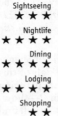

Sightseeing ★★★
Nightlife ★★★★
Dining ★★★★
Lodging ★★★★
Shopping ★★

The city's most recognizable sightseeing spot, the Bund, on the bank of Shanghai's Huangpu River, is lined with massive foreign buildings that predate 1949. Some of these buildings have been developed into hip "lifestyle" complexes with spas, restaurants, bars, galleries, and designer boutiques. The Bund is also an ideal spot for that photo of Pudong's famous skyline. Leading away from the Bund, Nanjing Dong Lu is a shadow of the stylish street it once was, but it's still a popular shopping spot for the locals. Some of the adjacent streets still have a faded glamour. The best time to visit is at night to stroll the neon-lit pedestrian road.

What's Here

People's Square station is the best place to begin. Head out exit three, following the signs to **Raffles City.** You can indulge in a bit of retail therapy in this mall before stepping out into **Xizang Nan Lu.** At **Nanjing Dong Lu,** gaze up at the austere art-deco grandeur of the **Shanghai No. 1 Department Store.** You can take this famous shopping street to get to the **Bund.** It may currently look a bit down on its luck, but, as is clear from the massive construction going on, this is probably set to change and hopefully the area will be returned to its former glory. If your feet are complaining, jump on the tourist train.

Try to look upward to catch glimpses of the wonderful architecture above the shop signs and in between the neon.

Before you head under the road to the promenade, stop to check out the **Peace Hotel.** The Northern Building is the more distinctive with its green tiled pitched roof. Inside, the lobby is a wonderful timepiece of

A BRIEF HISTORY

The district's name is derived from the Anglo-Indian and literally means "muddy embankment." In the early 1920s the Bund became the city's foreign street: Americans, British, Japanese, French, Russians, Germans, and other Europeans built banks, trading houses, clubs, consulates, and hotels in styles from neoclassical to art deco. As Shanghai grew to be a bustling trading center in the Yangzi Delta, the Bund's warehouses and ports became the heart of the action. With the Communist victory, the foreigners left Shanghai, and the Chinese government moved its own banks and offices here.

art-deco design. You can wander undisturbed up to the roof garden on the 11th floor. The bar and rooftop garden here are a bit underwhelming—Astroturf does not make a stylish statement—but the view across the **Bund** and to **Pudong** is lovely.

It's a rather impressive view either looking back at the old colonial buildings or at the sweep of modern construction across the river in **Pudong.** At the north end of the **Bund** is **Huangpu Park,** once banned to Chinese, and now just a little grotty. Underneath the **Memorial to the Heroes of the People** is the **Bund History Museum,** which has been under renovation. Heading south toward the ferry terminal, you'll pass a large statue of Chen Yi, Shanghai's first post-1949 mayor.

The **Bund Museum** is housed in a former observation tower. It's tiny, but the reproduction photos of the Bund through time are quite interesting for a quick look. The building itself was moved 22.4 meters (73 feet) to make way for construction. Just past the museum and the ferry terminal is the **I Love Shanghai** bar, where, if it's open, you can pick up an I LOVE SHANGHAI T-shirt.

Back along the other side of the road are the monumental buildings that make the **Bund** so famous. Several of them have been done up in recent years to create homes for trendy expensive bars, boutiques, and restaurants. One of the nicest places to sit and enjoy the view is **New Heights** at **Three on the Bund** or you can check out **Laris,** also in the same building.

Some streets in Shanghai still specialize in certain merchandise and **Fuzhou Lu** was once Shanghai's books and stationery street. There are still quite a few bookstores and some great buildings along this street. Pop into the little gallery, **Studio Rouge,** to see what's happening in Chinese art and get your feet reshod in embroidered shoes at **Suzhou Cobblers.** For some great milk tea and decorative ceilings, go to the **Xinwang Teahouse** on **Shandong Lu** and **Hankou Lu.** At the end of **Fuzhou Lu,** you'll end up back at your starting point, **People's Square,** from where you can take the metro to your next location.

Alternatively, you can head to the **Banyan Tree Spa** at the **Westin** in the **Bund Centre** to have yourself spoiled rotten.

GETTING ORIENTED

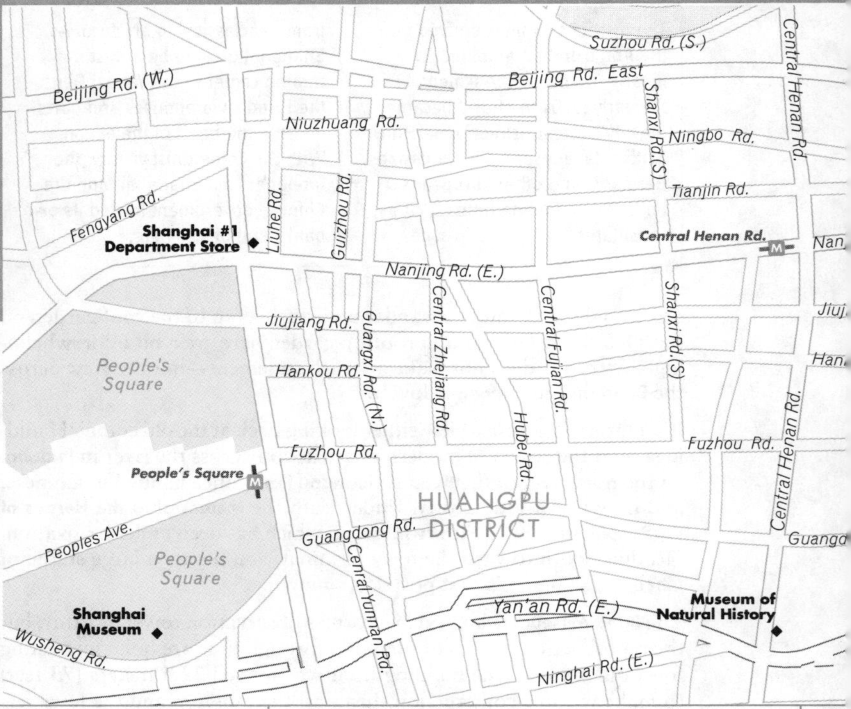

GETTING HERE

The simplest way to get here is to take metro Line 2 to Henan Zhong Lu station, and then head east for the Bund, or west for the main shopping area of Nanjing Dong Lu. Alternatively, you can get off at People's Square station and walk east.

TOP REASONS TO GO

- **The Bund:** this icon of Shanghai is fast becoming a stretch of sophisticated shopping, dining, and drinking.
- **Peace Hotel:** Victor Sassoon's famous hotel is a museum piece of art-deco design both inside and out.
- **M on the Bund:** the food may not always be great, but it was the first restaurant with a wonderful view over the river. Its newly expanded Glamour Bar, on the floor below hosts a wonderful array of local and international musicians, writers, and other interesting people.
- **Three on the Bund:** possibly the hippest lifestyle complex on the Bund. The restaurant and bar on the top, New Heights, is a lovely place to while away an evening.
- **Fuzhou Lu:** a stroll down this street might turn up a few good books, a quirky shoe store, and some spottings of old-style buildings. It's also a pleasant alternative to get from the Bund to People's Square while avoiding Nanjing Dong Lu.

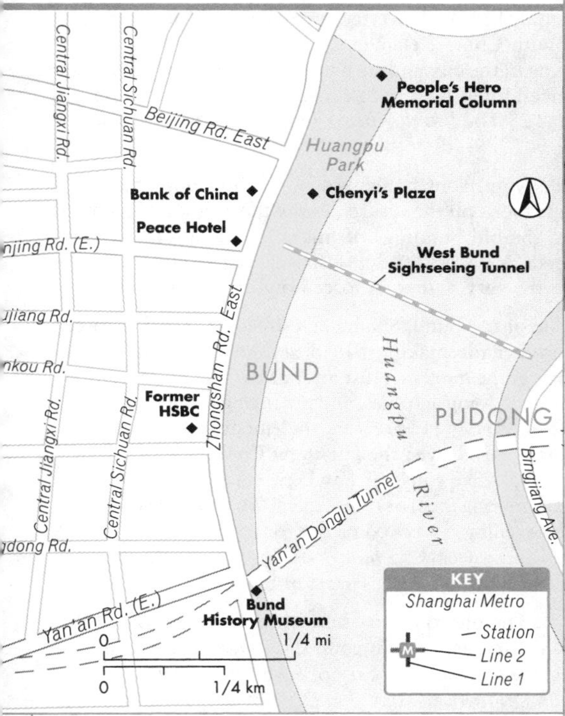

QUICK BITES

I Love Shanghai (✉ 155 Zhongshan Dong Er Lu, Huangpu District ☎ 021/6355-8058) is tucked away near the ferry terminal. There are often drink specials, and it's a cozy place to hang out. The main reason to come here is to get your I LOVE SHANGHAI T-shirt. Intellectual Property Rights, eat your heart out.

Laris's (✉ 6/F Three on the Bund, 17 Guangdong Lu, Huangpu District ☎ 021/6321-9922) all white interior is a beautiful place to have lunch, and they have a decent set menu that won't break the bank. The food is modern fusion and pretty tasty to boot. If you want a good view, book in advance.

M on the Bund (✉ 7/F 5 The Bund, 20 Guangdong Lu, Huangpu District ☎ 021/6350-9988) is somewhat of a Shanghai institution as it was the first foreign restaurant to take up shop on the Bund. The food is hit or miss, but the Glamour Bar is a great place to gather.

MAKING THE MOST OF YOUR TIME

This excursion is a relatively easy stroll as it takes about 20 minutes to walk up Nanjing Dong Lu. You can also combine this area with either a trip to Pudong or to the sights around People's Square to make a day's worth of exploring.

SAFETY

As in any tourist area, there are pickpockets. Not so much a safety issue as an annoyance are the "art students" who invite you to see a display of paintings; avoid this at all costs as not only will you be subject to the hard sell, but the paintings are also overpriced and usually poor quality. Also be wary of the moneychangers who loiter outside the Peace Hotel and the Bank of China. Some may be reputable, but some may not.

A GOOD WALK

Join in with the throng and stroll the Bund promenade from Huangpu Park to the ferry terminus. Despite the other people, it can be quite romantic, especially at night.

What to See

Bank of China. Here, old Shanghai's Western architecture (British art deco in this case) mixes with Chinese elements. In 1937 it was designed to be the highest building in the city and surpassed the neighboring Cathay Hotel (now the Peace Hotel) by a hair, except for the green tower on the Cathay's roof. ☒ *23 The Bund, Zhongshan Dong Yi Lu, Huangpu District* ☎ *021/6329–1979.*

Fodor'sChoice
★
The Bund. Shanghai's waterfront boulevard best shows both the city's pre-1949 past and its focus on the future. Today the municipal government has renovated the old buildings of this most foreign face of the city, highlighting them as tourist attractions, and even tried for a while to sell them back to the very owners it forced out after 1949.

On the riverfront side of the Bund, Shanghai's street life is in full force. The city rebuilt the promenade, making it an ideal gathering place for both tourists and residents. In the morning, just after dawn, the Bund is full of people ballroom dancing, doing aerobics, and practicing kung fu, qi gong, and tai chi. The rest of the day people walk the embankment, snapping photos of the Oriental Pearl Tower, the Huangpu River, and each other. Be prepared for the aggressive souvenir hawkers; while you can't completely avoid them, try ignoring them or telling them *"bu yao,"* which means "Don't want." In the evenings lovers come out for romantic walks amid the floodlit buildings and tower. ☒ *5 blocks of Zhongshan Dong Yi Lu between Jinling Lu and Suzhou Creek, Huangpu District.*

Bund History Museum. The photo gallery here chronicles the role of the Bund in Shanghai's history: as an architectural showcase, as a commercial hub, and as a stage for the political upheaval of the 1920s to the '40s. ☒ *1 Zhongshan Dongyi Lu, Huangpu District* ☎ *021/6321–6542* ☞ *Free* ☉ *Daily 10 AM–2 AM.*

Bund Museum. The white-and-red observation tower has held watch over the weather and the Huangpu River since 1884. The base, now home to this tiny museum, was built 19 years earlier. Photos along the walls present a round-up of the Bund's most famous buildings, both past and present. ☒ *Unit A, 1 Zhongshan Erlu, The Bund, Huangpu District* ☎ *No phone* ☞ *Free* ☉ *Daily 9–5.*

Former Hong Kong and Shanghai Bank Building (HSBC). One of the Bund's most impressive buildings—some say it's the area's pièce de résistance—the domed structure was built by the British in 1921–23, when it was the second-largest bank building in the world. After 1949 the building was turned into Communist Party offices and City Hall; now it is used by the Pudong Development Bank. In 1997 the bank made the news when it uncovered a beautiful 1920s Italian-tile mosaic in the building's dome. In the 1950s the mosaic was deemed too extravagant for a Com-

> **WORD OF MOUTH**
>
> "To see the Bund at night with its distinctive colonial architecture is simply not to be missed—a dramatically different look than seen in daylight." —Airlawgirl

TREAT YOURSELF

Housed in the Westin Hotel, which incidentally is one of Shanghai's nicest, the Banyan Tree Spa is a decadent way to indulge with single treatments such as massages right up to deluxe packages. The spa has elegantly decorated treatment rooms representing the five Chinese elements. ✉ *Level 3, The Westin, 88 Henan Zhong Lu, Huangpu District* ☎ *021/6335-1888.*

munist government office, so it was covered by white paint, which protected it from being found by the Red Guards during the Cultural Revolution. It was then forgotten until the Pudong Development Bank renovated the building. If you walk in and look up, you'll see the circular mosaic in the dome—an outer circle painted with scenes of the cities where the HSBC had branches at the time: London, Paris, New York, Bangkok, Tokyo, Calcutta, Hong Kong, and Shanghai; a middle circle made up of the 12 signs of the zodiac; and the center painted with a large sun and Ceres, the Roman goddess of abundance. ✉ *12 The Bund, Zhongshan Dong Yi Lu, Huangpu District* ☎ *021/6161-6188* *Free* *Daily 9–6.*

Huangpu Park. The local government paved over what once was a lovely green garden to create this park. During colonial times Chinese could not enter the park; a sign at the entrance allegedly said, NO DOGS OR CHINESE ALLOWED. From its location at the junction of Suzhou Creek and the Huangpu River, it offers views of both sides of the river. Beneath the park's **Memorial of the Heroes of the People** obelisk is a sweeping relief of China's liberation. ✉ *North end of Bund, beside the river, Huangpu District* ☎ *021/5308-2636* *Free* *May–Oct., daily 6 AM–10 PM; Nov.–Apr., daily 6 AM–6 PM.*

★ **Peace Hotel** (Heping Fandian). This hotel at the corner of the Bund and Nanjing Lu is among Shanghai's most treasured old buildings. If any establishment will give you a sense of Shanghai's past, it's this one. Its high ceilings, ornate woodwork, and art-deco fixtures are still intact, and the ballroom evokes old Shanghai cabarets and gala parties.

The south building was formerly the Palace Hotel. Built in 1906, it is the oldest building on the Bund. The north building, formerly the Cathay Hotel, built in 1929, is more famous historically. It was known as the private playroom of its owner, Victor Sassoon, a wealthy landowner who invested in the opium trade. The Cathay was actually part of a complete office and hotel structure collectively called Sassoon House. Victor Sassoon himself lived and entertained his guests in the green penthouse. The hotel was rated on a par with the likes of Raffles in Singapore and the Peninsula in Hong Kong. It was *the* place to stay in old Shanghai; Noel Coward wrote *Private Lives* here. In the evenings, the famous Peace Hotel Old Jazz Band plays in the German-style pub on the 1st floor. ✉ *20 Nanjing Dong Lu, Huangpu District* ☎ *021/6321-6888* 🌐 *www.shanghaipeacehotel.com.*

FORMER FRENCH CONCESSION

Sightseeing ★★★
Nightlife ★★★★
Dining ★★★★
Lodging ★★★
Shopping ★★★★

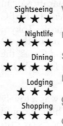

With its tree-lined streets and crumbling old villas, the Former French Concession is possibly Shanghai's most atmospheric area. It's a wonderful place to go wandering and make serendipitous discoveries of stately architecture, groovy boutiques and galleries, or cozy cafés. Here, much of Shanghai's past beauty remains, although many of the old buildings are in desperate states of disrepair. One of the major roads through this area, Huaihai Lu, is a popular shopping location with shops selling international and local brands. It's also where many of Shanghai's restaurants, bars, and clubs are located, so if you are looking for an evening out, this is a good area to head for.

What's Here

From **Huangpi Lu** or **Shaanxi Nan Lu** station, head down **Huaihai Lu** to **Sinan Lu.** At the corner of these two roads is the **Epsite Gallery,** a small gallery attached to the Benetton clothing store, which always has an interesting photographic exhibition or two and is free of charge.

On shady **Sinan Lu,** you'll find wonderful old villas set in small gardens and lots of trees. Further down **Sinan Lu** is the entrance to **Sun Yat-sen's Former Residence** where you'll be taken through a rather hurried guided tour; however, it's a good opportunity to get a look inside an old house. To the west down **Gaolan Lu** is **Fuxing Park,** a pleasant place during the day, but it really comes alive on weekend nights due to the two popular clubs, **Park 97** and **Guandi** located here.

A BRIEF HISTORY

The French were first granted permission to settle in Shanghai by the Qing in 1844. Although originally established by the French and run by their municipal government, by the 1930s the area was largely populated by Russians and Chinese. It also became a place of gangster activity including opium trade and prostitution. Today the area is a charming historic district known for its atmosphere and beautiful old architecture.

Further down the road is the home of the former prime minister during Mao's time, Zhou Enlai. Here you can wander around by yourself. If you've been bitten by the shopping bug, the **Taikang Antique Market** is worth a look, especially as it's usually quiet and you can sometimes turn up some interesting items, particularly from the revolutionary period. Continue down **Taikang Lu,** and you'll come across the small artistic community that has set up there with studios and some funky design shops. Take a break in the courtyard at **Kommune,** which serves an excellent breakfast.

Head in the general direction of the intersection of **Maoming Lu** and **Huaihai Lu** through tranquil backstreets where modern development has been relatively subdued. On **Maoming Lu,** once a notorious bar street, there's an entrance to the former **Morriss Estate,** now **Ruijin Park,** which is a lovely spot to settle at one of the cafés or bars for a quiet drink. **Face,** a bar in an old mansion within the grounds is particularly charming and also serves afternoon tea. At the intersection, there is the **Cathay Cinema,** a recently restored art-deco movie theater which is still in use. Those interested in architecture can continue down **Maoming Lu** to check out the **Jinjiang Hotel** and the **Lyceum Theatre.**

You might want to walk down **Huaihai Lu** to browse the shops with the crowds, or slip down **Changle Lu** or **Julu Lu** to avoid them. At **Fenyang Lu,** you can pop into the **Arts and Crafts Research Centre,** which although somewhat dusty and lackluster, is still an opportunity to see people working on traditional Chinese crafts such as paper cutting.

Happy hour in the garden at **Sasha's,** a stately old home once belonging to businessman TV Soong (brother of Soong Qingling and Soong Meiling who were married to Sun Yat-sen and Chiang Kai-shek respectively), is a very pleasant experience and the lounge-bar is cozy when the weather is cold. Further down Hengshan Road is the **International Cathedral,** which still holds services. If you want to check your e-mail, the **Shanghai Library** has Internet access in the basement for Y4 per hour.

Finally, head further down **Huaihai Lu** to check out the **Former Residence of Soong Qingling.**

What to See

Cathay Cinema. Once part of millionaire Victor Sassoon's holdings, the art-deco Cathay Cinema was one of the first movie theaters in Shang-

GETTING ORIENTED

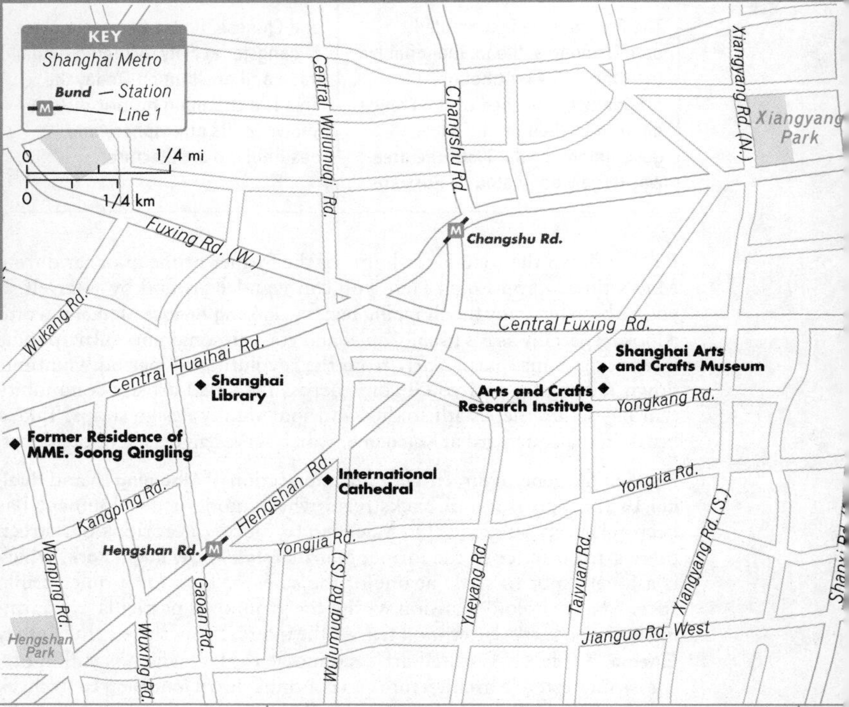

GETTING HERE

Any of the four Line 1 metro stops (Huangpi Nan Lu, Shaanxi Nan Lu, Changshu Lu, or Hengshan Lu) will land you somewhere in the French Concession area. There are usually plenty of taxis except on rainy days or at peak hours.

SAFETY

Along **Huaihai Lu,** the number of pickpockets has risen recently. Keep an eye on your belongings, even when in cafés.

TOP REASONS TO GO

- **Walking tree-lined avenues:** tree-lined streets with old buildings make for a pleasant walk. Poke your head into compounds and snap the architecture while it's still there.

- **Taikang Lu:** this small artistic community of bars, cafés, studios, and boutiques situated around a laneway makes for an alternative break to Shanghai's malls and shopping streets.

- **Ruijin Park:** relax in an elegant park that was formerly the Morriss Estate. Face is best of the bars and cafés inside, and afternoon tea facing the lawn here is respite from Shanghai's endless activity.

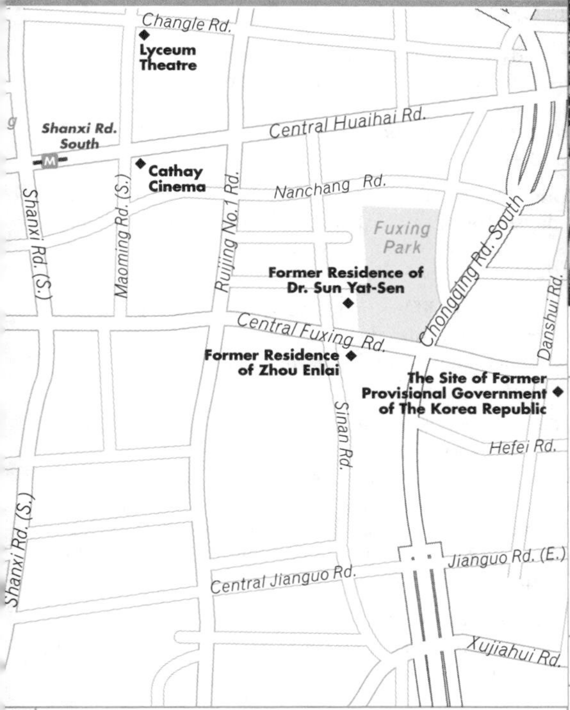

MAKING THE MOST OF YOUR TIME

This is really a lovely area to walk around, so it might be best to leave cabs behind and go on foot. The only site that is at a distance is Soong Qingling's Former Residence, which is a bit further down Huaihai Lu. It's a pleasant way to while away a morning or an afternoon.

NEAREST PUBLIC RESTROOMS

Your best bets are the malls on Huaihai Lu such as at Times Square or Hong Kong Plaza. Don't forget the toilet paper.

A GOOD WALK

The walk from **Shaanxi Nan Lu** or **Huangpi Nan Lu** metro station to the **Taikang Lu** artists' community is a good one because it encompasses many of Shanghai's different personalities—the consumerism of **Huaihai Lu,** the old-world avenue of **Sinan Lu,** and the funky and alternative feel of **Taikang Lu.** Without stopping at the sites, this walk should take about 20 minutes.

QUICK BITES

Arch (✉ 439 Wukang Lu, Xuhui District ☎ 021/6466-0807) is a little out of the way, but so worth the journey. Situated on the ground floor of a grand old French-style building, this café is a favorite particularly among the expat community for its hip decor, wireless access, and great food.

Face (✉ Building 4, Ruijin Guest House, 118 Ruijin Er Lu, Xuhui District ☎ 021/6466-4328) is a bar and restaurant in an old mansion set in Ruijin Park. Decorated with Asian antiques including opium beds for lounging, it has an air of colonial decadence. Cocktails or afternoon tea are the most chic ways to enjoy the atmosphere.

Secret Garden (✉ 333 Changle Lu, Xuhui District ☎ 021/5405-0789) is hidden away, but is worth seeking out to enjoy elegantly presented Chinese food amongst antique-style furniture, silk cushions, and candlelight in an old villa.

hai. The building still serves as a theater, showing a mix of Chinese and Western films. ✉ *870 Huaihai Zhonglu, at Maoming Nan Lu, Luwan District* ☎ *021/5404–1122.*

Fuxing Park. The grounds of this European-style park—known as French Park before 1949—provide a bit of greenery in crowded Shanghai. Here you'll find people practicing tai chi and lovers strolling hand in hand. ✉ *105 Fuxing Zhong Lu, Luwan District* ☎ *021/5386–1069* 🎫 *Free* ⏲ *Daily 6 AM–6 PM.*

International Cathedral. This small ivy-covered cathedral dates to Shanghai's Concession days. Today it's called the Shanghai Community Church and holds weekly Protestant services. ✉ *53 Hengshan Lu, Xuhui District* ☎ *021/6437–6576.*

Lyceum Theatre. In the days of old Shanghai, the Lyceum was the home of the British Amateur Drama Club. The old stage got a face-lift in 2003 and is still in use as a concert hall. ✉ *57 Maoming Nan Lu, Luwan District* ☎ *021/6217–8530.*

Shanghai Arts and Crafts Research Institute. It's a little dusty, run-down, and bare bones, but you can watch Shanghai's artisans as they create traditional Chinese arts and crafts. Works you can purchase include everything from paper cuts to snuff bottles, but prices can be a bit high compared to quality. Formerly, the old French mansion housed an official of the Concession's pre-1949 government. ✉ *79 Fenyang Lu, Xuhui District* ☎ *021/6437–0509* 🎫 *Y8* ⏲ *Daily 9–5.*

Soong Qingling's Former Residence. While she first came to national attention as the wife of Dr. Sun Yat-sen, Soong Qingling became revered in her own right for her dedication to the Communist Party. Indeed, many mainland Chinese regard her as the "Mother of China." (On the other hand, Soong's sister, Meiling, married Chiang Kai-shek, who was the head of the Nationalist government from 1927 to 1949, at which point the couple fled to Taiwan.) This three-story house, built in 1920 by a German ship owner, was Soong's primary residence from 1948 to 1963. It has been preserved as it was during her lifetime and includes her 4,000 books in the study and furniture in the bedroom that her parents gave as her dowry. The small museum next door has some nice displays from Soong Qingling and Sun Yat-sen's life, including wedding pictures from their 1915 wedding in Tokyo. ✉ *1843 Huaihai Zhonglu, Xuhui District* ☎ *021/6431–4965* 🎫 *Y8* ⏲ *Daily 9–4:30.*

Sun Yat-sen's Former Residence. Dr. Sun Yat-sen, the father of the Chinese republic, lived in this two-story house for six years, from 1919 to 1924. His wife, Soong Qingling, continued to live here after his death until 1937. Today it's been turned into a museum, and tours are conducted in Chinese and English. ✉ *7 Xiangshan Lu, Luwan District* ☎ *021/6437–2954* 🎫 *Y8* ⏲ *Daily 9–4:30.*

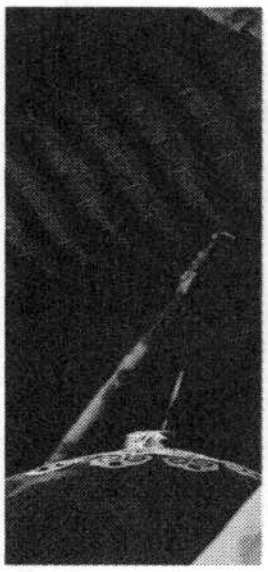

NANJING XI LU & JING'AN

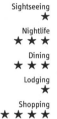

Sightseeing ★
Nightlife ★ ★ ★
Dining ★ ★ ★
Lodging ★
Shopping ★ ★ ★ ★

Shanghai's glitziest malls and some five-star hotels are along the main street in this area, Nanjing Xi Lu. So, if you're into designer threads, luxury spas, or expensive brunches, you can satisfy your spending urges and max out your credit here. For those of a more spiritual bent, Jingan Temple, although still being reconstructed, is one of Shanghai's largest temples. The small Jingan Park across the street is popular with couples. Behind the temple is an interesting network of back streets.

What's Here

Sights are a bit thin on the ground in this area, but if you like international designer labels, this is where you can work the plastic. Coming out from **Jingan Si** metro station on Line 2, you'll be close to **Jingan Temple.** Across the street is **Jingan Park** inside, which has an Indonesian restaurant, Bali Laguna in a rather romantic setting if you can ignore the **Yanan Lu** flyover behind you.

Behind the temple is the **Paramount,** a restored dance hall with three daily sessions of dancing at various prices. If you don't have a partner, don't worry—you can rent one. Behind the **Paramount** and **Jingan Temple** is a network of backstreets that make for interesting wandering.

Further up **Nanjing Xi Lu,** you'll pass shiny malls with high-end designer stores, and five-star hotels as well as the monumental Soviet-inspired **Shanghai Exhibition Center.**

What to See

Jingan Temple. Originally built about AD 300, the Jingan Temple has been rebuilt and renovated numerous times. The sound of power tools often

GETTING ORIENTED

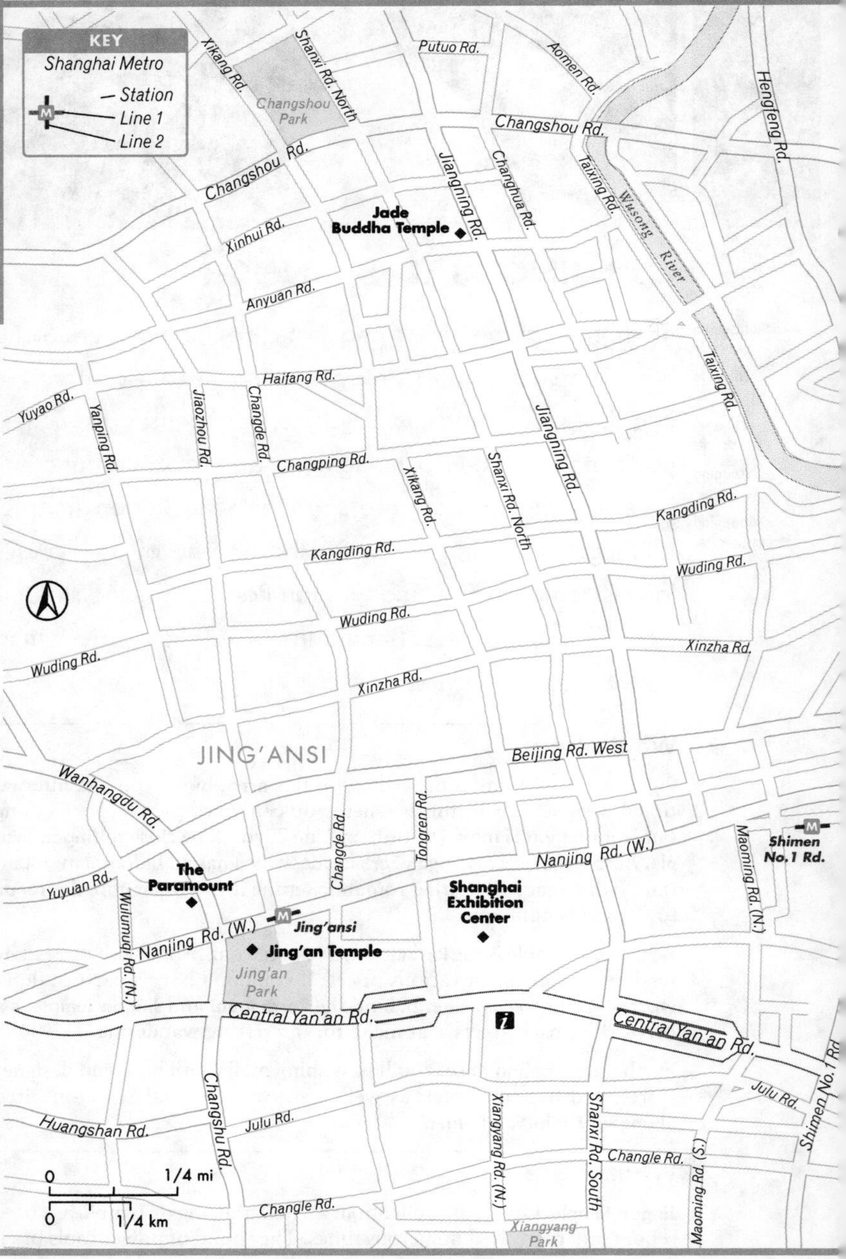

GETTING HERE

Metro Line 2 takes you to **Jingan Si** station. If you want to take a taxi afterward, joining the queue at the **Shanghai Centre/Portman Ritz-Carlton** is a good idea, especially when it's raining.

TOP REASONS TO GO

- **Jingan Temple:** although not Shanghai's best temple, this is the main sight in this area and one of Shanghai's larger inner-city temples.

- **Designer shopping:** If you have the funds, the designer shopping here is currently the best in Shanghai; all the big high-end brands fill posh-looking malls.

QUICK BITES

Situated in Jingan Park, **Bali Laguna** (✉ 1649 Nanjing Xi Lu, inside Jingan Park, Jingan District ☎ 021/6248-6970) is a romantic setting overlooking a small pool that is particularly pretty at night when the lights twinkle and reflect in the water. The food does not live up to the atmosphere, so stick to the drinks.

Bi Feng Tang (✉ 1333 Nanjing Lu, Jingan District ☎ 021/6279-0738) serves up cheap Cantonese-style food with lots of choices. It's open until 5 AM so it's perfect for midnight snacking. The menu is big on dim sum and you might get to sit in one of the replica boats.

Element Fresh (✉ :Rm 112, Shanghai Centre, 1376 Nanjing Xi Lu, Jingan District ☎ 021/6279-8682) is very popular for its large breakfasts, great salads, and fresh juices. Be prepared to wait for a table on weekends and during office lunch hours.

MAKING THE MOST OF YOUR TIME

This area can be covered very quickly—in an hour or so—as there isn't much to see. **Jingan Si** metro is on Line 2, so if you don't get caught up in a shopping frenzy, head to **People's Square, Henan Zhong Lu,** or the **Bund** afterward.

SAFETY

There are often a few beggars along this strip, but they aren't overly aggressive and not really a threat to your safety. It's entirely up to you whether you give them money or not—some are in real need and others are professionals who belong to "beggar rackets."

NEAREST PUBLIC RESTROOMS

Malls are your best bets for decent clean toilets. The ones in CITIC Square are particularly recommended.

A BRIEF HISTORY

In the past, home to Shanghai's ultrarich such as the Kadoories and the Hardoons, Nanjing Xi Lu was once Bubbling Well Road and also the site of some of Shanghai's more famous clubs of the 1930s. Jingan Park was once Bubbling Well Cemetery. The street and the cemetery take their name from a well that used to exist in the area and was apparently first used in the 3rd century AD. The first temple was built at this site around the same time, but the one you see today is a shiny new reproduction that's typical of the Chinese habit of tearing down buildings and replacing them with reconstructions.

drowns out the monks' chanting. The temple's Southern-style halls, which face a central courtyard, gleam with new wood carvings of elephants and lotus flowers, but the hall interiors have stark, new concrete walls, and feel generally antiseptic. The temple's main draw is its copper Hongwu bell, cast in 1183 and weighing in at 3.5 tons. ✉ *1686 Nanjing Xi Lu, next to the Jingan Si subway entrance, Jingan District* ☎ *021/6256–6366* 🎫 *Y10* 🕗 *Daily 7:30–5.*

Paramount. Built in 1933, socialites referred to the Paramount as the finest dance hall in Asia. Now, at night, the domed roof of this art-deco dance hall glow blue and inside people dance the afternoon and the night away. ✉ *218 Yuyuan Lu, Jingan District* ☎ *021/6249–8866* 🎫 *Varies depending on the dance session time* 🕗 *Daily.*

Shanghai Exhibition Center. This mammoth piece of Russian architecture was built as a sign of Sino-Soviet friendship after 1949. Today, it hosts conventions and special touring exhibitions. The complex has a restaurant that caters largely to tour groups. ✉ *1000 Yanan Zhonglu, Jingan District* ☎ *021/6279–0279* 🕗 *Daily 9–4.*

Giant Buddha Statue, Leshan

THE AGE OF EMPIRES

When asked his opinion on the historical impact of the French Revolution, Chairman Mao quipped, "It's too early to tell." Though a bit tongue in cheek, China does measure its history in millennia, and in its grand timeline, interactions with the West have been mere blips.

According to historical records, Chinese civilization stretches back to the 15th century BC—markings found on turtle shells carbon dated to around 1500 BC bear some similarity to modern Chinese script. China then resembled city-states rather than a unified nation. Iconic figures such as Lao Tzu (the father of Taoism), Sun Tzu (author of the *Art of War*), and Confucius lived during this period. Generally, 221 BC is accepted as the beginning of Imperial China, when the city-states united under various banners.

Over the next 2,200 years (give or take a few), China alternated between periods of harmony and political upheaval. Its armies conquered new territory and were in turn conquered by external invaders (most of whom wound up themselves being assimilated).

By the early 18th century, the long, slow decline of the Qing—the last of China's Imperial dynasties—was already in progress, making the ancient nation ripe for exploitation by rising European powers. The Imperial era ended with the forced abdication of child Emperor Puyi (whose life is chronicled in Bernardo Bertolucci's *The Last Emperor*), and it's here that the history of modern China, first with the founding of the republic under Sun Yat-sen and then with the establishment of the People's Republic under Mao Zedong, truly begins.

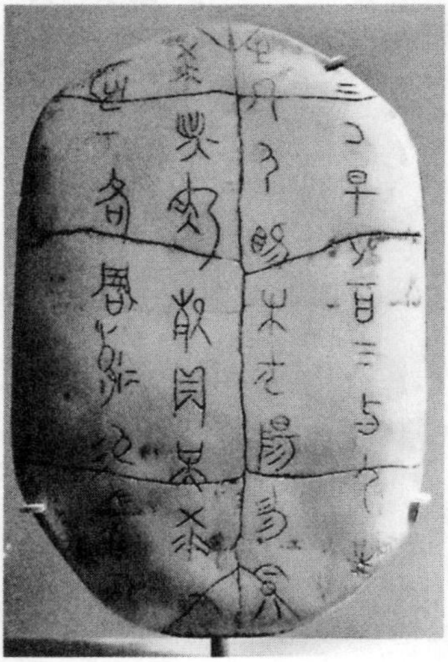

(left) Oracle shell with early Chinese characters. (top, right) The Great Wall stretches 4,163 miles from east to west. (bottom, right) Confucius was born in Qufu, Shandong.

circa 1500 BC

Writing Appears

The earliest accounts of Chinese history are still shrouded in myth and legend, and it wasn't until 1959 that stories were verified by archaeological findings. For millennia, people formed communities in the fertile lands of what is now central China. The first recorded Chinese characters are said to have been developed 3,500 years ago. Though sometimes referred to as the Shang Dynasty, this period was more of a precursor to modern Chinese dynasties than a truly unified kingdom.

722–475 BC

The Warring States Period

China was so far from unified that these centuries are collectively remembered as the Warring States Period. As befitting such a contentious time, military science progressed, iron replaced bronze, and weapons material improved. Some of China's greatest luminaries lived during this period, including the father of Taoism, Lao-tzu, Confucius, and Sun-Tzu, one of the greatest military tacticians and the author of the infamous *Art of War,* which is still studied in military academies around the world.

221–207 BC

The First Dynasty

The Qin Dynasty eventually defeated all of the other warring factions thanks to their cutting edge military technology, namely the cavalry. The Qin were also called Ch'in, which may be where the word China first originated. The first Emperor, Qin Shi-huang, unified much of the lands and established a legal code and vast bureaucracy to hold it together. The Qin dynasty also standardized the written and spoken language and introduced a common currency.

(left) Terra-cotta warriors in Xian, on the Silk Road. (top right) Buddha statue, Maijishan Cave in Tianshui, Gansa. (bottom left) Sun Tzu, author of The *Art of War*.

In order to protect his newly unified country, Qin Shi-huang ordered the creation of the massive Great Wall of China, which was built and rebuilt over the next 1,000 years. He was also a sculpture enthusiast and commissioned a massive army of stone soldiers to follow him into the afterlife. Buried with him, these terra-cotta warriors would remain hidden from the eyes of the world for two thousand years, until they were found by a farmer digging in a field just outside of Xian. These warriors are among the most important archaeological finds of the 20th century.

220–265 BC

Buddhism Arrives

Emperor Qin's dreams of a unified China fell apart, and eventually the kingdom split into three warring factions. But what was bad for stability turned out to be good for literature. The Three Kingdoms Period is still remembered in song and story. *The Romance of the Three Kingdoms* is as popular among Asian bookworms as the *Legend of King Arthur* is among western readers. It's still widely read and has been translated into almost every language. Variations of the story have been adapted for manga, television series, and video games.

The Three Kingdoms period was filled with court intrigue, murder, and massive battles that, while exciting to read about centuries later, weren't much fun at the time. Armies ravaged the countryside, and most people lived and died in misery. Perhaps it was the carnage and disunity of the time that turned the country into a magnet for forces of harmony; it was during this period that Buddhism was first introduced into China, traveling over the Himalayas from India, via the Silk Road.

(left) Genghis Khan conquered much of China. (top, right) Islamic lecture at madrassa classroom inside Dongguan mosque, Xinning. (bottom, right) Kublai Khan was the first Mongol Emperor of China.

618–845

Religion Diversifies

Chinese spiritual life continued to diversify. Nestorian Monks from Asia Minor arrived bearing news of Christianity, and Saad ibn Abi Waqqas (a companion of the Prophet Muhammad) supposedly visited the Middle Kingdom to spread the word of Islam. During this era, Wu Zetian, one-time concubine, seized power from the Tang Dynasty and became the first (and only) woman to assume the title of emperor. She ruled for 25 years through puppet emperors and finally, for 15 years as Emperor Shengshen.

1271–1368

Ghengis Invades

In Xanadu did Kublai Khan a stately pleasure dome decree ...

Or so goes the famed Coleridge poem. But Kublai's grandfather Temujin (better known as Ghengis Khan) had bigger things in mind. One of the greatest war tacticians in history, he united the restive nomads of Mongolia's grassy plains and eventually sacked, looted, and pillaged much of the known west and most of the Chinese landmass. By the time Ghengis died in 1227, his grandson was well-tutored and ready to take on the rest of China.

By 1271, Kublai had established a capital in a landlocked city that would only much later become known as Beijing. This marks the beginning of the first (but not last) non-Han dynasty. Kublai Khan kept fighting southward and by 1279, Guangzhou fell to the Mongols, and Khan became the ultimate monarch of China. Though barbarians at heart, the Mongols must be credited for encouraging the arts and a number of early public works projects, including extending the highways and grand canals.

(left) Statue of admiral Zheng He. (top right) Forbidden City in Beijing. (bottom right) Child emperor Puyi.

1368–1644

Ming Dynasty

Many scholars believe that the Mongols' inability to relate with the Han is what ultimately pushed the Han to rise up and overthrow them. The reign of the Ming Dynasty was the last ethnically Han Dynasty to rule over a unified China. At its apex, the Bright Empire encompassed a landmass easily recognized as China, even by today's mapmakers. The Ming Emperors built a huge army and navy, refurbished the agricultural system, and printed many books using movable type long before Gutenberg. In the 13th century, Emperor Yongle began construction of the famous Forbidden City in Beijing, a veritable icon of China.

Also during the Ming Dynasty, China's best known explorer, Zheng He, plied the seven seas in massive treasure fleets that dwarfed in size and range the ships of Christopher Columbus. A giant both in stature and persona, Admiral Zheng (who was also a eunuch) spent two decades expanding China's knowledge of the world outside of its already impressive borders. He traveled as far as India, Africa, and (some say) even the coast of the New World.

1644–1911

Qing Dynasty

The final dynasty represented a serious case of minority rule. They were Manchus from the northeast. The early Qing dynasty was a brutal period as forces loyal to the new emperor crushed those loyal to the old. The Qing Dynasty peaked in the mid-to-late 18th century but soon after, its military powers began to wane. In the 19th century, Qing control weakened and prosperity diminished. By 1910 China was fractured, a baby sat on the Imperial throne, and the Qing Dynasty was on its deathbed.

(left) Portrait of Marshal Chiang Kai-shek with his wife. (top, right) Mao Zedong on December 6, 1944. (bottom, right) Sun Yat-sen.

1834–1860

The Opium Wars

European powers were hungry to open new territories up for trade, but the Qing weren't buying. The British East India Company, strapped for cash, realized they could sell opium in China at huge profits. The Chinese government quickly banned the nefarious trade and in response, a technologically superior Britain declared war. After a humiliating defeat in the first Opium War, China was forced to cede Hong Kong. Other foreign powers followed with territorial demands of their own.

1912–1949

Republican Era

China's Republican period was chaotic and unstable. The revolutionary Dr. Sun Yat-sen —revered by most Chinese as the father of modern China— was unable to build a cohesive government without the aid of regional warlords and urban gangsters. When he died of cancer in 1925, power passed to Chiang Kai-shek, who set about unifying China under the Kuomintang. What began as a unified group of both left-and-right wingers quickly deteriorated, and by the mid-1920s, civil war between the Communists and Nationalists was brewing.

The '30s and '40s were bleak decades for the Chinese people, caught between a vicious war with Japan and periodic clashes between Kuomintang and Communist forces. After Japan's defeat in 1945, China's civil war kicked into high gear. Though the Kuomintang were armed with superior weapons and backed by American money, the majority of Chinese people rallied behind the Communists. Within four years, the Kuomintang were driven off the mainland to Taiwan, where the Republic of China exists to the present day.

(top left) Illiterate soldiers are taught about Mao's *Little Red Book* in Beijing on December 1966.
(top right) Central Shenzhen, Guangdong.
(bottom left) Poster of Mao's slogans.

1949–Present

The People's Republic

On October 1, 1949, Mao Zedong declared from atop Beijing's Gate of Heavenly Peace that "The Chinese People have stood up." And so the People's Republic of China was born. The Communist party set out to overhaul China's ancient feudal system, emphasizing class struggle, redistribution of wealth, and elimination of foreign dominance. The next three decades would see a massive, often painful transformation of Chinese society from feudalism into the modern age.

The Great Leap Forward was a disaster—Chinese peasants were encouraged to cram 100 years of industrial development into as many weeks. Untenable decisions led to industrial and agricultural ruin, widespread famine, and an estimated 30 million deaths. The trauma of this period, however, pales in comparison to The Great Proletarian Cultural Revolution. From 1966–76, fear and zealotry gripped the nation as young revolutionaries heeded Chairman Mao's call to root out class enemies. During this decade, millions died, millions were imprisoned, and much of China's accumulated religious, historical, and cultural heritage literally went up in smoke.

Like a phoenix rising from its own ashes, China rose from its own self-inflicted destruction. In the early 1980s, Deng Xiao-ping took the first steps in reforming China's stagnant economy. With the maxim "To Get Rich is Glorious," Deng loosened central control on the economy and declared Special Economic Zones, where the seeds of capitalism could be incubated. Two decades later, the nation is one of the world's most vibrant economic engines. Though China's history is measured in millennia, her brightest years may well have only just begun.

PUDONG

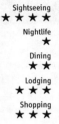

Sightseeing ★★★★
Nightlife ★
Dining ★★
Lodging ★★★
Shopping ★★★

Shanghai residents used to say that it was better to have a bed in Puxi than an apartment in Pudong, but the neighborhood has come a long way in recent years from a rural area to one that represents a futuristic city of wide boulevards and towering skyscrapers topped (although soon to be out-floored) by the pagodalike elegance of the Jinmao Tower. Apartments here are some of the most expensive in Shanghai. Although a little on the bland side, it is home to expat compounds designed in a medley of bizarre architectural styles, international schools, and malls. However, there are quite a few sites here worth visiting, particularly if you have children.

What's Here

As you stagger out from the bewildering light show of the **Bund Tourist Tunnel,** head toward the **Oriental Pearl Tower.** Directions are not a problem, as you really couldn't miss it if you tried. Its oversized pink "pearls" loom over the shoreline. You can head up to the top of this tower to see the view of Shanghai stretching out forever on a pollution-free day—which is a rarity. However, it is expensive, so you might want to save your money for the **Jinmao Tower.** Close to the **Oriental Pearl Tower** is the **Shanghai Ocean Aquarium** where the kids can have a great time hanging with the fish. Across the road in an obscure office building is a branch of **Wagas** for morning heart-starter coffee or their afternoon tea special.

You'll probably need to take a taxi to see the rest of the sights. Head over to the **Science and Technology Museum** where the whole family can enjoy the hands-on experiences offered or take a look at a film in one

A BRIEF HISTORY

Up until 1990, Pudong was an endless expanse of rural area with squat ramshackle housing, fields, and run-down warehouses. Check out the Shanghai Urban Planning Center photos if you can't visualize it looking at the massive banks of glass and steel that now glitter from across the Huangpu. Its lightning transformation happened after the Chinese government announced that Shanghai was to play an important role in China's economic development and that Pudong was to be a Special Economic Zone. Nowadays, scores of expats live in the area and some of the largest business interests are located there. For some Puxi dwellers, though, it remains an unexplored land.

of the IMAX cinemas. Alternatively, if the weather is good, opt for **Century Park** where you can picnic, cycle, or just stroll.

Back toward the Huangpu River are the **Jinmao Tower** where for a much cheaper price than the **Oriental Pearl Tower,** you can go to the dazzlingly high 88th floor observation deck. If you are there in the evening, the **Cloud Nine** bar at the **Grand Hyatt,** although lacking in atmosphere, is a top spot for a drink and a view of the lights. The cover charge (which includes drinks) is a bit steep though.

Until recently Asia's largest mall, the **Superbrand Mall** overlooks the Huangpu and has 10 floors of movies, restaurants, and shops. Once you have shopped 'til you drop, cross over the street to the **Riverside Promenade** where you can stroll or grab a bite at one of the restaurants there. At night the view across to the Bund is really lovely.

What to See

Bund Tourist Tunnel. For a look at Shanghai kitsch at its worst, you can take a trip across—actually, under—the Huangpu in plastic, capsular cars. The accompanying light show is part Disney, part psychedelic, complete with flashing strobes, blowing tinsel, and swirling hallucinogenic images projected on the concrete walls. The five-minute ride will make your head spin; you'll wonder if the Chinese central government isn't giving Shanghai just a little too much money. ✉ *Entrances are on the Bund at Nanjing Dong Lu and in Pudong near the Riverside Promenade* ☎ *021/5888–6000* 🎫 *Y30 one-way, Y40 round-trip* ⏲ *May–Oct., daily 8 AM–10:30 PM; Nov.–Apr., daily 8 AM–10 PM.*

Century Park. This giant swathe of green in Pudong is a great place to take children as it has a variety of vehicles for hire, good flat paths for rollerblading, and pleasure boats. On a fine day, pack a picnic as there are also designated picnic areas as well as woods and grass to play on. ✉ *1001 Jinxiu Lu, Pudong* ☎ *021/3876–0588* 🎫 *Y10* ⏲ *Daily 7 AM–6 PM.*

★ **Jinmao Tower.** (Jinmao Dasha). This gorgeous 88th-floor (8 being the Chinese number implying wealth and prosperity) industrial art-deco pagoda

GETTING ORIENTED

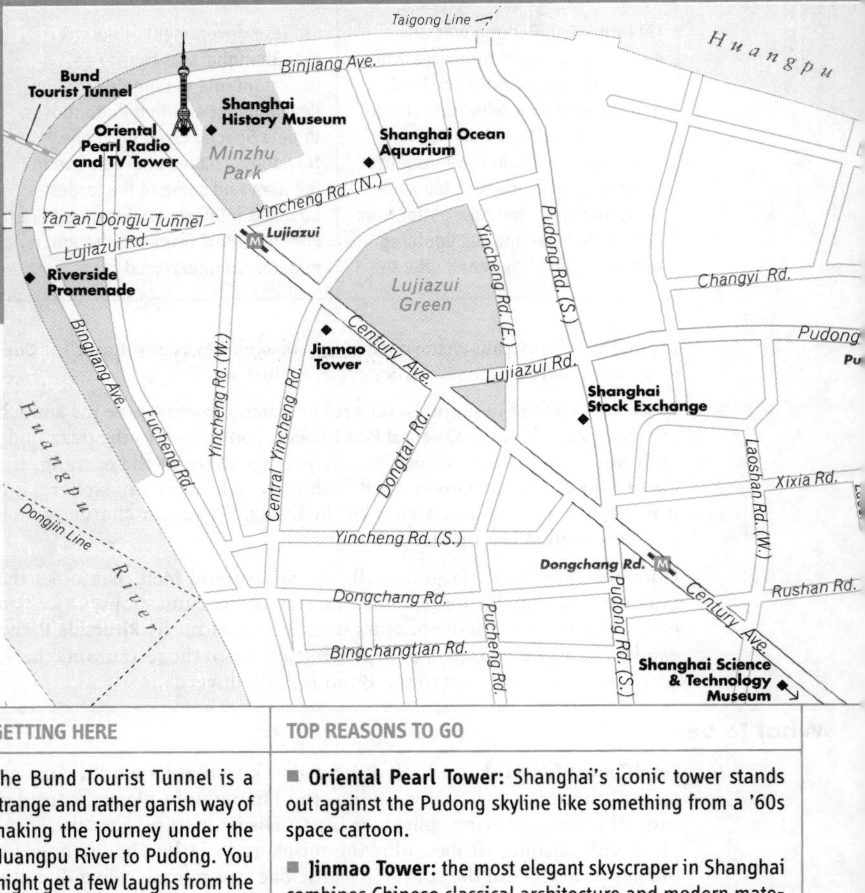

GETTING HERE	TOP REASONS TO GO
The Bund Tourist Tunnel is a strange and rather garish way of making the journey under the Huangpu River to Pudong. You might get a few laughs from the light displays. Otherwise you can take the metro on Line 2 to Lujiazui, or catch the ferry from the Bund.	■ **Oriental Pearl Tower:** Shanghai's iconic tower stands out against the Pudong skyline like something from a '60s space cartoon. ■ **Jinmao Tower:** the most elegant skyscraper in Shanghai combines Chinese classical architecture and modern materials. ■ **Shanghai Science and Technology Museum:** is an absorbing and hands-on place to take children. ■ **Century Park:** this huge park in Pudong has a variety of areas and activities including boats, bicycles, and trains.

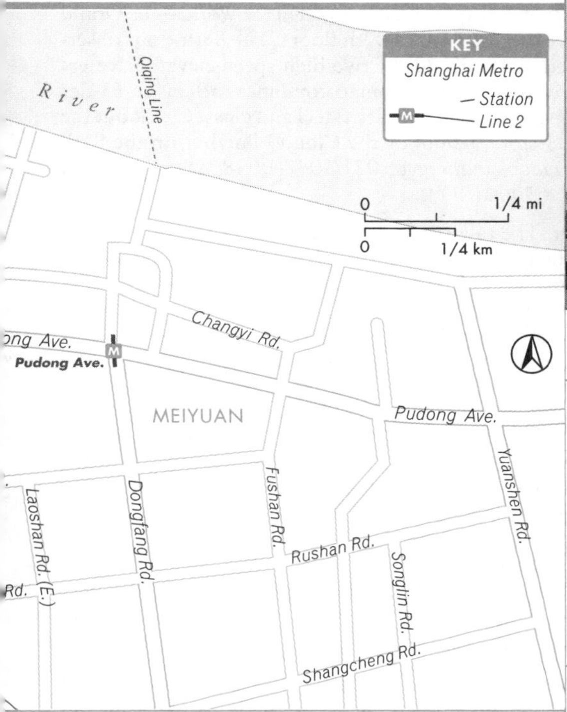

MAKING THE MOST OF YOUR TIME

Pudong is not a walking-friendly area as there are large, rather featureless distances between the sights. You can either take the metro to get around, or jump in a cab. If you visit all the sights, you could easily spend a day out here. For some Puxi residents, it's like a journey to another country.

SAFETY

Pudong is a pretty safe area and the only thing to keep a look out for is the cars as you cross the impossibly wide boulevards.

NEAREST PUBLIC RESTROOMS

All the major sites have facilities. Some are located past the ticket booth, but the ones at the Shanghai Aquarium are in the foyer before you go in.

A GOOD WALK

An evening stroll along the Riverside Promenade provides a good view back across to the Bund. There are a choice of bars and cafés if you feel peckish or thirsty.

QUICK BITES

The beer at **Paulaner Brauhaus** (✉ Binjiang Fengguangting 2967, Fudu Duan, Pudong ☎ 021/6888-3935) is particularly good. It's located on the Riverside Promenade, and at night, you get a spectacular view across to the Bund.

Wagas (✉ Rm G102, 1233 Lujiazui Huan Lu, Pudong ☎ 021/5879-4235) is one of a chain of Australian-owned groovy cafés that have made many a homesick expat happy. Serving decent-sized pastas, sandwiches, burgers, salads, and some great cakes, they also have a range of special deals at different times of the day.

Super Brand Mall (✉ 168 Lujiazui Lu Pudong ☎ 021/6887-7888) has a large food hall with a wide enough variety of restaurants to satisfy all stomachs including the popular American fast-food chains such as KFC.

is among the five tallest buildings in the world and the tallest in China—at least for the time being, as a massive skyscraper being built next door will soon eclipse it. In it is also the highest hotel in the world—the Grand Hyatt Shanghai takes up the 53rd to 87th floors. The 88th-floor observation deck, reached in 45 seconds by two high-speed elevators, offers a 360-degree view of the city. The Jinmao combines the classic 13-tier Buddhist pagoda design with postmodern steel and glass. Check out the Hyatt's dramatic 33-story atrium or the Cloud Nine bar on the 87th floor. ✉ *88 Shiji Dadao, Pudong* ☎ *021/5047–0088* 🎫 *Observation deck Y50* ⏲ *Daily 8:30 AM–9 PM.*

★ **Oriental Pearl Tower.** The tallest tower in Asia (1,535 feet or 468 meters) has become the pride and joy of the city, a symbol of the brashness and glitz of today's Shanghai. This UFO-like structure is especially kitschy at night, when it flashes with colored lights against the classic beauty of the Bund. Its three spheres are supposed to represent pearls (as in "Shanghai, Pearl of the Orient"). An elevator takes you to observation decks in the tower's three spheres. Go to the top sphere for a 360-degree bird's-eye view of the city or grab a bite in the Tower's revolving restaurant. On the bottom floor is the Shanghai History Museum. ✉ *1 Shiji Da Dao, Pudong* ☎ *021/5879–1888* 🎫 *Y135, all three spheres plus museum; Y70 and Y85 for the lower spheres* ⏲ *Daily 8 AM–9:30 PM.*

> **WORD OF MOUTH**
>
> "The kids will probably enjoy the fast elevator up the Oriental Pearl Tower and the stunning view from the observation floor." –Neil_Oz

Riverside Promenade. Although the park that runs 2,750 yards (2,514 meters) along the Huangpu River is sugary-sterile in its experimental suburbia, it still offers the most beautiful views of the Bund. You can stroll on the grass and concrete and view a perspective of Puxi unavailable from the west side. If you're here in the summer, you can ENJOY WADING, as a sign indicates, in the chocolate-color Huangpu River from the park's wave platform. ✉ *Bingjiang Dadao, Pudong* 🎫 *Free.*

★ **Shanghai History Museum.** This impressive museum in the base of the Pearl Tower recalls Shanghai's pre-1949 history. Inside you can stroll down a re-created Shanghai street circa 1900 or check out a streetcar that used to operate in the concessions. Dioramas depict battle scenes from the Opium Wars, shops found in a typical turn-of-the-20th-century Shanghai neighborhood, and grand Former French Concession buildings of yesteryear. ✉ *1 Shiji Dadao, Pudong* ☎ *021/5879–1888* 🎫 *Y35* ⏲ *Daily 8–9:30.*

Shanghai Ocean Aquarium. As you stroll through the aquarium's 12,000-foot-long, (3,658 meters) clear, sightseeing tunnel, you may feel like you're walking your way through the seven seas—or at least five of them. The aquarium's 10,000 fish span 300 species, 5 oceans, and 4 continents. You'll also find penguins and species representing all 12 of the Chinese zodiac animals, such as the tiger barb, sea dragon, and seahorse. ✉ *158*

Yincheng Bei Lu, Pudong ☎ 021/5877–9988 🌐 www.aquarium.sh.cn 🎟 Y110 adults, Y70 children ⏲ 9 AM–9 PM; last tickets sold at 8:30.

Shanghai Science and Technology Museum. This museum, a favorite attraction for kids in Shanghai, has more than 100 hands-on exhibits in its 6 main galleries. Earth Exploration takes you through fossil layers to the earth's core for a lesson in plate tectonics. Spectrum of Life introduces you to the animal and plant kingdoms within its simulated rain forest. Light of Wisdom explains basic principles of light and sound through interactive exhibits, and simulators in AV Paradise put you in a plane cockpit and on television. Children's Technoland has a voice-activated fountain and miniature construction site. In Cradle of Designers, you can record a CD or assemble a souvenir. Two IMAX theaters and an IWERKS 4D theater show larger-than-life movies, but mostly in Chinese. All signs are in English; the best times to visit are weekday afternoons. ✉ *1388 Lujiazui Huan Lu, Pudong* ☎ *021/6854–2000* 🎟 *Y60; there are separate prices for the IMAX and IWERKS* ⏲ *Tues.–Sun. 9–4:30.*

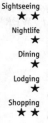

NORTH SHANGHAI

Sightseeing ★★
Nightlife ★
Dining ★
Lodging ★
Shopping ★★

Although often neglected in favor of their more glamorous neighboring areas, the northern Shanghai districts of Putuo, Hongkou, and Zhabei still offer some interesting sights. Hongkou District, particularly, is still relatively undeveloped and unchanged, and buildings from the past are still visible behind cheap clothing stores. An area with an interesting history, it has the most sights worth seeing as well as the lush green sweep of Lu Xun Park. The old buildings and warehouses around Suzhou Creek, which feeds into the Huangpu, are slowly being turned into a hip and happening arty area, particularly the M50 development. Also in Putuo District is another one of Shanghai's main temples, the Jade Buddha Temple.

What's Here

At the end of the **Bund** is the **Garden Bridge,** which crosses **Suzhou Creek.** Just over the bridge are the **Pujiang Hotel,** which was once the site of the very fashionable Astor House, and **Broadway Mansions,** an imposing art-deco apartment block, now **Shanghai Mansions** and a substandard hotel. As you go down **Sichuan Bei Lu,** you will see many architectural gems including the old **Post Office.** If you have been to the **Shanghai Urban Planning Center** and looked at the past and present photos, you will notice that much around this area has not changed.

Toward the end of this long road is **Duolun Lu,** a "cultural" street where famous writers such as **Lu Xun** used to wander. At the entrance of the street is a rather harsh looking modern-art gallery, the **Doland Gallery**

A BRIEF HISTORY

Hongkou was originally the American Settlement, but later joined with the British to form the International Settlement. At the turn of the 20th century Shanghai was not only an international port but also an open one, where anyone could enter regardless of nationality. As the century wore on and the world became riddled with war, Jews, first fleeing the Russian Revolution and then escaping Hitler, arrived in Shanghai from Germany, Austria, Poland, and Russia. From 1937 to 1941 Shanghai became a haven for tens of thousands of Jewish refugees. In 1943 invading Japanese troops forced all the city's Jews into the "Designated Area for Stateless Refugees" in Hongkou District, where they lived until the end of the war. Today you can still see evidence of their lives in the buildings and narrow streets of the area.

Further north, Zhabei District was decimated during the fighting with the Japanese in Shanghai during the 1930s. The now leafy green area of Zhabei Park was also used as an execution ground for Communists in the 1920s.

of Modern Art, which holds a varied range of exhibitions. If you continue down **Duolun Lu,** you will see some fine examples of old Shanghai architecture including a great church, built in "temple-style" complete with Chinese upturned eaves. There are some interesting junk/antique stores along here, so take time to browse.

At the end of **Duolun Lu,** head for the **Lu Xun Park,** named after China's most famous writer who lived in the area at various times in his life. In the park, you will find locals engaged in all sorts of activities as well as Lu Xun's tomb and a museum. If you are a real fan, you can head to his former residence in **Shanyin Lu,** which is worth checking out for the atmospheric laneway it is situated in alone.

A little further away are remnants of Shanghai's Jewish settlement at the **Ohel Moishe Synagogue** and **Huoshan Park.** Shanghai was one of the few places willing to accept Jewish refugees fleeing from persecution under the Nazi rule.

While you are in the area, you might want to go to **Qipu Lu,** a large indoor market, which is a mecca for cheap clothing, shoes, and accessories.

What to See

Duolun Lu. Designated Shanghai's "Cultural Street," Duolun Road takes you back in time to the 1930s, when the 1-km- (½-mi-) long lane was a favorite haunt of writer Lu Xun and fellow social activists. Bronze statues of those literary luminaries dot the lawns between the well-preserved villas and row houses, whose 1st floors are now home to antiques shops, cafés, and art galleries. As the street takes a 90-degree turn, its architecture shifts 180 degrees with the seven-story stark gray **Shang-**

GETTING ORIENTED

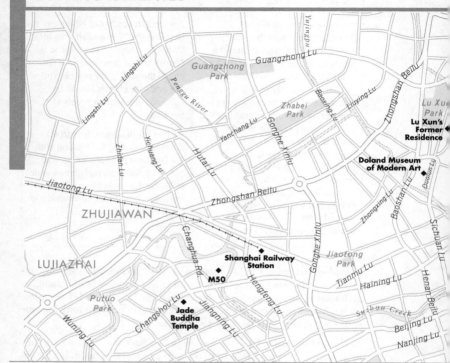

GETTING HERE

For the Jade Buddha Temple and M50, you can hop off the metro Line 1 at Shanghai Railway Station, but you still have to get across Suzhou Creek. You can take the Pearl Line to East Baoxing Lu and Hongkou Stadium for Lu Xun Park and Duolun Lu. The best way to get around these areas is by taxi.

TOP REASONS TO GO

- **Lu Xun Park:** a great place for people-watching and for kids to let loose for a bit, the park buzzes with activity all day long.
- **Doland Museum of Modern Art:** Shanghai's first modern art museum still holds an eclectic mix of exhibitions.
- **M50:** full of small and firmly established galleries, M50 is being developed as Shanghai's new art center and is. This is one of the best places to see what is happening in Chinese contemporary art in Shanghai.
- **Jade Buddha Temple:** this serene temple outside festivals and holidays is home to a precious Buddha statue.

QUICK BITES

Bandu Music Cafe (✉ Building 11, 50 Moganshan Lu, Putuo ☎ 021/6276-8267) is chilled during the day and a spot to pick up Chinese classical folk music. At night, especially on Saturday, there are often free performances.

MAKING THE MOST OF YOUR TIME

North Shanghai's sights are in three distinct areas. The galleries at M50 open later in the morning, so it may be best to head to some other sites first. Qipu Lu also gets very busy as the day goes on and is unbearable on weekends.

SAFETY

Qipu Lu in particular is notorious for pickpockets in the crowded narrow corridors of some of the markets, it's very easy for someone to slip their hand unnoticed into your pocket.

NEAREST PUBLIC RESTROOMS

Inside the gate of Lu Xun Park are some reasonable public toilets. The toilet entrance fee is 5 mao.

A GOOD WALK

If you're a good walker, it's an interesting but long journey down Sichuan Bei Lu, a block or two from Garden Bridge, to Lu Xun Park as some of the area has changed little over the years. Also, wandering around the backstreets of the area around Lu Xun Park will turn up some architectural gems.

hai Doland Museum of Modern Art. ✉ *Off Sichuan Bei Lu, Hongkou District.*

★ **Jade Buddha Temple.** Completed in 1918, this temple is fairly new by Chinese standards. During the Cultural Revolution, in order to save the temple when the Red Guards came to destroy it, the monks pasted portraits of Mao Zedong on the outside walls so the Guards couldn't tear them down without destroying Mao's face as well. The temple is built in the style of the Song Dynasty, with symmetrical halls and courtyards, upturned eaves, and bright yellow walls. The temple's great treasure is its 6½-foot-high, (2-meter)-pound seated Buddha made of white jade with a robe of precious gems, originally brought to Shanghai from Burma. Other Buddhas, statues, and frightening guardian gods of the temple populate the halls, as well as a collection of Buddhist scriptures and paintings. The 100 monks who live and work here can sometimes be seen worshipping. It's madness at festival times. ✉ *170 Anyuan Lu, Putuo District* ☎ *021/6266–3668* 🎫 *Y10 plus an extra Y10 for the Jade Buddha* ⏲ *Daily 8–4:30.*

Lu Xun Park and Memorial. Lu Xun (1881–1936)—scholar, novelist, and essayist—is considered the founder of modern Chinese literature. He is best known for his work *The True Story of Ah Q*. The park holds his tomb and a statue of the writer, as well as a **museum** of manuscripts, books, and photos related to his life and career. The park is usually full of pockets of people chatting, playing badminton, or doing a myriad of other activities. ✉ *2288 Sichuan Bei Lu, Hongkou District* ☎ *021/6540–0009* 🎫 *Museum, Y10* ⏲ *Park, daily 5 AM–7 PM; memorial and museum, daily 9–5, last entrance 4.*

M50 is a cluster of art galleries and artists studios by Suzhou Creek. This is home to some of Shanghai's hottest galleries and where you will see works from China's best artists as well as new and not so well-known ones. There are also a couple of shops selling music and art supplies and a branch of Shirtflag. Don't be shy about nosing around—there are galleries in many floors of these old factories and warehouses and sometimes artists will be around for a chat. ✉ *50 Moganshan Lu, Putuo District* 🎫 *Free* ⏲ *Daily although most galleries are closed on Mon. Opening times vary depending on the gallery.*

Ohel Moishe Synagogue and Huoshan Park. Currently called the Jewish Refugee Memorial Hall of Shanghai, the Ohel Moishe Synagogue served as the spiritual heart of Shanghai's Jewish ghetto in the 1930s and '40s. In this sanctuary-turned-museum, the lively 85-year-old narrator Wang Faliang provides colorful commentary for the black-and-white photo collection depicting daily life for the 30,000 Jews—academics, writers, doctors, musicians—who flooded into the Hongkou District from Europe.

An attic bedroom is frozen in time, with photos and a menorah left behind by residents who moved on after World War II. Around the corner, down a lane just as well preserved, Huoshan Park bears a memorial tablet in the immigrants' honor. The museum's art gallery best conveys the refugees' lasting gratitude to their Chinese hosts, a bond made most clear by a crystal Star of David, engraved with Chinese characters.

✉ *62 Changyang Lu, Hongkou District* ☎ *021/6541–5008* 🎫 *Y50* ⏲ *Mon.–Sat. 9 AM–4 PM.*

Shanghai Doland Museum of Modern Art. Opened in December 2003, this is Shanghai's first official venue for modern art. The six-story museum's 14,400 square feet of exhibition space include a tiny shop selling art books and a metal spiral staircase that's a work of art in itself. The exhibitions, which change frequently, are cutting edge for Shanghai. They've showcased electronic art from American artists, examined gender issues among Chinese, and featured musical performances ranging from Chinese electronica to the *dombra,* a traditional Kazak stringed instrument. ✉ *27 Duolun Lu, Hongkou District* ☎ *021/6587–2530* 🌐 *www.duolunart.com* 🎫 *Varies according to the exhibition* ⏲ *Daily 10–5:30.*

XUJIAHUI & SOUTH, HONGQIAO & GUBEI

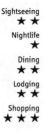

Sightseeing ★★
Nightlife ★
Dining ★★
Lodging ★★
Shopping ★★★

Buyers throng into the large malls in the shopping precinct at Xujiahui, which shines with neon and giant billboard advertisements. Further down the road are the districts of Hongqiao and Gubei where wealthy expats live in high-walled compounds and drive huge SUVs. You're likely to find a larger concentration of Western-style restaurants and supermarkets here if you are feeling homesick.

What's Here

Worship at the temple of commerce at Xujiahui among its Tokyo-like neons and the giant malls. Then jump in a taxi in order to worship at another temple, but this time a much more spiritual one at **Longhua.** Here you can light your free incense and pray to Buddha, see the monks wandering around or ring the giant bell for good fortune. The Longhua Pagoda across the way is not accessible to tourists, but is nicely photogenic. Next door is the serene yet more somber Longhua Martyrs Cemetery in commemoration of those who died for the Communist Cause including those executed in the Guomindang round-up in 1927. Wander around its shady paths and marvel at giant Soviet-style sculptures. Further away from the center you can wander among the plants of the Shanghai Botanic Gardens.

What to See

Longhua Martyrs Cemetery may seem a tranquil place now, but it has had a bloody history. It has been the execution site of many Communists, particularly during the Guomingdang crackdown in 1927. Nowadays, it's full of large Soviet-style sculpture and immaculate lawns. The most chilling is the small, unkempt, grassy execution area accessed by a tunnel where the remains of murdered Communists were found with leg irons still on

A BRIEF HISTORY

Xu Guangqi, a Catholic convert living in Shanghai during the 16th and 17th centuries, and his family once owned large parts of the Xujiahui area. They donated much of the land to the Jesuits who established a cathedral and various other buildings, such as orphanages and monasteries. Xuhui College, which was built in 1850, offered the first fully Western curriculum in China. Once the Communists seized power from the Nationalists, Catholicism was no longer tolerated and the Jesuits left China for safer places like Macau.

in the 1950s. ✉ *180Longhua Lu, Xuhui District* ☎ *021/6468–5995* 🎫 *Y1 with an extra Y4 to enter the museum* ⏲ *Daily 6–5, Museum 9–4.*

★ **Longhua Temple** (Longhua Si). Shanghai's largest and most active temple has as its centerpiece a seven-story, eight-sided pagoda. While the temple is thought to have been built in the 3rd century, the pagoda dates from the 10th century; it's not open to visitors. Near the front entrance of the temple stands a three-story bell tower, where a 3.3-ton bronze bell is rung at midnight every New Year's Eve. Along the side corridors of the temple you'll find the Longhua Hotel, a vegetarian restaurant, and a room filled seven rows deep with small golden statues. The third hall is the most impressive. Its three giant Buddhas sit beneath a swirled red and gold dome. ✉ *2853 Longhua Lu, Xuhui District* ☎ *021/6456–6085 or 021/6457–6327* 🎫 *Y10 with free incense and an extra Y50 to strike the bell* ⏲ *Daily 7–4:30.*

Shanghai Botanical Garden. Spread over 200 acres, the garden has separate areas for peonies and roses, azaleas, osmanthus, bamboo and orchids, and medicinal plants. Its Penjing Garden is among the world's best. *Penjing* translates as "pot scenery," and describes the Chinese art of creating a miniature landscape in a container. More than 2,000 bonsai trees line the Penjing Garden's courtyards and corridors. The Chinese Cymbidium Garden has more than 300 varieties. Within the Grand Conservatory are towering palms and more than 3,500 varieties of tropical plants. Admission to the garden is free on the 10th of each month. ✉ *1111 Longwu Lu, Xuhui District* ☎ *021/5436–3369* 🎫 *Y15 for entrance through main gate only* ⏲ *Daily 7–5.*

Soong Qingling Mausoleum. Unlike her beleaguered sister, Soong Meiling who married the wrong guy, Chiang Kai-shek, and escaped to Taiwan, Soong Qingling is a heroine in China. She was buried in the Wanguo Cemetery in 1981 and the cemetery was renamed in her honor. Now you can visit her grave, along with that of her maid and her parents and a small display of her personal items. ✉ *21 Songyuan Lu, Xuhui District* ☎ *021/6275–8080* 🎫 *Y3* ⏲ *Daily 8:30 AM–4:30 PM.*

Xujiahui Cathedral. Built by the Jesuits in 1848, this Gothic-style cathedral still holds regular masses in Chinese. Stained-glass artist Wo Ye designed the new windows for the entire cathedral. ✉ *158 Puxi Lu, Xuhui District* ☎ *021/6469–0930* ⏲ *Daily. Tours weekends at 1:30.*

GETTING ORIENTED

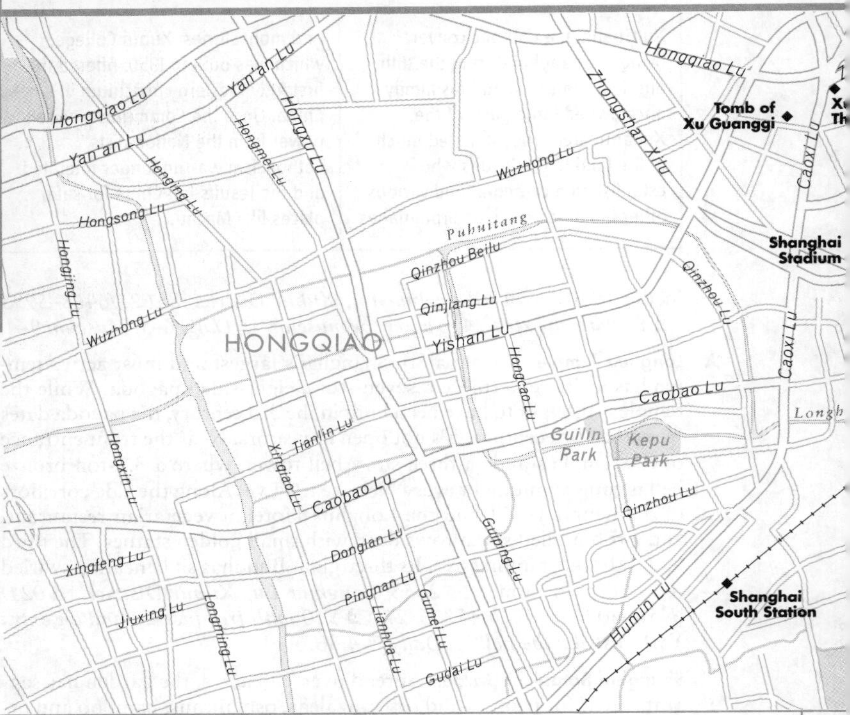

GETTING HERE

Metro Line 1 takes you right into the depths of the Grand Gateway Mall at Xujiahui. For the other sights, they are fairly far-flung, so it might be a good idea to jump into a taxi. If you are going to places like the Shanghai Botanical Gardens from the center of town, be prepared for a large taxi bill. Otherwise, you can get off at Shanghai South Railway Station.

SAFETY

Temples can get very crowded during festivals and this can be very unpleasant due to the pushing and shoving.

TOP REASONS TO GO

- **Longhua Temple and Pagoda:** take your free incense at the door and pray in the four directions with the locals at one of Shanghai's larger temple complexes—and the only one that is still fully active.
- **Longhua Martyrs Cemetery:** besides being historically interesting, there is also some amazing Soviet-style sculpture work in this pleasant garden.

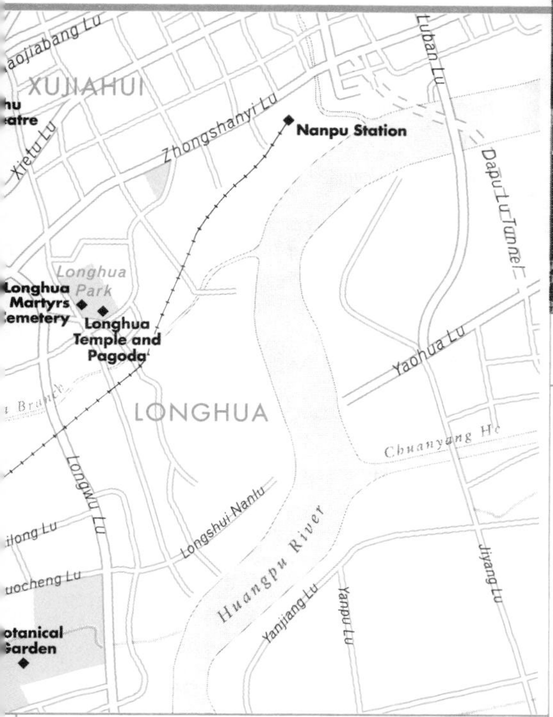

QUICK BITES

Longhua Vegetarian Hall (✉Longhua Temple, 2853 Longhua Lu Xuhui ☎ 021/6456-6085) is where you can pull up a Formica table and a stool and get stuck into some temple food. This is a basic vegetarian place mostly serving noodles.

Sushi Tei (✉ Unit 1-28, 1/F Metro City, 1111 Zhaojiabang Lu Xuhui ☎ 021/6426-7280) is one of Shanghai's better sushi restaurants (the super-expensive ones aside) and you can sit at the sushi train in a cozy little chair for two.

MAKING THE MOST OF YOUR TIME

There isn't much to see out in the southern suburbs, so there's no need to make it a large part of your trip. Getting there will take the longest time. The sights themselves will take an hour or two, unless you are deeply interested in botany and wish to linger at the Shanghai Botanical Gardens. Likewise, if you like malls and shopping, you could spend a lot of time wandering around Grand Gateway and the like at Xujiahui. Avoid Xujiahui on the weekends if possible.

TOURING TIP

Make sure to take the walk through the chilling tunnel to the bluntly named Martyrs Dying Ground at the Longhua Martyrs Cemetery. You will emerge at the extremely poignant sight where many people lost their lives. It may not be the most cheerful event of your day, but it will certainly fill you with a sense of awe at the senselessness of these events in history.

At a Glance

ENGLISH	PINYIN	CHINESE CHARACTERS
POINTS OF INTEREST		
Bank of China	zhōngguó yínháng	中国银行
Bund	wàitān	外滩
Bund History Museum	wàitān lìshǐ bówùguǎn	外滩历史博物馆
Bund Museum	wàitān bówùguǎn	外滩博物馆
Bund Tourist Tunnel	wàitān rénxìng guānguāng suìdào	外滩人行观光隧道
Customs House	hǎiguān dà lóu	海关大楼
Former Hong Kong and Shanghai Bank Building	pǔdōng fāzhǎn yínháng	浦东发展银行
Fuzhou Lu	fúzhōu lù	福州路
Hankou Lu	hànkǒu lù	汉口路
Henan Zhong Lu	hénán zhōng lù	河南中路
Huangpu Park	huángpǔ gōngyuán	黄埔公园
Huangpu River	huángpǔ jiāng	黄浦江
I Love Shanghai	wǒ aì shànghǎi	我爱上海
Jinling Lu	jīnlíng lù	金陵路
Laris	lùwéixuān	陆唯轩
Memorial of the Heroes of the People	rénmín yīngxióng jìniàn bēi	人民英雄纪念碑
Peace Hotel	hépíng fàndiàn	和平饭店
Raffles City	láifúshì guǎngchǎng	来福士广场
Shandong Lu	shāndōng lù	山东路
Shanghai No. 1 Department Store	dìyī bǎihùo	第一百货
Studio Rouge	hóngzhài dāngdài yìshù huàláng	红寨当代艺术画廊
Suzhou Cobblers	sūzhōu xiéjiàng	苏州鞋匠
Suzhou Creek	sūzhōu hé	苏州河
Xinwang Tea House	xīnwàng chá cāntīng	新旺茶餐厅
Xizang Nan Lu	xīzàng nán lù	西藏南路
Zhongshan Dong Yi Lu	zhōngshān dōng yī lù	中山东一路
Zhongshan Er Lu	zhōngshān èr lù	中山二路

Shopping

Shanghai Super Brand Mall

WORD OF MOUTH

"Tailor shops can be found easily in Shanghai. If you can ask help from a native, I believe the quality of your clothing can be well guaranteed. Usually the clothing can be finished within three days, if there are not many people waiting for their clothing in the shops."

–Vanessa

SHOPPING PLANNER

Start Shopping!

When in Shanghai, do as the locals do and hit the shops hard. Ask someone in the street their favorite hobby, and if they don't say basketball or PC games, they will probably say shopping. New stores open each day—from glittering luxury behemoths to tiny boutiques with barely any breathing room.

Great Souvenirs

- Revolutionary propaganda depicting Chairman Mao
- Handmade shoes
- A mah-jongg set
- Old advertising posters
- Yixing teapots
- An inflatable Shanghai Oriental Pearl Tower
- Baijiu (and the accompanying hangover)
- Brightly colored Wuxi clay dolls
- Cricket cage
- Silk brocade with dragon or bamboo motifs
- Miao embroidery

Top Places to Shop

Duolun Lu is a pedestrian street in Shanghai's historic Hongkou. Not only is it lined with examples of old architecture and home to a modern-art gallery, but its stalls and curio stores are ripe for browsing.

Moganshan Lu, a complex near Aomen Lu, once housed poor artists. It is now being developed and repackaged as M50, a hot new art destination with galleries, cafés, and boutiques moving in to make this a happening place to shop and hang out.

Taikang Lu is a former factory district that's now home to artists and designers. It has a hip and laid-back vibe and is fast becoming Shanghai's SoHo. You won't find Andy Warhols at the International Artists Factory, but there is definitely some worthwhile shopping.

In **Xintiandi,** exclusive and expensive stores are housed in reproduction traditional Shikumen buildings. Get ready to work that plastic.

Xujiahui, complexes where six major shopping malls and giant electronics in Puxi converge, looks like it's straight out of Tokyo. Shop 'til you drop, or play with the gadgets and compare prices at the electronics shops.

Yu Garden, a major tourist haunt in the Old Town area of Shanghai, can be overwhelming, but hard bargaining brings rewards. The amount and variety of goods for sale here is phenomenal. It is continually expanding as vendors move out of old buildings in the surrounding areas.

Also check out these streets that specialize in specific traditional products: **Fenyang Lu** and **Jinling Lu** for musical instruments; **Changle Lu** and **Maoming Lu** for *qipao* (Chinese-style dresses); and **Fuzhou Lu** for books and art supplies, including calligraphy supplies.

Avoid Scams

■ Fake antiques are often hidden among real treasures and vice versa. Some stores may tell you whether a piece is old or new, but you only have their word to prove it. Also be aware of age; the majority of pieces date from the late Qing Dynasty (1644–1911). Technically, only items dated after 1795 can be legally exported. In some stores, only domestic customers may purchase these items to prevent illegal exportation.

■ China is famous for its silk, but some unscrupulous vendors will try to pass off synthetics at silk prices. Ask the shopkeeper to burn a small scrap from the bolt you're considering. If the burned threads bead up and smell like plastic, the fabric is synthetic. If the threads turn into ash and smell like burned hair, the fabric is real silk. (The same goes for wool.) For brocade silk, fair-market prices range from Y30 to Y40 a meter; for synthetics, Y10 to Y28. You'll pay more in retail shops.

■ On tourist stretches such as the Yu Gardens and Nanjing Dong Lu, you may be approached by young people claiming to be students who invite you to an "art exhibition." Unless you are in the market for imitation artwork at high prices, decline and keep moving.

■ Check for fake pearls before purchasing. Real pearls will feel gritty when you bite them, and they also feel cool to the touch. Taking a knife to the surface to see if it scrapes off or burning the pearl are common tactics used by vendors to show that it is real.

■ Real jade makes a distinctive chiming sound when struck and will stick slightly to your hand when under water.

SHOPPING HOURS

Shanghai gets up late and opening hours really vary. Local supermarkets open early, but malls don't usually open until 10 and boutiques at 11 AM. The upside is stores tend to stay open later, with many closing at 10 PM. Markets generally start earlier, at around 8:30 or 9:30 AM, and close at around 6 PM. Most stores are open seven days a week.

■ TIP→ **Shopping here is a voyage of discovery that is best done on foot so as to discover the little surprises, especially in areas like the former French Concession.**

Sample Costs in Shanghai

ITEM	PRICE (IN YUAN)
DVD on the street	Y8
DVD in a store	Y10
Mao's Little Red Book (new)	Y40
Fake designer sunglasses	Y30
Silk brocade	Y35 per meter
Pearls	Y40 for a basic strand

Revised by
Elyse Singleton

Because of Shanghai's commercial status as China's most open port city, it has the widest variety of goods to be found in the nation after Hong Kong. Ritzy chrome shopping malls stand alongside dingy state-run stores and around the corner from local markets, inundating the intrepid shopper with both foreign name brands and domestic goods. Take some time to browse the curio stands and do some window-shopping on Nanjing Lu, China's premier shopping street.

OLD CITY

Souvenirs

Old Street of Yu Gardens. Souvenir shops, tourists, and vendors touting for business fill this street. Some of the merchandise is of dubious taste, but there are still some shops selling unusual or good quality products. **Shop 368** sells pretty embroidered shoes, belts, and spangles; **Shop 385** has overpriced yet tempting retro pieces; **Shop 408** sells old books, some dating back to the Ming Dynasty; **Shop 424** has calligraphy supplies and chops starting at Y8 (uncut); **Shop 430** sells opera costumes, including amazing headdresses and the obligatory fake beards. ✉ *Fangbang Lu, Huangpu District.*

XINTIANDI & CITY CENTER

Antiques

Shanghai Art Deco. It looks like an old junk shop but Shanghai Art Deco has a wonderful selection of radios, old tin advertising signs, furniture, and retro household items like Revolution-era teapots and double happiness trays. ✉ *107 Dongtai Lu, Luwan* ☎ *021/6387–6048.*

★ **Zhen Zhen.** Friendly owner Mr. Liu sells a range of lamps, gramophones, fans, and other electrical equipment salvaged from Shanghai's glorious

ULTIMATE SHOPPING TOUR

Shopping in Shanghai requires comfortable shoes and regular stops for sustenance. To beat the crowds (which increase as the day progresses), start at around 9 AM at **Yu Garden,** and fuel up with a coffee at **La Casbah** on Lishui Lu. Yu Garden is the best place in Shanghai for standard Chinese items such as chopsticks, name chops (stone stamps carved with names and characters), painted bottles, and teapots.

Avoid the stores inside the bewildering main complex and concentrate on slightly cheaper ones around **Fangbang Lu.** Dive into side streets and forage among the large buildings on the edges, such as the market at **Fuyou Gate.**

Revive with steamed buns from street vendors and grab a taxi to **Dongtai Lu** (about Y15) for more eclectic Chinese items such as cricket cages, old qipao, and odd pieces from the 1930s and '40s. Enjoy the surroundings: old men playing chess and babies in spilt pants toddling about. Stop at **Xintiandi,** a short walk away, for lunch and window-shopping.

You can walk from here to **Taikang Lu** to take in the wonderful buildings along Sinan Lu, but it's a long haul, especially with all those bags, so take a cab if you're not up to the walk. Taikang Lu has a more modern and arty edge. Buy T-shirts at **insh** or **Shirtflag,** or listen to Miao women singing as they embroider at the **Harvest Studio.** Around the corner, **Taikang Antique Market** may be devoid of customers, but has some interesting finds. Finally, collapse in a heap at **Kommune,** a café in the yard off Lane 210.

past. Some of his stock has been bought by chic restaurants like M on the Bund, and most are in some kind of working order. A small glass lamp base will set you back about Y100. ✉ *11 Dongtai Lu, Luwan* ☎ *021/6385–8793.*

Books & Art Supplies

Chaterhouse Books. An oasis for the starved reader, this bookstore stocks a good range of magazines in English and other languages and English books, including children's books and a comprehensive selection of travel guides. ✉ *Shop B1-E Shanghai Times Square, 99 Huaihai Zhong Lu, Luwan* ☎ *021/6391–8237.*

Gifts

Fodor's Choice ★ **Shanghai Museum Shop.** The selection of books on China and Chinese culture at the main store is impressive, and there are some children's books. Expensive reproduction ceramics are available as well as smaller gift items such as magnets, scarves, and notebooks. Cool purchases like a Chinese architecture–ink stamp (Y90) make great gifts. A delicate bracelet with Chinese charms costs Y150. ✉ *Shanghai Museum, 201 Renmin Dadao, Huangpu* ☎ *021/6372–3500* ✉ *123 Taicang Lu, Luwan* ☎ *021/6384–7900.*

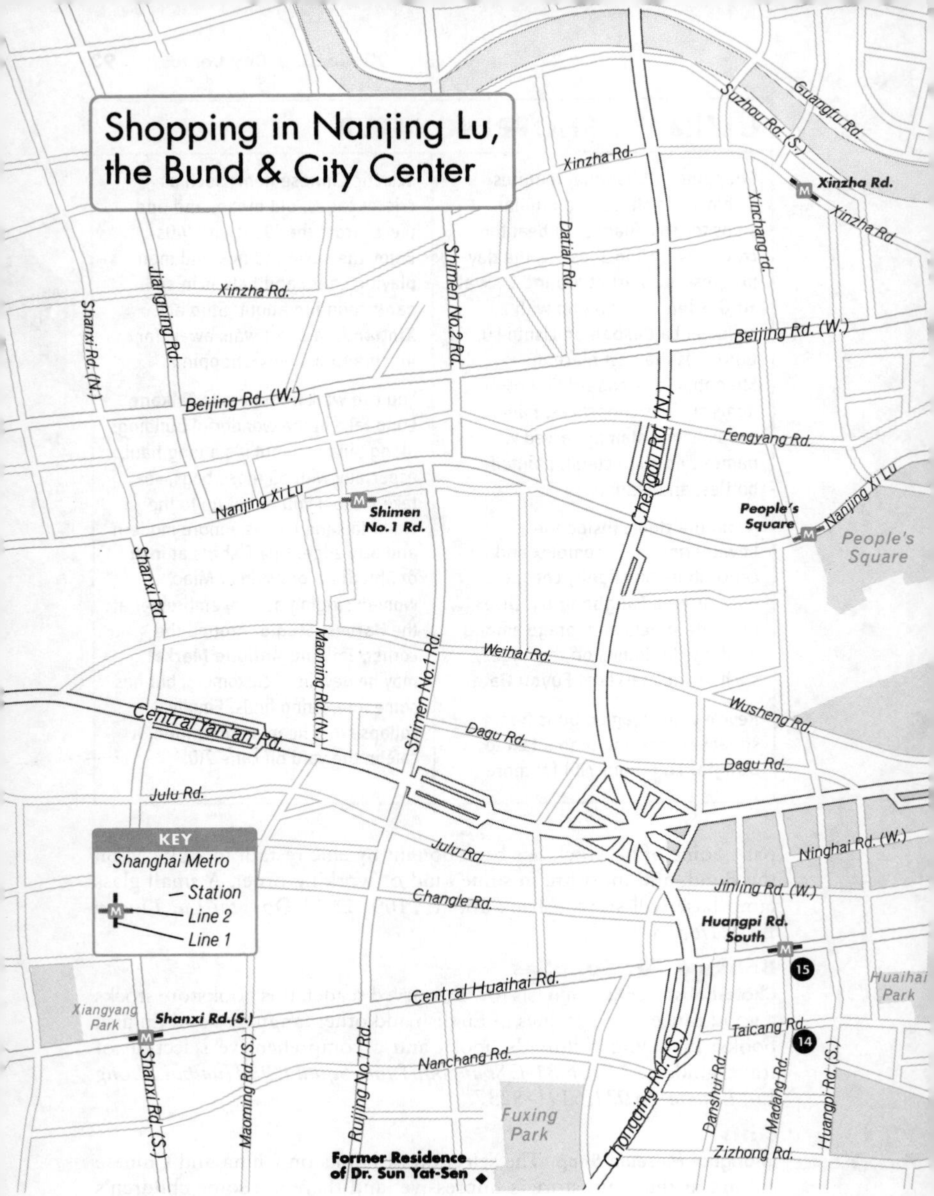

Brilliance Shimao 8
Bund 18 6
Foreign Language Bookstore 4
Raffles City 3
Shanghai #1 Department Store 1
Shanghai #1 Dispensary . .2
Shanghai Antique 11
Shanghai Art Deco 13
Shanghai Museum 9
Super Brand 14
Suzhou Cobblers 7
Three on the Bund 10
Xavier 15
Yangzhenhua Bizhuang 5
Zhen Zhen 12

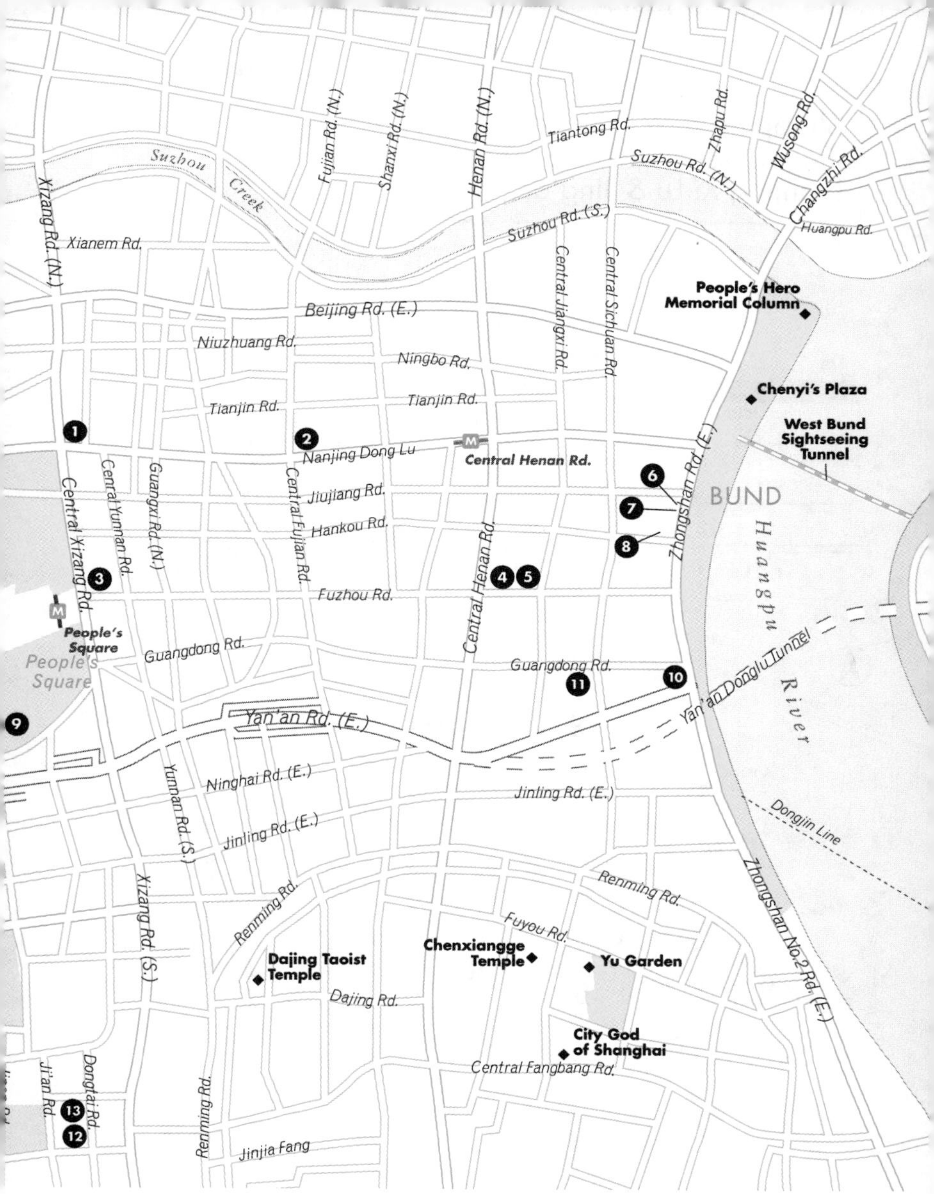

Suzhou Creek
Fujian Rd. (N.)
Shanxi Rd. (N.)
Henan Rd. (N.)
Tiantong Rd.
Zhapu Rd.
Wusong Rd.
Suzhou Rd. (N.)
Changzhi Rd.
Huangpu Rd.
Suzhou Rd. (S.)
Xizang Rd. (N.)
Xianem Rd.
Central Jiangxi Rd.
Central Sichuan Rd.
People's Hero Memorial Column
Beijing Rd. (E.)
Niuzhuang Rd.
Ningbo Rd.
Chenyi's Plaza
Tianjin Rd.
Tianjin Rd.
West Bund Sightseeing Tunnel
Nanjing Dong Lu
Central Henan Rd.
Central Yunnan Rd.
Guangxi Rd. (N.)
Central Fujian Rd.
Central Xizang Rd.
Jiujiang Rd.
Hankou Rd.
Zhongshan Rd. (E.)
BUND
Huangpu River
Central Henan Rd.
Fuzhou Rd.
People's Square
People's Square
Guangdong Rd.
Guangdong Rd.
Yan'an Donglu Tunnel
Yan'an Rd. (E.)
Yunnan Rd. (S.)
Ninghai Rd. (E.)
Jinling Rd. (E.)
Jinling Rd. (E.)
Dongjin Line
Xizang Rd. (S.)
Renming Rd.
Renming Rd.
Fuyou Rd.
Zhongshan No.2 Rd. (E.)
Dajing Taoist Temple
Chenxiangge Temple
Yu Garden
Dajing Rd.
City God of Shanghai
Central Fangbang Rd.
Ji'an Rd.
Dongtai Rd.
Renming Rd.
Jinjia Fang

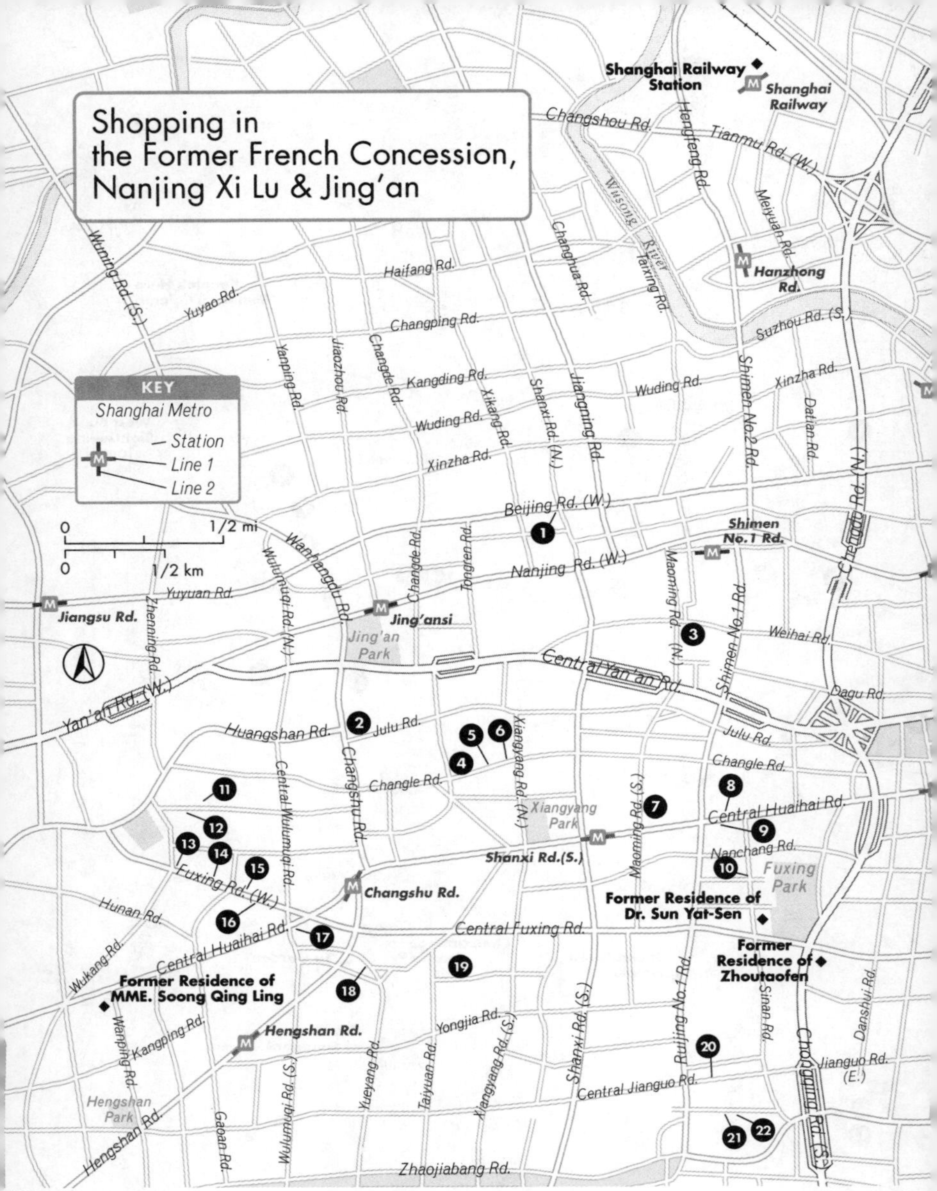

- Art Scene Warehouse . . . **16**
- Arts & Crafts Research Institute **19**
- Asian View **1**
- Boutique Cashmere Lover **22**
- Eawe **12**
- insh **21**
- Larosin Tree **3**
- Madame Mao's Dowry **14**
- 1918 Artspace **10**
- QiongZi **2**
- Paddy Field **20**
- Rouge Baiser Elise **13**
- Shanghai Huangshan Tea Company **8**
- Shanghai Tang **7**
- Shirtflag **4**
- Silk King **9, 17**
- Simply Life **18**
- Skylight **15**
- The Thing **5**
- Torana House **6**
- Village Girl **11**

NANJING DONG LU & THE BUND

Antiques

Shanghai Antique and Curio Store. A pleasant departure from the touristy shops in the area, this government-owned store is an excellent place to gauge whether you are being taken for a ride elsewhere. Goods start as low as Y20 for small pieces of embroidery, and items range from ceramics to wedding baskets (traditionally used to hold part of the bride's dowry). Be aware that some of the pieces may not be taken out of the country, as a sign in the ceramics store warns. ✉ *192–246 Guangdong Lu, Huangpu* ☎ *021/6321–5868.*

Art

★ **Studio Rouge.** A small but well-chosen collection of mainly photography and paintings by emerging and established artists crowd this simple shop. Look for Studio Rouge Black Box opening up at M50 in Moganshan Lu; it will house the works of more international artists. Prices start at US$600 for a limited-edition silk screen. ✉ *17 Fuzhou Lu, Huangpu* ☎ *021/6323–0833.*

Books & Art Supplies

Foreign Languages Bookstore. On the 1st floor, find a selection of English-language books about China and Chinese language. Head to the 4th floor for English-language classic novels and children's books. Prices start at Y10 for paper-cut cards. ✉ *390 Fuzhou Lu, Huangpu* ☎ *021/6322–3200, 021/6322–3271, or 021/6322–3219.*

Yangzhenhua Bizhuang. Calligraphy supplies at excellent prices—fine brushes start at just Y2—can be purchased at this long-established shop. It still has the original glass counters and dark-wood shelves, and a staff that relaxes at the back with tea and pumpkin seeds. ✉ *290 Fuzhou Lu, Huangpu* ☎ *021/6322–3117.*

Ceramics

Blue Shanghai White. The eponymous colored ceramics here are designed and hand-painted by the owner, and are made in Jingdezhen, once home to China's imperial kilns. Some larger pieces are made with wood salvaged from demolition sites around Shanghai, such as a wooden bureau with ceramic drawer fronts. Prices start at Y60 for a cup to Y30,000 for a screen with ceramic panels. ✉ *17 Fuzhou Lu, Room 103, Huangpu* ☎ *021/6323–0856* ✉ *369 Zizhong Lu, Luwan* ☎ *021/6385–5406.*

Chinese Medicine

Shanghai No. 1 Dispensary. If you've got an illness, this place has something to cure it. The flagship store on Nanjing Dong Lu carries Eastern and Western medicines from ginseng to hairy antler, and aspirin to acupuncture needles. ✉ *616 Nanjing Dong Lu, Huangpu* ☎ *021/6322–4567.*

Clothing & Shoes

Bund 18. The glamorous collection of shops here sell high-end designer clothing and accessories such as Marni, Ermenegildo Zegna, Cartier, and Giorgio Armani. The boutique **Younik** stands out by specializing in Shanghai-based designers, including Lu Kun. ✉ *18 Zhongshan Dong Yi Lu, Huangpu* ☎ *021/6323–7066.*

Larosin Tree. Clothing, cute toy animals, and accessories are handmade with real wax batik. ■ **TIP→ Wax batik is a process of decorating fabric using wax, and is sometimes printed rather than made using actual wax.** Designs have vintage and ethnic influences. ✉ *Peace Hotel, 20 Nanjing Dong Lu, Huangpu* ☎ *021/6321–6888 or 021/6321–6614* ✉ *127B Maoming Nan Lu, Luwan District* ☎ *021/5403–3202* 🌐 *www.larosintree.com.*

★ **Suzhou Cobblers.** Beautifully embroidered handmade shoes and slippers with quirky designs such as cabbages are sold alongside funky bags made from rice sacks. Women's shoes start at Y480 and can be made to order for an extra Y50. Children's shoes are also available. Also sold here are sweet knitted toys and children's sweaters. ✉ *17 Fuzhou Lu, Room 101, Huangpu* ☎ *139–181–877–60 (mobile)* 🌐 *www.suzhou-cobblers.com.*

Three on the Bund. Like Bund 18 (*above*), Three on the Bund is a luxury complex that stocks mainly European-designer brands. ✉ *3 Zhongshan Dong Yi Lu, Huangpu* ☎ *021/6323–0101.*

Department Stores

Shanghai No. 1 Department Store. Shanghai's largest state-owned store attracts masses of Chinese shoppers, especially on weekends. It sells everything from porcelain dinnerware to badminton racquets and is popular with much of Shanghai's male population who want no-nonsense, one-stop shopping. ✉ *830 Nanjing Dong Lu, Huangpu* ☎ *021/6322–3344.*

Malls

Brilliance Shimao International Plaza. This mall near People's Square (it was finished in 2006) stocks some high-end designers such as Givenchy mixed in with midrange ones such as Lacoste and Esprit. ✉ *829 Nanjing Dong Lu, Huangpu* ☎ *021/3313–4718.*

Raffles City. Near People's Square, Raffles City has midrange foreign and local designer stores including funky streetwear such as Miss Sixty, Roxy, and FCUK. It also has a movie theater showing both Chinese and foreign films, and a food court in the basement with snacks and drinks. ✉ *268 Xizang Zhong Lu, Huangpu* ☎ *021/6340–3600.*

Pearls & Jewelry

Ling Ling Pearls & Jewelry. Traditional pearl necklaces and inexpensive fashion jewelry stand out for being hipper than the competition. Contemporary-looking pearl and stone combinations are priced high, but large discounts are often given sans haggling. ✉ *2F, Pearl City, 558 Nanjing Dong Lu, 2nd fl., Huangpu* ☎ *021/6322–9299* 🌐 *www.linglingspearl.com.*

Pearl City. Many stalls here—including ⇨ Ling Ling Pearls & Jewelry—sell pearls and other jewelry. ✉ *558 Nanjing Dong Lu, 2nd fl., Huangpu.*

FORMER FRENCH CONCESSION

Antiques

Brocade Country. The English-speaking owner, Liu Xiao Lan, has a Miao mother and a broad knowledge of her pieces. The Miao sew their history into the cloth and she knows the meaning behind each one. Many pieces are antique-collector's items and Ms. Liu has also started designing more wearable items. Antique embroidery can go as high as Y20,000, but mounted new embroidery pieces start at Y150 and are flat and easy to slip into a suitcase. ✉ *616 Julu Lu, Xuhui* ☎ *021/6279–2677.*

WHO ARE THE MIAO?

Famous for their intricate embroidery work, the Miao are one of the oldest ethnic-minority groups in China and one of the largest groups still in southwest China. The Miao may have existed as early as 200 BC, in the Han Dynasty. It's not only the Miao, however, who are accomplished embroidery artists. Many ethnic-minority groups in southwestern China make pieces of similar quality.

Jin. This packed little store sells furniture that's up to 100 years old. Compared to the larger antiques warehouses, prices are quite competitive. Good buys include tiny little stools at Y150 and wooden mooncake (traditional cakes eaten at the mid-autumn festival) molds for Y100. The shop doesn't arrange shipping. ✉ *614 Julu Lu, Jing'an* ☎ *021/6247–2964.*

★ **Madame Mao's Dowry.** This covetable collection of mostly revolutionary-propaganda items from the '50s, '60s, and '70s is sourced from the countryside and areas in Sichuan province and around Beijing and Tianjin. Mixed in are hip designs from local and international designers. Although this could be your one-stop shopping experience, remember this is communism at capitalist prices: Y800 for a small Revolution-era teapot and around Y1,800 for a Revolution-era mirror. ✉ *70 Fuxing Xi Lu, Xuhui* ☎ *021/6437–1255* ✉ *Gallery: 50 Moganshan Lu, Building 6, 5th fl., Putuo* ☎ *021/6276–9932.*

Art

Art Scene. A 1930s French Concession villa serves as a beautiful, albeit contrasting, backdrop for this gallery's contemporary Chinese artwork. Like the established and emerging artists it represents, the gallery is making a name for itself internationally, having participated in Art Chicago and the San Francisco International Art Exposition. ✉ *No. 8, La. 37, Fuxing Xi Lu, Xuhui* ☎ *021/6437–0631.*

1918 Artspace. Excellent up-and-coming artists such as Jin Shan are showcased at this independent gallery. The old villa, with its lush garden, makes for great openings and is a showcase in itself. It's open by appointment only. The gallery has a newer warehouse space as well. ✉ *6 Xiangshan Lu, Luwan District* ☎ *021/5306–8030* 🌐 *www.1918artspace.com* ✉ *78 Changping Lu, Putuo* ☎ *021/5228–6776.*

Carpets

Torana House. Two stories here are filled with carpets handmade by Tibetan artisans in rural areas using top-quality wool and featuring auspicious symbols. This is also a good place to pick up an antique piece from Tibet or Xinjiang. ✉ *La. 339, Changle Lu, No. 15, Xuhui* ☎ *021/5404–7787* 🌐 *www.toranahouse.com.*

CLOSE UP

Qipao Aplenty

You'll find dozens of *qipao* (traditional Chinese dress) shops on **Changle Lu** between Maoming Nan Lu and Shaanxi Nan Lu. These two streets are also home to many tiny boutiques in the blocks just north and south of Huaihai Lu. They sell ready-to-wear and many offer a tailoring service. However, the prices will probably be lower at the **South Bund Soft Spinning Material Market** (⇨ Markets *below*), where a qipao costs around Y500 (including fabric).

Other places that create tailor-made qipao: **Feel** (⇨ *above*), which charges from around Y1,000 for a silk qipao; **Xiu Zhuang** (✉ 318 Julu Lu, Luwan ☎ 021/6217–5169), whose hand-embroidered qipao cost a whopping Y6,000; and **Hanyi** and **Tailor Chen** (⇨ Tailor-Made for You box, *below*).

In general, it takes around three to seven days for a qipao to be made at any of these shops.

Clothing & Shoes

Boutique Cashmere Lover. The small collection of wickedly soft cashmere and blends is contemporary in design; some have Chinese details. Made to order is available. A man's pure-cashmere sweater is around Y1,580. ✉ *200 Taikang Lu, Room 409, Luwan* ☎ *021/6473–7829.*

Eawe. Owned by a Japanese- and Thai-design duo, this tiny shop has witty Shanghai-focused T-shirts that include the Good Citizen line and a small selection of women's dresses. T-shirts cost Y180. ✉ *151 Anfu Lu, Xuhui* ☎ *021/5404–7111* 🌐 *www.eawe.cn.*

Feel. The qipao may be a traditional Chinese dress, but Feel makes it a style for modern times as well. Pop across the lane to Feel Handicrafts, which has great lamps. ✉ *La. 210, No. 3, Room 110, Taikang Lu, Luwan* ☎ *021/5465–4519/6466–8065.*

insh (In Shanghai). A local designer sells cheeky clothes that are not for the fainthearted. Skirts barely cover bottoms but there are cute takes on traditional qipao. It's a good place for T-shirts featuring stylish Chinese-inspired designs. T-shirts cost Y188. ✉ *200 Taikang Lu, Luwan* ☎ *021/6466–5249* 🌐 *www.insh.com.cn.*

La Vie. Asian-style and more eclectic pieces—some quite unusual—are sold here. There is a lot of attention to detail; for example, a crisp turquoise shirt with phoenix embroidery at Y590. ✉ *Courtyard 7, La. 210, Taikang Lu, Luwan District* ☎ *021/6445–3585* ✉ *Bund 18, 18 Zhongshan Yi Lu, 2nd fl., Huangpu* 🌐 *www.lavie.com.cn.*

L'Atelier Mandarine. Clothing and accessories focus on the home and lounging. The French designer uses natural fabrics such as silk, cotton, and cashmere and old embroidery techniques. The simple and chic designs let the quality of the fabric speak for itself. ✉ *Studio No. 318, No.3 La. 210, Taikang Lu, Luwan* ☎ *021/6473–5381.*

QiongZi. The Hubei-born designer personally sources fabrics from different parts of the world for her feminine designs, which have strong Chinese and Japanese influences. Ready-to-wear starts at Y1,200. ✉ *620 Julu Lu, Xuhui* ☎ *021/6473–5465.*

Rouge Baiser Elise. Yet another French designer in Shanghai, Rouge Baiser Elise has beautiful linen and cotton homeware and clothing, including children's clothes. Items can be made to order in your choice of color, and children's names can be sewn onto clothing for no extra cost. Handmade pieces have subtle embroidery, and everything looks distinctly French. Go just to check out the beautiful building. Prices start at Y150 for socks. ✉ *299-2 Fuxing Xi Lu, Xuhui* ☎ *021/6431–8019* 🌐 *www.rougebaiser-elise.com.*

3

★ **Shanghai Tang.** This is one of China's leading fashion brands with distinctive acid-bright silks, soft as a baby's bottom cashmere, and funky homeware. Sigh at the beautiful fabrics and designs and gasp at the prices. ✉ *Xintiandi 15, North Block 181, Taicang Lu, Luwan* ☎ *021/6384–1601* ✉ *JinJiang Hotel, Shop E, 59 Maoming Nan Lu, Luwan* ☎ *021/5466–3006* ✉ *Shangri-La Hotel, Lobby Level, 33 Fucheng Lu, Pudong* ☎ *021/5877–6632* 🌐 *www.shanghaitang.com.*

★ **Shanghai Trio.** Chinese fabrics mixed with French flair, irresistible children's clothes in bright colors and sweet little kimonos, great utilitarian satchels that scream urban chic, and crafty necklaces are the stars of this range. The most luxurious item is a Y3,000 cashmere qipao-style coat. ✉ *Xintiandi 181, Taicang Lu, Luwan* ☎ *021/6355–2974.*

★ **Shirtflag.** A hipper-than-thou collection of witty and slickly designed T-shirts, accessories, and notebooks at this fun shop takes on propaganda art with a humorous and funky edge. Get Mao's head on a pair of Converse-style canvas sneakers for Y150. ✉ *Room 8, No.7, La. 210 Taikang Lu, Luwan* ☎ *021/6466–7009* ✉ *330 Nanchang Lu, Luwan* ☎ *021/5465–3011* ✉ *Room 505, 168 Lujiazui Lu, Pudong* ☎ *021/5047–1650* ✉ *336 Changle Lu, 1st fl., Xuhui* ☎ *021/6255–7699* 🌐 *www.shirtflag.com.*

The Thing. Find strange yet compelling graphics with a 1970s art feel or a Chinese twist printed on bags, sneakers, tees, and sweats. The designs are increasingly popular with Shanghai fashionistas. ✉ *266 Changle Lu, Luwan* ☎ *021/6384–5207.*

Village Girl. Hand-selected by the owner, the clothing, shoes, embroidery pieces, and other items—vintage and new—sold here are made by people (mostly women) of China's ethnic minorities who live in small villages in Guizhou, Guangxi, and Hunan. The most interesting is a reasonable selection of fabrics. If you're going on to southwest China, wait to buy there. Fabric starts at Y50 per meter. ✉ *155 Anfu Lu, Xuhui* ☎ *021/5403–5754.*

Xavier. Head here for your Mrs. Robinson–style, cocktails-by-the-pool outfits and for wild hats, including some extravagant feathered concoctions. The Australian designer also has a small line of wool carpets priced at around Y8,000. ✉ *119 Madang Lu, Unit 603, Luwan* ☎ *021/6328–7111* 🌐 *www.shanghai-xavier.com.*

CLOSE UP

Tailor-Made for You

Tailors usually charge a flat fee per type of garment and may require a deposit, with the balance paid upon satisfactory completion of the garment. If you can, bring in a picture of what you want made or an existing garment for them to copy. Usually, copying is the most successful. Try to allow enough time for an initial and follow-up fitting as tailors are accustomed to working with Chinese bodies and may need to adjust the garment a bit more to achieve a proper fit on Western frames.

Dave's Custom Tailoring. Now in its 40th year of operation, Dave's has an English-speaking staff and skilled tailoring, making it a favorite among expats and visiting businesspeople. The shop specializes in men's dress shirts and wool suits, which require around 10 days and 2 fittings to complete. ✉ *No. 6, 288 Wuyuan Lu, Xuhui* ☎ *021/5404-0001* 🌐 *www.tailordave.com.*

Hanyi. A well-respected qipao shop, Hanyi has a book of styles that its tailors can make in three days, or more complex, finely embroidered patterns that require a month for proper fitting. Prices range from Y1,000 to Y1,800. ✉ *221 Changle Lu, Luwan* ☎ *021/5404-4727* 🌐 *www.shanghai1888.com.*

Tailor Chen. One phone call and a return-taxi fare will bring Mr. Chen to your hotel room for measurements. His translator will help with the details. He's known for his women's suits and qipao. ☎ *138/1667-5781 English line (cell phone), 021/5218-0621 or 138/1738-2017 (cell phone).*

Furniture

Asian View. A longtime favorite among expats for Chinese furniture, Alex Zheng has broadened his focus with this store devoted to furnishings from throughout Asia. Reasonably priced and beautifully made tables, beds, and accessories from Indonesia, India, Malaysia, and Thailand fill the 1,219-square-meter (4,000-square-foot) showroom. ✉ *233 Shaanxi Nan Lu, Luwan* ☎ *021/6474–1051* 🌐 *www.asianview.com.cn.*

Paddy Field. Ready-made and made-to-order furniture features a blend of Southeast Asian and Chinese influences. The modern and the ancient are also combined in designs, and quality materials such as teak and elm are used. Custom-made furniture takes around three weeks. ✉ *273 Jianguo Xi Lu, Xuhui District* ☎ *021/6467–4128.*

Tibet Treasure. This small shop has a chilled vibe and lots of brightly colored, painted Tibetan furniture as well as swirling Indian embroidered skirts. The walls are hung with Thankas for in-store karma. A small painted wooden cabinet goes for Y780. ✉ *96 Xiangyang Nan Lu, Xuhui* ☎ *021/6431–3150* 🌐 *www.tibettreasure.com.*

Gifts & Housewares

Harvest Studio. Drop in for an embroidery class or just to watch the Miao women with their distinctive hair knots embroidering, and sometimes singing. This studio sells Miao-embroidered pillows, purses, and cloth-

Continued on page 110

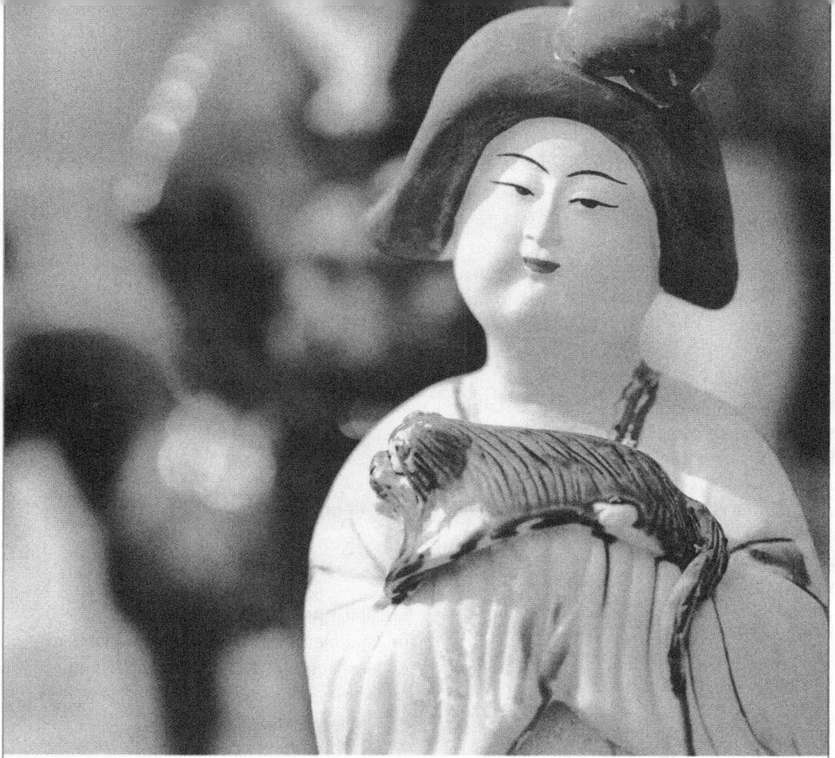

MARKETS

A GUIDE TO BUYING SILK, PEARLS & POTTERY

Chinese markets are hectic and crowded, but great fun for the savvy shopper. The intensity of the bargaining and the sheer number of goods available are pretty much unsurpassed anywhere else in the world.

Nowadays wealthier Chinese may prefer to flash their cash in department stores and designer boutiques, but generally, markets are still the best places to shop. Teens spend their pocket money at cheap clothing markets. Grandparents, often toting their grandchildren, go to their local neighborhood food market almost daily to pick up fresh items such as tofu, fish, meat, fruit, and vegetables. Markets are also great places to mix with the locals, see the drama of bargaining take place, and watch as the Chinese banter, play with their children, challenge each other to cards, debate, or just lounge.

Some markets have a mish-mash of items, whereas others are more specialized, dealing in one particular ware. Markets play an essential part in the everyday life of the Chinese and prices paid are always a great topic of conversation. A compliment on a choice article will often elicit the price paid in reply and a discussion may ensue on where to get the same thing at an even lower cost.

GREAT FINDS

The prices we list below are meant to give you an idea of what you can pay for certain items. Actual post-bargaining prices will of course depend on how well you haggle, while pre-bargaining prices are often based on how much the vendor thinks he or she can get out of you.

PEARLS

Many freshwater pearls are grown in Taihu; seawater pearls come from Japan or the South Seas. Some have been dyed and others mixed with semiprecious stones. Designs can be pretty wild and the clasps are not of very high quality, but necklaces and bracelets are cheap. Post-bargaining, a plain, short strand of pearls should cost around Y40.

ETHNIC-MINORITY HANDICRAFTS

Brightly colored skirts from the Miao minority and embroidered jackets from the Yunnan area are great boho souvenirs. The heavy, elaborate jewelry could decorate a side table or hang on a wall. Colorful children's shoes are embellished with animal faces and bells. After bargaining, a skirt in the markets should go for between Y220 to Y300, and a pair of children's shoes for Y40 to Y60.

RETRO

Odd items from the hedonistic '20s to the revolutionary '60s and '70s include treasures like old light fixtures and tin advertising signs. A rare sign such as one banning foreigners from entry may cost as much as Y10,000, but small items such as teapots can be bought for around Y250. Retro items are harder to bargain down for than mass-produced items.

"MAOMORABILIA"

The Chairman's image is readily available on badges, bags, lighters, watches, ad infinitum. Pop-art–like figurines of Mao and his Red Guards clutching red books are kitschy but iconic. For soundbites and quotes from the Great Helmsman, buy the Little Red Book itself. Pre-bargaining, a badge costs Y25, a bag Y50, and a ceramic figurine Y380. Just keep in mind that many posters are fakes.

CERAMICS

Most ceramics you'll find in markets are factory-made, so you probably won't stumble upon a bargain Ming Dynasty vase, but ceramics in a variety of colors can be picked up at reasonable prices. Opt for pretty pieces decorated with butterflies, or for the more risqué, copulating couples. A bowl-and-plate set goes for around Y25, a larger serving plate Y50.

BIRDCAGES

Wooden birdcages with domed roofs make charming decorations, with or without occupants. They are often seen being carried by old men as they promenade their feathered friends. A pre-bargaining price for a medium-sized wooden cage is around Y180.

PROPAGANDA AND COMIC BOOKS

Follow the actions of Chinese revolutionary hero, Lei Feng, or look for scenes from Chinese history and lots of *gongfu* (Chinese martial arts) stories. Most titles are in Chinese and often in black and white, but look out for titles like *Tintin and the Blue Lotus*, set in Shanghai and translated into Chinese. You can bargain down to around Y15 for less popular titles.

SILK

Bolts and bolts of silk brocade with blossoms, butterflies, bamboo, and other patterns dazzle the eye. An enormous range of items made from silk, from purses to slippers to traditional dresses, are available at most markets. Silk brocade costs around Y35 per meter, a price that is generally only negotiable if you buy large quantities.

JADE

A symbol of purity and beauty for the Chinese, jade comes in a range of colors. Subtle and simple bangles vie for attention with large sculptures on market stalls. A lavender jade Guanyin (Goddess of Mercy) pendant runs at Y260 and a green jade bangle about Y280 before bargaining.

MAH-JONGG SETS

The clack-clack of mah-jongg tiles can be heard late into the night on the streets of most cities in summer. Cheap plastic sets go for about Y50. Far more aesthetically pleasing are ceramic sets in slender drawers of painted cases. These run about Y250 after bargaining, from a starting price of Y450. Some sets come with instructions, but if not, instructions for the "game of four winds" can be downloaded in English at www.mahjongg.com.

SHOPPING KNOW-HOW

When to Go

Avoid weekends if you can and try to go early in the morning, from 8 AM to 10 AM, or at the end of the day just before 6 PM. Rainy days are also good bets for avoiding the crowds and getting better prices.

Bringin' Home the Goods

Although that faux-Gucci handbag is tempting, remember that some countries have heavy penalties for the import of counterfeit goods. Likewise, that animal fur may be cheap, but you may get fined a lot more at your home airport than what you paid for it. Counterfeit goods are generally prohibited in the United States, but there's some gray area regarding goods with a "confusingly similar" trademark. Each person is allowed to bring in one such item, as long as it's for personal use and not for resale. For more details, go to the travel section of www.cbp.gov. The HM and Revenue Customs Web site, www.hmrc.gov.uk, has a list of banned and prohibited goods for the United Kingdom.

⚠The Chinese government has regular and very public crackdowns on fake goods, so that store you went to today may have different items tomorrow. In Shanghai, for example, pressure from the Chinese government and other countries to protect intellectual property rights led to the demise of one of the city's largest and most popular markets, Xiangyang.

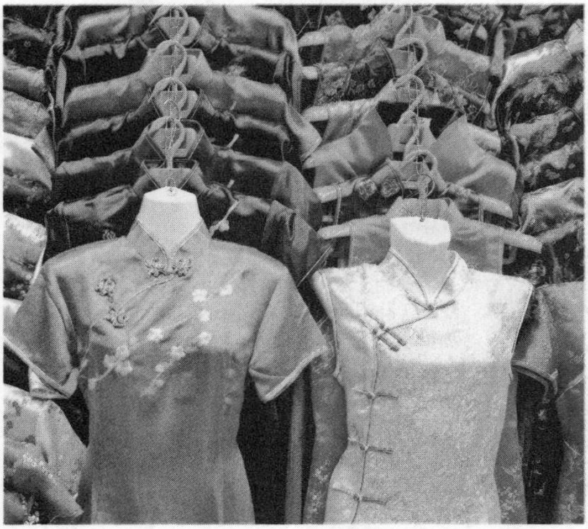

BEFORE YOU GO

- Be prepared to be grabbed, pushed, followed, stared at, and even to have people whispering offers of items to buy in your ear. In China, personal space and privacy are not valued in the same way as in the West, so the invasion of it is common. Move away but remain calm and polite. No one will understand if you get upset anyway.
- Many Chinese love to touch foreign children, so if you have kids, make sure they're aware of and prepared for this.
- Keep money and valuables in a safe place. Pickpockets and bag-slashers are becoming common.
- Pick up a cheap infrared laser pointer to detect counterfeit bills. The light illuminates the hidden anti-counterfeit ultraviolet mark in the real notes.
- Check for fake items, e.g. silk and pearls.
- Learn some basic greetings and numbers in Chinese. The local people will really appreciate it.

HOW TO BARGAIN

Successful bargaining requires the dramatic skills of a Hollywood actor. Here's a step-by-step guide to getting the price you want and having fun at the same time.

DO'S

Browsing in a silk shop

- Start by deciding what you're willing to pay for an item.
- Look at the vendor and point to the item to indicate your interest.
- The vendor will quote you a price, usually by punching numbers into a calculator and showing it to you.
- Here, expressions of shock are required from you, which will never be as great as those of the vendor, who will put in an Oscar-worthy performance at your prices.
- Next it's up to you to punch in a number that's around 75% of the original price—or lower if you feel daring.
- Pass the calculator back and forth until you meet somewhere in the middle, probably at up to (and sometimes less than) 50% of the original quote.

DONT'S

Chinese slippers at a ladies' market

- Don't enter into negotiations if you aren't seriously considering the purchase.
- Don't haggle over small sums of money.
- If the vendor isn't budging, walk away; he'll likely call you back.
- It's better to bargain if the vendor is alone. He's unlikely to come down on the price if there's an audience.
- Saving face is everything in China. Don't belittle or make the vendor angry, and don't get angry yourself.
- Remain pleasant and smile often.
- Buying more than one of something gets you a better deal.
- Dress down and leave your jewelry and watches in the hotel safe on the day you go marketing. You'll get a lower starting price if you don't flash your wealth.

SHANGHAI MARKETS

Antiques Market of Shanghai Old Town God Temple. (Huabao Building). Prices are high due to the prime location of this basement market in the main Yu Garden shopping complex. Shop No. 22 has revolution-era materials, including an original Little Red Book for Y180. No. 200 has textiles and embroidery starting at Y50 for a 5-cm-square patch. ✉ *Yu Garden, 265 Fangbang Zhonglu, Huangpu* ✥ *On the corner of Fangbang Lu* ☎ *021/6355–9999* ⏲ *Daily 10 AM–6 PM.*

Cang Bao Antiques Building (Cang Bao Lou). During the week, you can browse four floors of booths that sell everything from Mao paraphernalia to real and fake antique porcelain. There are pearls in a wide range of colors and styles, starting from Y10 for a simple bracelet. Curios and other jewelry are on the ground floor, and check out the third floor for old photos, clothing, books, and obscure household kitsch. On Sunday the action starts long before sunrise when, according to a local saying, only ghosts should be awake, hence the market's nickname: *guishi* or "ghost market." Hawkers from the provinces arrive early to lay out their goods on the sidewalk or inside on the fourth floor. Ivory, jade, and wood carvings are among the many goods sold here, all at negotiable prices. ✉ *457 Fangbang Zhonglu, Huangpu* ✥ *End of Fangbang Lu near the gate to Henan Zhong Lu* ⏲ *Weekdays 9–5:30, weekends 6 AM–5:30 PM.*

★ Fodor's Choice **Dongtai Lu Market.** Mao statues, tiny shoes for women with bound feet (though foot-binding is rarely practiced in China anymore), ethnic minority-crafted clothing and embroidery, ceramic bracelets, gramophones —it's all here. This is one of the best places in town to buy gifts and souvenirs, and it's within walking distance of the shops at Xintiandi. Most of the stalls sell similar items, so your bargaining power is high as you can just walk to another store if you don't like the price. Real antiques are rare. Squeeze behind the stalls to check out the shops in the back. ✉ *1266 Nanjing Xi Lu, Jing'an* ☎ *021/5306–8888* ✥ *Just west of Xizang Lu* ⏲ *Daily 9–6.*

Fuyou Gate Market. This department-store-meets-market with a wild variety of items spreads over three floors. On the ground floor, shop No. 156 sells Nepali and Indian clothing and jewelry; No. 186 sells brightly colored Chinese folk textiles, including children's shoes; and on the second floor, shop No. 1 sells Korean stationery. ✉ *427 Fuyou Lu, Huangpu* ✥ *Take bus No. 66 from Xizang Nan Lu* ⏲ *Daily 7 AM–5:30 PM.*

Fuyuan Market. The first floor of this market, also in theYu Garden area, specializes in Chinese medicine. You can get jujube seeds for insomnia and kudzu vine flower for hangovers, or just wander around and marvel at the weird-looking ginseng. ✉ *338 Fuyou Lu, Huangpu* ✥ *Across the street and just east of Fuyou Gate Market* ⏲ *Daily 8 AM–5:30 PM.*

Pu'an Lu Children's Market. A mecca for parents, children, and doting relatives, this underground market sells toys, accessories, shoes, and clothing for kids. Hunt out French and Swedish clothing brands, and big-name toy manufacturers such as Lego and Barbie, as well as some beautiful Japanese wooden toys. You might find a pretty dress for Y29 or a small wooden Noah's ark for Y35. ✉ *10 Pu'an Lu Lu, Luwan* ✢ *Take metro line 1 to Huangpi Nan Lu and walk east down Huaihai Lu a few blocks, then turn left* ⏲ *Daily 9:30 AM–6:30 PM.*

Qi Pu Clothing Wholesale Market. Three large buildings (and counting) are stuffed to the rafters with cheap clothing here. It's good for children's clothes, but women's clothing tends to be very petite, and shoe lovers with big feet will be heartbroken. You're most likely to come away with fake designer sneakers and a T-shirt printed with misspelled or vaguely obscene English. ✉ *168 and 183 Qipu Lu, by Henan Bei Lu, Zhabei* ✢ *Take bus No. 66 from Xizang Nan Lu to Qipu Lu, or take the long walk north from the Henan Zhong Lu metro stop* ☎ *021/5102–0001* ⏲ *Daily 6 AM–6 PM.*

★ Fodor's Choice **South Bund Soft-Spinning Material Market.** The unusual name alludes to the veritable treasure chest of fabrics, from lurid synthetics to silk brocades, spread over three floors. Shop No. 313 can produce embroidery based on a digital image for Y40, while Nos. 231, 399, 353, 161 are Aladdin's caves of buttons and braids. No. 189 has masses of silk brocade from a negotiable Y35 per meter. Most stores have a tailoring service with prices starting at Y40 for a shirt and Y50 for a pair of pants. Be warned: the tailoring is very hit or miss. Opt for a tailor whose display clothes are similar to those you want to have made. ✉ *399 Lujiabang Lu, Huangpu* ✢ *Near the Zhongshan Er Lu end of Lujiabang Lu* ⏲ *Daily 8:30 AM–6:30 PM.*

Taikang Antiques Market. Here on lovely Sinan Lu, owners lounge around and smoke as you wander under the low ceilings. It makes a nice change from the tourist scramble of Yuyuan and Dongtai Lu. There are a lot of ceramics, some furniture, and plenty of junk. Shop C28 is crammed with revolutionary propaganda, B113 has old pictures and photos, and C6 has old *qipao* and silks. ✉ *113 Sinan Lu, Luwan* ✢ *About 6 blocks south of Huaihai Lu* ⏲ *Daily 9:30 AM–6 PM.*

Wenmiao Book Market. The Sunday book market at Shanghai's only Confucian temple is worth a look for old propaganda material, comic books, and other cheap paperbacks mainly in Chinese. Look about under the tables for the cheapest items or flip through someone else's photo album. You can pick up a propaganda magazine for Y15 and then head out to the street to eat or have sticker photos made. ✉ *Wenmiao Lu, off Huaihai Lu, Huangpu* ⏲ *Sun. 10 AM–4 PM* 🎫 *Y1.*

WHERE TO EAT

Street vendors selling snacks and meals surround most markets. Wenmiao market has a particularly good selection of street food, including cold noodles served from carts, fried meat on sticks, and in summer, fresh coconut milk. At the South Bund Soft-Spinning Market, on Nancang Jie, you'll find similar offerings. Rumor has it that you can even eat snake there; look for the baskets outside the small food vendors' stores. Dongtai Lu is close to Xintiandi, where you can choose from a wide selection of cafés, bars, and restaurants.

■ TIP→→ **Avoid tap water, ice, and uncooked food. Cooked food from street vendors is generally safe unless it looks like it has been sitting around for a while.**

ing as well as the silver jewelry that traditionally adorns the Miao ceremonial costume. ✉ *3 La. 210, Room 118, Taikang Lu, Luwan* ☎ *021/6473–4566.*

Jooi. This Danish-owned design studio has luxurious cushions in oriental fabric and boho evening bags that are heavy on beading and embroidery. Some clothing is sold and there are great sample sales. Prices start at Y68 for a funky felt coin purse. ✉ *Studio 201, International Artist Factory, La. 210, Taikang Lu, Luwan* ☎ *021/6473–6193* 🌐 *www.jooi.com.*

Simply Life. Popular buys include chunky, shiny red-glazed pottery and delicate bone porcelain painted with Chinese iconic items such as Ming vases and ancient clothing. Better values can be found elsewhere, but it's a good place for lazy shoppers. The flagship store is at the Xintiandi location. ✉ *Unit 101, Xintiandi, 159 Madang Lu, Luwan* ☎ *021/6387–5100* ✉ *9 Dongping Lu, Xuhui* ☎ *021/3406–0509* 🌐 *www.simplylife-sh.com.*

Pearls & Jewelry

★ **Amy Lin's Pearls and Jewelry.** Friendly owner Amy Lin has sold pearls to European first ladies and American presidents but treats all her customers like royalty. Her shop just near the old Xiangyang Market has inexpensive trinket bracelets, strings of seed pearls, and stunning Australian seawater pearl necklaces. ✉ *77 Xiangyang Nan Lu, Xuhui* ☎ *021/5403–9673 or 021/6275–3954* 🌐 *www.amy-pearl.com.*

Lilli's. Here you'll find pearls, dainty silver bracelets with Chinese characters, and mah-jongg–tile bracelets. There's a pricey selection of swank silk photo albums and purses. A sexy clutch in acid-dyed silk costs Y300, and a pearl-adorned cell-phone accessory costs Y120. ✉ *"Le Passage," ground fl., 174 Xiangyang Nan Lu, Xuhui* ☎ *021/6474–5336* ✉ *Maosheng Mansion, Suite 1D, 1051 Xinzha Lu, Jing'an* ☎ *021/6215–5031* ✉ *Shanghai Center, Suite 605, 1376 Nanjing Xi Lu, Jing'an* ☎ *021/6279–8987* ✉ *The Gatehouse, Dong Hu Villas, 1985 Hongqiao Lu, Changning* ☎ *021/6270–1585.*

Skylight. Beautiful Tibetan jewelry is on display at Skylight. Although you could probably get it cheaper at the Yu Gardens or even from street vendors, at least you know it's real. You can also buy breathtaking photos of Tibet and her people taken by the owner. Mounted images start from Y25. A second store is opening up down the road at No. 133. ✉ *28 Fuxing Xi Lu, Xuhui* ☎ *021/6473–5610.*

Photography

Wei Ma Kodak Professional. Good quality prints are hard to find in Shanghai. This store produces professional-quality contact sheets for black-and-white photos, digital prints, and prints from film. They are also able to add white borders and sometimes stock hard-to-find Ilford film. ✉ *459 Wulumuqi Lu, Xuhui* ☎ *021/6248–2187.*

Silk

Silk King (Shanghai Silk Commercial Company). With so many branches, it seems that there's a Silk King on every corner, and for good reason. The shop is respected for its quality silk and wool, and the average price of silk is Y138 per meter. But though the quality may be guaranteed, the patterns are a little dowdy. ✉ *139 Tianping Lu, Xuhui District* ☎ *021/6282–5013* ✉ *590 Huaihai Zhonglu, Luwan District* ☎ *021/6372–0561* ✉ *1226 Huaihai Zhonglu, Xuhui* ☎ *021/6437–3370.*

Souvenirs

Arts and Crafts Research Institute. Shanghai artisans create pieces of traditional Chinese arts and crafts such as embroidery and paper-cutting right before your eyes at this institute. You can purchase everything from paper-cuts to snuff bottles, although at prices higher than you'll pay at the stalls around Yu Garden. ✉ *79 Fenyang Lu, Xuhui* ☎ *021/6437–2509* *Y8.*

Tea

Shanghai Huangshan Tea Company. The nine Shanghai locations of this teashop sell traditional Yixing teapots as well as a huge selection of China's best teas by weight. The higher the price the better the tea. ✉ *605 Huaihai Zhonglu, Luwan* ☎ *021/5306–2974.*

WORD OF MOUTH

"The tea [at Huangshan Tea Company] is packaged nicely for gifts and they had very pretty flowering jasmine. Next door is a little bakery called Lily's. They had excellent egg custard tarts with really flaky pastry! What a nice treat."
-quimbymoy

PUDONG

Malls

Next Age. This veritable behemoth of a department store–meets-mall has loads of foreign brands, especially in the beauty department. ✉ *501 Zhangyang Lu, Pudong* ☎ *021/5830–1111.*

Super Brand Mall. At 10 stories, this is one of Asia's largest malls. It has a massive Lotus supermarket along with a mind-boggling array of shops and food stops, and a movie complex. It can be overwhelming if you don't love to shop. ✉ *168 Lujiazui Lu, Pudong* ☎ *021/6887–7888.*

Times Square. The high-end products—and prices—at Times Square result in fewer customers than at most malls. Brand names such as Escada and Loewe have stores here. ✉ *500 Zhangyang Lu, Pudong* ☎ *021/5836–7777.*

Xinmei Union Square. Smaller, newer, and funkier than Pudong's other malls, Xinmei focuses on hip foreign brands such as Miss Sixty, G-Star Raw, Fornarina, and Swatch. ✉ *999 Pudong Nan Lu, Pudong* ☎ *021/5134–1888.*

NORTH SHANGHAI

Antiques

Henry Antique Warehouse. Named the number-one shop in Shanghai by *Shanghai 8 Days,* an expat magazine, this company is the antique Chinese–furniture research, teaching, and training institute for Tongji University. Part of the showroom sometimes serves as an exhibition hall for the modern designs created jointly by students and the warehouse's 50 craftsmen. Wandering through the pieces on display is a trek through Chinese history; from intricately carved traditional altar tables to 1920s deco furniture. ✉ *796 Suining Lu, Changning* ☎ *021/5219–4871* 🌐 *www.antique-designer.com.*

BUDDHIST PARAPHERNALIA

Around the **Jade Buddha Temple** (✉ Yufo Si, corner of Anyuan Lu and Jiangning Lu, Putuo) are a cluster of stores selling Buddhist items including monks' clothing, prayer beads, lotus lamps, and candles and incense for the temple. Get an embroidered monk's bag for Y15.

Art

Art Scene Warehouse. A comprehensive collection of mostly local works—from installations to photography to sculpture—fills this spacious gallery. ✉ *50 Moganshan Lu, Building 4, 2nd fl., Putuo* ☎ *021/6277–4940* 🌐 *www.artscenewarehouse.com.*

★ **M50.** This complex on Moganshan Lu is soon going to be one of the hippest places in Shanghai. Get down to these old warehouses before the crowds do. It's a great place to spend time wandering around the smaller galleries, chatting to the artists, and seeing China's more established artists' work as well. ✉ *50 Moganshan Lu, Putuo* ☎ *No phone.*

ShanghArt. The city's first modern-art gallery, ShanghART is *the* place to check out the work of art-world movers and shakers such as Ding Yi, Xue Song, and Shen Fan. Here you can familiarize yourself with Shanghai's young contemporary avant-garde artists, who are garnering increasing international attention. The gallery represents 30 local artists as well as putting on great shows and openings in its adjacent H Space. They sell some catalogs of artists they represent and of past shows. ✉ *50 Moganshan Lu, Putuo* ☎ *021/6359–3923* 🌐 *www.shanghartgallery.com.*

Shine. This stylish gallery usually showcases one or two artists at a time, and places an emphasis on painting. ✉ *50 Moganshan Lu, Block 9, Putuo* ☎ *021/6266–0605* 🌐 *www.shineartspace.com.*

Souvenirs

Friendship Store. This state-owned chain for foreigners started in major Chinese cities as a sign of friendship when China first opened to the outside world. The prices, however, are not very friendly. Still, it's a good, quick source of Chinese silk clothes, snuff bottles, carpets, calligraphy, jade, porcelain, and other traditional items that are certified as authentic. There's no bargaining, but there are occasional sales. ✉ *1188 Changshou Lu, Changning* ☎ *021/6252–0330* 🌐 *www.bund-sfs.com.*

Tea

Tianshan Tea City. This place stocks all the tea in China and then some. More than 300 vendors occupy the three floors. You can buy such famous teas as West Lake dragon well tea and Wuyi red-robe tea, and the tea set to serve it in. ✉ *520 Zhongshan Xi Lu, Changning* ☎ *021/6228–6688* 🌐 *www.dabutong.com.*

XUJIAHUI & SOUTH SHANGHAI

Antiques

★ **Hu & Hu Antiques.** Co-owner Marybelle Hu worked at Taipei's National Palace Museum as well as Sotheby's in Los Angeles before opening this shop with sister-in-law Lin in 1998. Their bright, airy showroom contains Tibetan chests and other rich furniture as well as a large selection of accessories, from lanterns to mooncake molds. Their prices are a bit higher than their competitors, but so is their standard of service. ✉ *Alley 1885, 8 Caobao Lu, Minhang* ☎ *021/3431–1212* 🌐 *www.hu-hu.com.*

Malls

Grand Gateway. Look for the dome; beneath you'll find more than 1.4 million square feet of shopping and entertainment, including a movie complex, restaurants, and floor after floor of clothing stores, plus a large number of Shanghai's shoppers. ✉ *1 Hongqiao Lu, Xuhui* ☎ *021/6407–0115.*

HONGQIAO & GUBEI

Gifts

Lee's Decor. Photo albums, bags, and other gifts are made using a range of Chinese brocades. Lee's is a cut above the rest due to the unusual patterns of the fabric and its range of gorgeous lamps, including one made from a birdcage and another shaped like a giant lotus. A small business-card file costs Y40 and cute ponytail holders are Y18. ✉ *1038 Guyang Lu, Changning* ☎ *021/6219–9230* ✉ *633 Biyun Lu, Suite C3, Pudong* ☎ *021/5030–5733.*

3

At a Glance

ENGLISH	PINYIN	CHINESE CHARACTERS
POINTS OF INTEREST		
1918 Artspace	yījiǔyībā yìshù kōngjiān	一九一八艺术空间
Amy Lin's Pearls and Jewelry	aìmǐnlínshì zhūbǎo	艾敏林氏珠宝
Art Scene	yìshù jǐng	艺术景
Arts and Crafts Research Institute	shànghǎi gōngyì měishù yánjiū suǒ	上海工艺美术研究所
Asian View	yìyùdǎ jiājù	异域岛家具
Blue Shanghai White	hǎishàng qīnghuā	海上青花
Brilliance Shimao International Plaza	bǎilián shìmào guójì guǎngchǎng	百联世茂国际广场
Brocade Country	jǐnxiùfāng	锦绣纺
Bund 18	wàitān shíbāhào	外滩十八号
Chaterhouse Books	sānlián shūdiàn	三联书店
CITIC Square	zhōngxìn tàifù guǎngchǎng	中信泰富广场
Feel	jīnfěn shìjiā	金粉世家
Foreign Languages Bookstore	wàiwén shūdiàn	外文书店
Friendship Store	yǒuyì shāngdiàn	友谊商店
Grand Gateway	gǎnghuì guǎngchǎng	港汇广场
Guan Long Photography	guànlóng qìcái diàn	冠龙器材店
Hanyi	hànyì	瀚艺
Harvest Studio	shànghǎi yíngjiāfǎng gōngzuòshǐ	上海盈稼坊工作室
Henry Antique Warehouse	hànruì gǔdiǎn jiājù	汉瑞古典家具
Hu & Hu Antiques	gǔyuè jiājù	古悦家具
Insh	yīngshàng gōngmào	莺裳工贸
Jin	jīnfěn shìjiā	金粉饰家
Jooi	ruìyì	瑞逸
KaDe Club	kǎdí	卡迪
Kodak Professional	wēimǎ zhuānyè xǐyìn	威马专业洗印
La Vie	shēng zhífǎng	生织纺
Larosin Tree	lán sōngshù	蓝松树
Lee's Decor	lìshì	力饰
Lei Yun Shang	léi yǔn shàng	雷允上
Ling Ling Pearls & Jewelry	línglíng zhūbǎo	玲玲珠宝

M50	Chūnmíng yìshù chǎnyèyuán	春明艺术产业园
Madame Mao's Dowry	máotaì shèjì	毛太设计
Maison Mode	měiměi bǎihuò	美美百货
Mr. Yang's Calligraphy Store	yángzhènhuá bǐzhuāng	杨振华笔庄
Next Age	dìyī bābǎibàn	第一八佰伴
O-Store	ōushíduō	欧实多
Paddy Field	dào	稻
Pearl City	shànghǎi lǚyóupǐn shāngshà	上海旅游品商厦
Plaza 66	hénglóng guǎngchǎng	恒隆广场
Qiong Zi	qíong zī	琼子
Raffles City	láifúshì guǎngchǎng	来福士广场
Shanghai Antique and Curio Store	shànghǎi wénwù shāngdiàn	上海文物商店
Shanghai Art Deco	shànghǎi huáijiù	上海怀旧
Shanghai Hongqiao Friendship Shopping Centre	shànghǎi hóngqiáo yǒuyì shāngchéng	上海虹桥友谊商城
Shanghai Huangshan Tea Company	shànghǎi huángshān cháyè yǒuxiàn gōngsī	上海黄山茶叶有限公司
Shanghai Museum Shop	shànghǎi bówùguǎn shāngdiàn	上海博物馆商店
Shanghai No. 1 Department Store	dìyī bǎihùo	第一百货
Shanghai No. 1 Dispensary	yīyào yī diàn	医药一店
Shanghai Tang	shànghǎi tān	上海滩
Shanghai Trio	shànghǎi zǔhé	上海组合
ShanghArt	xiāng gé nà huàlàng	香格纳画廊
Shine	shēng yìshù kōngjiān	升艺术空间
Shirtflag	zédōng shíshàng	泽东时尚
Silk King	zhēnsī dàwáng	真丝大王
Simply Life	yìjū shēnghuóguǎn	逸居生活馆
Skylight	tiānlài	天籁
Studio Rouge	hóngzhài dāngdài yìshù huàlàng	红寨当代艺术画廊
Super Brand Mall	zhèngdà guǎngchǎng	正大广场
Tianshan Tea City	dàbùtóng tiānshān chāchéng	大不同天山茶城
Tibet Treasure	zàngbǎo	藏宝

Times Square	shídià guǎngchǎng	时代广场
Tom's Gallery	héng gǔ táng	恒古堂
Village Girl	cūngū xiùwū	村姑绣屋
Westgate Mall	méilóngzhèn guǎngcǎng	梅龙镇广场
Xinmei Union Square	xīnméi liánhé guǎngchǎng	新梅联合广场
Zhen Zhen	zhēn zhēn gǔwān diàn	珍珍古玩店
MARKETS		
Antiques Market of Shanghai Old Town	huábǎo lóu	华宝楼
Cangbao Antiques Building	cángbǎo lóu	藏宝楼
Cybermart	sàibó shùmǎ guǎngchǎng	赛博数码广场
Dongtai Lu Antiques Street	dōngtái lù	东台路
Fuyou Gate Market	fúyòu mén shāngshà	福佑门商厦
Fuyuan Building	fúyuán shāngshà	福源商厦
Pu'an Lu Children's Market	níhóng értóng guǎngchǎng	霓虹儿童广场
Taikang Antique Market	tàikāng gǔwán shìchǎng	泰康古玩市场
The South Bund Soft-spinning Material Market	shànghǎi nán wàitān qīngfǎng miànliào shìchǎng	上海南外滩轻纺面料市场
Wenmiao Temple Book Market	wénmiào shūchéng	文庙书城
Xiangyang Market	xiāngyáng shìchǎng	襄阳市场

Arts & Nightlife

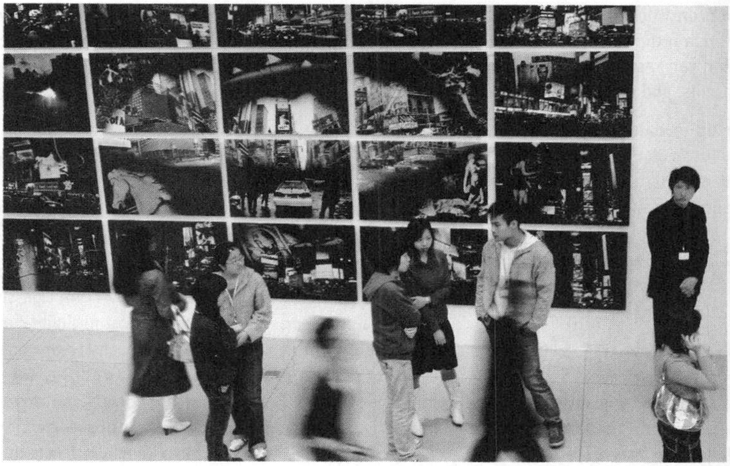

WORD OF MOUTH

"While in Shanghai, be sure to hear the Peace Hotel's famous jazz band. This band has been playing for nearly 50 years and (it is rumored) had to play in secret during the Cultural Revolution. The bar is lovely, and there is dancing."

–Suzanne

"The Chinese Acrobat Show at Shanghai Center was great—the kids loved it!"

–Lindsey

www.fodors.com/forums

ARTS & NIGHTLIFE PLANNER

What's Happening Now

Nightlife is a difficult business in Shanghai, and, aside from a few stalwarts, venues can open and close faster than the speed of apartment block construction, and even places that retain the same name and location can rapidly change owners, concepts, and clientele.

For up-to-date information, check out *That's Shanghai* and *City Weekend*, monthly and biweekly expatriate magazines available at Western bars, restaurants, and hotels throughout town; or *Shanghai Daily*, the English-language newspaper.

Safety After Dark

Overall, Shanghai is very safe, but bar districts are full of beggars and flower sellers who may grab for an unguarded wallet. Take the same precautions you would take anywhere, and refrain from overindulging unless you have a trusted companion to tuck you safely into bed. Also, be wary of the too-friendly girls at the bar streets, since odds are they are interested in your purse strings, not your winning personality.

Top After-Dark Spots

Cotton's. A cozy, friendly, unassuming little bar in an old house with a garden, Cotton's is one of the most popular hangout spots in town.

Mint. Dance the night away at Shanghai's trendiest club.

Shanghai Dramatic Arts Center. Experience the latest in Chinese drama at the city's only professional theater.

The Door. Head to the Door for a truly eclectic experience: contemporary interpretations of traditional Chinese music played in a room filled with antique furniture and modern accents.

Yuyintang Warehouse. This unassuming concert space showcases Shanghai rock at its edgiest.

Getting Around

Although downtown Shanghai is fairly compact, suburban sprawl is creeping in nefariously. Most nightlife destinations are downtown, but pockets of activity are creeping up in farther-flung areas. Go by taxi: it's fairly safe and fairly affordable. Prices are rising, and some drivers will take advantage of drunk or ignorant passengers and go the "scenic" route, so be sure to keep your wits about you and your eyes on the route. Also, many taxi drivers are new and from out of town, so some simply do not know where they are going.

What to Wear

The Shanghai dress code is fairly laid-back, and even nicer establishments are unlikely to turn away the casually dressed. Women in Shanghai like to doll it up, and are very brand-conscious, but one need not feel obliged to follow suit; men usually head out in jeans and a tee or polo shirt. Smoking is universal in China's bars and clubs, so wear clothing that washes well or that you don't mind carrying a souvenir fragrance of smoke and stale beer.

Updated by
Lisa Movius

Fueled equally by expatriates and an increasingly adventurous population of locals, Shanghai boasts an active and diverse nightlife. It's hardly the *buyecheng* (city that never sleeps) of the 1930s—most places peter out after 1 or 2 AM—but until then there's a bit of something for everyone.

Offerings range from world-class swank to dark and dingy dens or from young Shanghainese kids screaming experimental punk to Filipino cover bands singing "Hotel California" in a hotel basement. Prices, scenes, crowds, and ambiance can range just as wildly.

When it comes to the arts, Shanghai lacks the sort of performing-arts scene one would expect from a city its size, but it's getting there. The city has two world-class, state-of-the-art spaces in the Shanghai Grand Theater and the Oriental Art Center, but stodgy government management means their offerings are spotty at best. Recent years have witnessed an enthusiasm for importing popular Broadway shows, such as *Les Misérables* and *The Lion King,* and international music acts like the Rolling Stones and Nora Jones have also descended here. However, such events are few and far between. Things like acrobatics are solely of interest to tourists, and unrelated to this modern city's cultural life, however traditional forms of Chinese opera remain popular with older citizens and are even enjoying resurgences with the younger generation. The city also has several competent symphonies. The Shanghai Ballet and the Shanghai Folk Dance Troupe are excellent, although forced by official directive to restrain their creativity; both perform at the various theaters around town.

THE ARTS

For modern culture more in tune with Shanghai's vibe, head to the Shanghai Dramatic Arts Center. Despite being a state-owned institution, it manages to offset sumptuous historical epics with small, provocative plays that examine burning social issues like infidelity, divorce, finances, and AIDS. The center also does projects in conjunction with the city's handful of struggling but plucky modern-dance pioneers, who also perform at underground venues like Hi and Xihemi Warehouse, plus occasionally on the larger stages.

MAKING A COMEBACK

Traditional forms of Chinese opera remain popular with older citizens and are even enjoying a resurgence with the younger generation.

Acrobatics

Shanghai Acrobatics Troupe. The Shanghai Acrobatics Troupe performs remarkable gravity-defying stunts at both the Shanghai Center Theater and Shanghai Circus World, a glittering gold and green dome located in the center of Jing'an that seats more than 1,600 people. ✉ *Shanghai Center Theater, 1376, Nanjing Lu, Jing'an* ☎ *021/6279–8945* ✉ *Shanghai Circus World 2266 Gong He Xin Lu, Zhabei* ☎ *021/6652–7750* ⏲ *Shows daily at 7:30 PM* 🎫 *Y50–Y150.*

Chinese Opera

Kunju Opera Troupe. Kun opera, or Kunju, originated in Jiangsu Province more than 400 years ago. Because of the profound influence it exerted on other Chinese opera styles, it's often called the mother of Chinese opera. It's located in the lower part of the Former French Concession. ✉ *9 Shaoxing Luwar Lu* ☎ *021/6437–1012* 🎫 *Y20–Y50* ⏲ *Performances Sat. at 1:30.*

Yifu Theatre. Not only Beijing Opera, but also China's other regional operas, such as Huju, Kunju, and Yueju, are performed regularly at this theater in the heart of the city center. Considered the marquee theater for opera in Shanghai, it's just a block off People's Square. Call the box office for schedule and ticket information. ✉ *701 Fuzhou Lu, Huangpu* ☎ *021/6351–4668.*

Dance & Classical Music

Xintiandi & City Center

Shanghai Concert Hall. City officials spent $6 million in 2003 to move this 73-year-old hall two blocks to avoid the rumble from the nearby highway. Only then did they discover that they had moved it to sit over an even more rumbly subway line. Oops. It's the home of the Shanghai Symphony Orchestra and also hosts top-level classical musicians from around China and the world. ✉ *523 Yanan Dong Lu, Jing'an* ☎ *021/6386–9153.*

Shanghai Grand Theatre. The premier venue in town, this spectacular stage hosts top-billed domestic and international music and dance performances. In 2003 the theater hosted *Riverdance* and the Vienna Boys' Choir. ✉ *300 Renmin Dadao, Huangpu* ☎ *021/6372–8701, 021/6372–8702, or 021/6372–3833.*

Former French Concession

Jing An Hotel. Every Sunday, the Shanghai Symphony Orchestra performs chamber music in the lobby of the Jing An Hotel. Past concerts have included pieces by Bach, Ravel, and Chinese composer Huang Yongxi. ✉ *San Diego Hall, Jing An Hotel, 370 Huashan Lu, Jing'an* ☎ *021/6248–1888 Ext. 687* 🎫 *Y20.*

Shanghai Conservatory of Music. A renovation in 2003 boosted the stature of this 780-seat hall as a top venue for acoustic performances. The hall showcases the conservatory's talented students and occasionally hosts visiting Asian and Western musicians. ✉ *20 Fenyang Lu, Xuhui* ☎ *021/6431–8756.*

4

Pudong

Shanghai Oriental Art Center. Designed to resemble a white magnolia in full bloom, the glass-shrouded Shanghai Oriental Art Center is an attempt to kick-start Pudong's performing-art scene, although thus far it has featured mostly unimpressive acts. This $94-million center hopes eventually to rival the Shanghai Grand Theater and includes a 2,000-seat symphony hall, 1,100-seat theater, and 300-seat auditorium. ✉ *425 Dingxiang Lu, Pudong* ☎ *021/3842–4800.*

Nanjing Xi Lu & Jing'an

Shanghai Center Theater. This stage serves as a home to tourist favorites the **Shanghai Acrobatic Troupe** and has hosted performers such as the Israel Contemporary Dance Group and Wynton Marsalis. The building's distinct bowed front was designed to resemble the Marriott Marquis Theater in New York's Times Square. ✉ *Shanghai Center, 1376 Nanjing Xi Lu, Jing'an* ☎ *021/6279–8663.*

Xujiahui & South Shanghai

Shanghai Grand Stage. Built in 1975, this 12,000-seat arena usually hosts sports events and rock and pop concerts. In 2004 the venue got a multimillion-dollar face-lift thanks to the return of favorite son Yao Ming in an NBA exhibition match. ✉ *1111 Caoxi Bei Lu, inside Shanghai Stadium Xuhui* ☎ *021/6473–0940.*

★ **Xiahemi Warehouse.** Experimental-dance troupe Niao and other avant-garde performers use this small, underground space for rehearsals and occasional performances. ✉ *Longcao Lu, La. 200, No. 100, 3rd fl. Xujiahui* ☎ *021/5448–3368.*

Theater

Xintiandi & City Center

Shanghai Grand Theater. As the premier stage in town, the Shanghai Grand Theater hosts top national and international performances. When Broadway shows come to Shanghai—such as *The Lion King* in 2006—they play here. ✉ *300 Renmin Dadao, Huangpu* ☎ *021/6372–8701, 021/6372–8702, or 021/6372–3833.*

Former French Concession

Lyceum Theatre. Although the recent renovation of Shanghai's oldest theater sadly replaced the sumptuous dark wood with glaring marble and glass, the design of the space makes for an intimate theater experience. The Lyceum regularly hosts drama and music from around China as well as smaller local plays and Chinese opera performances. ✉ *57 Maoming Nan Lu, Luwan* ☎ *021/6217–8539.*

> **WORD OF MOUTH**
>
> The Lyceum Theatre [is] a fabulous art-deco building from the 30s. It's really fun just to be inside the theater that has seen so much of Shanghai's rise and fall from the glory days. -Andrea

Fodor'sChoice ★ **Shanghai Dramatic Arts Center.** Shanghai's premier theater venue and troupe, with several busy stages, the Dramatic Arts Center presents an award-winning lineup of its own original pieces, plus those of other cutting-edge groups around China. It also stages Chinese-language adaptations, sometimes very inventive, of Western works, such as a festival of Samuel Beckett works reinterpreted through Chinese opera. It also invites a steady lineup of renowned international performers, such as the Royal Shakespeare Company. Despite being a state-owned institution, the Shanghai Dramatic Arts Center manages to offset sumptuous historical epics with small, provocative plays that examine burning social issues like infidelity, divorce, finances, and AIDS. ✉ *288 Anfu Lu, Xuhui* ☎ *021/6473–4567.*

Nanjing Xi Lu & Jing'an

Shanghai Theatre Academy. The academy's performance hall presents a full schedule of student and professional works. ✉ *670 Huashan Lu, Jing'an* ☎ *021/6248–2920 Ext. 3040.*

★ **Majestic Theatre.** Once Asia's largest movie theater, this elegantly restored, beautiful 1930s art-deco gem regularly presents top-ticket theater from China's major troupes, as well as novelty acts and some Western performances. The venue does not have an affiliated drama troupe, so the space is open to all sundry comers. ✉ *66 Jiangning Lu, Jing'an* ☎ *021/6217–4409.*

North Shanghai

Hi Theatre. Shanghai's only private, independent experimental-theater space, Hi gives Shanghai's blossoming avant-garde a platform as well as bringing in creative projects from around Asia. ✉ *Inside Hi-Shanghai, Feihong Lu, La. 568, No. 49, Zhabei* ☎ *021/5448–3368.*

NIGHTLIFE

Once exclusive province of downtown, bars and clubs now dot all parts of Shanghai. There are, however, a few concentrations for those hoping to hop conveniently.

Maoming Nan Lu has long been Shanghai's nightlife hub, with the slightly seedy offerings of the main drag contrasting with the classy, upscale venues—most notably, **Face**—in the adjacent Ruijin Guest House, a hotel complex that takes up an entire city block. Threats to shut it down have yet to materialize, but much of the action has migrated elsewhere, to the new **Tongren Lu** bar street. Tongren Lu does have some good clubs for those who like their nightlife on the wild side. The infamous **Julu Lu** bar street is still going strong. All three of these are crowded with "fishing girls," who ask gents to give them money to buy drinks in exchange for their company (or something more)—and then they either pocket the money or take a cut from the bar.

Those looking for less-blatant sexual commerce should head to the popular bar, restaurant, and shopping complex of **Xintiandi,** an old Shanghai pastiche with an array of clean and pleasant but pricey bars. **The Bund** is gradually emerging as a center for upscale dining and drinking, and several new spaces slated to open in the upcoming years will serve to cement its position. **Hengshan Lu** and **Fuxing Park** also offer concentrations of bars and clubs.

Bars

Xintiandi & City Center

Barbarossa. Above the lily pond in People's Park and next to the MoCA, this beautiful Moroccan restaurant switches into a bar at night. Usually quiet and classy, it becomes crowded and crazy on Thursday, when women drink free. ✉ *231 Nanjing Xi Lu, Huangpu* ☎ *021/6318–0220.*

TMSK. Short for Tou Ming Si Kao, this exquisitely designed little bar is an aesthete's dream. Glisteningly modern, TMSK is stunning—as are the prices of its drinks. ✉ *Xintiandi North Block, Unit 2, House 11, 181 Taicang Lu, Luwan* ☎ *021/6326–2227.*

Nanjing Dong Lu & the Bund

Bar Rouge. The gem in the crown of the trendy, upscale Bund 18 complex, Bar Rouge is the destination du jour of Shanghai's beautiful people. It has retained that distinction for a surprisingly long time, considering the fickle nature of Shanghai's denizens of the dark. Pouting models and visiting celebrities are amongst the regular clientele. ✉ *Bund 18 7F, 18 Zhongshan Dong Lu, Huangpu* ☎ *021/6339–1199.*

Glamour Bar. The lounge of the perennial favorite **M on the Bund,** Glamour Bar offers beautiful decor in a classy, low-key setting. However, ■ TIP→ **bar patrons are forbidden from visiting the restaurant's balcony and enjoying the view that made the place famous, so visitors not planning to eat should head to other Bund locations instead.** ✉ *7F, 20 Guangdong Lu, Huangpu* ☎ *021/6350–9988.*

Number Five. One of the few unpretentious bars on the Bund, Five wears its position in the basement of the Glamour Bar with pride. Affordable drinks, generously proportioned pub food, Wednesday Swing-dancing nights, and sports broadcasts attract a crowd of dedicated regulars. ✉ *20 Guangdong Lu, BF, the Bund, Huangpu* ☎ *021/6289–9108.*

★ **Three on the Bund.** The sophisticated Three complex, suitably enough, encloses three different bars: the swanky, dark-wood paneled **Bar JG** on the 4th floor; the sleek white **Laris** on the 6th floor; and topped off by the more casual **New Heights/Third Degree** on the 7th floor. ✉ *3 Zhongshan Dong Lu, Huangpu* ☎ *021/6321–0909.*

Former French Concession

★ **Arch Bar and Café.** For an artsy expatriate circle, head to Arch. Its location in Shanghai's copy of the Flatiron building and in a popular residential district attracts architects and design professionals. ✉ *439 Wukang Lu, Xuhui* ☎ *021/6466–0807.*

The Blarney Stone. The friendly Irish bartenders and lively chatter make the Blarney Stone one of the best places for drinking alone in Shanghai. ✉ *5A Dongping Lu, Xuhui* ☎ *021/6415–7496.*

Buddha Bar. A heavy hangover from Maoming Lu's glory days, Buddha Bar continues to please a dedicated clientele with trance music and other intoxicants. ✉ *172 Maoming Lu, Xuhui* ☎ *021/6415–2688.*

Fodor's Choice ★ **Cotton's.** This friendly, laid-back favorite moved many times before settling into the current old garden house. Busy without being loud, Cotton's is a rare place where you can have a conversation with friends—or make some new ones. ✉ *132 Anting Lu, Xuhui* ☎ *021/6433–7995.*

Face. Once the see-and-be-seen place in Shanghai, Face's hipster clientele have mostly moved to Manifesto with former owner Charlie, leaving it mostly a tourist destination. But it's still beautiful: candlelit tables outside and a four-poster bed inside are the most vied-for spots in this colonial villa with Indonesian furnishings. ✉ *Bldg. 4, Ruijin Hotel, 118 Ruijin Er Lu, Luwan* ☎ *021/6466–4328.*

Guandii. Opened by several Hong Kong celebrities, Guandii's minimalist low-slung bar attracts terminally hip Chinese who flash their wealth by ordering bottles of one of the 30 champagnes on the drink menu. ✉ *Fuxing Park, 2 Gaolan Lu, Luwan* ☎ *021/5383–6020.*

O'Malley's. The most beloved of Shanghai's Irish pubs—not that there's much competition—O'Malley's has the requisite Guinness on tap and live Irish music. Its outdoor beer garden packs in crowds in the summer and during broadcasts of European soccer and rugby matches. Popularity with expatriate professionals makes the place expensive even by Shanghai standards. ✉ *42 Taojiang Lu, Xuhui* ☎ *021/6474–4533.*

Sasha's. A favorite with longtime expatriates, Sasha's promises dependable drinks and food in a sumptuous villa that was once Song Meiling's home. Its rolling garden is one of the nicest places to cool off on a hot summer's night. ✉ *9 Dongping Lu, House 11, Xuhui* ☎ *021/6247–2400.*

★ **Time Passage.** Shanghai has always been a place more inclined toward slick nightclubs and posh wine bars than mellow, conversation dives, but Time Passage has always been the exception. Cheap beers, friendly service, and a cool, if grungy, atmosphere makes it the best way to start—or end—a night on the town. ✉ *Huashan Lu, La. 1038, No. 183, by Fuxing Lu, Xuhui* ☎ *021/6240–2588.*

Windows. Shanghai's budget-drinking chain, Windows lures patrons with Y10 drinks. Packed solid on weekends, chill on weekdays, it's the place to meet foreign students and hard-core booze hounds. ✉ *Windows Roadside: 186 Maoming Nan Lu, Luwan* ☎ *021/6445–7863* ✉ *Windows Scorecard: 681 Huaihai Zhong Lu 3F, Xuhui* ☎ *021/5382–7757*

LOCAL BREWS

Northern Chinese swear by their Baijiu, a strong, usually sweet clear liquor, but Shanghainese opt for milder poison. Most beloved is Huangjiu, a brown brew from Shaoxing with a mild taste that resembles whiskey, which may explain why the latter is the most popular foreign liquor among locals. Huangjiu's quality is determined by whether it was brewed 2, 5, or 10 years ago. It is usually served warm, sometimes with ginger or dried plum added for kick.

Beer is also widely consumed; although there is a Shanghai Beer brand, it is cheap, very bitter, and mostly found in the suburbs. More common are Suntory, or Sandeli, a local brewery opened by the Japanese brand, and Reeb (yes, it's meant to be "beer" spelled backward), or Li Bo. Most bars, however, serve Qingdao and imports like Tiger, Heineken, and Budweiser, which are more expensive. More premium imported beers can also be had, but the markup is steep. For example, expect to pay Y60 for a pint of Guinness.

4

✉ *Windows Tembo: 66 Shaanxi Bei Lu, Jing'an* ☎ *021/5116–8857* ✉ *Windows Too: J104, Jingan Si Plaza J104, 1669 Nanjing Xi Lu, Jing'an* ☎ *021/3214–0351.*

Zapata's. This Mexican restaurant and cantina thumps all night with ample margaritas and go-go dancers on the bars. Popular with the young party crowd, its ladies' nights and other specials are well attended. ✉ *5 Hengshan Lu, Xuhui* ☎ *021/6433–4104.*

Pudong

Dublin Exchange. Dublin Exchange is a great place for a Pudong pint. Its upmarket Irish banker's-club ambience caters to the growing wannabe Wall Street that is Lujiazui. ✉ *HSBC Bldg., 2nd fl., 101 Yincheng Dong Lu, Pudong* ☎ *021/6841–2052.*

Nanjing Xi Lu & Jing'an

Blue Frog. The multiple locations of Blue Frog are popular among Westerners primarily for their hearty pub food. The chummy chill-out pads serve up more than 100 shots and well-mixed cocktails. ✉ *86 Tongren Lu, near Yanan Xilu, Jing'an* ☎ *021/6445–6634* ✉ *206-7 Maoming Nan Lu, Luwan* ☎ *021/6445–6634* ✉ *Green Sports & Leisure Center, R3-633 Biyun Lu, Pudong* ☎ *021/5030–6426* ✉ *Hongmei Entertainment St. #30, 3888 Hongmei Lu, Gubei* ☎ *021/6445–6634.*

Long Bar. In the Shanghai Center, the narrow, horseshoe-shape Long Bar has a loyal expat-businessman clientele. Rousing rounds of liar's dice, a big-screen TV, and chest-thumping conversations among executives provide the entertainment, but the real attraction is the nightly "model show." ✉ *1376 Nanjing Xi Lu, Jing'an* ☎ *021/6279–8268.*

Malone's American Café. A magnet for Western expats and travelers, Malone's is always packed. A cover band belts out pitch-perfect versions of Van Morrison and No Doubt. TVs broadcast sporting events, and pool tables draw people upstairs to the 2nd floor. The Shanghai Comedy Club brings in English-speaking comedians one weekend each month to the makeshift 3rd-floor stage. ✉ *255 Tongren Lu, Jingan* ☎ *021/6247–2400.*

★ **Manifesto.** The mastermind behind Face opened this coolly minimalist yet warmly welcoming space and took most of his clientele with him. Popular with foreigners and local white-collars alike, it serves up standard cocktails plus excellent tapas from its sister restaurant Mesa. ✉ *748 Julu Lu, Jing'an* ☎ *021/6289–9108.*

Hongquiao & Gubei

Fodor's Choice ★ **The Door.** The stunningly extravagant interior of the Door distracts from the bar's overpriced drinks. Take in the soaring wood-beam ceilings, sliding doors, and the museum's worth of antiques as you listen to the eclectic house band, which plays modern, funky riffs on Chinese music on the *erhu, pipa,* and other traditional instruments. ✉ *4F, 1468 Hongqiao Lu, Changning* ☎ *021/6295–3737.*

Hotel Bars

Xintiandi & City Center

JW Lounge. At the top of the JW Marriott, this lounge has a panoramic view of downtown Shanghai. ✉ *JW Marriott, 40F, 399 Nanjing Xi Lu, Huangpu* ☎ *021/5359–4969.*

Nanjing Dong Lu & the Bund

Jazz Bar. Within the historic and romantic Peace Hotel, this German-style pub has earned its fame due to the nightly performances (tickets, Y80) of the Peace Hotel Old Jazz Band. The musicians, whose average age is above 70, played jazz in dance halls in pre-1949 Shanghai. However, they're not quite as swingin' as in their prime, and a sense of tradition, rather than the quality of the music, has sustained these performances. ✉ *Peace Hotel, 20 Nanjing Dong Lu, Huangpu* ☎ *021/6321–6888.*

Former French Concession

Ye Lai Xiang (The Garden Hotel Bar). Few people know the real name of the Garden Hotel's terrace bar. Considered one of the most romantic spots in town for a drink when the weather is nice, this 3rd-floor terrace overlooks the fountain and hotel's namesake 2-acre garden. ✉ *Okura Garden Hotel, 58 Maoming Nan Lu, Luwan* ☎ *021/6415–1111.*

Pudong

B.A.T.S. (Bar at the Shangri-La). Tucked away in the basement of the Shangri-La, B.A.T.S.'s crowd ebbs and flows depending on the quality of the band. The cavelike brick-walled space has diner-style booths arranged around a large central bar. ✉ *Pudong Shangri-La, 33 Fucheng Lu, Pudong* ☎ *021/6882–8888.*

★ **Cloud 9.** Perched on the 87th floor of the Grand Hyatt, Cloud 9 is the highest bar in the world. It has unparalleled views of Shanghai from among—and often above—the clouds. The sky-high views come with sky-high prices: ■ TIP→ **there's a two-drink minimum in the evening, so go in the late afternoon to avoid this.** The class is offset with kitsch, as Chinese fortune-tellers and various artisans ply their skills to customers. ✉ *Grand Hyatt, 88 Shiji Dadao, Pudong* ☎ *021/5049–1234.*

★ **Jade on 36.** This gorgeous, swanky new spot in the new tower of the Pudong Shangri-La has swish drinks in a swish setting. Exquisite design and corresponding views (when Shanghai's pollution levels cooperate) have made Jade popular with the in set. ✉ *Pudong Shangri-La, Tower 2, 36F 33 Fucheng, Pudong* ☎ *021/6882–3636.*

Patio Bar. No skyline views here, just a dazzling, dizzying view of the Grand Hyatt's soaring 33-story atrium. It's an expensive, but impressive, stop for a pre- or post-dinner drink. ✉ *Grand Hyatt, 88 Shiji Dadao, Pudong* ☎ *021/5049–1234.*

Pu-J's. In the Grand Hyatt, Pu-J's offers a variety of musical styles on various dance floors, plus a quiet bar area, sometimes with live jazz, and rentable karaoke rooms upstairs. ✉ *Grand Hyatt, 3rd fl., 88 Shiji Dadao, Pudong* ☎ *021/5049–1234 Ext. 8732.*

Nanjing Xi Lu & Jing'an

★ **Jazz 37.** The Four Seasons' jazz bar matches its penthouse view with a stylish interior. Grab a canary-yellow leather chair by the white grand piano for some top-quality live jazz. ✉ *The Four Seasons, 37F, 500 Weihai Lu, Jing'an* ☎ *021/6256–8888.*

Ritz-Carlton Bar. Like an airline's first-class lounge, the Ritz-Carlton Bar is the domain of a high-flying executive clientele. Cigar smoke, specialty Scotches, and some of the best jazz in town cap the elite atmosphere. ✉ *The Portman Ritz-Carlton, 1376 Nanjing Xi Lu, Jing'an* ☎ *021/6279–8888.*

Gay–Lesbian Bars & Clubs

The gay and lesbian scene in Shanghai is low-profile, staying under the gaydar of China's still-conservative social norms. Bars and clubs usually list under the euphemism of "alternative," and some of the more popular spots have been forced to move repeatedly. Contrary to the usual clichés, the pick-up scene in Shanghai's gay bars—and there are a lot more gays than lesbians at them—is much more laid-back and low-key than the supercharged sexuality at most "mainstream" clubs. The more aggressive pick-up scenes play out at public toilets, parks, and some bathhouses. The following are all in the Former French Concession.

Eddy's. Flamboyant, occasional drag queen Eddy has had to move his male-friendly bar all over the city over the years, but has found an apparently permanent home on this quiet stretch of Huaihai. ✉ *1877 Huaihai Zhong Lu, Luwan* ☎ *021/6841–2052.*

Home. Pretty boys are always welcome at this happening home of the men's pick-up scene. ✉ *18 Gaolan Lu, Xuhui* ☎ *021/5383–2208.*

Vogue in Kevin's. At the heart of Shanghai's "alternative"—that is, gay—scene, Vogue in Kevin's is a popular party and pick-up spot. The circu-

CLOSE UP

Old Shanghai's Dance Halls

Most Shanghainese are not dedicated drinkers, and they rarely go out simply to drink and converse. Instead, they prefer to drink over dinner or KTV, and even at regular bars, games and other diversions are popular. This multitasking approach to entertainment has deep roots in Shanghai's nightlife traditions.

Prior to 1949, the evening entertainment de rigueur was dancing, and swanky dance halls like Ciros and the Majestic were where the 1930s' glitterati flocked to see and be seen. Young women worked as "taxi dancers," and clients would buy books of dance tickets for the pleasure of their company. As with today's KTV parlors, additional forms of "company" were available for purchase at some establishments. Some of the most iconic images of that era's Shanghai capture Qipao-clad taxi dancers awaiting business, and many a vintage film depicts such clubs or romanticizes the travails of taxi dancers.

Though the dance halls were shuttered in 1949, and few of their original edifices remain, the art-deco Paramount Theater was reopened as an old-style dance hall, complete with floor shows, and in a modern twist offers male as well as female taxi dancers. Community dance halls remain popular with older Shanghainese, and every evening at dusk, dancers overrun neighborhood parks, fox-trotting to boom boxes.

lar bar is a good perch for people-watching and scoping out prospective partners. ✉ *House 4, 946 Changle Lu, Xuhui* ☎ *021/6248–8985.*

Dance Clubs

Xintiandi & City Center

Babyface. An outpost of the popular Guangzhou nightclub chain, Babyface draws a well-dressed crowd of wannabes and already-ares who don't mind waiting outside along the velvet rope before dancing to progressive house and hard trance. ✉ *Shanghai Square Unit 101 138 Huaihai Zhong Lu, Luwan* ☎ *021/6375–6667.*

Pegasus. It began life as just another dance club, but Pegasus took wing after restyling itself into the top place for aspiring hip-hop DJs to battle it out. Regular mix-off competitions really pull in the crowds. ✉ *Golden Bell Plaza 2F, 98 Huaihai Zhong Lu, Luwan* ☎ *021/5385–8187.*

Rojam. A three-level techno behemoth, Rojam is like a never-ending rave that bulges with boogiers and underground lounge lizards from the under-30 set. ✉ *4/F, Hong Kong Plaza, 283 Huaihai Zhong Lu, Luwan* ☎ *021/6390–7181.*

Former French Concession

California Club. Celebrity guest DJs play everything from tribal to disco for the bold and beautiful crowd at this hip establishment. The club is part of the Lan Kwai Fong complex at Park 97, which also includes Baci and Tokio Joe's restaurants. ✉ *Park 97, 2A Gaolan Lu, Luwan* ☎ *021/5383–2328.*

HISTORIC BAR: MINT

When it opened in 2000, Mint allowed architecture buffs a long-desired glimpse into the interior of one of Shanghai's urban gems. While art-deco designs of all eras were popular in Old Shanghai and remain numerous now, only a few Bauhaus structures were erected. Of those, the most striking remainder is the curving, three-storied Wu Tongwen House, which once housed the Shanghai City Planning Institute and now houses Mint. Ladislaus Edward Hudec constructed the building in 1938 as a residence for Shanghainese tycoon Wu Tongwen, an in-law of architect I. M. Pei. Wu chose the location because the names of intersecting streets at the time, Hatong Lu and Aiwen Yilu, contained the characters of his given name. Also known as Laszlo, the Hungarian native Hudec lived in Shanghai from 1918 to 1945 and designed many of the city's most interesting modernist landmarks, most notably Nanjing Road's Park Hotel, which upon its construction in 1934 was the tallest building in Asia, and the adjacent Grand Theater.

Fabrique. In the hip Bridge 8–design district, Fabrique is one of Shanghai's favorite spots for cool DJs and the dancers who love them. ✉ *8 Jianguo Lu, Xuhui* ☎ *021/6415–1600.*

Judy's Too. A veteran on the club scene, Judy's Too is infamous for its hard-partying, meat-market crowd. The den of iniquity was memorialized in Wei Hui's racy novel *Shanghai Baby,* among others. ✉ *176 Maoming Nan Lu, by Yongjia Lu, Luwan* ☎ *021/6473–1417.*

Real Love. Still going strong despite the fickleness of Shanghai's nightlife patrons, Real Love remains the most popular place for young Shanghainese to bop to pop tunes. It is worth going just to watch the sincere, eager young crowd—quite a contrast from the jaded clientele at most of the city's clubs. Such is the popularity that it creates traffic jams on Hengshan Lu most nights. ✉ *10 Hengshan Lu, Xuhui* ☎ *021/6474–6830.*

YY's. The small, mellow YY's is long past its glory days, but remains a favorite for some, and sometimes revives for big all-out parties. Named for the ancient Chinese yin-and-yang symbol, the club balances a quiet lounge with a techno dance floor that's popular with members of both sexes. ✉ *125 Nanchang, Luwan* ☎ *021/6466–4098.*

Nanjing Xi Lu & Jing'an

The Lab. A conceptual space for Shanghai's DJs to practice their craft, the Lab also has special events and occasional barbecues on their rooftop terrace. ■ TIP→ **Patrons should bring their own booze,** as no alcohol is served here. The tradeoff is that most events are free. Enjoy the music while lolling on the terrace, or take a turn at showing off your spinning prowess. ✉ *343 Jiaozhou Lu, Jing'an* ☎ *021/5213–0877.*

Fodor'sChoice ★ **Mint.** One of Shanghai's most popular clubs, as much for its location in a gorgeous old Bauhaus mansion as for its dance music, Mint has special guest DJs most weekends. ✉ *333 Tongren Lu, 2F, Jing'an* ☎ *021/6247–9666.*

North Shanghai

★ **Pier One.** Looking to single-handedly transform the Suzhou Creek district from an artists' colony into a clubbing destination, Pier One occupies a cavernous historic warehouse. The space includes a dance club, **Minx,** with schedules online at www.minx.com.cn, an **Art Deco** lounge bar, **Jacuzzi Monsoon,** and the **Mimosa Supperclub** restaurant. ✉ *82 Yi Chang Lu, next to Suzhou Creek at Shaanxi Bei Lu, Zhabei* ☎ *021/5155–8310.*

Karaoke

Karaoke is ubiquitous in Shanghai; most nights, the private rooms at KTV (Karaoke TV) establishments are packed with Shanghainese crooning away with their friends. Many KTV bars employ "KTV girls" who sing along with (male) guests and serve cognac and expensive snacks. (At most establishments, KTV girls are also prostitutes.) That said, karaoke is a popular—and sometimes legitimate—pastime among locals. Many bars also have KTV rooms, but these places are dedicated karaoke establishments.

Haoledi. Crowded at all hours with locals of all ages crooning pop favorites, the popular Haoledi chain has branches virtually everywhere. These listed are just a few of the outlets downtown. ✉ *1111 Zhaojiabang Lu, Xuhui* ☎ *021/6311–5858* ✉ *180 Xizang Zhong Lu, Luwan* ☎ *021/6311–5858* ✉ *438 Huaihai Zhong Lu, Luwan* ☎ *021/6311–5858.*

Party World. This giant establishment is one of Shanghai's most popular KTV bars, and among the few that's dedicated to the KTV instead of the KTV girls. Its warren of rooms is packed nightly. ✉ *459 Wulumuqi Bei Lu, Jing'an* ☎ *021/6374–1111* ✉ *109 Yandan Lu, inside Fuxing Park, Luwan* ☎ *021/5306–3888* ✉ *68 Zhejiang, Huangpu* ☎ *021/6374–1111.*

Live Music

Shanghai has a burgeoning alternative-music scene. Several bars have good live music nightly, and far more put on interesting concerts over the weekend. Any given Saturday, Shanghai has at least five worthy gigs to choose between. Although the alternative recording industry remains stagnant, Shanghai has scores of active original bands giving voice to the city's evolution, and stylistically there is a bit of someone for everyone.

Xintiandi & City Center

JAZZ **CJW.** The acronym says it all: cigars, jazz, and wine are what this swank lounge is all about. Its second location atop the Bund Center throws in a breathtaking view of the river. ✉ *Xintiandi, House 2, 123 Xingye Lu, Luwan* ☎ *021/6385–6677* ✉ *Bund Center 50F, 222 Yanan Dong Lu, Huangpu* ☎ *021/6329–9932.*

Former French Concession

JAZZ ★ **Club JZ.** Reincarnated in a new venue, JZ continues its role as the king of Shanghai's jazz offerings. Most nights the solid house band grooves, but occasionally guest performers from around the world take the stage. ✉ *46 Fuxing Xi Lu, Xuhui* ☎ *021/6431–0269.*

Cotton Club. A dark and smoky jazz and blues club, the Cotton Club is an institution in Shanghai and still one of the best places to catch live jazz. The house band is a mix of Chinese and foreign musicians with a sound akin to Blues Traveler. ✉ *8 Fuxing Xi Lu, Xuhui* ☎ *021/6437–7110.*

★ **House of Blues and Jazz.** Decked out in memorabilia from Shanghai's jazz era of the 1930s, Blues and Jazz would be a great bar even without the music. But the several nightly sets make it a must visit. Owner Lin Dongfu, a local television personality, ensures a steady stream of minor celebrities, if the band isn't entertainment enough. ✉ *158 Maoming Nan Lu, Luwan* ☎ *021/6437–5280.*

4

ROCK ★ **Tanghui.** Weekends at Tanghui see some of Shanghai rock's perennial favorites rocking out downstairs. The rest of the week brings a more eclectic lineup. Lounges on the 2nd and 3rd floors facilitate DJ parties or just hanging out. ✉ *85 Huating Lu, Xuhui* ☎ *021/6281–5646.*

North Shanghai

CHINESE FOLK **Bandu Music.** An unpretentious café and bar in the M50 art compound, Bandu sells hard-to-find CDs and holds concerts of traditional Chinese folk music every Saturday night. ✉ *50 Moganshan Lu, Unit 11, 1F, Zhabei* ☎ *021/6431–0269.*

ROCK **021 Live House.** Take-no-prisoners grunge is the motif of this dingy, proudly underground-music dive. The clientele is mostly drawn from the nearby student population, as are most of the acts, but occasionally they attract better-known Chinese rock bands. For a performance schedule, visit www.shrock.cn. ✉ *2893 Yangshupu Lu, 2F, Yangpu* ☎ *139/1801–5880.*

Live Bar. Another grungy rock dive catering to students and serving up cheap beer and loud music, Live Bar features mainly heavy punk, metal, and hardcore sounds. ✉ *721 Kunming Lu, Zhabei* ☎ *021/2833–6764.*

Xujiahui & South Shanghai

Fodor'sChoice ★ **Yuyintang Warehouse.** No one or thing has done as much to bring Shanghai rock out from the underground and into the open than the Yuyintang collective. Headed by sound engineer and former musician Zhang Haisheng, the group started organizing regular concerts around town and eventually opened their own space. Regular concerts, usually on Friday and Saturday nights or Sunday afternoons, spotlight the best and latest in Chinese music. Visit www.yuyintang.com for a schedule. ✉ *Longcao Lu, La. 200, No. 100, 1F, Xuhui* ☎ *021/6436–0072.*

At a Glance

ENGLISH	PINYIN	CHINESE CHARACTERS
POINTS OF INTEREST		
021 Live House	021 Jiǔ bā	021酒吧
Arch Bar and Café	Jiǔjiān Jiǔbā	玖间酒吧
B.A.T.S.	Biānfú Jiǔbā	蝙蝠酒吧
Bandu Music	Bàndù Yīnyuè	半度音乐
Barbarossa	Bābālùshā Jiǔbā	巴巴路莎酒吧
Blue Frog	Lánwā Xīcāntīng	蓝娃西餐厅
Buddha Bar	Bùdábā Jiǔbā	布达吧酒吧
California Club	Jiālìfúníyà Jiǔbā	加利福尼亚酒吧
CJW	CJW Juéshìyuè Jiǔbā	CJW爵士乐酒吧
Cloud 9	Jiǔxiāo Jiǔbā	九霄酒吧
Club JZ	Chúncuì Juéshìyuè Jiǔbā	纯粹爵士乐酒吧
Cotton Club	Miánhuā Jùlèbù	棉花俱乐部
Cotton's	Miánhuā Jiǔbā	棉花酒吧
Dublin Exchange	Dōubólín Kāfēiguǎn	都柏林咖啡馆
Fabrique	Lèfǎbèi Jiǔbā	乐法贝酒吧
Fuxing Park	Fùxīng Gōngyuán	复兴公园
Glamour Bar	Mèilì Jiǔbā	魅力酒吧
Guandii	Guāndǐ Jiǔbā	官邸酒吧
Haoledi	Hǎolèdì KTV	好乐迪KTV
Hengshan Lu	Héngshān Lù	衡山路
Hi Theatre	Hǎishànghǎi Xiǎojùchǎng	海上海小剧场
House of Blues and Jazz	Bùlǔsī Yǔ Juéshì Zhīwū	布鲁斯与爵士之屋
Jade on 36	Fěicuì 36 Jiǔbā	翡翠36酒吧
Jazz 37	Juéshì 37 Jiǔbā	爵士37酒吧
Jazz Bar	Juéshì Bā	爵士吧
Julu Lu	Jùlù Lù Jiǔbājiē	巨鹿路酒吧街
Kunju Opera Troupe	Shànghǎi Kūnjùtuán	上海昆剧团
Live Bar	Xiànchǎng Jiǔbā	现场酒吧
Long Bar	Chánglláng Jiǔbā	长廊酒吧
Lyceum Theatre	Lánxīn Dàxìyuàn	兰馨大戏院
Majestic Theatre	Měiqí Dàxìyuàn	美琪大戏院
Malone's American Café	Mǎlóng Měishì Cāntīng	马龙美式餐厅

Maoming Nan Lu	Màomíngnán Lù Jiǔbājiē	茂名南路酒吧街
Number Five	Wàitān Wǔhào Jiǔbā	外滩五号酒吧
O'Malley's	Oumǎlì Jiǔbā	欧玛莉酒吧
Party World	Qiánguì KTV	钱柜KTV
Patio Bar	Tiāntíng Jiǔbā	天庭酒吧
Pier One	Yīhào Mǎtóu	一号码头
Real Love	Zhēnài Jiǔbā	真爱酒吧
Ritz-Carlton Bar	Lìjiā Jiǔbā	丽嘉酒吧
Rojam	Luójié Jiǔbā	罗杰酒吧
Sasha's	Sà Shā	萨莎
Shanghai Acrobatics Troupe	Shànghǎi Zájìtuán	上海杂技团
Shanghai Center Theater	Shànghǎi Shāngchéng Jùyuàn	上海商城剧院
Shanghai Concert Hall	Shànghǎi Yīnyuètīng	上海音乐厅
Shanghai Conservatory of Music	Shànghǎi Yīnyuè Xuéyuàn	上海音乐学院
Shanghai Dramatic Arts Center	Shànghǎi Huàjù Yìshù Zhōngxīn	上海话剧艺术中心
Shanghai Grand Stage	Shànghǎi Dàwǔtái	上海大舞台
Shanghai Grand Theatre	Shànghǎi Dàjùyuàn	上海大剧院
Shanghai Oriental Art Center	Shànghǎi Dōngfāng Yìshù Zhōngxīn	上海东方艺术中心
Shanghai Theatre Academy	Shànghǎi Xìjù Xuéyuàn	上海戏剧学院
Tanghui	Tánghuì Jiǔbā	堂会酒吧
The Blarney Stone	Bùlā'nísīdòng Cāntīng	布拉尼斯栋餐厅
The Door	Qiánmén Jiǔbā	乾门酒吧
The Lab	Shí Yàn Shì	实验室
Time Passage	Shíguāng Tōngdào Jiǔbā	时光通道酒吧
TMSK	Tòumíng Sīkǎo Jiǔbā	透明思考酒吧
Tongren Lu	Tóngrén Lù Jiǔbājiē	同仁路酒吧街
Xiahemi Warehouse	Xiàhé Mǐcāng	下河米仓
Ye Lai Xiang (The Garden Hotel Bar)	Yèláixiāng Jiǔbā	夜来香酒吧
Yifu Theatre	Yìfū Wǔtái	逸夫舞台
Yuyintang Warehouse	Yù Yīn Táng	育音堂

Where to Eat

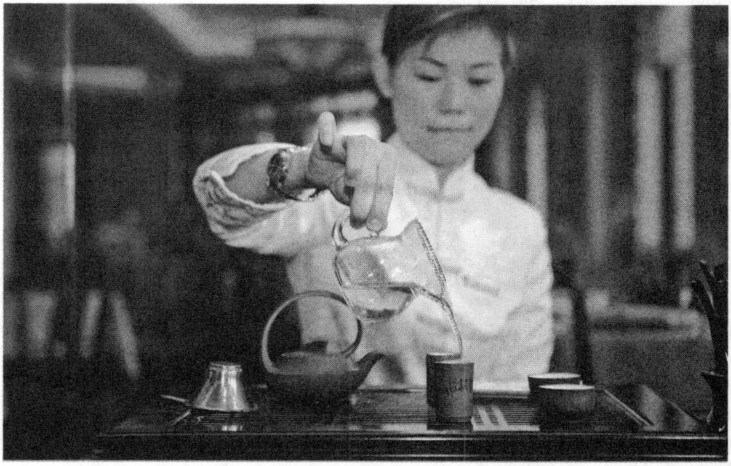

Tea ceremony in Whampoa Club at Three on the Bund

WORD OF MOUTH

"Shintori Null II: Shintori is a well-kept secret. Visitors may find this restaurant a bit mysterious, but it's well worth puzzling out."

–Heather, USA

"T8: Impeccable service, outstanding food, and a Western wine list in an authentic teahouse. Upon entering you know immediately that this place is quietly in a different world."

–Don, Sacramento

www.fodors.com/forums

DINING PLANNER

Dining Hours

Dining in Shanghai can be a protracted affair. Dinner hours in restaurants begin at around 5 PM, but often carry on late into the night. Many of the classic, local restaurants popular with the Shanghainese only close after the last diners have left, which sometimes keeps them open until the wee hours of the morning. Generally, though, dinner is eaten between 6 and 11 PM, with fine dining generally happening later than casual meals.

Reservations & Dress

Reservations are always a good idea: we mention them only when they're essential or not accepted. Book as far ahead as you can, and reconfirm as soon as you arrive. Generally, we mention dress only when men are required to wear a jacket or a jacket and tie. Many upmarket restaurants don't require a jacket or tie, but have a no shorts or sandals policy. This can be a problem in the extreme summer heat, so call ahead to confirm the dress code.

Top 5 Restaurants

- **T8.** Innovative, elegant, and classy T8 is the star performer in the very competitive Xintiandi restaurant market. It has excellent food, impeccable service, and beautiful surroundings.
- **Mesa.** Nestled on Julu Lu in the Old French Concession, this place is a little hard to find. But with minimalist decor, spectacular food, and some of the best service in Shanghai, it's well worth the effort.
- **Jade on 36.** This opulent restaurant is an experience second to none, and has a spectacular 36th-floor view across the Huangpu to the historical sights of the Bund.
- **Sens & Bund.** Modern interpretations on traditional Mediterranean fare are presented by the award-winning Pourcel brothers. Sens & Bund serves impeccable food in a beautifully decorated historic location.
- **Yin.** A series of Japanese and Chinese restaurants stacked on top of each other, Yin has some of the best Asian food in town.

On the Menu

Shanghainese food is fairly typical Chinese, with dark, sweet, and oily dishes served in great abundance. The dish sizes can be quite small, so be careful when ordering—it's not unusual for two diners to polish off six dishes plus rice. The drink of choice with Shanghainese food is *huangjiu*, or yellow wine. It's a mild-tasting sweetish rice wine, which pairs well with the local cuisine.

Shanghai is full of fine restaurants from around the world, but sometimes, the finest dining experience in the city can be had with a steamer tray of *xiaolongbao* (Shanghai's signature dumplings—small steamed buns filled with pork and crab meat in broth) matched with a cold beer. River fish is often the highlight (and most expensive part) of the meal, and hairy crab is a seasonal delicacy. It may not be the finest dining, but it's an enjoyable and genuine taste of the city.

Prices

From an American or European point of view, fine dining in Shanghai can be very economical. Even in the fanciest restaurants, main courses are unlikely to cost more than US$35. However, in Shanghai, like everywhere else, fame is on par with price. The famous restaurants charge as much as the international market will bear—prices that often don't reflect the quality of the dining experience.

If you're looking for an excellent meal and you don't care about the restaurateur's name, then exceptional dining experiences can be had for half the price, without sacrificing quality or ambience. Sadly, the difference between $$$$ and $$$ is often just fame and face rather than quality.

For the adventuresome, great local food can be found everywhere for laughably cheap prices, even in fairly nice restaurants. The food is good and inexpensive ($1 to $5 per dish), and the experience of eating at a small, unknown restaurant is pure China. We recommend you try it at least once.

Paying & Tipping

Credit cards are becoming more widely accepted, but this is still a cash economy. Hotels and upmarket international restaurants will take plastic, but when in doubt, bring cash. Don't worry about being caught out without cash in hand–ATMs are everywhere.

China is not a tipping nation, so tip carefully! Most hotels add a service charge (usually 15%) onto the bill–check the fine print on the menu. If the service has been very good, tipping 5% to 15% is a welcome gesture. Bear in mind that some restaurants will not allow the staff to accept tips, whereas in others the tips are seized by management.

WHAT IT COSTS In Yuan

	$$$$	$$$	$$	$	¢
AT DINNER	over Y300	Y151–Y300	Y81–Y150	Y40–Y80	under Y40

Prices are for a main course at dinner.

Revised by
David Taylor

When eating out, you'll notice most Chinese restaurants in Shanghai have large, round tables. The reason will become clear the first time you eat a late dinner at a local restaurant and are surrounded by jovial, laughing groups of people toasting and topping off from communal bottles of beer, sharing cigarettes, and spinning the lazy Susan loaded with food.

Dining out with friends and family isn't just a favorite social activity; it's a ritual. Whether feting guests or demonstrating their growing wealth, hosts will order massive, showy spreads. Although take-away boxes for leftovers are starting to become popular, proud hosts wouldn't deign to use them.

Shanghai's standing as China's most international city is reflected in its dining scene. You can enjoy *jiaozi* (dumplings) for breakfast, foie gras for lunch, and Kobe beef teppanyaki for dinner.

It's traditional to order several dishes, plus rice, to share among your party. Tipping is not expected, but sophistication still comes at a price. Although you can easily eat as the locals do at Chinese restaurants for less than Y40, even simple Western meals will cost you a more Western price.

Most restaurants in Shanghai offer set lunches—multicourse feasts—at a fraction of the usual price. It's the best dining deal going, allowing you to eat at local Chinese restaurants for Y25 or less and at such places at M on the Bund without completely blowing your budget. Also, check out the "Restaurant Events" section of *That's Shanghai,* or *SH Magazine,* which list dining discounts and promotions around town.

OLD CITY

Narrow and crowded, the Old City is all that's left of old Chinain Shanghai. The area is home to the spectacular Yuyuan Gardens, and can be a good location to find some traditional-style food in an authentic environment. The surroundings of the Yuyuan may be spectacular, but it is still a tourist hub. We recommend that the adventurous go out into the side streets around Fangbang Lu in search of authentic Chinese snacks. ■ TIP→ **When dining in these small local restaurants always ask the price first—with no English menu, many sellers in this area aren't above raising the price after your first bite.**

WORD OF MOUTH

"Definitely eat soup dumplings from the Nan Xiang in the Yu Gardens shopping area across from the teahouse in the center. You can't miss it. It will have a line of people waiting to get dumplings to go. Just go up the stairs to the 3rd floor, share a table, and enjoy. We had the crab dumpling set and they were incredible. First suck the juice out and then gobble them down." -iammurphy

Chinese

$–$$$ ✕ **Lu Bo Lang.** A popular stop for visiting dignitaries, Lu Bo Lang is a perfect photo op of a restaurant. The traditional three-story Chinese pavilion with upturned eaves sits next to the Bridge of Nine Turnings in the Yu Garden complex. The food is good but not great, with many expensive fish choices on the menu. Among the best dishes are the crab meat with bean curd, the braised eggplant with chili sauce, and the sweet *osmanthus* cake, made with the sweetly fragrant flower of the same name. ✉ *115 Yuyuan Lu, Huangpu* ☎ *021/6328–0602* ✍ *Reservations essential* 💳 *AE, DC, MC, V.*

Indian

$ ✕ **Masala Art.** A rising star of the Indian dining scene, Masala Art is a little hard to find but worth the effort. Serving excellent breads and sublime curries in an understated dining area, Masala Art wins praise for fine food at very reasonable prices. ✉ *397 Dagu Lu, Huangpu* ☎ *021/6327–3571* ✍ *Reservations essential* 💳 *AE, DC, MC, V.*

Mediterranean

¢–$ ✕ **Mediterranean Café.** Buried in the east end of town, the Med is a hidden gem. Small and unpretentious, it is one of the few places in town serving authentic Mediterranean food. With highlights of genuine bagels (one of the only places to find them in town), kosher-deli foods, feta and falafels, this is a perfect lunch destination. We recommend the pita falafel—hot, green, and crunchy, served with an Israeli salad—and the latkes, which are perfectly fried potato pancakes served with sour cream. ✉ *415 DaGu Rd., Huangpu* ☎ *021/6327–0897 or 021/6295–9511* 💳 *No credit cards.*

XINTIANDI & CITY CENTER

The center of the gastronomic city, the City Center and Xintiandi contain some of the finest restaurants of the city, for any type of cuisine. Named after their stone entranceways, the beautifully restored traditional *shikumen* (stone gatehouse) dwellings of Xintiandi now house world-class restaurants like T8, and in the area surrounding People's Square are popular spots such as the JW Marriott's restaurants and the trendy Middle Eastern food of Barbarossa.

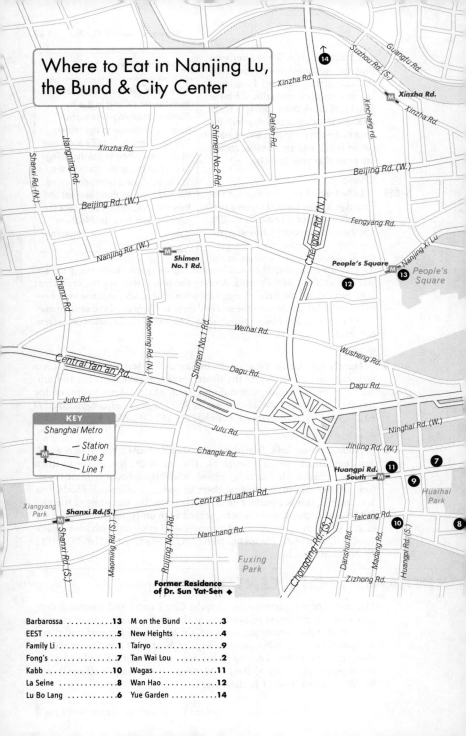

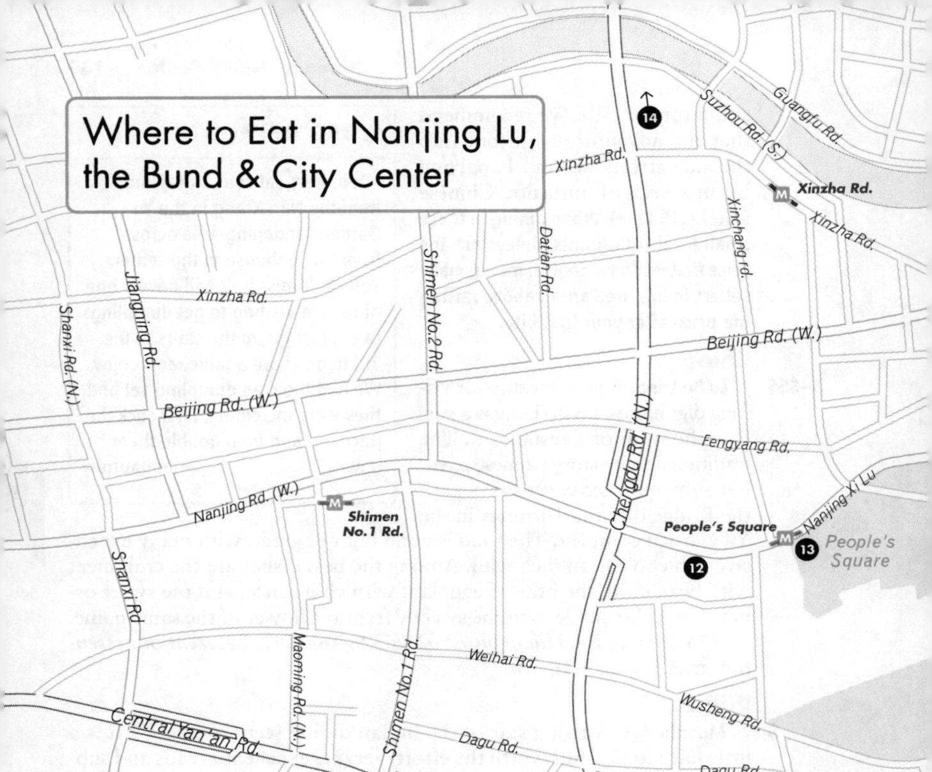

Barbarossa 13
EEST 5
Family Li 1
Fong's 7
Kabb 10
La Seine 8
Lu Bo Lang 6
M on the Bund 3
New Heights 4
Tairyo 9
Tan Wai Lou 2
Wagas 11
Wan Hao 12
Yue Garden 14

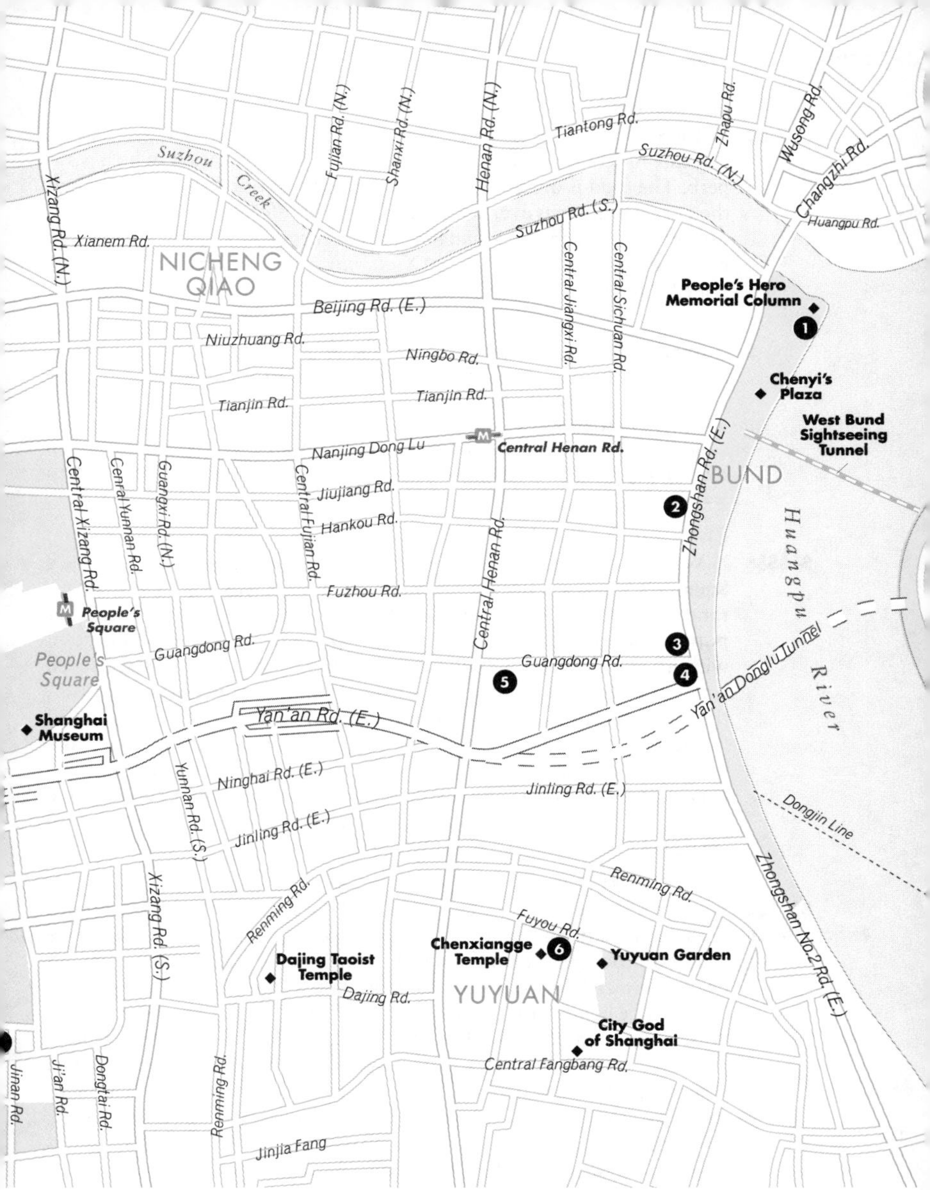

NICHENG QIAO
BUND
YUYUAN
Suzhou Creek
Huangpu River
Tiantong Rd.
Suzhou Rd. (N.)
Suzhou Rd. (S.)
Zhapu Rd.
Wusong Rd.
Changzhi Rd.
Huangpu Rd.
Fujian Rd. (N.)
Shanxi Rd. (N.)
Henan Rd. (N.)
Xizang Rd. (N.)
Xianem Rd.
Central Jiangxi Rd.
Central Sichuan Rd.
Beijing Rd. (E.)
Niuzhuang Rd.
Ningbo Rd.
Tianjin Rd.
Tianjin Rd.
Nanjing Dong Lu
Central Henan Rd.
Jiujiang Rd.
Hankou Rd.
Fuzhou Rd.
Guangdong Rd.
Guangdong Rd.
Central Xizang Rd.
Central Yunnan Rd.
Guangxi Rd. (N.)
Central Fujian Rd.
Central Henan Rd.
Zhongshan Rd. (E.)
People's Hero Memorial Column
1
Chenyi's Plaza
West Bund Sightseeing Tunnel
2
3
4
5
People's Square
People's Square
Shanghai Museum
Yan'an Rd. (E.)
Yan'an Donglu Tunnel
Ninghai Rd. (E.)
Jinling Rd. (E.)
Jinling Rd. (E.)
Yunnan Rd. (S.)
Xizang Rd. (S.)
Dongjin Line
Zhongshan No.2 Rd. (E.)
Renming Rd.
Renming Rd.
Fuyou Rd.
Chenxiangge Temple
6
Yuyuan Garden
Dajing Taoist Temple
Dajing Rd.
City God of Shanghai
Central Fangbang Rd.
Renming Rd.
Jinan Rd.
Ji'an Rd.
Dongtai Rd.
Jinjia Fang

American

$–$$ ✕ **Kabb.** Serving burgers, salads, and other standards of American food, this café in Xintiandi is distinguished mostly for its location, which is superb. The food is unremarkable, being good without distinction, though the portions are massive. Service is slightly indifferent, and the pricing is rather high for such pedestrian fare. However, it does fill the bill for a quick lunch on the sidewalk tables. ✉ *Xintiandi, 181 Taicang Lu, 5 Xintiandi Bei Li, Luwan* ☎ *021/3307–0798* 💳 *AE, DC, MC, V.*

Cafés

¢–$ ✕ **Wagas.** Serving sandwiches, salads, and coffees, Wagas is a popular lunch stop. The food is decent, and the service adequate, but there is little distinctive about this easily accessible chain café. It's popular with locals for its reasonable prices, English menus, and speedy service and is good for a quick refill when shopping. ✉ *Hong Kong New World Plaza, 300 Huaihai Zhong Lu, Luwan* ☎ *021/6335–3739* 💳 *No credit cards.*

Chinese

$–$$$$ ✕ **Wan Hao.** On the 38th floor of the JW Marriott overlooking People's Square, Wan Hao is an elegant and relatively inexpensive Chinese restaurant. It specializes in Cantonese dishes, though the menu contains other popular options like Peking Duck and spicy chicken. The food is good without being exceptional, the ambience is pleasant, and the staff is well trained and helpful. Look to the seasonal dishes for the freshest options; the kitchen team is always updating the menu to reflect the flavors of the season. Servings tend to be on the small side—Chinese-style—despite the Western place settings, so expect to order several dishes per person. If you're unsure about your order, the staff is happy to help. ✉ *JW Marriott at Tomorrow Square, 38th fl., 399 Nanjing Xi Lu, Luwan* ☎ *021/5359–4969* 💳 *AE, DC, MC, V.*

Contemporary

$$–$$$ **Fodor'sChoice ★** ✕ **T8.** A favorite haunt for celebrities, T8 has garnered its share of headlines for its stunning interior and inspired contemporary cuisine. The restaurant occupies a traditional shikumen house within Xintiandi and has modernized the space with raw stone floors, carved-wood screens, and imaginative lighting that transforms shelves full of glasses into a modern-art sculpture. The show kitchen turns out such Thai- and Chinese-inspired dishes as a slow-cooked, Sichuan-flavored lamb pie, and nori-wrapped sashimi-grade tuna. Like the clientele, the wine list is exclusive, with many labels unavailable elsewhere in Shanghai. ✉ *House 8, North Block, Xintiandi, 181 Taicang Lu, Luwan* ☎ *021/6355–8999* ✍ *Reservations essential* 💳 *AE, DC, MC, V* ⏲ *No lunch Tues.*

French

$–$$$ ✕ **La Seine.** Its stylish dining room and authentic contemporary fare make La Seine a perfect place to savor and contemplate the intricacies of French cuisine. Royal purple reigns, in the linens, flower arrangements, suede chairs, and the throw pillows on the generously sized booths. The artfully presented dishes range from the expected escargot and foie gras to delicate seafood like tilapia in mustard-cream sauce. The weekday lunch

BORDERS.

BORDERS #383
BOOKS MUSIC AND CAFE
650 Ponce De Leon, Suite 500
Atlanta, GA 30308
(404) 607-7903

STORE: 0383 REG: 02/23 TRAN#: 1758
SALE 09/17/2008 EMP: 00725

FODORS SHANGHAI
8600314 QP T 18.95

	Subtotal	18.95
	GEORGIA 8%	1.52
1 Item	Total	20.47
	VISA	20.47

ACCT # /S XXXXXXXXXXXX9632
AUTH: 04485B
NAME: ERNEST/HENRY P

09/17/2008 02:48PM

store receipt, Borders Gift Receipt, or presented for return beyond 30 days from date of purchase, must be carried by Borders at the time of the return. The lowest price offered for the item during the 6 month period prior to the return will be refunded via a gift card.

Opened videos, music discs, cassettes, electronics, and audio books may only be exchanged for a replacement of the original item.

Periodicals, newspapers, out-of-print, collectible, pre-owned items, and gift cards may not be returned.

Returned merchandise must be in saleable condition.

BORDERS®

Returns to Borders Stores

Merchandise presented for return, including sale or marked-down items, must be accompanied by the original Borders store receipt or a Borders Gift Receipt. Returns must be completed within 30 days of purchase. For returns accompanied by a Borders Store Receipt, the purchase price will be refunded in the medium of purchase (cash, credit card or gift card). Items purchased by check may be returned for cash after 10 business days. For returns within 30 days of purchase accompanied by a Borders Gift Receipt, the purchase price (after applicable discounts) will be refunded via a gift card.

Merchandise unaccompanied by the original Borders store receipt, Borders Gift Receipt, or presented for return beyond 30 days from date of purchase, must be carried by Borders at the time of the return. The lowest price offered for the item during the 6 month period prior to the return will be refunded via a gift card.

Opened videos, music discs, cassettes, electronics, and audio books may only be exchanged for a replacement of the original item.

Periodicals, newspapers, out-of-print, collectible, pre-owned items, and gift cards may not be returned.

Returned merchandise must be in saleable condition.

semi-buffet (pairing an entrée with salad and dessert bar), weekend brunch buffet, and dinner prix-fixe menus are the best deals. Be sure to stop in the patisserie, where the heavenly scent will inspire you to buy some truffles and croissants for the way home. ✉ *8 Jinan Lu, Luwan* ☎ *021/6384–3722* ✍ *Reservations essential* ▭ *AE, DC, MC, V.*

Fusion

$$–$$$$ ✕ **California Grill.** The JW Marriott's "Western" dining option serves California-style fusion. The steaks are exceptional, with tender Black Angus beef. Everything else is fairly standard, with a wide selection of sampler plates available. The desserts are at the five-star standard, with the exception of the Cohiba, a chocolate cigar and "cigar-flavored" crème brûlée served in an ashtray. It's about as tasty as it sounds, and is worth avoiding. ✉ *JW Marriott at Tomorrow Square, 40th fl., 399 Nanjing Xi Lu, Luwan* ☎ *021/5359–4969* ▭ *AE, DC, MC, V.*

5

Japanese

$–$$ ✕ **Tairyo.** Teppanyaki has invaded Shanghai. More down to earth than a sophisticated sushi bar, teppanyaki (Japanese barbecue) is a gastronomic experience serving sushi, sashimi, barbecued meats, and a wide variety of Western and Eastern dishes. It does have à la carte, but at Y150 for all you can eat and drink, Tairyo's main attraction is obvious. Just walk in, take a seat at the grill, and indulge while the chef prepares your dinner as you watch. We recommend the Mongolian King Steak, but the menu has English and pictures, so pick and choose. This is a perfect no-effort dinner destination. Private rooms are available for groups larger than seven (reservations essential). ✉ *Hong Kong New World Plaza, South Building, 283 Huaihai Rd., 3rd fl., Luwan* ☎ *021/6390–7244* ▭ *AE, DC, MC, V.*

Middle Eastern

$–$$ ✕ **Barbarossa.** Modern Middle Eastern food in a setting taken from the *Arabian Nights*, Barbarossa is rapidly becoming a destination of choice. The decoration is amazing, albeit possibly flammable, with billowing draperies swathing the space, and the food is good and reasonably priced. At around 10 PM, Barbarossa becomes a club, so don't aim for a late dinner unless you like mingling with the party people. ✉ *People's Square, 231 Nanjing Xi Rd., next to the Shanghai Art Museum, Luwan* ☎ *021/6318–0220* ▭ *AE, DC, MC, V.*

Vietnamese

$–$$ ✕ **Fong's.** Don't be deterred by Fong's location in an office plaza. Inside, chirping birds, gauze curtains, bamboo furniture, and hostesses wearing *ao dai* (a long Vietnamese dress with side slits worn over pants) set a romanticized scene for Fong's excellent French-style Vietnamese cuisine. The English menu (with photos) focuses on traditional dishes like spring rolls and a wonderfully smoky fried vermicelli with seafood, but it also includes bouillabaisse and other French specialties. Service is adequate but may seem distant in this busy and justifiably popular restaurant. ✉ *Lippo Plaza, 222 Huaihai Zhonglu, 2nd fl., Luwan* ☎ *021/6387–7228* ▭ *AE, DC, MC, V.*

NANJING DONG LU & THE BUND

The Bund is the spiritual heart of modern Shanghai, with the colonial history of Puxi facing the towering steel and glass of Pudong. The stellar view of the river and Pudong has attracted some of the finest restaurant development in town, including the showcase restaurants at Bund18, Sens & Bund, and Three on the Bund. However, many visitors complain that the Bund restaurants are more style than substance, and rely too heavily on their fame and location. We find that though service and quality can occasionally lapse, it's well worth your effort to experience what this area has to offer.

American

★ **$–$$$** ✕ **New Heights.** Perched atop prestigious Three on the Bund, New Heights is a surprisingly unpretentious restaurant. With a gorgeous terrace overlooking the river and a solid menu of generally North American standard fare, this is an excellent destination for the weary Bund tourist. We recommend it for a late lunch basking in the afternoon sun on the terrace. Try the hamburger with a cold beer. ✉ *Three on the Bund, 7th fl., 3 Zhong Shan Dong Yi Rd., Huangpu* ☎ *021/6321–0909* ▭ *AE, DC, MC, V.*

Chinese

$$$$ ✕ **Family Li Imperial Cuisine.** This spectacular restaurant, a newer branch of the famous Beijing Imperial restaurant, deserves a visit despite high prices (set menus begin at Y1,000). Using family recipes smuggled from the Forbidden City a century ago, Family Li gives the closest thing to a taste of imperial food. There are only nine rooms, and only set menus are served. Reservations more than 24 hours in advance are a must. ✉ *Huangpu Park, 500 East Zhongshan Yi Rd., Huangpu* ☎ *021/5308–1919* ✍ *Reservations essential* ▭ *AE, DC, MC, V.*

$$–$$$$ ✕ **Whampoa Club.** A new addition to the Bund scene, Whampoa Club is nouveau Chinese at its best. With a focus on fresh seafood and interesting interpretations of Shanghai classics, this is a destination worth checking out. As befits a celebrity venue, prices are steep, but generally worth the expense. ✉ *Three on the Bund, 4th fl., 3 Zhongshan Dong Yi Lu, Huangpu* ☎ *021/6323–3355* ✍ *Reservations essential* ▭ *AE, DC, MC, V.*

$$–$$$$ ✕ **Tan Wai Lou.** Bund18's signature Chinese restaurant, Tan Wai Lou serves up nouveau-Cantonese cuisine in a refined setting. The food is good and well presented, though the non-Chinese service (dishes are presented in courses and not shared) can be a little jarring for a diner expecting a classic Chinese meal. Still, the seafood is very fresh and the view of the Huangpu spectacular. ✉ *Bund18, 5th fl., 18 Zhongshan Dong Yi Rd., Huangpu* ☎ *021/6339–1188* ✍ *Reservations essential* ▭ *AE, DC, MC, V.*

Contemporary

$$–$$$$ ✕ **Laris.** The signature restaurant of star Australian chef David Laris, this is one of the few Bund restaurants with the owner/chef in residence. The innovative continental-inspired cuisine is good and well presented,

Continued on page 151

A CULINARY TOUR OF CHINA

For centuries, the collective culinary fragrances of China have drifted far beyond its borders and tantalized the entire world. In the decades following the revolution, most Westerners couldn't get anything close to genuine Chinese cuisine. But with China's arms now open to the world, a vast variety of Chinese flavors are more widely accessible than ever.

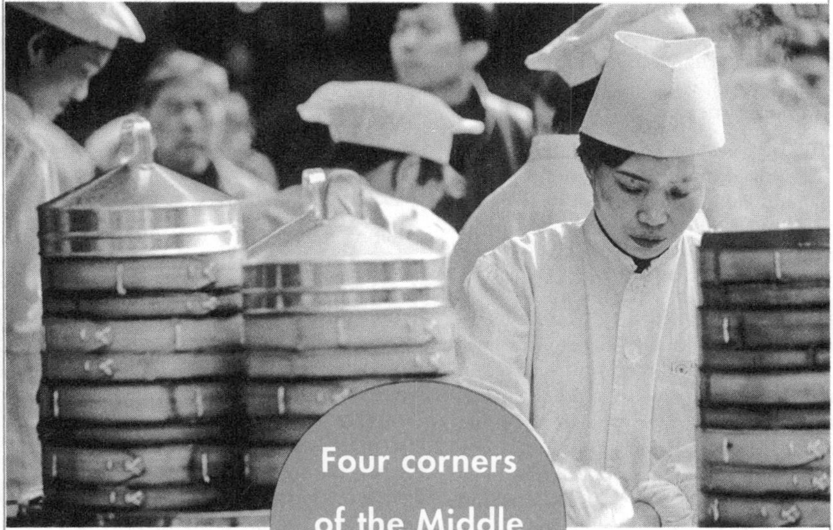

Four corners of the Middle Kingdom

In dynasties gone by, a visitor to China might have to undertake a journey of a thousand li just to feel the burn of an authentic Sichuanese hotpot, and another to savor the crispy skin and juicy flesh of a genuine Beijing roast duck. Luckily for us, the vast majority of regional Chinese cuisines have made successful internal migrations. As a result, Sichuanese cuisine can be found in Guangzhou, Cantonese dim sum in Urumuqi, and the cumin spiced lamb-on-a-stick, for which the Uigher people of Xinjiang are famous, is now grilled all over China.

Before you begin your journey, remember, a true scholar of Middle Kingdom cuisine should first eliminate the very term "Chinese food" from their vocabulary. It hardly encompasses the variety of provincial cuisines and regional dishes that China has to offer, from succulent Shanghainese dumplings to fiery Sichuanese hotpots.

To guide you on your gastronomic journey, we've divided the country's gourmet map along the points of the compass—North, South, East, and West. Bon voyage and *bon appétit!*

NORTH

THE BASICS

Cuisine from China's Northeast is called *dongbei cai,* and it's more wheat than rice based. Vegetables like kale, cabbage, and potatoes are combined with robust, thick soy sauces, garlic (often raw), and scallions.

Even though many Han Chinese from southern climates find mutton too gamey, up north it's a regular staple. In many northern cities, you can't walk more than a block without coming across a small sidewalk grill with *yang rou chua'r,* or lamb-on-a-stick.

NOT TO BE MISSED

The most famous of all the northern dishes is Peking duck, and if you've ever had it well prepared, you'll know why Beijingers are proud of the dish named for their city.

The fowl is cleaned, stuffed with burning millet stalks and other aromatic combustibles, and then slow-cooked in an oven heated by a fire made of fragrant wood. Properly cooked, Peking duck should have crispy skin, juicy meat, and none of the grease. Peking duck is served with pancakes, scallions and a delicious soy-based sauce with just a hint of sweetness.

The ultimate window dressing.

LEGEND HAS IT

Looking for the best roast duck in Beijing? You won't find it in a luxury hotel. But if you happen to find yourself wandering through the Qianmendong hutong just south of Tiananmen Square, you may stumble upon a little courtyard home with a sign in English reading LIQUN ROAST DUCK. This small and unassuming restaurant is widely considered as having the best Peking roast duck in the capital. Rumor has it that the late leader Deng Xiaoping used to send his driver out to bring him back Liqun's amazing ducks.

THE CAPITAL CITY'S NAMESAKE DISH

SOUTH

(left) Preparing for the feast. (top right) Dim sum as art. (bottom right) Meat-filled Beijing dumplings.

THE BASICS

The dish most associated with Southern Chinese Cuisine is dim sum, which is found in great variety and abundance in Guangdong province, as well as Hong Kong and Macau. Bite-sized dim sum is usually eaten early in the day. Any good dim sum place should have dozens of varieties. Some of the most popular dishes are *har gao,* a shrimp dumpling with a rice flour skin, *siu maai,* a pork dumpling with a wrapping made of wheat flour, and *chaahabao,* a steamed or baked bun filled with sweetened pork and onions. Adventerous eaters should order the chicken claws. Trust us, they taste better than they look.

The Cantonese saying *"fei qin zou shou"* roughly translates to "if it flies, swims or runs, it's food."

For our money, the best southern food comes from Chaozhou (Chiuchow), a coastal city only a few hours drive north of its larger neighbors. Unlike dim sum, Chaozhou cuisine is extremely light and understated. Deep-fried bean curd is also a remarkably fresh Chaozhou dish.

NOT TO BE MISSED

One Chaozhou dish that appeals equally to the eye and the palate is the plain-sounding mashed vegetable with minced chicken soup. The dish is served in a large bowl, and resembles a green and white yin-yang. As befitting a dish resembling a Buddhist symbol, a vegetarian version substituting rice gruel for chicken broth is usually offered.

SOUTHWEST AND FAR WEST

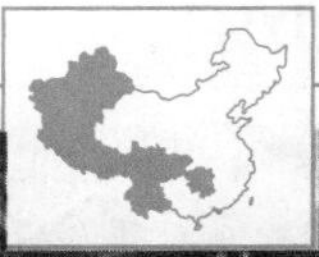

Southwest

THE BASICS

When a person from the Southwest asks you if you like spicy food, consider your answer well. Natives of Sichuan and Hunan take the use of chilies, wild pepper, and garlic to blistering new heights. These two areas have been competing for the "spiciest province in China" title for centuries. The penchant for fiery food is likely due to the weather—hot and humid in the summer and harshly cold in the winter. But no matter what the temperature, if you're eating Sichuan or Hunan dishes, be prepared to sweat.

Southwest China shares some culinary traits with both Southeast Asia and India. This is likely due to the influences of travelers from both regions in centuries past. Traditional Chinese medicine also makes itself felt in the regional cuisine. Theory has it that sweating expels toxins and equalizes body temperature.

As Chairman Mao's hometown province, Hunan has a number of dishes with revolutionary names. The most popular are red-cooked Hunan fish *(hongshao wuchangyu)* and red-cooked pork *(hongshao rou)*, which was said to have been a personal favorite of the Great Helmsman.

The hotter the better.

NOT TO BE MISSED

One Sichuan dish you won't want to miss out on is *mala zigi*, or "peppery and hot chicken." It's one part chicken meat and three parts fried chilies and a Sichuanese wild pepper called *huajiao* that's so spicy it effectively numbs the tongue. At first it feels like eating Tiger Balm, but the hot-cool-numb sensation produced by crunching on the pepper is oddly addictive.

KUNG PAO CHICKEN

One of the most famous Chinese dishes, Kung Pao chicken (or *gongbao jiding*), enjoys a legend of its own.

Though shrouded in myth, its origin exemplifies the improvisational skills found in any good Chinese chef. The story of Kung Pao chicken has to do with a certain Qing Dynasty era (1644-1911) provincial governor named Ding Baozhen, who arrived home unexpectedly one day with a group of friends in tow. His cook, caught in between shopping trips, had only the chicken breast and a few vegetables he was planning to cook for his own dinner. The crafty chef diced the chicken into tiny bits and fried it up with everything he could find in the cupboard—some peanuts, sugar, onion, garlic, bits of ginger, and a few handfuls of dried red peppers—and hoped for the best.

(top left) Chowing down at Kashgar's Sunday Market. (center left) Eat, drink, and be merry! (bottom left) Monk stirring tsampa barley. (right) Juggling hot noodles in the Xinjiang province.

Far West

THE BASICS

Religion is the primary shaper of culinary tradition in China's far west. Being a primarily Muslim province, chefs in Xinjiang don't use pork products of any kind. Instead, meals are likely to be heavy on spiced lamb. Baked flat breads coated in sesame seeds are a specialty. Whole lamb roasted on a spit, fine spicy tomato salads, and lightly spiced mutton and vegetable soups are also favorites.

NOT TO BE MISSED

In Tibet, climate is the major factor dictating cuisine. High and dry, the Tibetan plateau is hardly suited for rice cultivation. Whereas a Han meal might include rice, Tibetan cuisine tends to include tsampa, a ground barley usually cooked into a porridge. Another staple that's definitely an acquired taste is yak butter tea. Dumplings, known as *momo,* are wholesome and filling. Of course, if you want to go all out, order the yak penis with caterpillar fungus.

EAST

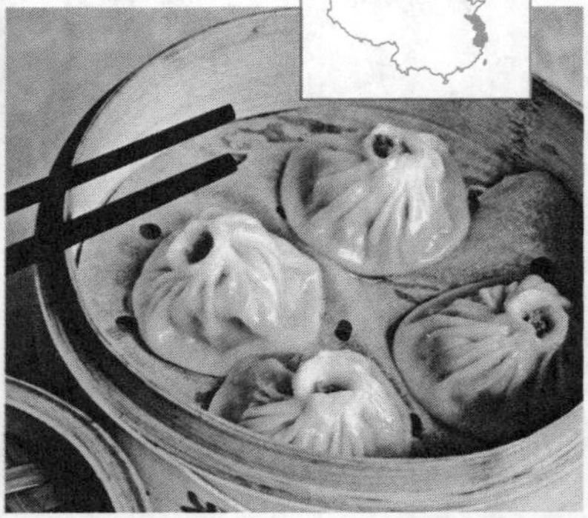

(top left) Flash cooking with the wok. (top right) Juicy steamer dumplings. (bottom right) Harvesting China's staple. (bottom left) Shanghai's sublime hairy crab.

THE BASICS

The rice, seafood and fresh vegetable-based cooking of the southern coastal provinces of Zhejiang and Jiangsu are known collectively as *huiyang cai*. As the area's biggest city, Shanghai has become a major center of the culinary arts. Some popular dishes in Shanghai are stir-fried freshwater eels and finely ground white pepper, and red-stewed fish—a boiled carp in sweet and sour sauce. Another Shanghai favorite are *xiaolong bao*, or little steamer dumplings. Similar to Cantonese dim sum, xiaolong bao tend to be more moist. The perfect steamed dumpling is meant to explode in your mouth in a juicy burst of meat.

NOT TO BE MISSED

Drunken anything! Shanghai chefs are known for their love of cooking with wine. Dishes like drunken chicken, drunken pigeon, and drunken crab are all delectable meals cooked with prodigious amounts of Shaoxing wine. People with an aversion to alcohol should definitely avoid these. Another meal not to be missed is hairy freshwater crabs, which only come into season in October. One enthusiast of the dish was 15th century poet and essayist Li Yu, who wrote of the dish in near-erotic terms. "Meat as white as jade, golden roe . . . to use seasoning to improve its taste is like holding up a torch to brighten the sunshine."

though service can often be problematic, with complaints about sloppy service and haughty staff being all too common. In our opinion, Laris survives more on hype than on substance. ✉ *Three on the Bund, 6th fl., 3 Zhongshan Dong Yi Lu, Huangpu* ☎ *021/6321–9922* ⚠ *Reservations essential* ▭ *AE, DC, MC, V.*

$$–$$$$ ✕ **M on the Bund.** The original international restaurant on the Bund, M has long had a reputation of being a place to see and be seen. However, it's been fading somewhat of late, in the face of the new competitors nearby. Still, the brunch is a landmark affair, business lunches are good, and the food can occasionally reach dizzying heights. ✉ *20 Guangdong Lu, 7th fl., Huangpu* ☎ *021/6350–9988* ⚠ *Reservations essential* ▭ *AE, DC, MC, V* ⏲ *No lunch Mon.*

French

$$–$$$$ ✕ **Jean Georges.** One of the fine-dining warhorses of the Bund, Jean Georges is the Shanghai project of celebrity Chef Jean Georges Vongerichten. The dark and intimate dining room in the historic Three on the Bund brings the right note of class to the experience, though the service can occasionally be lacking. The contemporary French cuisine is generally well executed, although very expensive. This is a showcase restaurant and at its best, Jean Georges is on the top of the scene; however, it's too often that it falls just a little short of perfection. ✉ *Three on the Bund, 4th fl., 3 Zhong Shan Dong Yi Rd., Huangpu* ☎ *021/6321–7733* ▭ *AE, DC, MC, V.*

$$–$$$$ ✕ **Sens & Bund.** The Shanghai branch of the France-based Jardin du Sens Group, Sens & Bund serves contemporary Mediterranean cuisine that is a study in elegant contrasts. The food is good, the service well-trained, and the ambience relaxing. The prices are quite high, but the overall quality and consistency makes this a better choice than many of its neighbors. ✉ *Bund 18, 1 Zhongshan Dong Yi Rd., 6th fl., Huangpu* ☎ *021/6323–9898* ▭ *AE, DC, MC, V.*

Japanese

$–$$$$ ✕ **EEST–The Crystal Garden.** This impressive three-in-one venue has full Japanese, Cantonese, and Thai menus, though the execution occasionally leaves something to be desired. Although the sushi bar and teppanyaki grill make it easy to zero-in on the Japanese offerings, sampling across the menus is the best approach. Shark-fin dumpling, *pomelo* salad, and rice with green tea and crabmeat are among the treasures buried in the pages of possibilities. The restaurant is in a sunny glass-roofed garden with retracting overhead shades, which cool you during the day and allow you to stargaze at night. ✉ *The Westin Shanghai, 88 Henan Zhonglu, Huangpu* ☎ *021/6335–1888* ▭ *AE, DC, MC, V.*

FORMER FRENCH CONCESSION

Steeped in history and brimming with fine-dining options, the Old French Concession is the place to go for diverse dining, from traditional French to local Shanghainese. With its maze of tree-lined streets and small bistros, the Concession is an excellent area to explore the cuisine and the city.

CLOSE UP

Where to Refuel Around Town

WHEN ALL YOU WANT IS A QUICK, INEXPENSIVE BITE, look for these local chains. They all have English menus and branches in Shanghai's tourist areas.

Ajisen Noodles: This Japanese-style noodle joint has an English menu with photos, and fast service.

Bi Feng Tang: Dim sum is the sum of the menu, from chickens' feet to less exotic items such as shrimp wontons and barbecue pork pastries.

Sumo Sushi: Sit along the carousel and watch the chefs slice and dice fresh made-to-order sushi. You can order set lunches, à la carte, or all you can eat.

Gino Café: The inexpensive Italian fare at this café chain includes pizza, pasta, sandwiches, and good desserts.

Manabe: This Japanese coffeehouse chain serves Western fast food, such as club sandwiches and breakfast fare, as well as Japanese snacks and a long list of teas.

American

¢–$ ✕ **Café Keven.** No-frills, Café Keven (as on the sign) or Kevin (as in the listings) is a simple café at the border of the Old French Concession and Xujiahui. The decor is café-standard wooden tables and chairs, the menus bilingual, and the service mostly attentive. Evidenced in Keven's clientele—mainly local expats having a cup and reading the paper—the food is pretty predictable: American breakfasts, sandwiches, and omelets. The coffee is cheap and fairly good, and the small courtyard can be a nice place to sit back and relax. ✉ *525 Hengshan Lu, Xuhui* ☎ *021/6433–5564* ▭ *AE, DC, MC, V.*

Cantonese

¢ ✕ **Shen Yue Xuan.** Dim sum is the big draw at Shen Yue Xuan. It's the featured fare at breakfast and lunch and has its own separate menu. The restaurant's Cantonese–Shanghainese dinner menu has a healthy slant, though the amount of grease often counteracts these efforts. The two-story restaurant is nestled in Dingxiang Garden, a verdant 35-acre playground the late Qing Dynasty–mandarin Li Hongzhang gave to his concubine Ding Xiang. There's outdoor seating on a large terrace, and the 2nd floor overlooks the garden. Book early if you want a table by the window. ✉ *849 Huashan Lu, Xuhui* ☎ *021/6251–1166* ✍ *Reservations essential* ▭ *AE, DC, MC, V.*

Chinese

$–$$ ✕ **Quan Ju De.** The original Beijing branch of this restaurant has been *the* place to get Peking duck since 1864. This Shanghai branch opened in 1998, but the Peking duck is just as popular here. Few dishes are more definitively Chinese than Peking duck, the succulent, slow-roasted bird that is never quite prepared properly overseas. The ambience here is "old Chinese" to the point of absurdity, complete with hostesses dressed in traditional imperial outfits including platform tasseled shoes and flashy headpieces, and with lattice screens scattered throughout the dining room.

The menu has both pictures and English text to explain the different types of duck available. One minor drawback is the size of the portions. There are no half-ducks on the menu, and a full duck is rather a lot for two people. ✉ *786 Huaihai Zhonglu, 4th fl., Luwan* ☎ *021/5404–5799* *Reservations essential* ▭ *AE, DC, MC, V.*

★ ¢–$ ✕ **Grape.** Entry-level Chinese food at inexpensive prices has been the Grape's calling card since the mid-1980s. This cheerful two-story restaurant remains a favorite among expatriates and travelers wandering the Former French Concession. The English menu, with photos, includes such recognizable fare as sweet-and-sour pork and lemon chicken as well as delicious dishes like garlic shrimp and *jiachang doufu* (home-style bean curd), all of which are served with a smile. ✉ *55 Xinle Lu, Luwan* ☎ *021/5404–0486* ▭ *No credit cards.*

¢–$ ✕ **Hot Pot King.** *Huo guo,* or hotpot, is a popular Chinese ritual of at-the-table cooking, in which you simmer fresh ingredients in a broth. Hot Pot King reigns over the hotpot scene in Shanghai because of its extensive menu as well as its refined setting. The most popular of the 17 broths is the yin-yang, half spicy red, half basic white pork-bone broth. Add in a mixture of veggies, seafood, meat, and dumplings for a well-rounded pot, then dip each morsel in the sauces mixed tableside by your waiter. The minimalist white and gray interior has glass-enclosed booths and well-spaced tables, a nice change from the usual crowded, noisy, hotpot joints. ✉ *1416 Huaihai Rd., 2nd fl., Xuhui* ☎ *021/6473–6380* ▭ *AE, DC, MC, V.*

5

Contemporary

$$–$$$ ✕ **Mesa.** Nestled on the quiet residential street Julu Lu, Mesa is a little hard to find. The unassuming facade is backed with a stark minimalist decor, which belies the sophistication of the seasonal menu. The cuisine is contemporary, meaning the chef has been allowed to experiment, and the results are impeccable. The wine list is comprehensive, with an excellent by-the-glass selection, and not overpriced. That, combined with some of the best service in Shanghai, makes finding Mesa well worth the effort. ✉ *748 Julu Lu, Luwan* ☎ *021/6289–9108* ▭ *AE, DC, MC, V.*

★ $–$$ ✕ **Azul and Viva.** In creating his continent-hopping New World cuisine, owner Eduardo Vargas drew upon his globe-trotting childhood and seven years as a restaurant consultant in Asia. As a result, the menus in Azul, the tapas bar downstairs, and Viva, the restaurant upstairs, feature a delicious, delicate balance of flavors that should please any palate. Classics like beef carpaccio contrast cutting-edge dishes like coffee-glazed pork. Lunch and weekend brunch specials are lower priced. The relaxed, romantic interior—dim lighting, plush pillows, and splashes of color against muted backdrops—invites you to take your time on your culinary world tour. ✉ *18 Dongping Lu, Xuhui* ☎ *021/6433–1172* ▭ *AE, DC, MC, V.*

WORD OF MOUTH

"Azul was one of the highlights of the trip: funky dj-in', great tapas (especially the calamari and as Paddies we really appreciated the magnificant mashed spuds!), cool cocktails, and laid-back vibe."

–Jenny, Ireland

$–$$ **Fodor's Choice ★** ✕ **A Future Perfect.** Hidden away down a little lane off Huashan Road, AFP has the kind of terrace space that most Shanghai-restaurant owners can only dream of: spacious, tranquil, yet intimate. It is a must for those hot afternoons and evenings in Shanghai when you need a break from shopping and sightseeing, and deserve some good food and good drinks. We recommend being adventurous; try the caviar blinis and Tuna-ba-lulla (a large portion of excellently prepared tuna) if you like seafood, or the 300 T (300 grams of tenderloin) for a carnivorous treat. The menu is fresh and there is plenty to satisfy any tastes. AFP has an on-site bakery, and serves breakfast every morning. ✉ *16, La. 351 Huashan Lu, Xuhui* ☎ *021/6248–8020* 💳 *AE, DC, MC, V.*

German

$$–$$$$ ✕ **Paulaner Brauhaus.** There's a shortage of good German food in Shanghai. Paulaner Brauhaus does its best to fill the void with a menu of classic German dishes; Wiener schnitzel, bratwurst, and apple strudel, accompanied by the house-brewed lager. The food isn't inspiring, and seems pricy, but the beer is excellent. The Fenyang Lu location is more laid-back, with a courtyard beer garden in the summer. The Xintiandi branch, open for lunch, is great for people-watching. ✉ *150 Fenyang Lu, Xuhui* ☎ *021/6474–5700* ⏲ *No lunch* ✉ *House 19-20, North Block Xintiandi, 181 Taicang Lu, Luwan* ☎ *021/6320–3935* 💳 *AE, DC, MC, V.*

Indian

$–$$$ ✕ **The Tandoor.** Don't miss the unbelievable *murgh malei kebab* (tandoori chicken marinated in cheese and yogurt mixture) or try some vegetable curries—*palak aloo* (spinach with peas) or *dal makhani* (lentil). Decorated with mirrors, Indian artwork, and Chinese characters dangling from the ceiling, the restaurant is ingeniously designed to show the route of Buddhism from India to China. The management and staff, all from India, remain close at hand throughout the meal to answer questions and attend to your needs. ✉ *Jinjiang Hotel, South Building, 59 Maoming Nan Lu, Luwan* ☎ *021/6472–5494* ✍ *Reservations essential* 💳 *AE, DC, MC, V.*

★ $ ✕ **Vedas.** In the heart of the Old French Concession, Vedas is a popular destination for quality Indian food at affordable prices. Decor is dark and comfortable. The menu focuses on northern Indian cuisine, and the hand-pulled naan bread, thick and succulent curries, fiery vindaloos, and house-made chutneys are excellent. Vedas is extremely popular, and always bustling. Don't expect an intimate, tranquil dining experience, but do expect spectacular food and great service in a pleasant if busy environment. ✉ *550 Jianguo Xi Lu, Xuhui* ☎ *021/6445–8100* ✍ *Reservations essential* 💳 *AE, DC, MC, V.*

¢–$ ✕ **Indian Kitchen.** The Indian chefs working their magic in the show kitchen provide the entertainment while you wait for a table at this tremendously popular restaurant. Delicious butter chicken marsala and tandoor-cooked chicken tikka taste as good as they look in the picture menu, which is packed with classic Indian dishes. The many bread selections include melt-in-your-mouth spring onion *parotas* (fried flat bread). Two blocks from the Hengshan Lu metro station and bar neighborhood, In-

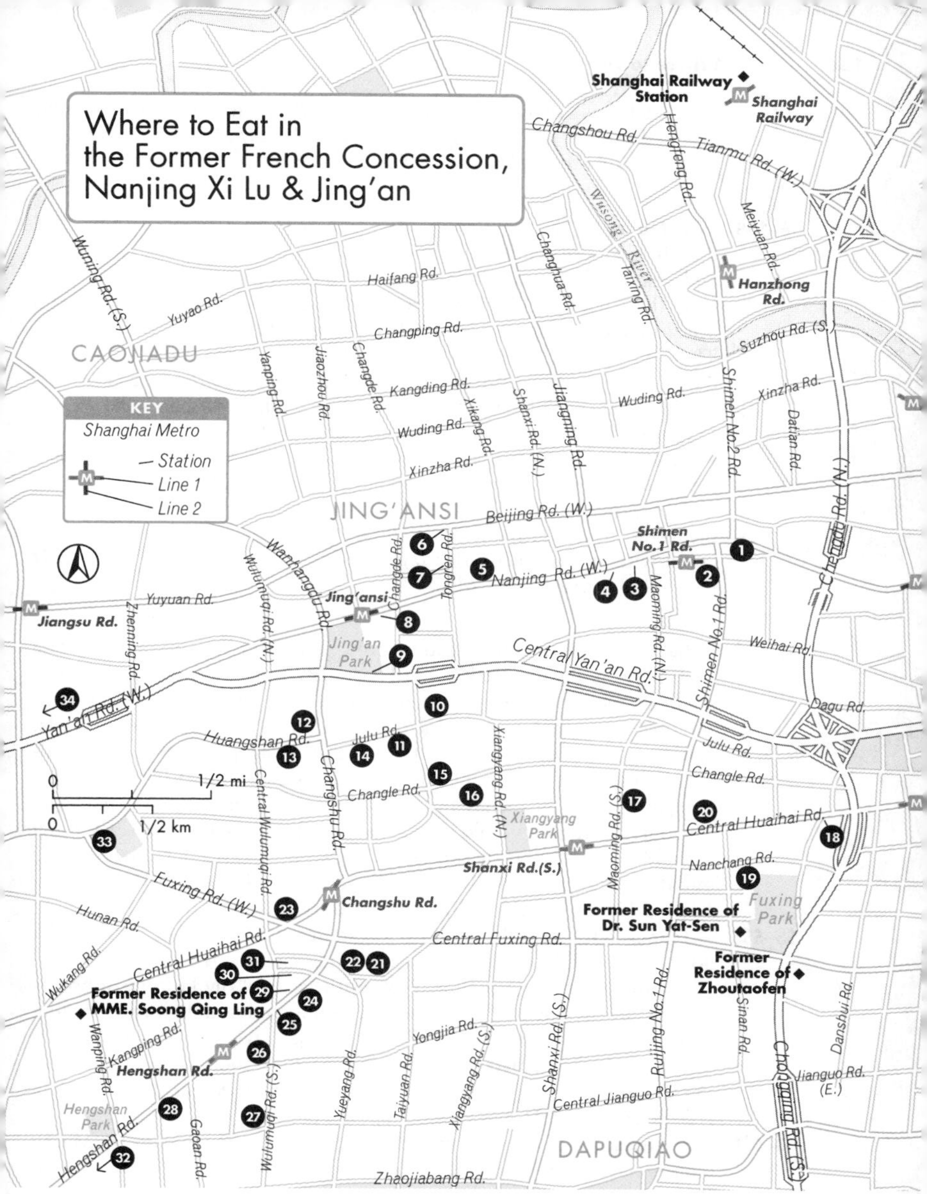

A Future Perfect 13
Baci 19
Bali Laguna 9
Bao Lu 15
Brasil 8
Café Keven 28
Da Marco 18
Dagama 32
Element Fresh 5
Gongdelin 1
Grape 16
Hot Pot King 23
Indian Kitchen 26
Leonardo's 12
Malone's 6
Meilongzhen 4
Mesa 10
Nepali Kitchen 14
O'Malley's 22
1221 34
Onion 3
Paulaner Brewhaus 21
Quan Ju De 20
Shen Yue Xuan 33
Shintori Null II 11
Simply Thai 24
South Beauty 31
Sumo Sushi 29
Taco Paco 7
Tairyo 30
Tandoor 17
239 2
Vedas 27
Yang's Kitchen 25

dian Kitchen is a convenient dining spot and the perfect start to an evening out on the town. ✉ *572 Yongjia Lu, Xuhui* ☎ *021/6473–1517* ✍ *Reservations essential* ▭ *AE, DC, MC, V.*

Irish

$–$$$ ✕ **O'Malley's.** With a fire in the hearth, a super-friendly Irish staff, and a band playing traditional tunes from the balcony, O'Malley's feels every bit like an authentic Irish pub. The old French mansion has lots of dark, cozy corners, and the huge outdoor patio is packed to capacity during broadcasts of European football (soccer) and rugby matches. The requisite Guinness and Kilkenny are on tap and complement the meat-and-potatoes menu, but all come with rather steep price tags. ✉ *42 Taojiang Lu, Xuhui* ☎ *021/6474–4533* ▭ *AE, DC, MC, V.*

> **WORD OF MOUTH**
>
> "This is a great expat hangout. Come here to watch football games or F1 races. . . . Unfortunately drinks are overpriced and food is not good at all. Come here for the atmosphere and events only!"
>
> –Slacker, American expat in Shanghai

Italian

$$–$$$ ✕ **Baci.** Good Italian food can be difficult to find in Shanghai, but one such place is Baci at Park 97 in Fuxing Park, the Shanghai entertainment complex of Hong Kong's famous Lan Kwai Fong Group. The restaurant itself is elegant and subdued, with intimate booths lining the walls. The impressive wine list includes wines from around the world, available by the glass and the bottle. The staff is courteous and knowledgeable, discussing the dishes and providing advice on good wine pairings. The only complaint would be the clubs next door in the Lan Kwai Fong complex: after 10 PM, it can get noisy, so be aware that a late dinner mightn't be so tranquil. ✉ *Fuxing Park, 2A Gaolan Rd., Xuhui* ☎ *021/5383–2328 or 021/5383–2208* ▭ *AE, DC, MC, V.*

$$–$$$ ✕ **Leonardo's.** The Hilton's Italian restaurant, Leonardo's is unusually good, with solid interpretations of Italian classics. The service is five-star standard, though the location, at the rear of the Hilton's lobby, is slightly inconvenient. The menu is seasonal, and matched with an adequate wine list, though wines are on the expensive side. The easy chairs in the da Vinci–themed dining room are a little too comfortable, making it slightly difficult to sit at table. ✉ *Hilton Shanghai, 250 Huashan Rd., Luwan* ☎ *021/6248–0000* ▭ *AE, DC, MC, V.*

$–$$$ ✕ **Da Marco.** Its reasonably priced authentic Italian fare makes Da Marco a universal favorite in Shanghai. The original location, on Dong Zhu An Bang Lu, is a magnet for Italian expats in search of a late dinner, whereas the Yandang Lu location attracts a mix of locals, expats, and tourists. Lasagna, ravioli, Caprese salad, and pizza (11 types) are among the classic dishes on the menu. The wine list includes many selections under Y200. Three-course set lunches are a popular option. You can choose alfresco dining under the bright orange awning or a comfy seat on the banquette in the sunshine-yellow dining room. ✉ *62 Yandang Lu, Luwan* ☎ *021/6385–5998* ✍ *Reservations essential* ▭ *AE, DC, MC, V.*

Japanese

$$–$$$ ✕ **Shintori Null II.** The restaurant's plain gray wall facing Julu Lu belies the futuristic design masterpiece that lies behind it. With its magic sliding doors, etched glass, and concrete airplane hangar of a dining room, the restaurant is often compared to a set from *Blade Runner.* The French-influenced Japanese cuisine uses curry and foie gras to dress up the sushi, sashimi, tempura, and noodle dishes. ✉ *803 Julu Lu, Jing'an* ☎ *021/5404–5252* ✍ *Reservations essential* ▭ *AE, DC, MC, V* ⊙ *No lunch weekdays.*

$–$$ ✕ **Tairyo.** After indulging in the Y150 all-you-can-eat teppanyaki special at Tairyo, you might feel as big as the three sumo wrestlers in the restaurant's wall-sized mural. While locals seem to prefer the cheaper à la carte menu, Westerners come here for the endless delicious servings of sashimi, scallops, lemon prawns, and some of the best beef in town. Beer, sake, wine, and plum wine are included in the price, too. ✉ *139 Ruijin Yi Lu, Luwan District* ☎ *021/5382–8818* ✉ *15 Dongping Rd., Xuhui* ☎ *021/6445–4734* ✍ *Reservations essential* ▭ *AE, DC, MC, V.*

5

Korean

¢ ✕ **Gao Li Korean Restaurant.** Hidden on a small lane, Gao Li is a bit of a hole in the wall, but its eight tables are packed with patrons until 2 AM. It serves great, cheap food and specializes in tender and delicious grilled meats. You do the cooking, placing thin cuts of meat on a small gas grill and then wrapping them in a lettuce leaf and adding chili sauce. The noodle dishes are some of the best in town: try the cold Korean noodles for dessert. ✉ *No. 1, 181 Wuyuan Lu, Xuhui* ☎ *021/6431–5236* ▭ *AE, DC, MC, V.*

Nepalese

¢ ✕ **Nepali Kitchen.** An intimate space with low tables and cushions upstairs, and paper-lamp-lit small tables downstairs, Nepali Kitchen is a cozy spot to sample the subtleties of Nepalese fare. In addition to the curries and naan found at most Indian restaurants, there are tasty starters like fried cheese balls and potato chili. ✉ *La. 819, 4 Julu Rd., Xuhui* ☎ *021/5404–6281* ✍ *Reservations essential* ▭ *No credit cards* ⊙ *Closed Mon.*

Shanghainese

¢–$$ ✕ **Yang's Kitchen.** Traditional Shanghainese food without the usual *renao* (hot and noisy atmosphere) draws customers down the narrow laneway to the restored villa that's now home to Yang's Kitchen. The 19-page menu includes familiar dishes like mandarin fish, the obligatory *xiaolongbao,* as well as 22 soups. An apricot-and-white side

> **WORD OF MOUTH**
>
> "One place where you won't have to worry about being surrounded by the Americans you saw on the Bund. A true local hangout. Enormous, noisy and authentic. Go with a group, the bigger the better But study the gigantic menu carefully. "Shredded chicken" is a pigeon in seven pieces, including the head. With anything you order, you'll be tasting the 'real thing.' "
>
> –John Mihalec, Connecticut

dining room with small tables spaced widely for privacy is popular among couples and solo diners seeking a quiet and inexpensive meal. ✉ *No. 3, 9 Hengshan Lu, Xuhui* ☎ *021/6445–8418* ▭ *AE, DC, MC, V.*

¢–$ ✕ **Bao Luo.** Although its English menu caters to tourists, Bao Luo is Chinese dining as the Chinese enjoy it, a fact confirmed by the usual long wait for a table. The freshness of the ingredients comes through in every dish, from perfectly steamed broccoli to tender stewed crab and pork meatballs. Tables are packed tightly in this small two-story restaurant, and the light-wood interior merely serves as backdrop to the can't-miss cuisine. However, look closely for the red-scroll neon sign with a tiny BL, or you may miss the restaurant altogether. ✉ *271 Fumin Lu, by Changle Lu, Jing'an* ☎ *021/5403–7239* ⚠ *Reservations essential* ▭ *No credit cards.*

Sichuan

$$–$$$ ✕ **Sichuan Court.** Get a sky-high view of the city at this upscale eatery at the top of the Hilton. As a starter, the Sichuan treasure box combines several delicacies: cold sliced garlic pork, sliced suckling pig, sliced duck, and some cold vegetables. The Chengdu tea-smoked duck, *mapo doufu* (spicy tofu), and *dan dan* (noodles) are typical of the Sichuan dishes served here. ✉ *Shanghai Hilton, 250 Huashan Lu, Jing'an* ☎ *021/6248–0000* ⚠ *Reservations essential* ▭ *AE, DC, MC, V.*

★ $–$$ ✕ **South Beauty.** The elegant interior and spicy fare are both worth beholding at South Beauty. As the sliding-glass front door opens—revealing a walkway between two cascading walls of water—it splits the restaurant's trademark red Chinese-opera mask in two. Likewise, the menu is split down the middle between cooler Cantonese cuisine and sizzling hot Sichuan fare. Don't be fooled: even dishes with a one-pepper rating, like sautéed baby lobster, will singe your sinuses. ✉ *28 Taojiang Lu, Xuhui* ☎ *021/6445–2581* ⚠ *Reservations essential* ▭ *AE, DC, MC, V.*

Spanish

$$ ✕ **Le Garçon Chinois.** This dimly lit restaurant in an old French villa is a favorite spot for couples on a date. The walls are painted in warm hues, the art-deco fittings are tasteful, and large windows frame surrounding trees and old mansions. Run by a Japanese–European couple, the restaurant presents a predominantly Spanish menu, with several tapas and paella selections. ✉ *No. 3, La. 9, Hengshan Lu, Xuhui* ☎ *021/6445–7970* ⚠ *Reservations essential* ▭ *AE, DC, MC, V* ⊙ *No lunch.*

Thai

¢–$$ ✕ **Simply Thai.** Unpretentious Thai fare at moderate prices has earned
Fodor's Choice ★ this restaurant a loyal expat clientele. Customers flock to the tree-shaded patio to savor such favorites as green and red curries (on the spicy side) and stir-fried rice noodles with chicken (on the tame side). The appetizers are all first-rate, especially the crispy spring rolls and samosas. The wine list includes a half-dozen bottles under Y200 ($25), a rarity in Shanghai. The branch in Xintiandi is a bit noisier but features the same great food and prices. ✉ *5C Dongping Rd., Xuhui* ☎ *021/6445–9551* ⚠ *Reservations essential* ▭ *AE, DC, MC, V.*

PUDONG

Steep and shining, the skyscraper-rich financial district of Pudong is home to a surprising number of high-class eateries. The many five-star hotels are modern and luxurious, and boast some of Shanghai's most popular restaurants, including the Shangri-la's Yi Café and the Hyatt's towering Cloud 9.

Contemporary

$-$$$ ✕ **Cloud 9.** Pudong can be an intimidating concrete jungle, with little respite in sight. If you're looking for refreshment on your Pudong safari, try Cloud 9 on the 87th floor of the Hyatt. Be aware, this is not a cheap lounge—there is a Y120 minimum and dress code, but the view is spectacular. Kick back and drink in the city laid out beneath you, while nibbling at their tasty Asian-inspired tapas and snacks. ✉ *Grand Hyatt, 87th fl., 88 Shiji Dadao, Pudong* ☎ *021/5049–1234* ✍ *Reservations essential* 💳 *AE, DC, MC, V.*

5

Continental

$$-$$$$ ✕ **Grand Café.** Two of the Grand Hyatt's restaurants (the other is the Grill, *below*) present continental cuisine with absolutely spectacular views of Shanghai—unless the building is shrouded in fog. The sophisticated 24-hour restaurant touts its "show kitchen" buffet, which includes appetizers, daily specials, fresh seafood, and desserts. ✉ *Grand Hyatt, 88 Shiji Dadao, Pudong* ☎ *021/5049–1234* ✍ *Reservations essential* 💳 *AE, DC, MC, V.*

$$-$$$$ ✕ **The Grill.** Part of the Hyatt's three-in-one, open-kitchen restaurant concept, the Grill shares the 56th floor with two other restaurants (serving Japanese and Italian cuisine). At the Grill you can feast on a great seafood platter or unbelievably tender steak. ✉ *Grand Hyatt, 88 Shiji Dadao, Pudong* ☎ *021/5049–1234* ✍ *Reservations essential* 💳 *AE, DC, MC, V.*

WORD OF MOUTH

"I was looking for a good steak, and The Grill delivered! There is not a more magnificent view anywhere than at the Grand Hyatt Hotel, and if you want a good rib-eye steak, this is a can't miss in Shanghai."

–Dan Hooker, New Jersey

International

$$$$ ✕ **Jade on 36.** This is a restaurant that must be experienced to be believed. Perched on the 36th floor of the Shangri-La tower, the Jade lounge/restaurant is simply beautiful. There is no à la carte menu; instead, diners choose from a selection of set menus named simply for colors and sizes. The cuisine is innovative and extremely fresh, the service impeccable, and the view pleasant. Menus vary from five to eight courses, with an emphasis on fresh seafood and tender meats. The jumbo shrimp in a jar is especially enjoyable, as is the signature lemon tart. It's an expensive indulgence, but worth every penny. ✉ *Pudong Shangri-La, 36th fl., 33 Fu Cheng Lu, Pudong* ☎ *021/6882–8888* 💳 *AE, DC, MC, V.*

Fodor's Choice ★

Cloud 9 5
Danieli's 9
Grand Cafe 7
The Grill 6
Itoya 8
Jade on 36 4
Nadaman 2
South Beauty . . . 1
Yi Cafe 3

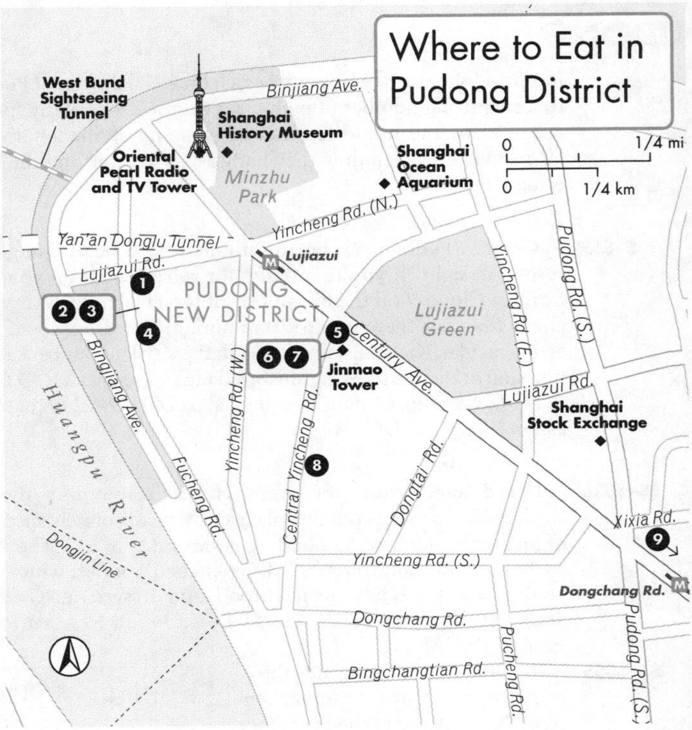

$$$ ✕ **Yi Café.** Popular and busy, the Yi Café at the Shangri-La is open-kitchen dining at its finest, serving a world of cuisines. The Yi Café is very popular with the Lujiazui business set, as well as local diners for the quality and variety of the food. It's a great place to people-watch over a selection of the finest dishes Asia has to offer. This experience doesn't come cheap, at Y268 per person, but it's worth it. The restaurant is slightly underrepresented in Western cuisine, focusing more on Asian dishes. ✉ *Pudong Shangri-La, 2nd fl., 33 Fu Cheng Lu, Pudong* ☎ *021/6882–8888* 💳 *AE, DC, MC, V.*

Italian

★ **$$–$$$** ✕ **Danieli's.** This is one of the finest Italian restaurants in the city, and worth the commute to Pudong. The intimate dining area is spacious without being overwhelming, and the staff is very well trained. Their business lunch is famed for its speed and quality, but it is at dinner that Danieli's really shines. The menu is well balanced with seasonal dishes, and boasts an excellent five-course set menu. Prices can be expensive, especially for wine, but it is worth the money. We recommend the set menu with a bottle of the superb Green Point by Chandon sparkling wine. ✉ *St. Regis, 889 Dongfang Lu, Pudong* ☎ *021/5050–4567* ✍ *Reservations essential* 💳 *AE, DC, MC, V.*

Japanese

$$–$$$$ ✕ **Nadaman.** Sleekly elegant and stylized, Nadaman is modern Japanese dining taken to its extreme. The accents of raw granite merged into a formalized designer interior shows the signs of the restaurant's origins in the modern Tokyo, looking almost overdesigned. With a focus on freshness and presentation, Nadaman gives diners superb cuisine at a price tag to match. The sushi is some of the finest in the city. ✉ *Pudong Shangri-La, 2nd fl., 33 Fu Cheng Lu, Pudong* ☎ *021/6882–8888* ✍ *Reservations essential* ▭ *AE, DC, MC, V.*

$–$$ ✕ **Itoya.** The waitstaff's precision teamwork makes dining at Itoya a pleasure. Servers pause to greet all guests in unison. You're handed a hot towel upon sitting down and instantly after finishing your meal. The menu sticks to traditional Japanese fare: tempura, sushi, sashimi. In line with its location directly across from the Grand Hyatt's entrance, the restaurant also has several budget-busting items such as Kobe beef and lobster sashimi. ✉ *178 Huayuan Shiqiao Lu, Pudong* ☎ *021/5882–9679* ▭ *AE, DC, MC, V.*

5

Sichuan

$–$$ ✕ **South Beauty.** From its perch atop the top floor of the Super Brand Mall, the Pudong branch of South Beauty has a sweeping view of the beauty of the Bund. Although half of its menu is Cantonese, the restaurant is known for its sizzling hot Sichuan fare. Even dishes with a one-pepper rating will scorch your mouth. ✉ *Super Brand Mall, 10th fl., 168 Lujiazui Lu, Pudong* ☎ *021/5047–1817* ▭ *AE, DC, MC, V.*

NANJING XI LU & JING'AN

A business hub that is home to some of the finest hotels in the city, the Jing'an area is understandably heavy on Western-dining options. Familiar American franchises like Tony Roma's rub shoulders with Buddhist restaurants and popular expat destinations like Element Fresh and Malone's, making this a vibrant dining destination.

American

★ **$–$$** ✕ **Element Fresh.** Freshly made and generously portioned salads and sandwiches draw crowds of people to this bright lunch spot in the Shanghai Center. The creative menu of innovative sandwiches, light pasta dishes and excellent salads has made Element Fresh one of the most popular lunch destinations in the city. For the health-conscious, an equally creative drink menu has long lists of fresh fruit juices and smoothies. ✉ *Shanghai Center, 1376 Nanjing Xi Lu, Jing'an* ☎ *021/6279–8682* ▭ *AE, DC, MC, V.*

$–$$ ✕ **Malone's American Café.** An attempt at a classic American sports bar in Shanghai, Malone's is very popular with the expat crowd. Its substantial menu includes American favorites like buffalo wings, burgers, and pizza, as well as Asian dishes. The food isn't superb but it's satisfying as a casual meal in a cheerful bar setting. ✉ *255 Tongren Lu, Jing'an* ☎ *021/6247–2400* ▭ *AE, DC, MC, V.*

FODOR'S FIRST PERSON

Rachel King Berlin
Fodor's writer

I've stopped cooking since moving to Shanghai, preferring to wander out of my apartment to explore the small family-owned restaurants in my neighborhood in a quiet area of the Old French Concession. My favorite is the Harbin Dumpling House, a five-table hole-in-the-wall that sells boiled dumplings by the pound. The restaurant is cramped between a bicycle-repair shop and a dingy hair salon. The kitchen opens onto the street and there are always large bundles of green onions, Napa cabbage, and long cucumbers stacked on the sidewalk. Before going into the restaurant, I like to stop and watch the cooks in their dirty white uniforms as they expertly fold the dumplings and drop them into vats of boiling water.

During the lunch-hour rush, the owner, a tall man in his forties who chain smokes Double Happiness cigarettes, sets up folding tables on the sidewalk for the neighborhood's construction workers. They arrive at noon, their baggy blue clothes and orange safety helmets covered in dust. They have come from the countryside to find whatever work they can in Shanghai. They stare at me, laughing at our white skin and "tall" noses. But their laughter is not malicious and they always shout a hearty "Hallooo!" when they see us.

None of the Dumpling House's waitstaff speaks English and, even after three months, they are still excited to hear me speaking Chinese. I typically order edamame steamed with star anise, cucumber wedges with fermented bean and pork sauce, and two huge plates of steaming pork-and-cabbage dumplings that I dip in vinegar and hot chili oil. The bill for the whole meal comes to about US$1.50. I eat at the Dumpling House so often that if I don't show up for a couple days, the waitresses will ask us where we've been. Even after a year in Shanghai, having eaten at Jean-Georges and Laris, Crystal Jade and Meilongzhen, I still keep coming back to the Harbin Dumpling House, always preferring a plate of pork and cabbage dumplings to all the other fabulous food Shanghai has to offer.

Brazilian

$ ✕ Brasil Steak House. Shanghai has developed a taste for *churrascarias*, Brazilian-style barbecue restaurants. Brasil Steak House is perhaps the best, due in large part to the percentage of South Americans on staff. The all-you-can-eat lunches and dinners pair a salad bar with an unending rotation of waiters brandishing skewers of juicy chunks of meat for your consideration; just nod your approval and they'll slice off a piece for your plate. The large picture windows brighten up the room and let you observe the parade of people passing through Jing'an Park. ✉ *1649 Nanjing Xi Lu, Jing'an* ☎ *021/6255–9898* 💳 *AE, DC, MC, V.*

Cantonese

$$–$$$$ ✕ **Summer Pavilion.** Helmed by Ho Wing, the former chef of Hong Kong's famed Jockey Club, Summer Pavilion serves delicious Cantonese specialties ranging from simple dim sum to delicacies such as shark fin, bird's nest soup, and abalone. As befits the Portman Ritz-Carlton, the restaurant's dining room is elegant, with black and gold accents and a raised platform that makes you feel as though you're center stage—a sense heightened by the attentive servers, who stand close, but not too close, at hand, anticipating your needs. ✉ *Portman Ritz-Carlton, 2nd fl., 1376 Nanjing Xi Lu, Jing'an* ☎ *021/6279–8888* *Reservations essential* ▭ *AE, DC, MC, V.*

$–$$ ✕ **The Onion.** On the high-traffic sector of Nanjing Xi Lu, Onion is a simple concept Cantonese restaurant, serving quality Cantonese dishes at reasonable prices. The decor is light and airy, with well-spaced tables and efficient service. The menu is extensive and bilingual, with lunch specials and dim sum. This is a very low stress restaurant, and a great destination for a simple and satisfying meal. ✉ *881 Nanjing Xi Lu, 3rd fl., Jing'an* ☎ *021/6267–5477* ▭ *No credit cards.*

5

Chinese Vegetarian

¢–$ ✕ **Gongdelin.** A two-story gold engraving of Buddha pays tribute to the origins of the inventive vegetarian dishes this restaurant has served for 80 years. Chefs transform tofu into such surprising and tasty creations as mock duck, eel, and pork. The interior is just as inspired, with Ming-style, wood-and-marble tables; metal latticework; and a soothing fountain. Tables fill up quickly after 6 PM, so either arrive early or buy some goodies to go at the take-out counter. ✉ *445 Nanjing Xi Lu, Huangpu* ☎ *021/6327–0218* ▭ *AE, DC, MC, V.*

> **WORD OF MOUTH**
>
> "I would go back to Shanghai just to eat at this place—the vegetarian cuisine is amazing!!!"
>
> —Rebecca Schmal, Canada

French

$$–$$$ ✕ **Le Bouchon.** This charming French wine bar and bistro serves up tasty traditional French fare in a cozy 12-table hideaway. The Y350 degustation menu is a greatest hits of French cuisine: escargot, foie gras, and duck breast. The baked Alaska (ice cream over a sponge cake topped with meringue), a rare treat in Shanghai, must be ordered separately, and it's worth it. The wine list includes two dozen reasonably priced French selections. ✉ *1455 Wuding Xi Lu, Changning* ☎ *021/6225–7088* *Reservations essential* ▭ *AE, DC, MC, V* ⊙ *No lunch. Closed Sun.*

Fusion

$–$$$ ✕ **239.** A project of Eduardo Vargas, the man behind Azul and Viva, 239 is new concept European dining, with Asian-influenced French dishes served in the Chinese fashion. This shared-plate dining is a little unusual for the cuisine, but it works—and the more diners, the better. The service is well trained and attentive, and the dining room nicely designed. One gripe: with its entrance surrounded by an office-supply wholesaler, 239 can be a little difficult to find. A nice touch: there is a no-smoking policy in effect in the dining room until 10 PM. ✉ *239 Shimen Yi Rd., Jing'an* ☎ *021/6253–2837* ▭ *AE, DC, MC, V.*

Italian

$$–$$$ ✕ **Palladio.** As befits the showcase Italian Restaurant at the Ritz, the award-winning Palladio is simply excellent. With a seasonal menu and positively obsequious service, this restaurant will always satisfy your senses—though it might also deplete your wallet. Set lunches begin at Y198, and dinners soar into the heady heights. ✉ *Portman Ritz-Carlton, 1376 Nanjing West Rd., Jing'an* ☎ *021/6279–7188* ✍ *Reservations essential* ▭ *AE, DC, MC, V.*

Indonesian

$–$$ ✕ **Bali Laguna.** Overlooking the lily pond in Jing'an Park and with interior and alfresco dining, Bali Laguna is a popular choice for couples. Balinese music piped along the statue- and palm-lined walkway sets the mood even before the sarong-clad hostess welcomes you inside the traditional, three-story, Indonesian-style house or to a pondside table. The menu is heavy on seafood, such as grilled fish cakes and chili crab, which captures the fire of Indonesian cuisine. Quench it with a Nusa Dua Sunset or other Bali-inspired cocktail. ✉ *Jing'an Park, 189 Huashan Lu, Jing'an* ☎ *021/6248–6970* ✍ *Reservations essential* ▭ *AE, DC, MC, V.*

Japanese

$$–$$$ ✕ **Hanagatami.** Despite its location at the Ritz, Hanagatami is fairly average. The food is good, but lacks the flair expected of a showcase Japanese restaurant, especially considering the prices. Still, the seafood is very fresh and the service good, in a fairly traditional Japanese dining environment. ✉ *Portman Ritz-Carlton , 1376 Nanjing West Rd., Jing'an* ☎ *021/6279–8888* ▭ *AE, DC, MC, V.*

Korean

$$–$$$ ✕ **Arirang.** One of Shanghai's oldest Korean eateries, Arirang serves meat and seafood barbecued on smoky coals right before your eyes, along with *kimchi* (pickled cabbage), noodles, and cold appetizers. The meat dishes are a good choice here, as is the always delicious *congyoubing*, or onion pancake. ✉ *28 Jiangsu Bei Lu, 2nd fl., Changning* ☎ *021/6252–7146* ▭ *AE, DC, MC, V.*

Mexican

¢ ✕ **Taco Popo.** The tiny Taco Popo is packed around the clock with customers craving its Mexican fast-food fare. The dozen seats along the diner counter fill up the quickest—especially right after the bars have closed—but there's more seating upstairs. The menu is short but solid, with tacos, burritos, enchiladas, and quesadillas. Throw in another Y5 to Y10 for extras like sour cream or tortilla chips. ✉ *70–80 Tongren Lu, 3rd fl., Jing'an* ☎ *021/6289–3602* ✍ *Reservations not accepted* ▭ *No credit cards.*

Shanghainese

★ $–$$ ✕ **1221.** This stylish but casual eatery is a favorite of hip Chinese and expatriate regulars. The dining room is streamlined chic, its crisp white tablecloths contrasting the warm golden walls. Shanghainese food is the mainstay, with a few Sichuan dishes. From the extensive 26-page menu (in English, pinyin, and Chinese), you can order dishes like sliced *you tiao* (fried bread sticks) with shredded beef, a whole chicken in a green-onion soy sauce, and *shaguo shizi tou* (pork meatballs). ✉ *1221 Yanan Xi Lu, Changning* ☎ *021/6213–6585 or 021/6213–2441* ✍ *Reservations essential* ▭ *AE, DC, MC, V.*

$–$$$ Fodor'sChoice ★ ✕ **Meilongzhen.** Probably Shanghai's most famous restaurant, Meilongzhen is one of the oldest dining establishments in town, dating from 1938. The building served as the Communist Party headquarters in the 1930s, and the traditional Chinese dining rooms still have their intricate woodwork, and mahogany and marble furniture. The exhaustive menu has more than 80 seafood options, including such traditional Shanghainese fare as Mandarin fish, and dishes with a more Sichuan flair, like shredded spicy eel and prawns in chili sauce. Since this is a stop for most tour buses, expect a wait if you haven't booked ahead. ✉ *No. 22, 1081 Nanjing Xi Lu, Jing'an* ☎ *021/6253–5353* ✍ *Reservations essential* ▭ *AE, DC, MC, V.*

> **WORD OF MOUTH**
>
> "Meilongzhen is the most famous in the area for Shanghainese food. The huge menu makes your eyes water, yet every dish is delicious and well-presented."
>
> –Shanghaihese

Sichuan

¢–$$ ✕ **Ba Guo Bu Yi.** Its name translates as "Sichuan Common People," which describes both the restaurant's style of food and the local clientele it attracts. The menu is a greatest hits of Sichuan cuisine, including *mapo tofu,* braised tofu with chili and brown pepper, and *lazi ji,* chicken smothered in chili peppers. The two-story dining room is arranged like a traditional Chinese house, around a central courtyard. ✉ *1018 Dingxi Lu, Changning* ☎ *021/5239–7779* ✍ *Reservations essential* ▭ *No credit cards.*

Thai

$–$$$ ✕ **Irene's.** This traditional Thai teak house certainly stands out from its neighbors on Tongren Lu. The inside is just as distinctive, with pink and purple textiles, golden statues, and a platform with low tables and cushions on the floor. The food is good but not as inspired as the surroundings and somewhat overpriced. Spring rolls, pineapple rice, and papaya salad are among the best choices. Consider going on a Monday or Friday, when a Y150 all-you-can-eat special lets you sample across the menu. ✉ *263 Tongren Lu, Jing'an* ☎ *021/6247–3579* ✍ *Reservations essential* ▭ *AE, DC, MC, V.*

NORTH SHANGHAI

Often neglected, North Shanghai is a historic neighborhood, with several fine options for eating. This is not a place to go in search of Western dining, but it has a selection of good Chinese restaurants.

5

Chinese

¢–$ ✕ **Yue Garden.** In the Great Wall Wing of the Holiday Inn Downtown, Yue Garden serves Cantonese and Shanghainese classics. The dishes are well prepared and presented, and the service is always good. Close to the train station and reasonably priced, Yue Garden is a good option for travelers coming through. ✉ *Holiday Inn Downtown, 585 Heng Feng Rd., 2nd fl., Zhabei* ☎ *021/6353–8008* ▭ *AE, DC, MC, V.*

HONGQIAO & GUBEI

The neighborhoods of Hongqiao, with its conference centers and hotels, and Gubei, with its high-end residential properties, have a few great options. The most noteworthy is Giovanni's in the Sheraton, a solidly traditional Italian bistro that is often overlooked.

Café

¢–$ ✕ **Wagas.** Serving sandwiches, salads, and coffees, Wagas is a popular lunch stop and good for a quick refill when shopping. The food is decent and the service speedy, but there is little else that is distinctive about this easily accessible chain café. ✉ *Maxdo Building, 86 Xia Xia Lu, Luwan* ☎ *021/5208–1978* ▭ *No credit cards.*

Cantonese

$–$$ ✕ **The Dynasty.** Although its cuisine is mostly Cantonese, Dynasty does serve some other regional fare, such as first-rate Peking duck and Sichuan-influenced hot-and-sour soup. The Cantonese seafood dishes, especially the prawns and lobster, are particularly good, and the shrimp *jiaozi* (dumplings) are delicious. Keyhole cutouts in the subdued pewter walls showcase Chinese vases and artifacts. Thick carpets mute any hotel noise, but the prices quickly remind you this is indeed a hotel restaurant. ✉ *Renaissance Yangtze, 2099 Yanan Xi Lu, Changning* ☎ *021/6275–0000* ✍ *Reservations essential* ▭ *AE, DC, MC, V.*

Indian

¢ ✕ **Indian Kitchen.** The second outpost of Indian Kitchen (the other is in the Old French Concession, *above*) features the same great food but in a more attractive setting: the cozy rooms of a renovated house. Delicious butter chicken marsala and tandoor-cooked chicken tikka taste as good as they look in the picture menu, which is packed with classic Indian dishes. The many bread selections include yummy spring onion parotas. ✉ *House 8, 3911 Hongmei Lu, Changning* ☎ *021/6261–0377* ✍ *Reservations essential* ▭ *AE, DC, MC, V.*

Italian

★ $$–$$$ ✕ **Giovanni's.** Its Italian courtyard with a penthouse view provides a wonderful backdrop for Giovanni's traditional Italian fare. The antipasta and calamari are delicious, and the pastas are served perfectly al dente. Once dark and gloomy, Giovanni's has recently been renovated into a bright and colorful bistro. Seasonal promotions add a taste of Tuscany and other regions to the menu. ✉ *Sheraton Grand Tai Ping Yang, 27th fl., 5 Zunyi Nan Lu, Changning* ☎ *021/6275–8888* ✍ *Reservations essential* ▭ *AE, DC, MC, V.*

Taiwanese

¢–$ ✕ **Bellagio.** Taiwanese expatriates pack the bright, sunlit dining room of Bellagio for an authentic taste of home. Red fabric–covered chairs and black streamlined tables contrast the white walls and decorative moldings. Waiters, chic in black sweaters, move efficiently between the closely spaced tables. The menu includes such traditional entrées as three-cup chicken as well as 25 noodle dishes spanning all of Southeast Asia. Save room for dessert: shaved-ice snacks are obligatory Taiwanese treats and come in 14 varieties. ✉ *778 Huangjin Cheng Dao, by Gubei Lu, Changning* ☎ *021/6278–0722* ✍ *Reservations not accepted* ▭ *AE, DC, MC, V.*

XUJIAHUI & SOUTH SHANGHAI

5

Once solely a shopping destination for locals, Xujiahui has blossomed into the center of the southwest. Good dining is a little hard to find; the majority of restaurants still cater to Chinese-style fast food, but there are some diamonds in the rough.

American

¢–$ ✕ **Rendezvous Café.** With its inexpensive menu of juicy hamburgers and bacon-and-eggs breakfasts, Rendezvous Café is as close to an American diner as you'll find in Shanghai. Owner Richard Soo ran its namesake predecessor in San Francisco before pulling up stakes for Taiwan, then Shanghai. The café's coffee selections are equally satisfying, which is no surprise considering that Soo also owns a nearby coffee shop. ✉ *435 Jin Feng Lu, Minhang* ☎ *021/5226–4353* ▭ *MC, V.*

Brazilian

$–$$ ✕ **Dagama Barbeque.** This can't be considered fine dining, but it is good, and particularly satisfying for families who are shopped out after a long day. A churrascaria done Shanghai style, Dagama serves all-you-can-eat grilled meats carved at your table, has a buffet of sides and desserts, and occasionally a band plays Sino-pop versions of American classics. It's an excellent value for the money, especially if you've got a big appetite. ✉ *Metro City, 8th fl., by Caoxi Bei Lu, 1111 Zhaojiabang Lu, Xuhui* ☎ *021/6426–7056* ▭ *No credit cards.*

International

$–$$$ ✕ **Garden Court.** Open-kitchen buffet dining on the west end, the Garden Court is an acceptable option for an easy lunch or dinner. The food is good, though the selection limited, and the price is quite reasonable. Although the lobby of the hotel is a bit faded, the restaurant is newly renovated, and the service is well trained. ✉ *Huating Hotel, Caoxi Bei Lu, Xuhui* ☎ *021/6439–1000* ▭ *AE, DC, MC, V.*

STREET SNACKS

Shanghai's street snacks are the city's main culinary claim to fame. You'll see countless sidewalk stands selling the famed *xiaolongbao,* (Shanghai's signature steamed dumplings, filled with pork or crab and soup broth) as well as various types of *bing* (Chinese pancakes), and *baozi* (filled or unfilled steamed buns).

Middle Eastern

¢–$ ✕ **Shanghai Xinjiang Fengwei Restaurant.** You'll probably hear this restaurant before you see its blue-canopied entrance and street-side kabob stand; pounding Xinjiang (Middle Eastern) music throbs from the second-story windows. The lively singing waitstaff frequently recruits diners as dance partners; service often falters as a result. The traditional Xinjiang menu is heavy on lamb but also includes a few chicken and fish dishes. A bottle of Xinjiang black beer is a must to wash it all down. ✉ *280 Yishan Lu, Xuhui* ☎ *021/6468–9198* ▭ *No credit cards.*

Southeast Asian

$–$$ ✕ **Oriental.** Professing a cuisine called MTV—Myanmar (Burmese), Thai, and Vietnamese—Oriental has the most traditional Southeast Asian food in the city. The decorations, however, are quite modern. It's an unusually fine Asian restaurant for the Xujiahui area, and well worth checking out. ✉ *392 Tianping Rd., 3rd fl., Xuhui* ☎ *021/6447–6579* ▭ *AE, DC, MC, V.*

At a Glance

ENGLISH	PINYIN	CHINESE CHARACTERS
POINTS OF INTEREST		
Element Fresh	Xīn Yuánsù	新元素
Arirang	ā Lǐ Láng	阿里郎
Bali Laguna	Dōushì Táohuā Yuán	都市桃花源
Barbarossa	Bā Bā Lù Shā	芭芭露莎
Bellagio	Băi Lè Gōng	百乐宫
Brasil Steak House	Bā Xī Shāokăo Wū	巴西烧烤屋
Café Keven	Kăiwén Xī Cāntīng	凯文西餐厅
California Grill	Jiāzhōu Bā Fáng	加州扒房
Cameo	Kă Měi ào	卡美奥
Cloud 9	Jiŭ Chóng Tiān	九重天
Da Marco	Dà Mă Kě	大马可
Dagama Barbeque	Dá Jiā Mă	达加马
EEST–The Crystal Garden	Shuǐ Jīng Yuàn	水晶苑
Family Li Imperial Cuisine	Lì Jiā Cài	历家菜
Gao Li Korean Restaurant	Gāolì Cāntīng	高丽餐厅
Garden Court	Huā Yuán	花园
Giovanni's	Jí Fàn Ní Sī	吉范尼斯
Gongdelin	Gōngdé Lín	功德林
Grand Café	Jīnmào Jūnyuè Kāfēi Tīng	金茂君悦咖啡厅
Grape	Pútáo Yuán	葡萄园
Hanagatami	Huākuāng Rì Cāntīng	花筐日餐厅
Hot Pot King	Lái Fú Lóu	来福楼
Indian Kitchen	Yìndù Xiăo Chú	印度小厨
Irene's	Ōu Fēng Tàiguó Cāntīng	欧风泰国餐厅
Itoya	Yīténg Jiā	伊藤家
Jade on 36	Fěicuì Sān Shí Liù	翡翠36
Kabb	Kăi Bó Xī	凯博西
La Seine	Sāi Nà Hé	塞纳河
Laris	Lù Wéi Xuān	陆唯轩
Le Bouchon	Bó Xùn	勃逊
Lu Bo Lang	Lǜbō Láng Jiŭlóu	绿波廊酒楼
Malone's American Café	Mă Lóng Měishì Cāntīng	马龙美式餐厅

5

Masala Art	Xiāngliào Yìshù	香料艺术
Mediterranean Café	Dìzhōnghǎi Xīcān Tīng	地中海西餐厅
Meilongzhen	Méi Lóng Zhèn	梅龙镇
Mesa	Méi Sà Cāntīng	梅萨餐厅
Mexico Lindo	Língdé Mòxīgē Cāntīng	灵得墨西哥餐厅
Nadaman	Tān Wàn	滩万
Nepali Kitchen	Níbóěr Chúfáng	尼泊尔厨房
Oriental	Dōngfāng Yàzhōu Měishí Jīngcuì	东方亚洲美食精粹
Palladio	Pà Lán Duǒ	帕兰朵
Paulaner Brauhaus	Bǎoláinà Cāntīng	宝莱纳餐厅
Quan Ju De	Quán Jù Dé	全聚德
Rendezvous Café	Lǎng Dí Mǔ	朗迪姆
Sens & Bund	Yǎ Dé	雅德
Shanghai Xinjiang Fengwei Restaurant	Shànghǎi Xīnjiāng Fēngwèi Fàndiàn	上海新疆风味饭店
Shen Yue Xuan	Shēn Yuè Xuān	申粤轩
Shintori Null II	Xīdūlǐ Wú'èr Diàn	新都里无二店
Sichuan Court	Tiān Fǔ Lóu	天府楼
Simply Thai	Tiān tài Cāntīng	天泰餐厅
South Beauty	Qiào Jiāng Nán	俏江南
Summer Pavilion	Xià Yuàn	夏苑
Tairyo	Tài Láng	太郎
Tan Wai Lou	Tān Wài Lóu	滩外楼
The Dynasty	Mǎn Fú Lóu	满福楼
The Grill	Měishì Shāokǎo	美式烧烤
The Onion	Yángcōng Cāntīng	洋葱餐厅
The Tandoor	Tiāndūlǐ Yìndù Cāntīng	天都里印度餐厅
Wagas	Huá Jiā Sī	华佳思
Wagas Maxdo	Huá Jiā Sī (Huáihǎi Diàn)	华佳思（淮海店）
Wanjia Denghuo	Wàn Jiā Dēng Huǒ	万家灯火
Whampoa Club	Huáng Pǔ Huì	黄埔会
Yang's Kitchen	Yángjiā Chúfáng	杨家厨房
Yi Café	Yí Kāfēi	怡咖啡
Yue Garden	Yuè Yuán	粤园

Where to Stay

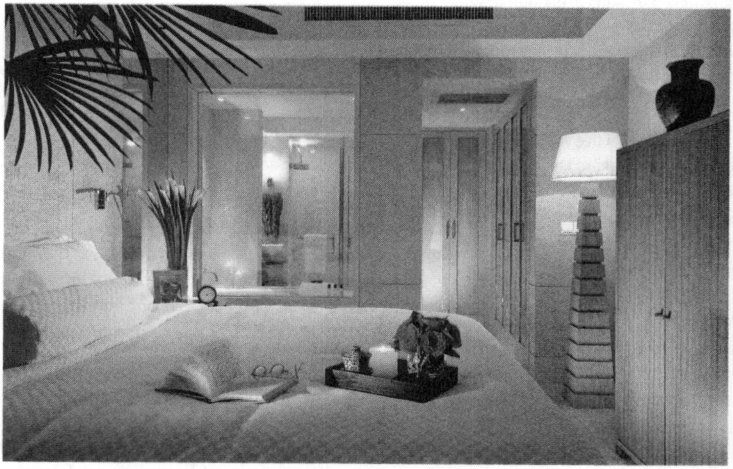

The Westin Bund Center

WORD OF MOUTH

"If you don't want to spend too much time in taxis . . . book [a hotel] in the central area even if it costs a bit more."

–Shanghainese

"When you leave your hotel, take a card with the name of your hotel—in Chinese—so if you get lost or just want to get back you can give it to a cab driver."

–gpotvin

www.fodors.com/forums

LODGING PLANNER

Cutting Costs

Since Shanghai's hotels target business travelers, there are often excellent deals available on weekends at many of the upmarket establishments. Reductions on room rates are widely available (November to March), except over Chinese New Year (mid-January to mid-February) when an influx of domestic tourists causes prices to spike.

Don't be shy to practice your bargaining skills when making reservations—the Chinese are used to the first price always being up for negotiation. That said, you probably don't want to stamp your foot and shout "Tai gui.le!" (Too expensive!) when making reservations at the Four Seasons. If you're staying for several nights, some three- or four-star hotels will throw in breakfast or give you a discounted rate, so always be sure to ask.

Facilities

Doubles in China often come with two twin beds, though most hotels offer queens or kings too, so be sure to state your preference when making reservations. All hotels listed have private baths and air-conditioning unless otherwise noted.

Top 5 Hotels

- **Westin.** The Westin wins hands down among the luxury hotels in Puxi, with its sleek elegance (and fabulous art), attentive service, and ultracomfortable rooms.
- **Old House Inn.** We love the Old House Inn as much for its local charm as its bargain prices.
- **St. Regis.** No other hotel in Shanghai can boast that it treats every one of its guests like VIPs—for the most sumptuous hotel experience in Shanghai, look no further.
- **Ramada Plaza.** With an ace location and fabulously priced rooms, the Ramada is the number-one hotel for discerning travelers seeking a moderately priced Western-style experience.
- **Pudong Shangri-La.** The Shangri-La's addition of a second tower means there are now twice the number of fabulous views available—if a breathtaking vista is what you're looking for, don't search any farther than this glam hotel right on the banks of the Huangpu River overlooking the iconic Bund and the Pearl TV Tower.

Prices

Rates are generally quoted for the room alone; breakfast, whether continental or full, usually is extra. We've noted at the end of each review if breakfast is included in the rate (CP for continental breakfast daily and BP for full breakfast daily). All hotel prices listed here are based on high-season rates. (We always list the facilities that are available, but we don't specify whether they cost extra. When pricing accommodations, always ask what's included and what costs extra.)

WHAT IT COSTS In yuan

	$$$$	$$$	$$	$	¢
FOR 2 PEOPLE	over Y1,800	Y1,401–Y1,800	Y1,101–Y1,400	Y700–Y1,100	under Y700

Prices are for two people in a standard double room in high season, excluding 10%–15% service charge.

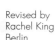

Revised by Rachel King Berlin

Although China has become a hot destination for leisure travelers, Shanghai's stature as China's business capital means that its hotels still cater primarily to business clientele and can be divided into two categories: modern Western-style hotels that are elegant and nicely appointed; or hotels built during the city's glory days, which became state-run after 1949. The latter may lack great service, modern fixings, and convenient facilities, but they often make up for it in charm, tradition, history, and value.

Judging by the number of five-star and Western chain hotels now in Shanghai, the city has proven just how grandly it has opened to the outside world. The Grand Hyatt, JW Marriott, Westin, Portman Ritz-Carlton, and St. Regis aren't merely hotels; they're landmarks on the Shanghai skyline and standard-bearers for all lodgings in town. Even the historic properties that make up the other half of Shanghai's hotel market feel the pressure to update their rooms and facilities. And as Shanghai speeds up its preparations for the World Expo in 2010, newcomers, like the Regent, are setting the bar even higher with their ultramodern settings and top-notch service. This increasing competition means there are bargains to be had, especially during the low season from November through March. Avoid traveling during the three national holidays—Chinese New Year (mid-January to mid-February), Labor Day (May 1), and National Day (October 1)—when rooms and prices will be at a premium.

OLD CITY

★ $$$$ **The Westin Shanghai.** With its distinctive room layouts, glittering glass staircase, and 90-plus works of art on display, the Westin Shanghai is a masterpiece, fittingly located near the majestic Bund. Crowne Deluxe rooms are miniature suites; sliding doors divide the sitting area, bathroom, and bedroom (the only problem is that all these divisions make

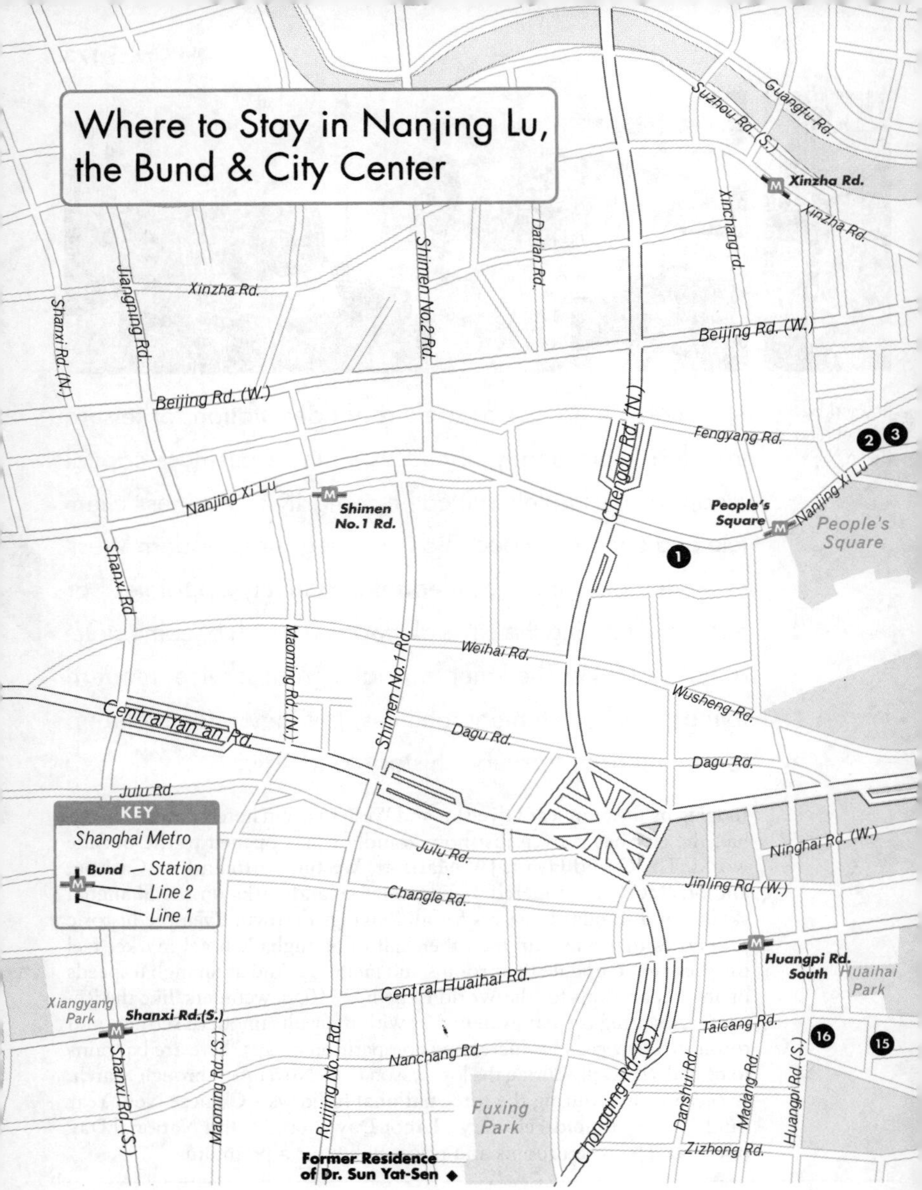

88 Xintiandi 16
Astor Hotel 10
Broadway Mansions Hotel . 8
Captain Hostel 12
JW Marriott 1
Nanjing Hotel 7
Pacific Hotel 3
Panorama Century Court 9
Park Hotel 2
Peace Hotel 11
Radisson Hotel New World 4
Ramada Plaza 5
Sofitel Hyland 6
Somerset Grand 15
The Westin 13
YMCA Hotel 14

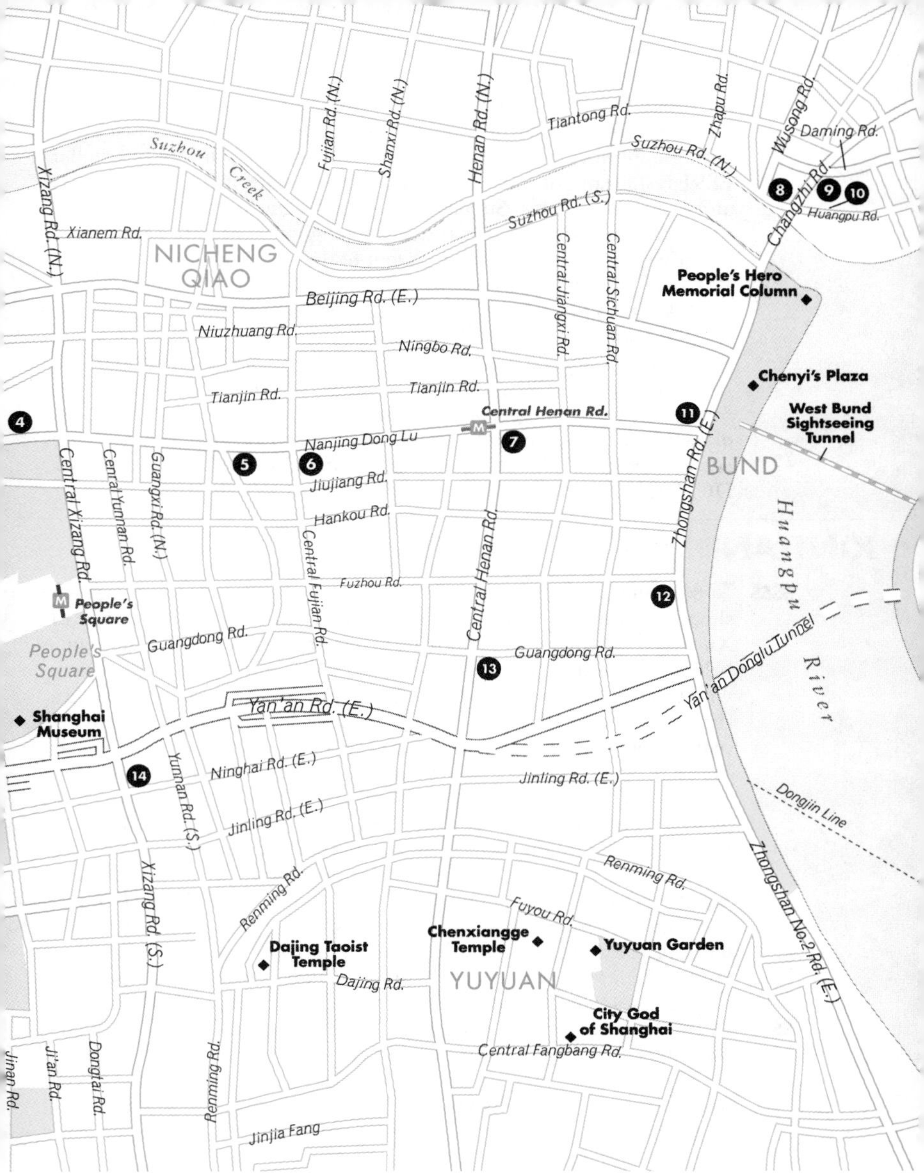
Suzhou Creek
Xizang Rd. (N.)
Xianem Rd.
NICHENG QIAO
Fujian Rd. (N.)
Shanxi Rd. (N.)
Henan Rd. (N.)
Tiantong Rd.
Zhapu Rd.
Wusong Rd.
Daming Rd.
Suzhou Rd. (N.)
Suzhou Rd. (S.)
Changzhi Rd.
Huangpu Rd.
Central Jiangxi Rd.
Central Sichuan Rd.
People's Hero Memorial Column
Beijing Rd. (E.)
Niuzhuang Rd.
Ningbo Rd.
Chenyi's Plaza
Tianjin Rd.
Central Henan Rd.
West Bund Sightseeing Tunnel
Nanjing Dong Lu
Zhongshan Rd. (E.)
BUND
Central Xizang Rd.
Central Yunnan Rd.
Guangxi Rd. (N.)
Jiujiang Rd.
Hankou Rd.
Central Fujian Rd.
Huangpu River
Fuzhou Rd.
Central Henan Rd.
People's Square
Guangdong Rd.
Yan'an Donglu Tunnel
People's Square
Guangdong Rd.
Shanghai Museum
Yan'an Rd. (E.)
Ninghai Rd. (E.)
Yunnan Rd. (S.)
Jinling Rd. (E.)
Jinling Rd. (E.)
Dongjin Line
Renming Rd.
Renming Rd.
Xizang Rd. (S.)
Fuyou Rd.
Chenxiangge Temple
Yuyuan Garden
Dajing Taoist Temple
Zhongshan No.2 Rd. (E.)
Dajing Rd.
YUYUAN
City God of Shanghai
Central Fangbang Rd.
Jinan Rd.
Ji'an Rd.
Dongtai Rd.
Renming Rd.
Jinjia Fang
4
5
6
7
8
9
10
11
12
13
14

the rooms feel on the small side). Luxurious amenities include rain-forest showers, extra deep tubs, and Westin's trademark Heavenly Bed. Pampering continues at the Banyan Tree spa—China's first—and stellar EEST restaurant, a sunny three-in-one venue with full Thai, Japanese, and Cantonese menus. Sunday champagne brunch at the Stage restaurant is considered the best in town by Shanghai's glitterati. Service is so attentive that extra staff stand in front of the check-in counter to assist. ✉ *Bund Center, 88 Henan Zhonglu, Huangpu 200002* ☎ *021/6335–1888 or 888/625–5144* 📠 *021/6335–2888* 🌐 *www.westin.com/shanghai* *276 rooms, 25 suites* *3 restaurants, grocery, patisserie, room service, in-room faxes, in-room safes, minibars, cable TV, in-room data ports, indoor pool, health club, hair salon, hot tub, sauna, spa, steam room, bar, lobby lounge, piano, shops, babysitting, dry cleaning, laundry service, concierge, concierge floor, Internet, business services, convention center, travel services, some free parking, no-smoking floors* 💳 *AE, DC, MC, V.*

XINTIANDI & CITY CENTER

$$$$ **88 Xintiandi.** Although it targets business travelers, 88 Xintiandi is a shopper's and gourmand's delight. The boutique hotel is in the heart of Xintiandi, its balconies overlooking the top-dollar shops and restaurants below. The rooms, all mini- or full-size suites with kitchens, are likewise upscale. Beds are elevated on a central, gauze-curtained platform; sitting areas have large TVs and DVD players. Stylish wood screens accent the rooms and common areas. Deluxe rooms and the executive lounge overlook man-made Lake Taipingqiao, and guests have access to the comprehensive Alexander City Club gym next door. Renovations will be complete by the end of 2007 and will add such amenities as plasma TVs, DVD players, foot massage machines, printers, scanners, and juicers to all rooms. ✉ *380 Huangpi Nan Lu, Luwan 200021* ☎ *021/5383–8833* 📠 *021/5353–8877* 🌐 *www.88xintiandi.com* *12 suites, 41 rooms* *Restaurant, room service, in-room faxes, in-room safes, kitchens, minibars, microwaves, refrigerators, cable TV, in-room VCRs, in-room data ports, indoor pool, gym, bar, babysitting, laundry service, concierge, business services, parking (fee), no-smoking floors* 💳 *AE, DC, MC, V.*

$$$$ **JW Marriott.** For the best views in Puxi, look no further. The JW Marriott's futuristic 60-story tower on the edge of People's Square turns heads with its 90-degree twist, which divides the executive apartments below from the 22-story hotel above. The interior follows classic lines with subtle Chinese accents. Celadon vases, wedding boxes, and ornamental jades complement the soft green-and-yellow palette and warm fiddle-back wood in the spacious rooms, but the real eye-catcher is the amazing cityscape vista from every room. The largely business clientele appreciates the one-touch "At Your Service" call button, and the Mandara Spa, indoor and outdoor pools, excellent restaurants, JW Lounge

> **WORD OF MOUTH**
>
> "In Shanghai, we stayed at the JW Marriott and were able to walk to the Bund daily. I'd recommend it highly. The hotel was splendid.
> —EllenLM

(with 60-plus martinis), and proximity to many of the major tourist attractions are big draws for leisure travelers. ✉ *399 Nanjing Xi Lu, Huangpu 200003* ☎ *021/5359–4969 or 888/236–2427* 🖷 *021/6375–5988* 🌐 *www.marriotthotels.com/shajw* *305 rooms, 37 suites* *3 restaurants, coffee shop, room service, some in-room faxes, in-room safes, minibars, cable TV, in-room data ports, 2 pools (1 indoor), health club, hot tub, sauna, spa, steam room, lobby lounge, lounge, library, piano, shops, babysitting, dry cleaning, laundry service, concierge, concierge floor, Internet, business services, convention center, travel services, parking (fee), no-smoking rooms, no-smoking floor* 💳 *AE, DC, MC, V.*

$$$$ **Radisson Hotel Shanghai New World.** A prominent figure not only on People's Square, but also on the Shanghai skyline, the dome-topped Radisson New World is best known for its revolving restaurant, Epicure on 45. Rooms are divided between the lower Park Tower and the higher City Tower. Park Tower rooms are more expensive, but have the best views, facing People's Square. Though the hotel caters primarily to business travelers, suites—each with a huge living room, kitchen/dining room, and spacious bath—are convenient for families. In addition, most rooms have flat-screen TVs, and DVD players are available by request. Many travelers still prefer the tranquil garden setting of the Radisson's Xingguo hotel in the French Concession, but it cannot compete with the New World's central location and city views. ■ TIP→ **Be sure to ask about special weekend packages.** ✉ *88 Nanjing Xi Lu, Huangpu 200003* ☎ *021/6359–9999* 🖷 *021/6358–9705* 🌐 *www.radisson.com* *429 rooms, 91 suites* *3 restaurants, patisserie, room service, in-room data ports, in-room safes, minibar, cable TV, indoor pool, gym, health club, hair salon, spa, virtual golf, squash, billiards, bar, lobby lounge, shops, babysitting, laundry service, concierge, Internet, business services, convention center, travel services, parking (fee), no-smoking floors* 💳 *AE, DC, MC, V.*

$$$ **Somerset Grand.** Designed as serviced apartments for expats, the Somerset Grand's suites are great for families wanting extra space plus the usual hotel amenities. The twin 34-story towers have 334 one- to three-bedroom suites, ranging from 890 to 2,500 square feet (762 sq. meters). (One-bedroom suites have only one king-size bed.) The units feel homey, with blue-and-pink floral comforters and rugs, and a small kitchen. Kids can burn off steam at the pool and in the playroom. There's a great French restaurant and coffee shop on the grounds; the hotel is two blocks from the restaurants, shops, and movie theater at Xintiandi and 10 minutes to the subway. ✉ *8 Jinan Lu, Luwan 200021* ☎ *021/6385–6888* 🖷 *021/6384–8988* 🌐 *www.the-ascott.com* *334 suites* *In-room safes, kitchen, minibars, refrigerators, cable TV, in-room data ports, 2 tennis courts, indoor pool, health club, hair salon, hot tub, massage, sauna, steam room, billiards, library, babysitting, playground, dry cleaning, laundry facilities, laundry service, concierge, Internet, business services, meeting rooms, travel services, parking (fee), no-smoking rooms* 💳 *AE, DC, MC, V.*

$$ **Park Hotel** (Guoji Fandian). Once Shanghai's tallest building, the 20-story Park Hotel is now dwarfed on the Puxi skyline and eclipsed by other hotels whose glory days are present instead of past. Recently named a

China Cultural Heritage Site, this 1934 art-deco structure overlooking People's Park still has great views and a musty charm, particularly in its restored marble lobby. Rooms are clean and bright, with prints of historic buildings from around the world. But bathrooms are tiny, and the hotel's limited English service and facilities have definitely slipped to second-rate. ✉ *170 Nanjing Xi Lu, Huangpu 200003* ☎ *021/6327–5225* 📠 *021/6327–6958* *225 rooms, 25 suites* *3 restaurants, in-room safes, minibars, cable TV, some in-room data ports, gym, hair salon, sauna, billiards, 2 bars, lobby lounge, piano, shop, dry cleaning, laundry service, concierge, Internet, business services, meeting rooms, travel services, some free parking, no-smoking rooms* ▭ *AE, DC, MC, V.*

$ **Pacific Hotel.** This 1926 property has done an admirable job of preserving its charm. The marble lobby and the downstairs bar, decorated with art-deco leather chairs and archived photos of 1920s Shanghai, sweep you back to the city's glory days. In the original Italian-style front building, 6th- and 7th-floor rooms have wood floors, ornate molded ceilings, and great views of People's Park. (Bathrooms, though, are rather institutional.) The smaller rooms in the rear building lack the fine detail and views but are still comfortable and are a bit quieter. Amenities fall short, and soundproofing could be better, but the hotel's proud history, prime location, and prices make it an appealing choice. ✉ *108 Nanjing Xi Lu, Huangpu 200003* ☎ *021/6327–6226* 📠 *021/6372–3634* 🌐 *www.pacifichotelsh.com* *177 rooms, 5 suites* *Restaurant, 2 bars, room service, minibars, cable TV, in-room data ports, Wi-Fi, some in-room safes, lobby lounge, shop, hair salon, spa, laundry service, dry cleaning, Internet, business services, meeting rooms, travel services, parking (fee)* ▭ *AE, DC, MC, V.*

¢–$ **YMCA Hotel.** Its central location within a 15-minute walk of People's Square, Xintiandi, and the Bund makes the YMCA Hotel a top destination for budget travelers. Built in 1929 as an actual YMCA, the 11-story brick building retains some of its original features: a temple-like exterior and painted ceiling beams on the 2nd floor. The four dormitory rooms have single beds, rather than bunks. This is also a good chance for you to practice your bargaining skills, as discounts are almost always available. ✉ *123 Xizang Nan Lu, Huangpu 200021* ☎ *021/6326–1040* 📠 *021/6320–1957* 🌐 *www.ymcahotel.com* *140 rooms, 6 suites, 4 rooms with shared bath* *2 restaurants, bar, coffee shop, grocery, room service, some in-room safes, in-room data ports, minibars, cable TV, gym (fee), hair salon, massage, billiards, Ping-Pong, recreation room, shops, laundry service, Internet, business services, meeting rooms, airport shuttle, travel services* ▭ *AE, DC, MC, V.*

NANJING DONG LU & THE BUND

$$$–$$$$ Fodor's Choice ★ **Ramada Plaza.** With its ornate lobby resembling a European opera house, the Ramada Plaza Shanghai brings a touch of grandeur to the Nanjing Road pedestrian walkway. Statues of Greek gods reign from atop intricate inlaid tables. Soaring marble columns direct the eye skyward toward a stained-glass skylight. Although the fair-size rooms lack any great views, they do face in toward a dramatic atrium, topped by yet another courtyard and the executive lounge. In 2005, an indoor swim-

WHICH NEIGHBORHOOD?

Shanghai may have an excellent subway system and cheap, plentiful taxis, but if you want to take full advantage of Shanghai's popular tourist sights, restaurants, and nightlife opt to stay in downtown **Puxi**, incorporating the quiet, leafy green Former French Concession, the historical promenade of the Bund, and the bustling shopping street of Nanjing Dong Lu. From these neighborhoods you'll have easy access to all of Shanghai's dynamic neighborhoods.

NANJING LU & THE BUND

Breathtaking views of the Pudong skyline, skyscrapers juxtaposed with Victorian architecture, and easy access to great shopping and some of the city's best restaurants are just a few reasons to stay here. Best of all, most major sites, from the Bund to the Shanghai Museum, are all within comfortable walking distance. If you want to see modern Shanghai, this is the place to be.

FORMER FRENCH CONCESSION

Sneak away from the city's frenetic energy in one of the historical hotels tucked down the Former French Concession's tree-lined streets. Excellent restaurants and shopping abound, the neighborhood's relaxing atmosphere can be a nice break after a hectic day of sightseeing. A short cab or metro ride takes you straight to any of the city's sights on Nanjing Lu and the Bund.

HONGQIAO DEVELOPMENT ZONE

Hongqiao is not a destination for leisure travelers. A combination of residential complexes and business offices, Hongqiao lacks many sights or restaurants. Unless business brings you here or you have an early flight from the Hongqiao airport, there aren't many reasons to stay so far from the action.

PUDONG

Although Pudong—with its shiny new skyscrapers and wide boulevards—can feel impersonal, and it's too far from downtown Puxi for some, it has some of the city's best hotels, all close to Pudong International Airport. Phenomenal views of the Bund are a major bonus. But if you stay here, be prepared to spend at least 30 minutes shuttling back and forth to Puxi (and it could take even longer during rush hour as millions of locals compete to flag down taxis or squeeze into subway cars almost overflowing with commuters).

ming pool, one of the largest in Shanghai, was added, housed inside an addition reminiscent of an ancient Chinese palace. Given the lush setting and ace location, the Ramada Plaza is a good value for the money, and you can usually get a room for less than the rack rate. ✉ *719 Nanjing Dong Lu, Huangpu 200001* ☎ *021/6350–0000 or 800/854–7854* 🖷 *021/6350–6666* 🌐 *www.ramadainternational.com* *376 rooms, 36 suites* *4 restaurants, patisserie, room service, in-room safes, minibars, cable TV, in-room data ports, some in-room hot tubs, indoor pool, gym, hair salon, massage, sauna, spa, steam room, billiards, lobby lounge, nightclub, shops, babysitting, dry cleaning, laundry service, concierge,*

concierge floor, Internet, business services, convention center, travel services, free parking, no-smoking floors ▭ *AE, DC, MC, V.*

> **STOP ON BY**
>
> The Peace Hotel is a great place to drop by for an evening drink at the Jazz Bar or have an afternoon coffee as an interlude during a tour of the Bund. That said, as a place to stay, many have found it an unfortunate disappointment.

$$–$$$$ **Peace Hotel.** The allure of the Peace Hotel is as one of Shanghai's most treasured historic buildings. That said, as a place to stay, it's an unfortunate disappointment. Though the art-deco lobby and international suites still retain some of the hotel's past glamour, the rooms tend toward small and stuffy, with nondescript worn furnishings. The south building, opened in 1906 as the Palace Hotel, is the oldest structure on the Bund, but its rooms are the hotel's most modern (and least expensive), with larger bathrooms and nicer furniture. There are rumors of renovations in 2007, but even that won't fix the staff's curt service. ✉ *20 Nanjing Dong Lu, Huangpu 200002* ☎ *021/6321–6888* 🖷 *021/6329–0300* 🌐 *www.shanghaipeacehotel.com* *411 rooms, 9 suites* *2 restaurants, room service, Wi-Fi, in-room safes, minibars, gym, hair salon, massage, sauna, spa, steam room, billiards, Ping-Pong, 2 bars, lobby lounge, piano, shops, babysitting, playground, dry cleaning, laundry service, concierge, concierge floor, convention center, travel services, free parking, no-smoking rooms* ▭ *AE, DC, MC, V.*

$$$ **Sofitel Hyland.** Directly on the Nanjing Road pedestrian mall, the Sofitel Hyland is a convenient base for shopping and exploring the city center and the Bund. The rooms in this 30-story French-managed hotel are somewhat small, but were spruced up in 2006 with prints of Chinese emperors and small replicas of terra-cotta warrior statues. The top-floor Sky Lounge serves Sunday brunch amid views of the Bund and downtown, and Le Pub 505 brews up its own beer. ✉ *505 Nanjing Dong Lu, Huangpu 200001* ☎ *021/6351–5888* 🖷 *021/6351–4088* 🌐 *www.accorhotels-asia.com* *299 rooms, 73 suites* *3 restaurants, room service, in-room safes, minibars, cable TV, in-room data ports, pool, gym, health club, hair salon, massage, sauna, spa, steam room, 2 bars, lobby lounge, pub, piano, shops, dry cleaning, laundry service, concierge floor, Internet, business services, convention center, airport shuttle, travel services, parking (fee), no-smoking floors* ▭ *AE, DC, MC, V.*

¢ **Captain Hostel.** One of the few hostels in Shanghai, backpackers choose Captain Hostel as much for its rooftop bar and restaurant as for its clean, bright rooms and convenient location a half-block west of the Bund. The dormitories accommodate 5 to 10 people per room in bunks resembling ships' berths, in keeping with the overall nautical theme in this 1920s hotel. The 20 first-class rooms are tired but fair-sized, with TVs and private bathrooms. Bunk rooms must be paid for in cash. ✉ *37 Fuzhou Lu, Huangpu 200002* ☎ *021/*

> **DRINK AND A VIEW**
>
> The hopping Noah's Bar on the 6th floor [of Captain Hostel] has views of the Pudong skyline that rival those from much pricier lodgings.

6323–5053 🖨 021/6321–9331 ⊕ *www.captainhostel.com.cn* 🛏 *20 rooms, 85 rooms with shared bath* ♿ *2 restaurants, café, some cable TV, laundry facilities, Internet, meeting rooms, no-smoking rooms; no phones in some rooms* 🖃 *MC, V.*

¢ 🖼 **Nanjing Hotel.** A frequent choice for budget tour groups, the Nanjing Hotel is only half a block yet a world away from the modern bustle of the Nanjing Dong Lu pedestrian walkway. Step out the front door and you'll see China as the locals do: fruit vendors balancing their loads, trash men ringing their hand bells. The hotel's proximity to the metro line and the Bund compensate for the street noise and lack of views. Built in 1931, the eight-story building is dated, yet rooms are fair-sized with Internet access and a few satellite channels. ■ **TIP→** **Though 5th-floor rooms were refurbished in 2006, opt for a room on the 6th floor, which is quieter.** ✉ *200 Shanxi Lu, Huangpu 200001* ☎ *021/6322–2888* 🖨 *021/6351–6520* ⊕ *www.nj-hotel.com* ♿ *Restaurant, room service, in-room safes, in-room data ports, minibars, cable TV, shops, laundry service, Internet, business services, meeting rooms, travel services* 🖃 *AE, DC, MC, V.*

FORMER FRENCH CONCESSION

6

$$$$ 🖼 **Crowne Plaza.** This hotel on the far western side of the Former French Concession makes up for its out-of-the-way location with service. The staff here is among the friendliest in town and makes guests, mostly business travelers, feel at home. Though the hotel's rooms are not as elegant as those of its competitors, it does have the biggest club lounge in Shanghai, with a mezzanine floor and a sleek black marble-topped bar. ✉ *400 Panyu Lu, Xuhui 200052* ☎ *021/6280–8888 or 800/227–6963* 🖨 *021/6280–3353* ⊕ *www.shanghai.crowneplaza.com* 🛏 *488 rooms, 12 suites* ♿ *4 restaurants, café, patisserie, room service, in-room safes, some in-room hot tubs, minibars, some kitchens, some microwaves, in-room data ports, cable TV, indoor pool, gym, hair salon, massage, sauna, steam room, 2 bars, lobby lounge, piano, shops, babysitting, concierge floor, Internet, business services, convention center, free parking, no-smoking floors* 🖃 *AE, DC, MC, V.*

$$$$ 🖼 **Jinjiang Hotel.** The former Cathay Mansions, Grosvenor Gardens, and Grosvenor House, now known collectively as the Jinjiang Hotel, are among the few art-deco buildings left standing in the city. It's here that President Nixon and Premier Zhou Enlai signed the Shanghai Communique in 1972 and all lobbies display photographs of the heads of state who have graced the hotel's grounds, giving the establishment a wonderful air of history. The fabulous luxury suites in the Grosvenor House start at $800 nightly. Rooms in the 1929 Cathay Building are plain but fair-sized with separate showers and tubs. Deluxe rooms are more stylish. The 5-floor Cathay Garden, which reopened in 2005 after extensive renovations, now houses the hotel's best non-suite room, with guests praising the spacious modern deco furnishings and deep soak bathtubs. For the best view, snag a room on the 4th or 5th floor. ✉ *59 Maoming Nan Lu, Luwan 200020* ☎ *021/6258–2582* 🖨 *021/6472–5588* 🛏 *328 rooms, 33 suites* ♿ *5 restaurants, room service, in-room safes, minibars, cable TV, in-room data ports, indoor pool, health club, hair salon, sauna, bowling, 2 bars, lobby lounge, shops, babysitting, Internet, business*

services, convention center, airport shuttle, travel services, free parking, no-smoking rooms, no-smoking floors ▭ *AE, DC, MC, V.*

$$$–$$$$ **Hilton Shanghai.** Opened in 1988 as Shanghai's first five-star hotel, the Hilton remains a local favorite among businessmen and airline crews. Rooms are comfortable with an understated sand-tone color scheme, but not as cutting-edge as the hotel's younger competitors. But what the Hilton lacks in modern decor it makes up for with its prime location near the restaurants and nightlife of Jing'an Temple and the Former French Concession and its low-key friendly service. The delectable Gourmet Corner now occupies a large storefront in the front lobby, whereas in the rear lies the much-lauded Italian restaurant Leonardo's and the sunlit 24-hour Atrium Café, which resembles a quiet Chinese garden. On the top floors, the conference center, Penthouse Bar, and stellar Sichuan Court restaurant all have stunning views of the ever-expanding Puxi skyline. ✉ *250 Huashan Lu, Xuhui 200040* ☎ *021/6248–0000 or 800/445–8667* 📠 *021/6248–3848* 🌐 *www.shanghai.hilton.com* *692 rooms, 28 suites* *6 restaurants, café, coffee shop, room service, some in-room faxes, minibars, cable TV, in-room data ports, tennis court, indoor pool, health club, hair salon, hot tub, Japanese baths, sauna, spa, steam room, squash, 3 bars, lobby lounge, shops, babysitting, dry cleaning, laundry service, concierge, concierge floor, Internet, business services, convention center, airport shuttle, travel services, parking (fee), no-smoking floors* ▭ *AE, DC, MC, V.*

$$$$ **Okura Garden Hotel.** Its parklike setting in the heart of the French Concession makes this 33-story Garden Hotel a favorite Shanghai retreat, especially for Japanese travelers familiar with the Okura Group name. The first three floors, which were once old Shanghai's French Club, have been restored, with cascading chandeliers, frescoes, and art-deco details at every turn. Average-size standard rooms are simply furnished with silk wallpaper and European-style furniture and, unlike deluxe rooms and suites, lack flat-screen TVs. The romantic 3rd-floor terrace bar overlooks the 2-acre garden, and the Japanese and French restaurants serve excellent but high-priced food. For those who want to stay connected, cell phones are available for rent at the concierge desk. ✉ *58 Maoming Nan Lu, Luwan 200020* ☎ *021/6415–1111* 📠 *021/6415–8866* 🌐 *www.gardenhotelshanghai.com* *478 rooms, 22 suites* *5 restaurants, room service, some in-room faxes, in-room safes, minibars, cable TV, in-room data ports, 2 tennis courts, indoor-outdoor pool, health club, hair salon, hot tub, massage, sauna, 3 bars, lobby lounge, shops, dry cleaning, laundry service, concierge, concierge floor, Internet, business services, convention center, airport shuttle, travel services, some free parking, no-smoking floors* ▭ *AE, DC, MC, V.*

WORD OF MOUTH

I ended up in the Okura Garden Hotel when my other choices were full. I ended up very impressed. The service was great, room service was good and reasonably priced and the little extras made it one of my favorites.

–Dina, New York, NY

$$$$ **Radisson Plaza Xing Guo.** This quiet garden property was once the government-owned Xing Guo Hotel, a villa complex where Chairman Mao frequently stayed. The modern 16-story Radisson Plaza sprouted up in 2002, its garden-view rooms overlooking the central lawn and Mao's legendary Villa No. 1. The comfortable beige-tone rooms have ample work space, with two club chairs and a large desk. The Clark Hatch Fitness Center has top-name equipment, an aerobics room, and an elevated pool. Although the hotel's location in the consular district means it's far from the subway and most attractions, many guests still prefer its tranquil setting over the hustle and bustle of downtown Puxi. ✉ *78 Xingguo Lu, Xuhui 200052* ☎ *021/6212–9998* 🖷 *021/6212–9996 or 888/201–1718* 🌐 *www.radisson.com* *150 rooms, 40 suites* *2 restaurants, café, room service, some in-room faxes, in-room safes, minibars, cable TV, in-room data ports, indoor pool, health club, hair salon, hot tub, massage, sauna, steam room, bowling, Ping-Pong, squash, bar, lobby lounge, library, shops, babysitting, dry cleaning, laundry service, concierge, concierge floor, Internet, business services, meeting rooms, airport shuttle, travel services, some free parking, no-smoking rooms* 💳 *AE, DC, MC, V.*

6

$$$$ **Regal International East Asia Hotel.** Its exclusive Shanghai International Tennis Center is the Regal's trump card among five-star hotels. The center has 10 tournament courts as well as one of the city's best health clubs (it's not only huge, but all cardio machines come with personal TVs). The spacious rooms were renovated in 2005 and have flat-screen TVs. Club rooms each have a curvilinear desk and ergonomic chair and a funky chaise longue; deluxe rooms have compact bathrooms with marble sinks and huge mirrors. The Hengshan Road metro station and bar/restaurant district are just a block away, but there's plenty of entertainment downstairs at the hotel's 12-lane bowling alley and gorgeous Fragrance Chinese restaurant. ✉ *516 Hengshan Lu, Xuhui 200040* ☎ *021/6415–5588* 🖷 *021/6445–8899* 🌐 *www.regal-eastasia.com* *278 rooms, 22 suites* *3 restaurants, coffee shop, patisserie, room service, some in-room faxes, in-room safes, some in-room hot tubs, minibars, cable TV, some in-room VCRs, in-room data ports, 10 tennis courts, indoor pool, health club, hair salon, hot tub, massage, sauna, steam room, billiards, bowling, Ping-Pong, squash, lobby lounge, piano, shops, babysitting, concierge, concierge floor, Internet, business services, convention center, travel services, free parking, no-smoking floors* 💳 *AE, DC, MC, V.*

$$–$$$$ **Donghu Hotel.** Just off the frenzied shopping street of Huaihai Road, the Donghu Hotel remains one of Shanghai's best preserved hotels from the city's 1920s heyday. The hotel's seven buildings have a surprising array of restaurants—Korean barbecue and Japanese, in addition to the standard Chinese and Western fare—an indoor pool, and a wide variety of room options. "Superior" rooms in Building 7 don't quite live up to their title and are simply furnished with twin beds and rather mismatched yellow wallpaper and red carpet. We suggest the Donghu deluxe rooms across the street at Building 1—with their traditional Chinese furniture and dark-wood paneling, these spacious rooms make you feel as if you've stepped back in time. ✉ *70 Donghu Lu, Xuhui*

200031 ☎ 021/6415–8158 📠 021/6415–7759 🌐 www.donghuhotel.com 🛏 240 rooms, 30 suites ♿ 6 restaurants, room service, some in-room safes, minibars, cable TV, in-room data ports, indoor pool, gym, hair salon, billiards, piano, dry cleaning, laundry service, concierge, Internet, business services, convention center, travel services, parking (fee) 💳 AE, DC, MC, V.

$$$–$$$$ **Jing An Hotel.** The weekly chamber-music concert in its lobby is just one example of how the Jing An Hotel has retained its elegance and charm after 70 years. In a 1½-acre garden, the Spanish-style main building's lobby has beautiful stained-glass windows. The ornate upstairs dining rooms often host prominent city officials. Although facilities are lacking compared to the newer hotels in town and the rooms in the Jing An New Building should be avoided at all costs (bathrooms are barely the size of a closet), the hotel's proximity to the subway line and its lush Former French Concession setting make this oft-overlooked property a winner. *✉ 370 Huashan Lu, Xuhui 200040 ☎ 021/6248–0088 📠 021/6249–6100 🌐 www.jinganhotel.net 🛏 210 rooms, 17 suites ♿ 2 restaurants, coffee shop, room service, in-room safes, minibars, cable TV, in-room data ports, gym, hair salon, massage, sauna, lobby lounge, piano bar, shops, babysitting, dry cleaning, laundry service, concierge, Internet, business services, meeting rooms, airport shuttle, travel services, parking (fee), no-smoking rooms 💳 AE, DC, MC, V.*

> **SIZE MATTERS**
>
> Elaborately carved wooden door frames and lintels [at Jing An Hotel] direct the eye upward toward the 10-foot (3-m) ceilings that make for some of the most spacious hotel rooms in Shanghai.

$$$–$$$$ **Shanghai Hotel.** Part of the Jinjiang-managed triumvirate that includes the Jing An Hotel and the Jing An New Building, the Shanghai Hotel has the most modern amenities of the three hotels. The executive floors are the hotel's best and executive double rooms all come with computers. Though the Shanghai hotel is not as charming as the adjacent Jing An Hotel, its stellar location near Jing'an Temple make it a good choice among midrange hotels and very popular with Chinese and Western tour groups. *✉ 505 Wulumuqi Lu, Xuhui 200040 ☎ 021/6248–0088 📠 021/6248–1056 🌐 www.shanghaihotel.net.cn 🛏 540 rooms, 3 suites ♿ 2 restaurants, café, room service, in-room data ports, some in-room faxes, in-room safes, minibars, cable TV, gym, hair salon, spa, billiards, shuffleboard, virtual golf, piano, business services, Internet, meeting rooms, dry cleaning, laundry service, shops, no-smoking rooms, parking (fee) 💳 AE, DC, MC, V.*

★ $$–$$$$ **Ruijin Guest House.** Formerly the Morriss Estate, the Ruijin Hotel showcases how opulently *taipans* (expatriate millionaire businessmen) lived in Shanghai's heyday of the 1930s. Rooms within the two preserved villas—No. 1 and Old No. 3—are rich with detail: high ceilings, ornate plaster molding, bamboo-etched glass. The two other buildings are significantly shorter on charm but still overlook the verdant grounds, which are shared with several top-notch restaurants (including the hip Face Bar) and provide direct access to the bars on Maoming Road. New

Where to Stay in the Former French Concession, Nanjing Xi Lu & Jing'an

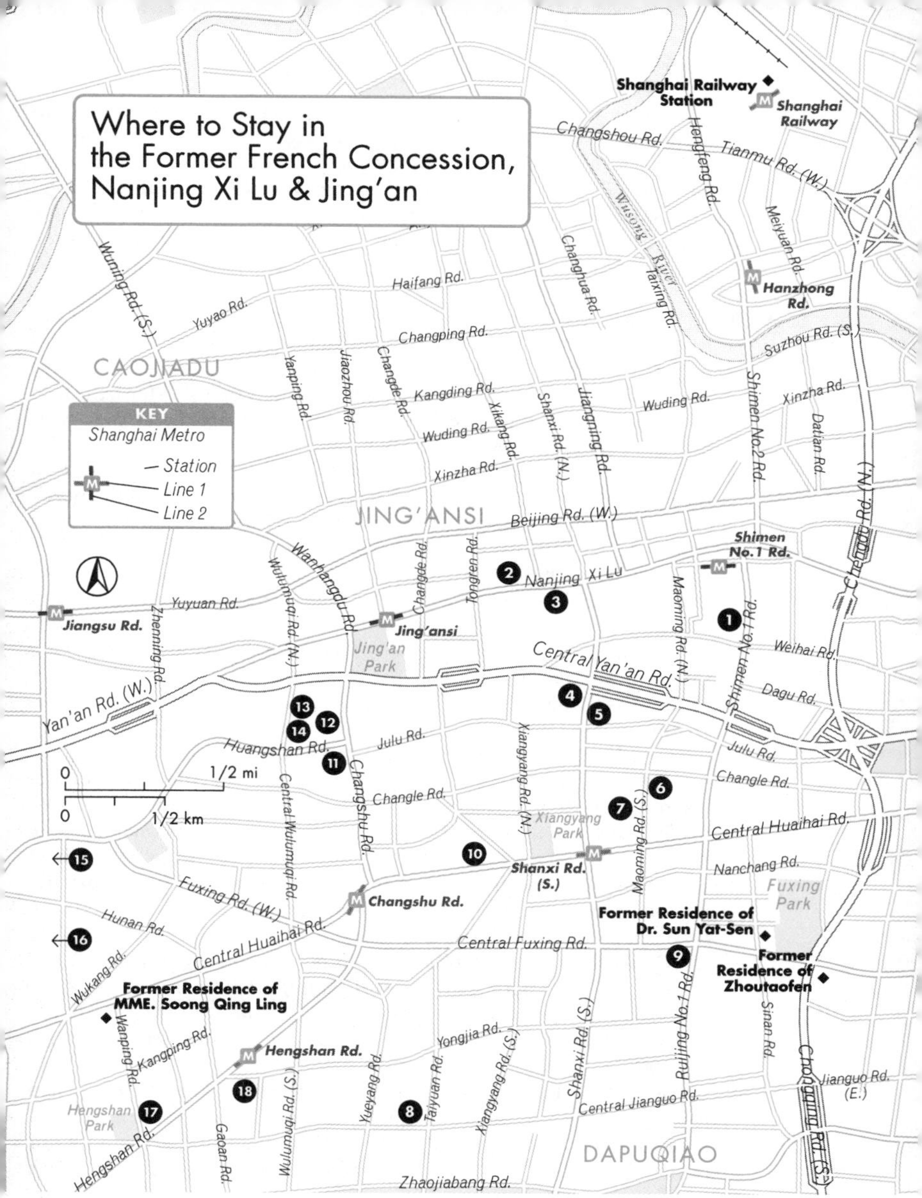

- Anting Villa Hotel **18**
- City Hotel **5**
- Crowne Plaza **16**
- Donghu Hotel **10**
- Four Seasons **1**
- Heng Shan Moller **4**
- Hilton Shanghai **12**
- Jing'an Hotel **14**
- Jinjiang Hotel Xin Guo **7**
- Okura Garden Hotel **6**
- Old House Inn **13**
- Portman Ritz-Carlton **2**
- Regal International East Asia Hotel **17**
- Ruijin Guest House **9**
- Shanghai Hotel **11**
- Shanghai JC Mandarin . . . **3**
- Shanghai Marriott Hongqiao **15**
- Taiyuan Villa **19**

No. 3 may lack the historic cache of the other buildings, but its standard rooms, which come with a king-size bed and Jacuzzi, are definitely a steal. ✉ *118 Ruijin Er Lu, Luwan 200020* ☎ *021/6472–5222* 🖷 *021/6473–2277* 🌐 *www.shedi.net.cn/outedi/ruijin* *62 rooms, 20 suites* *Restaurant, coffee shop, room service, in-room safes, minibars, cable TV, hair salon, 2 bars, lobby lounge, shops, laundry service, Internet, business services, convention center, free parking, no-smoking rooms* *AE, DC, MC, V.*

$$–$$$$ **Taiyuan Villa.** Nestled deep in a residential section of the Former French Concession, this offshoot of the Ruijin Hotel is a tranquil retreat from Shanghai's hustle and bustle. Once the residence of George Marshall (and the former stomping grounds of Madame Mao), the lush grounds surrounding the restored villa and the adjacent serviced apartments are planted with lush magnolia and palm trees. Rooms feel a bit worn, but are nonetheless charming, with spacious high ceilings and deco furniture. Be sure to take time to relax over a cup of tea on the porch overlooking the expansive lawn. ✉ *160 Taiyuan Lu, Luwan 200031* ☎ *021/6471–6688* 🖷 *021/6471–2618* *299 rooms, 73 suites* *4 restaurants, room service, in-room safes, minibars, cable TV, in-room data ports, pool, health club, hair salon, massage, sauna, spa, steam room, 2 bars, lobby lounge, pub, piano, shops, concierge floor, Internet, business services, convention center, airport shuttle, travel services, parking (fee), no-smoking floors* *AE, DC, MC, V.*

$$–$$$ **Somerset Xuhui.** The family-focused facilities of the all-suites Somerset Xuhui help compensate for its location: off the subway line, halfway between Xujiahui's shops and Former French Concession attractions. An indoor playroom, sizeable pool, and fitness center overlooking Zhaojiabang Road provide diversion for children and adults—as does the Starbucks downstairs. There are no restaurants, just small en-suite kitchens. All units were renovated in 2005 and range from one to three bedrooms, the latter having a room with twin beds for kids. Cozy living rooms and huge closets are two more reasons that this is a good spot for families in Shanghai. ✉ *888 Shaanxi Nan Lu, Luwan 200031* ☎ *021/6466–0888* 🖷 *021/6466–4646* 🌐 *www.the-ascott.com* *167 suites* *In-room data ports, in-room safes, kitchens, microwaves, refrigerators, cable TV, in-room VCRs, tennis court, indoor pool, gym, health club, laundry facilities, laundry service, Internet, business services* *AE, DC, MC, V.*

$$ **Anting Villa Hotel.** Two blocks from the metro and the Hengshan Road–nightlife district, the Anting Villa Hotel is a convenient and surprisingly quiet retreat tucked away down a small side street. Superior rooms in the 10-story hotel tower have been refurbished in a "Spanish style" with garishly bright red pillowcases and leather-covered furniture; some rooms now come with flat-screen TVs. It's worth it to pay a little extra for a garden-view room with vistas of the cedar-shaded grounds and namesake 1932 Spanish-style villa. Although English service is limited, the hotel's staff is eager and friendly. Full gym facilities, including a tennis court and pool, are planned for 2007. ✉ *46 Anting Lu, Xuhui 200031* ☎ *021/6433–1188* 🖷 *021/6433–9726* 🌐 *www.sinohotel.com* *135 rooms, 11 suites* *Restaurant, café, room service, in-room safes,*

CLOSE UP

Kid-Friendly Hotels in Shanghai

The **Somerset Grand,** in the Former French Concession, is the best option for families, with fully equipped kitchens in large apartmentlike suites. The hotel has a playroom and a pool, and it's within walking distance of the shops and movie theater at Xintiandi. The **City Hotel,** also in the Former French Concession, has smallish, somewhat tired rooms but there's an indoor playroom for kids. Rooms on the executive floors are larger and more up-to-date. The **Radisson Hotel Shanghai New World,** directly on Nanjing Lu by People's Square, has large (though pricey) family suites that come with spacious living rooms and dining areas. Suites with kitchens at competitive rates are the main draw at the **Somerset Xuhui,** between the Former French Concession and Xujiahui. It's a bit far from the action on Nanjing Lu, but there's an indoor playroom and a sizeable pool.

6

in-room data ports, minibars, cable TV, hair salon, massage, piano, shops, babysitting, laundry service, Internet, business services, meeting rooms, travel services, free parking, no-smoking rooms ▭ *AE, DC, MC, V.*

$–$$ **Mason Hotel.** Although it caters to business travelers, the Mason Hotel is conveniently located for leisure travelers: steps from the Shaanxi Nan Lu metro station and surrounded by the shops of Huaihai Lu. Soundproofing blocks most—but not all—the street noise from the fairly large, simply furnished rooms, which face in toward a sunny, quiet four-story courtyard. Facilities fall a bit short, but there's a Starbucks downstairs and a cozy sunroom up top in the Avenue Joffre restaurant. ✉ *935 Huaihai Zhonglu, Luwan 200020* ☎ *021/6466–2020* 🖷 *021/6467–1693* 🌐 *www.masonhotel.com* *115 rooms, 4 suites* *2 restaurants, room service, in-room safes, minibars, cable TV, in-room data ports, gym, hair salon, billiards, lobby lounge, piano, shops, laundry service, babysitting, concierge, Internet, business services, meeting rooms, travel services, free parking, no-smoking rooms* ▭ *AE, DC, MC, V.*

$ **Old House Inn.** Hidden down a small lane, Old House Inn is one of Shanghai's only boutique hotels and a must if you're looking for a personalized experience that the larger hotels just can't offer. What this tiny gem lacks in amenities (there's no elevator, gym, concierge, or business facilities), it makes up for with its authentic Chinese style and charm. All rooms are decorated with antique dark-wood furniture and traditional porcelains and the friendly staff is so eager to please that they'll even run down to the end of the lane and find you a taxi. Adjacent to the hotel is the swanky A Future Perfect restaurant, popular with both expats and trendy locals for its outdoor café. ■ TIP→ **Book well in advance to snag one of the moderately priced king-**

Fodor'sChoice ★

UNIQUE SPOT

Old House Inn is one of Shanghai's only boutique hotels and a must if you're looking for a personalized experience that the larger hotels just can't offer.

size rooms. ✉ *No. 16, Lane 351 Huashan Lu, Xuhui 200040* ☎ *021/6248–6118* 🖷 *021/6249–6869* 🌐 *www.oldhouse.cn* 12 rooms ♖ *Restaurant, bar, in-room data ports, in-room safes, minibars, cable TV, dry cleaning, laundry service, free parking* ▭ *AE, DC, MC, V.*

PUDONG

★ $$$$ **Grand Hyatt.** Views, views, views are what the world's highest hotel is all about—occupying floors 53 through 87 of the spectacular Jinmao Tower, the Grand Hyatt's interior is defined by art-deco lines juxtaposed with space-age grillwork and sleek furnishings and textures. The 33-story central atrium is a marvel in itself—a seemingly endless cylinder with an outer-space aura. Room amenities are space age as well: CAT 5 optical lines for laptop use; Internet connections on the flat-screen TV through a cordless keyboard; and three high-pressure shower heads in the bathroom. Views from the rooms are spectacular; corner rooms have two walls of pure glass for endless panoramas of the Oriental Pearl Tower, majesty of the Bund, and expanse of the city below. ■ TIP→ **But watch out—being that high up puts you literally in the clouds, and at the mercy of Shanghai's foggy weather.** ✉ *Jinmao Dasha, 88 Shiji Dadao, Pudong 200121* ☎ *021/5049–1234 or 800/233–1234* 🖷 *021/5049–1111* 🌐 *www.shanghai.grand.hyatt.com* *510 rooms, 45 suites* ♖ *5 restaurants, café, coffee shop, food court, room service, in-room safes, minibars, cable TV, in-room data ports, indoor pool, health club, hair salon, sauna, spa, steam room, 3 bars, lobby lounge, piano bar, nightclub, shops, dry cleaning, laundry service, concierge, concierge floor, Internet, business services, convention center, parking (fee), some free parking* ▭ *AE, DC, MC, V.*

$$$$ **Hotel InterContinental Pudong.** The pièce de résistance of the 24-story Intercontinental is a nearly 200-foot-high Italian Renaissance–inspired atrium decorated with red Chinese lanterns that shines natural light onto the 19 guest floors, six of which are executive floors. A vivid coat of red livens up the hallways and spacious guest rooms, which all have separate tub and shower. The restaurants cater to a wide range of tastes: Japanese, Cantonese, Shanghainese, Chaozhou, continental. The open kitchen of Level One restaurant turns out a great lunch buffet with samples of all those cuisines. ✉ *777 Zhangyang Lu, Pudong 200120* ☎ *021/5831–8888 or 800/327–0200* 🖷 *021/5831–7777* 🌐 *www.shanghai.intercontinental.com* *317 rooms, 78 suites* ♖ *4 restaurants, coffee shop, patisserie, room service, in-room safes, minibars, cable TV, in-room data ports, indoor pool, gym, hair salon, sauna, billiards, bar, piano, shops, babysitting, dry cleaning, laundry service, concierge, concierge floor, Internet, business services, convention center, parking (fee), no-smoking floors* ▭ *AE, DC, MC, V.*

$$$$ Fodor'sChoice ★ **Pudong Shangri-La.** The Shangri-La occupies one of the most prized locations in Shanghai: overlooking the Huangpu River, opposite the Bund, near the Pearl Tower in Lujiazui. The hotel's breathtaking water's-edge views, white-glove service, and spacious rooms attract a mix of business and leisure travelers. The addition of a second tower in 2005 made the Shangri-La the largest luxury hotel in Shanghai, with almost 1,000 guest rooms and 10 dining choices. Although rooms in Tower 2, behind

the original hotel, come with 32-inch plasma TVs, DVD players, and fax machines, many return guests still prefer the rooms in Tower 1 for their gloriously unobstructed views of the Bund. ✉ *33 Fucheng Lu, Pudong 200120* ☎ *021/6882–8888 or 800/942–5050* 🖷 *021/6882–6688* 🌐 *www.shangri-la.com* *916 rooms, 65 suites* *8 restaurants, patisserie, room service, in-room safes, minibars, cable TV, in-room data ports, some in-room faxes, tennis court, 2 indoor pools, 2 gyms, hair salon, hot tub, massage, sauna, steam room, spa, 2 bars, 2 lobby lounges, nightclub, shops, babysitting, dry cleaning, laundry service, concierge, concierge floor, Internet, business services, convention center, travel services, parking (fee), no-smoking floors* 💳 *AE, DC, MC, V.*

WORD OF MOUTH

"We stayed at the Pudong Shangri-La and loved it. From our room we had a view of the river with its neon boats cruising by and the Bund. We also discovered a great place to eat or just hang out right across the street and on the river. It's called Paulaner, a German brewhouse. We sat outside with a fabulous view, had fantastic food, and afterwards listened to the great house band." –banshee

6

$$$$ Fodor'sChoice ★ **St. Regis.** Every guest is a VIP at the St. Regis. The amphitheaterlike lobby sets the stage for the most indulgent hotel experience in Shanghai. The 318 rooms in this 40-story red-granite tower—its design lauded by *Architectural Digest*—spare no expense, with Bose wave radios, Herman Miller Aeron chairs, and rain-forest showers that give you the feeling of being under a waterfall. At 500 square feet (152 sq. m), standard rooms compare to other hotels' suites. The two women's-only floors are unique in Shanghai. Butlers address all your needs 24/7 (you can even contact them by e-mail) from in-room check-in to room service, and as part of a new program, they can arrange to escort guests personally to visit local artist studios. The hotel's location—15 minutes from the riverfront—is a drawback, but the fitness center and 24-hour gym, along with the remarkable Danieli's Italian restaurant add to this pampering property's appeal. ✉ *889 Dongfang Lu, Pudong 200122* ☎ *021/5050–4567 or 800/325–3589* 🖷 *021/6875–6789* 🌐 *www.stregis.com/shanghai* *274 rooms, 44 suites* *3 restaurants, room service, some in-room faxes, in-room safes, minibars, cable TV, in-room data ports, Wi-Fi, tennis court, indoor pool, health club, hair salon, hot tub, sauna, spa, steam room, 2 bars, lounge, shops, babysitting, dry cleaning, laundry service, concierge, Internet, business services, convention center, travel services, parking (fee), no-smoking floors* 💳 *AE, DC, MC, V.*

$$$–$$$$ **Holiday Inn Pudong.** In the commercial district of Pudong, this Holiday Inn is well-situated for travelers with business in the area and just a four-block walk to metro Line 2 into Puxi. Rooms are simply decorated—beige walls, bird's-eye maple furniture—but provide plenty of room to spread out your suitcases. The gym and indoor pool are quite large. For entertainment, there's a KTV (karaoke) club, a lobby piano bar, and an Irish pub with Guinness and Kilkenny on tap. ✉ *899 Dongfang Lu, Pudong 200122* ☎ *021/5830–6666 or 800/465–4329* 🖷 *021/5830–5555* 🌐 *www.holiday-inn.com* *285 rooms, 30 suites* *3*

restaurants, coffee shop, patisserie, in-room safes, minibars, cable TV, indoor pool, gym, hair salon, massage, sauna, steam room, billiards, 2 bars, piano bar, pub, babysitting, dry cleaning, laundry service, concierge, concierge floor, Internet, business services, convention center, travel services, parking (fee), no-smoking floors ☐ *AE, DC, MC, V.*

¢–$ **Changhang Merrylin Hotel.** The Merrylin Corporation is better known throughout China for its restaurants than its hotels, and Changhang Merrylin Hotel's exceptional Chinese restaurant overshadows its fair-size inexpensive rooms. Decor aspires to European grandeur but comes off as amusingly tacky. Reliefs and golden statues of frolicking nymphs dominate the lobby, and rooms are decked out in gold-flecked wallpaper and crackled white-painted fixtures. Service can be brusque, but the location is convenient, within 3 blocks of the 10-story Next Age Department Store and metro Line 2 to Puxi. ✉ *818 Zhangyang Lu, Pudong 200122* ☎ *021/5835–5555* 🖷 *021/5835–7799* *192 rooms, 32 suites* *3 restaurants, room service, minibars, cable TV, hair salon, lobby lounge, shops, dry cleaning, laundry service, concierge, Internet, business services, meeting rooms, airport shuttle, parking (fee)* ☐ *AE, DC, MC, V.*

NANJING XI LU & JING'AN

$$$$ **The Four Seasons.** With palm trees, fountains, and golden-hued marble as warm as sunshine, the lobby of the Four Seasons establishes the hotel's theme as an elegant oasis in bustling downtown Puxi. Opened in 2002, this 37-story luxury hotel caters to its largely business clientele. It has impeccable service, a 24-hour business center, a gym, and butler service. The spacious rooms—just 12 to 15 per floor—include safes big enough for a laptop, DVD/CD players, and marble showers and tubs (one of each). Nanjing Road and the Shanghai Museum are within a 10-minute walk, but there are convincing reasons to stay in: the Jazz 37 club; the exceptional Si Ji Xuan Cantonese restaurant; and **TIP→ you don't want to miss one of the spa's indulgent Balinese treatments.** ✉ *500 Weihai Lu, Jing'an 200041* ☎ *021/6256–8888 or 800/819–5053* 🖷 *021/6256–5678* 🌐 *www.fourseasons.com* *360 rooms, 79 suites* *4 restaurants, room service, some in-room faxes, in-room safes, minibars, cable TV, in-room VCRs, in-room data ports, Wi-Fi, pool, gym, hair salon, hot tub, spa, steam room, bar, lounge, shop, babysitting, dry cleaning, laundry service, concierge, concierge floor, Internet, business services, convention center, travel services, parking (fee), no-smoking floors* ☐ *AE, DC, MC, V.*

$$$$ **The Portman Ritz-Carlton.** Outstanding facilities and a high-profile location in the Shanghai Center have made the Portman Ritz-Carlton one of the city's top attractions since its opening in 1998. The 50-story hotel devotes three floors solely to its fitness center and another four to its executive club rooms. The two-story lobby—a popular networking spot and the location of the best afternoon tea in town—exudes cool refinement with its ebony, marble, and chrome touches. Renovations to be completed in 2007 will spruce up all guest rooms with plasma TVs and DVD players. In addition to the Shanghai Center's surrounding shops, banks, airline offices, and restaurants, the hotel has its own deli and four top-

notch restaurants. Though the hotel touts its consistent rankings as one of the best employers and hotels in Asia, there have been complaints that service has slipped and there are often long lines for the concierge and taxi stand. ✉ *1376 Nanjing Xi Lu, Jing'an 200040* ☎ *021/6279–8888 or 800/241–3333* 🖷 *021/6279–8887* 🌐 *www.ritzcarlton.com* *510 rooms, 68 suites* *4 restaurants, snack bar, room service, in-room safes, minibars, cable TV, in-room data ports, tennis court, indoor-outdoor pool, health club, hair salon, hot tub, massage, sauna, steam room, racquetball, squash, 2 bars, shops, babysitting, dry cleaning, laundry service, concierge, concierge floor, Internet, business services, convention center, helipad, parking (fee), no-smoking rooms* 💳 *AE, DC, MC, V.*

$$$$ **Shanghai JC Mandarin.** At the base of the JC Mandarin's 30-story blue-glass towers lies the most memorable lobby in Shanghai. Its five-story hand-painted mural depicts the voyage of the Ming Dynasty admiral Zheng Ho. Opened in 1991, the hotel overhauled most public areas in 2004 and 2005. The Mandarin Club Lounge now occupies an inviting space on the 2nd floor. The fitness center has added a spa. The Cuba cigar bar has carved a stylish lounge out of a former storeroom. Unfortunately, the spacious rooms are long overdue for an update. Though they are comfortable with earthy tones and natural wood, they lack the modern elegance of their five-star competitors. ✉ *1225 Nanjing Xi Lu, Jing'an 200040* ☎ *021/6279–1888 or 800/338–8355* 🖷 *021/6279–1822* 🌐 *www.jcmandarin.com* *476 rooms, 35 suites* *4 restaurants, café, patisserie, room service, in-room safes, minibars, cable TV, in-room data ports, tennis court, indoor pool, gym, hair salon, hot tub, massage, sauna, spa, steam room, squash, 2 bars, piano, shops, babysitting, dry cleaning, laundry service, concierge, concierge floor, Internet, business services, meeting rooms, parking (fee), no-smoking floors* 💳 *AE, DC, MC, V.*

$–$$$$ **Heng Shan Moller Villa.** Part gingerbread dollhouse, part castle, the Heng Shan Moller Villa was built by British businessman Eric Moller to resemble a castle his daughter envisioned in a dream. The family fled Shanghai in 1941, and after 1949 the house was the Communist Youth League's headquarters. Opened as a boutique hotel in 2002, the original villa has 11 deluxe rooms and has been ostentatiously restored with parquet floors, chintzy crystal chandeliers, and too much gold paint. Standard rooms in the new Building No. 2 are disappointingly plain and service is merely perfunctory. Guests have access to the neighboring Shanghai Grand Club's excellent fitness center. ✉ *30 Shaanxi Nan Lu, Luwan 200040* ☎ *021/6247–8881 Ext. 607* 🖷 *021/6289–1020* 🌐 *www.mollervilla.com* *40 rooms, 5 suites* *6 restaurants, coffee shop, some in-room safes, minibars, cable TV, in-room data ports, hair salon, shop, laundry service, Internet, business services, meeting rooms, free parking* 💳 *AE, DC, MC, V.*

NORTH SHANGHAI

$–$$$$ **Astor House Hotel.** The oldest hotel in China, the Astor House Hotel does an admirable job of capturing the feeling of Victorian Shanghai. The lobby's dark-wood columns and vaulted ceilings are accented by potted orchids and photos of famous visitors from the hotel's illustrious past (including Charlie Chaplin, Ulysses Grant, and Albert Einstein). The hotel has maintained its popularity with both budget and business travelers with its spacious, high-ceilinged rooms, often decorated with historical memorabilia, that more than compensate for the hotel's lack of views. We especially like Executive Room A, with its hardwood floors, oriental carpet, and rain shower. ■ TIP→ **Skip the renovated modern penthouse rooms—they lack the historical charm of the lower floors.** ✉ *15 Huangpu Lu, Hongkou 200080* ☎ *021/6324–6388* 🖷 *021/6324–3179* 🌐 *www.astorhotel.com* *127 rooms, 3 suites* *2 restaurants, café, room service, in-room data ports, some in-room faxes, some in-room safes, some minibars, cable TV, some in-room VCRs, gym, hair salon, bar, piano, shops, baby-sitting, dry cleaning, laundry service, concierge, Internet, business services, convention center, free parking, no-smoking rooms* ▭ *AE, DC, MC, V.*

$ **Broadway Mansions Hotel.** One of Shanghai's revered old buildings, the Broadway Mansions Hotel has anchored the north end of the Bund since 1934. Although the good-size rooms were last updated in 2001, the worn wood furniture, industrial bathrooms, and steam radiators betray their age. In contrast, business rooms are strikingly modern, with cool gray-and-tan interiors, glass-topped desks and nightstands, and separate marble showers and tubs. River-view rooms cost Y100 extra; request a higher floor to reduce the street noise. ✉ *20 Suzhou Bei Lu, Hongkou 200080* ☎ *021/6324–6260 Ext. 2326* 🖷 *021/6306–5147* 🌐 *www.broadwaymansions.com* *161 rooms, 72 suites* *2 restaurants, café, patisserie, room service, some in-room faxes, some in-room safes, minibars, cable TV, in-room data ports, gym, hair salon, massage, sauna, 2 bars, piano, babysitting, laundry service, concierge floor, Internet, business services, meeting rooms, airport shuttle, some free parking* ▭ *AE, DC, MC, V.*

$ **Panorama Century Court.** In a part of town dominated by historic properties, Panorama Century Court stands out for its modern facilities, competitive prices, and great Bund views from across the Waibaidu Bridge. The 32-story Accor-owned hotel attracts European tourists familiar with the brand as well as business travelers. One- to three-bedroom suites all include living rooms and tiny kitchens, but you'll have to request utensils. Standard rooms have thoughtfully designed bathrooms with handy shelves for toiletries. If you want to take full advantage of the view, ■ TIP→ **ask for a room above the 18th floor—otherwise your river view will be blocked by a billboard.** ✉ *53 Huangpu Lu, Hongkou 200080* ☎ *021/5393–0008* 🖷 *021/5393–0009* *62 rooms, 92 suites* *Restaurant, room service, in-room safes, some kitchens, minibars, microwaves, refrigerators, cable TV, in-room data ports, gym, sauna, steam room, lobby lounge, library, piano, laundry facilities, laundry service, concierge, Internet, business services, meeting rooms, free parking* ▭ *AE, DC, MC, V.*

HONGQIAO & GUBEI

$$$$ **The Regent.** This newcomer to town is already giving Shanghai's other five-star hotels a run for their money. All rooms come with 42" flat-screen TVs, luxurious rain showers, and dazzling city views. The

Regent's location outside the city center, on the edge of the Former French Concession, is more than compensated by the hotel's choice of eight restaurants, L'Institute de Guerlain Spa, and stunning infinity edge lap pool, where guests can feel as if they are swimming off into Puxi's cityscape. Guests also rave about the studio and corner suite's exceptional showers, which look out through a wall of glass to sweeping views of downtown Shanghai. An extensive gym and outdoor tennis courts add to the hotel's cache. ✉ *1116 Yan'an Xi Lu, Hongqiao 200052* ☎ *021/6115–9988* 🖷 *021/6115–9977* 🌐 *www.regenthotels.com* *511 rooms, 83 suites* *8 restaurants, patisserie, in-room data ports, in-room safes, minibars, some in-room hot tubs, in-room VCRs by request, 2 tennis courts, indoor pool, gym, health club, hair salon, spa, bar, lobby lounge, babysitting, dry cleaning, laundry service, concierge, concierge floor, Internet, business services, convention center, travel services, free parking, no-smoking rooms, no-smoking floors* 💳 *AE, DC, MC, V.*

$$$$ **Renaissance Yangtze.** Next door to the Sheraton Grand Tai Ping Yang, the Renaissance does not quite match its neighbor's detailed elegance and service (or lower prices, for that matter). It is nonetheless a great option in the Hongqiao area, with eight executive floors catering to conventioneers and corporate types with business at INTEX and Shanghai Mart. There's a good-size gym and pool and an often-overlooked cigar bar. The hotel's long-standing reputation for top-quality catering at its five restaurants is well deserved, particularly at its Chinese restaurant Dynasty. Rooms are warm, with sunrise-golden comforters and drapes, vermilion club chairs, and auburn-tiled bathrooms. The general manager is often to be found chatting with guests in the lobby or greeting staff by their first name, a surprisingly personal touch among Shanghai's five-star hotels. ✉ *2099 Yanan Xi Lu, Hongqiao 200336* ☎ *021/6275–0000 or 888/236–2427* 🖷 *021/6275–0750* 🌐 *www.renaissancehotels.com* *521 rooms, 23 suites* *5 restaurants, café, patisserie, room service, in-room safes, minibars, cable TV, in-room data ports, indoor pool, health club, hair salon, hot tub, massage, sauna, billiards, 2 bars, lobby lounge, piano, shops, babysitting, dry cleaning, laundry service, concierge, concierge floor, Internet, business services, convention center, travel services, some free parking, no-smoking floors* 💳 *AE, DC, MC, V.*

$$$$ **Shanghai Marriott Hongqiao.** With 8 stories and 325 rooms, the unpretentious Marriott Hongqiao feels like a boutique hotel compared to its soaring competitors in Hongqiao. The hotel is quiet; inside Premier rooms have balconies overlooking the 3rd-floor pool-side courtyard. Porcelain vases and Ming-influenced furniture add some Chinese flair to the generous-size rooms. The Manhattan Steakhouse serves tender, juicy steaks; the Marriott Café has an excellent Sunday brunch; and the Champions Bar offers many after-work promotions. When making reservations, be sure to ask about special rates and packages, especially on weekends. ✉ *2270 Hongqiao Lu, Gubei 200336* ☎ *021/6237–6000 or 800/228–9290* 🖷 *021/6237–6222* 🌐 *www.marriott.com* *312 rooms, 13 suites* *4 restaurants, patisserie, room service, in-room safes, minibars, cable TV, some in-room VCRs, in-room data ports, Wi-Fi, some in-room VCRs, tennis court, indoor pool, health club, hair salon, hot tub, massage, sauna, steam room, 2 bars, lobby lounge, sports bar,*

6

babysitting, dry cleaning, laundry service, concierge, concierge floor, Internet, business services, convention center, airport shuttle, travel services, free parking, no-smoking floors ▭ *AE, DC, MC, V.*

$$$$ **Sheraton Grand Tai Ping Yang.** Even after 16 years, the Sheraton Grand is still the go-to hotel for savvy business travelers staying in Hongqiao. Formerly the Westin, this Japanese-managed property has four club floors, one-touch service by phone, and golf privileges at Shanghai International Golf Club. Oriental rugs, antique pottery, folding Chinese screens, and wooden masks and statues, all chosen by the hotel's General Manager on his travels, add personal touches that cannot be found at any other hotel in town. Spacious standard rooms include large desks and ergonomic chairs, and the plush grand rooms have oriental carpets and overstuffed chairs in the separate bed and sitting rooms. A grand staircase sweeps you from the formal lobby up to the 2nd floor and the exceptional Bauernstube deli. Giovanni's serves Italian food as impressive as its views from atop the 27th floor. ✉ *5 Zunyi Nan Lu, Hongqiao 200336* ☎ *021/6275–8888 or 888/625–5144* 📠 *021/6275–5420* 🌐 *www.sheratongrand-shanghai.com* *474 rooms, 22 suites* *5 restaurants, café, coffee shop, room service, in-room safes, minibars, cable TV, some in-room faxes, some in-room hot tubs, in-room data ports, Wi-Fi, in-room VCRs by request, golf privileges, pool, tennis court, gym, health club, jogging track, hair salon, massage, sauna, steam room, 2 bars, lobby lounge, piano, library, shops, babysitting, dry cleaning, laundry service, concierge, concierge floor, Internet, business services, convention center, travel services, parking (fee), no-smoking floors* ▭ *AE, DC, MC, V.*

Fodor's Choice ★

$$–$$$$ **Cypress Hotel.** Once part of tycoon Victor Sassoon's estate, the Cypress Hotel's shaded, stream-laced grounds remain a tranquil retreat in noisy Shanghai. From the hotel's 149 rooms, you can look out over the garden and actually hear birdsong rather than car horns. The extensive health club boasts a swimming pool and outdoor tennis courts, which help to compensate for the hotel's limited English-speaking staff and location far, far away from downtown Puxi. ✉ *2419 Hongqiao Lu, Hongqiao 200335* ☎ *021/6268–8868* 📠 *021/6268–1878* *141 rooms, 8 suites* *2 restaurants, room service, in-room safes, minibars, cable TV, in-room data ports, driving range, putting green, 3 tennis courts, indoor pool, gym, hair salon, massage, sauna, steam room, fishing, basketball, billiards, bowling, Ping-Pong, squash, bar, shop, babysitting, dry cleaning, laundry service, Internet, business services, meeting rooms, airport shuttle, travel services, parking (fee), no-smoking rooms* ▭ *AE, DC, MC, V.*

At a Glance

ENGLISH	PINYIN	CHINESE CHARACTERS
POINTS OF INTEREST		
Anting Villa Hotel	Āntíng Biéshù Huāyuán Jiǔdiàn	安亭别墅花园酒店
Astor House Hotel	Pǔjiāng Fàndiàn	浦江饭店
Broadway Mansions	Shànghǎi Dàshà	上海大厦
Captain Hostel	Chuánzhǎng Qīngnián Jiǔdiàn**	船长青年酒店
Changhang Merrylin Hotel	Chángháng Měilín'gé Dàjiǔdiàn	长航美林阁大酒店
Crowne Plaza	Yínxīng Huángguān Jiàrì Jiǔdiàn	银星皇冠假日酒店
Cypress Hotel	Lóngbǎi Fàndiàn	龙柏饭店
Dong Hu Hotel	Dōnghú Bīnguǎn	东湖宾馆
Four Seasons Hotel	Sìjì Jiǔdiàn	四季酒店
Grand Hyatt	Shànghǎi Jīnmào Jūnyuè Dàjiǔdiàn	上海金茂君悦大酒店
Hengshan Moller Villa	Héngshān Mǎlè Biéshù Fàndiàn	衡山马勒别墅饭店
Hilton Hotel	Shànghǎi Jìng'ān Xī'ěrdùn Jiǔdiàn	上海静安希尔顿酒店
Holiday Inn Pudong Shanghai	Shànghǎi Pǔdōng Jiàrì Jiǔdiàn	上海浦东假日酒店
Hotel Intercontinental	Jǐnjiāng Tāngchén Zhōujì Dàjiǔdiàn	锦江汤臣洲际大酒店
JC Mandarin	Jǐncāng Wénhuà Dàjiǔdiàn	锦沧文化大酒店
Jin Jiang Hotel	Jǐnjiāng Fàndiàn	锦江饭店
Jing'An	Jìng'ān Bīnguǎn	静安宾馆
JW Marriott	J.W. Wànháo Jiǔdiàn	JW 万豪酒店
Mason Hotel	Měi Chén Dàjiǔdiàn	美臣大酒店
Nanjing Hotel	Nánjīng Fàndiàn	南京饭店
Okura Garden Hotel	Huāyuán Fàndiàn	花园饭店
Old House Inn	Lǎoshíguāng Jiǔdiàn	老时光酒店
Pacific Hotel	Jīnmén Dàjiǔdiàn	金门大酒店
Panorama Century Court	Hǎiwān Dàshà	海湾大厦
Park Hotel	Guójì Fàndiàn	国际饭店
Peace Hotel	Hépíng Fàndiàn	和平饭店

Pudong Shangri-la	Pǔdōng Xiānggélǐlā Jiǔdiàn	浦东香格里拉酒店
Radisson Hotel Shanghai New World	Xīnshìjiè Lìshēng Dàjiǔdiàn	新世界丽笙大酒店
Radisson Plaza Xing Guo Hotel Shanghai	Shànghǎi Xīngguó Bīnguǎn	上海兴国宾馆
Ramada Plaza	Nánxīn Yǎhuá Měidá Dàjiǔdiàn	南新雅华美达大酒店
Regal International East Asia	Fùháo Huánqiú Dōngyà Jiǔdiàn	富豪环球东亚酒店
Renaissance Yangtze Shanghai Hotel	Shànghǎi Yángzǐjiāng wànlì Dàjiǔdiàn	上海扬子江万丽达酒店
Ruijin Hotel	Ruìjīn Bīnguǎn	瑞金宾馆
Seagull Hotel	Hǎi'ōu Fàndiàn	海鸥饭店
Shanghai Hotel	Shànghǎi Bīnguǎn	上海宾馆
Shanghai Marriott Hongqiao	Shànghǎi Wànháo Hóngqiáo Dàjiǔdiàn	上海万豪虹桥大酒店
Sheraton Grand Tai Ping Yang	Shànghǎi Tàipíngyáng Dàfàndiàn	上海太平洋大饭店
Sofitel Hyland Hotel	Suǒfēitè Hǎilún Bīnguǎn	索菲特海仑宾馆
Somerset Grand	Shèngjiè Gāojí Fúwù Gōngyù	盛捷高级服务公寓
Somerset Xuhui	Xúhuì Shèngjié Fúwù Gōngyù	徐汇盛捷服务公寓
Tai Yuan Villa	Taìyuán Biéshù	太原别墅
The Portman Ritz-Carlton	Bōtèmàn Lìjiā Jiǔdiàn	波特曼丽嘉酒店
The Regent	Shànghǎi Lóngzhīmèng Lìjīng Dàjiǔdiàn	上海龙之梦丽晶大酒店
The St. Regis	Shànghǎi Ruìjí Hóngtǎ Dàjiǔdiàn	上海瑞吉红塔大酒店
Westin	Wēisītīng Dàfàndiàn	威斯汀大饭店
YMCA	Qīngniánhuì Bīnguǎn	青年会宾馆

Side Trips

Hangzhou's Buddhist Lingyin Temple Hall of the 500 Arhats

WORD OF MOUTH

"We visited Hangzhou, Suzhou, and a 'water town' called Zhouzhuang. We liked Suzhou the best, but we may have missed some of Hangzhou's charms. Zhouzhuang was very touristy, but pretty."

–Neil_Oz

www.fodors.com/forums

SIDE TRIPS PLANNER

Follow the Coast

Few tour routes these days have exclusive planners just for China's central coast, which is a pity. After all, the provinces of Zhejiang and Fujian have much on offer for bicyclists, hikers, ocean swimmers, and windsurfers. And as one of China's first Special Economic Zones, Xiamen is currently awash with cash but still hasn't lost its old-world charm. Fall and spring are the ideal times to visit the region. Spring, especially April and May, have very comfortable temperatures and the trees and flowers are in full bloom. Hot and muggy summer is not the best time to visit—many of the cities are uncomfortable from mid-June though August. The region has a long and very pleasant fall season—moderate weather and clear skies lasting into early December. Chinese tourists flood in during the two "Golden Week" holidays at the start of May and October, so try to avoid those two weeks. Most of the region's sights are open daily.

With the Kids

One of our favorite child-friendly places is the garden behind the **Pagoda of Six Harmonies** in Hangzhou. Start by climbing the stairs of the seven-story pagoda itself. The excellent views from the top look out onto the river and are worth the hike. Visit the garden and play among the miniature re-creations of China's most famous pagodas and temples—it's as educational as it is fun. With the tall trees and cozy benches, this park is an ideal place for a picnic. The best time to visit is about 4 PM, before the sun dips and the tower closes. There are also several gift shops next to the tower that sell everything from shell necklaces to kiddie qi-paos. If you want to avoid crowds remember, on the 18th day of the 8th lunar month, the pagoda is packed with people, all wanting the best seat for "Qiantang Reversal," when the river reverses itself and large waves form.

The pagoda is 2½ km (1½ mi) south of West Lake. ✉ *Fuxing Jie, on the Qiantang River* 🎫 *Y15* ⏲ *Daily 6 AM–6:30 PM.*

WHAT IT COSTS In Yuan

	$$$$	$$$	$$	$	¢
RESTAURANTS	over Y165	Y100–Y165	Y50–Y99	Y25–Y49	under Y25
HOTELS	over Y1,800	Y1,400–Y1,800	Y1,100–Y1,399	Y700–Y1,099	under Y700

Restaurant prices are for a main course, excluding tax and tips. Hotel prices are for a standard double room, including taxes.

Wonders of West Lake

A famous poem that says, "Of all the lakes, north, south, east and west, the one at West Lake is the best." Why? Because this ancient man-made lake casts the mold for scores of manicured lakes across China. How to explore it? One way is to start at where Pinghai Road meets Harbin Road in the northeastern part of the lake. There's a fabulous boardwalk with weeping willows, restaurants, and a lakeside teahouse.

Wending north, you can cross the street to ascend a small hill capped with the Baochu Pagoda. Here, the views of West Lake are some of the best in the city. Once you climb down, you can venture to the Baidi and Sudi Causeways, through the middle of the lake. Don't miss the classical Lingyin Temple, nestled in the nearby hills. Two of Lingyin's most famous halls include the Tianwang (Heavenly King) Hall and Mahavira Hall—they feature towering Buddhas and sword-carrying deities.

Take a guided boat from the southern shore by night, when the Three Pools Mirroring the Moon pagoda is alight. This stone pagoda has six incised circles. When candles are set inside them, the light appears as romantic moons. For romantic robes, visit the famed China National Silk Museum. The gift shop offers exquisite regional silks. And that's just the tip of the temple. It takes a lifetime to explore all of West Lake's charms. As Marco Polo once wrote, "In heaven there is paradise, on earth there is Hangzhou."

About the Restaurants & Hotels

Despite the fact that they are often portrayed as quaint, scenic marvels, Hangzhou and Suzhou are huge cities with several million residents. Western hotel chains are in both markets and cater as much to business travelers as to tourists. A few exceptional local hotels rival the quality standards of their foreign competitors; however, most are less-refined budget properties with fewer amenities.

On the Menu

Zhejiang cuisine is often steamed or roasted and has a more subtle, salty flavor; specialties include yellow croaker with Chinese cabbage, sea eel, drunken chicken, and stewed chicken. In Shaoxing locals traditionally start the day by downing a bowl or two of *huang jiu*—the true breakfast of champions. Shaoxing's most famous dish is its deep-fried *chou dofu*, or stinky tofu. Try it with a touch of the local chili sauce. Fujian cuisine is considered by some to have its own characteristics. Spareribs are a specialty, as are soups and stews using a soy and rice-wine stock. The coastal cities offer a wonderful range of seafood, including river eel with leeks, fried jumbo prawns, and steamed crab.

Mom-and-pop Chinese restaurants are the rule in the water towns. In Suzhou, the focus is on its storied centuries-old restaurants along Guanqian Jie; the few non-Chinese outlets (that aren't fast food) are found in hotels. Hangzhou's dining scene has progressed much farther; you'll find everything from tiny noodle shops to expensive Cantonese shark's-fin restaurants to outposts of Italian and Thai chains from Shanghai and Hong Kong.

By Will Thomson and Joshua Samuel Brown

It's easy to get Shanghai fatigue. The traffic, crowds, smog, and go-go pace of China's largest city can wear you down and leave you longing for someplace greener, more laid-back, and more reflective of China's past rather than its surge toward the future.

Water towns are the quickest escape. These living history museums along eastern China's vast canal system lie within a two-hour arc of Shanghai, down country roads and past fields still worked by hand, as they have been for centuries. City dwellers flock to the water towns to admire the ancient houses and simpler way of life—but then return to modernity and their own homes in time for dinner. Farther afield, the lakes, hills, gardens, and streams of eastern China provide a scenic reminder that Shanghai's urban canyon is not a natural, but a human-made, wonder, and that there are places where the greatest heights are peaks rather than skyscrapers.

Hangzhou

Residents of Hangzhou are immensely proud of their city, and will often point to a classical saying that identifies it as an "earthly paradise." Indeed, Hangzhou is one of the country's most enjoyable cities. The green spaces and hilly landscape that surround the city make Hangzhou unique in Eastern China. Add to the experience a thriving arts scene, sophisticated restaurants, and vibrant nightlife, and Hangzhou vies with nearby Shanghai as the hippest city in the East.

Exploring

West Lake (Xihu). With arched bridges stretching over the water, West Lake is the heart of leisure in Hangzhou. Originally a bay, the whole area was built up gradually throughout the years, a combination of natural changes and human shaping of the land. The shores are idyllic and imminently photographable, enhanced by meandering paths, artificial islands, and countless pavilions with upturned roofs.

Two pedestrian causeways cross the lake: **Baidi** in the north and **Sudi** in the west. They are both named for two poet–governors from different

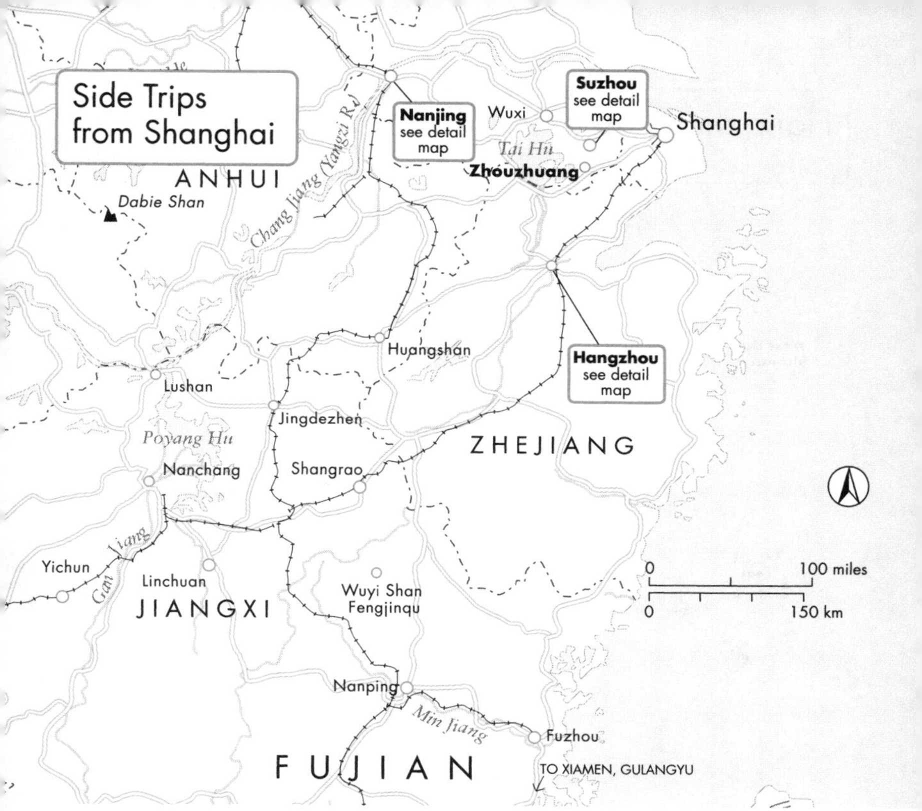

eras who invested in landscaping and developing the lake. Ideal for strolling or biking, both walkways are lined with willow and peach trees, crossed by bridges, and dotted with benches where you can pause to admire the views. ✉ *East of the city, along Nanshan Lu.*

❷ The Bai Causeway ends at the largest island on West Lake, **Solitary Hill Island** (Gushan). A palace for the exclusive use of the emperor during his visits to Hangzhou once stood here. On its southern side is a small, carefully composed park around several pavilions and a pond. A path leads up the hill to the **Seal Engraver's Society** (Xileng Yinshe) (☎0571/8781–5910 🎫Y5 ⏲Daily 9–5). Professional carvers here will

ZHEJIANG

The province of Zhejiang showcases the region's agricultural prowess and dedication to nature, even as it is one of the most populous urban regions of China. Zhejiang's farms are also among the most prosperous, and rural incomes are some three to four times higher than in many other areas of the country. Geographically, the river-basin plains in the north near Shanghai give way to mountains in the south of the province. Besides grain, the province also is recognized in China for its tea, crafts, silk production, and long tradition of sculpture and carving.

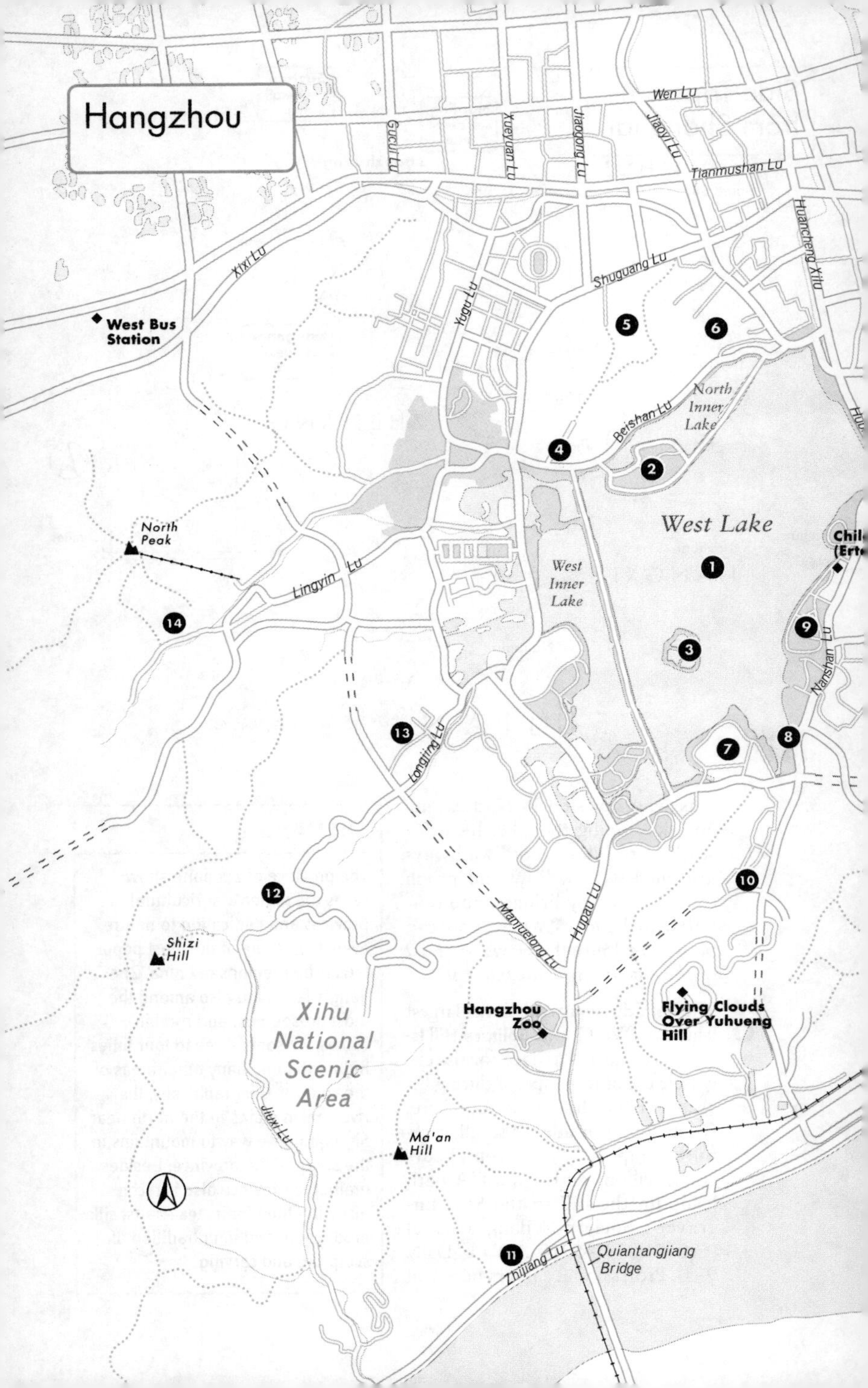

Hangzhou
Wen Lu
Jiaoyi Lu
Jiaogong Lu
Xueyuan Lu
Gucui Lu
Tianmushan Lu
Huancheng Xilu
Shuguang Lu
Xixi Lu
West Bus Station
Yugu Lu
North Inner Lake
Beishan Lu
West Lake
West Inner Lake
North Peak
Lingyin Lu
Nanshan Lu
Longjing Lu
Manjuelong Lu
Hupau Lu
Shizi Hill
Xihu National Scenic Area
Hangzhou Zoo
Flying Clouds Over Yuhueng Hill
Jiuxi Lu
Ma'an Hill
Zhijiang Lu
Quiantangjiang Bridge
1
2
3
4
5
6
7
8
9
10
11
12
13
14

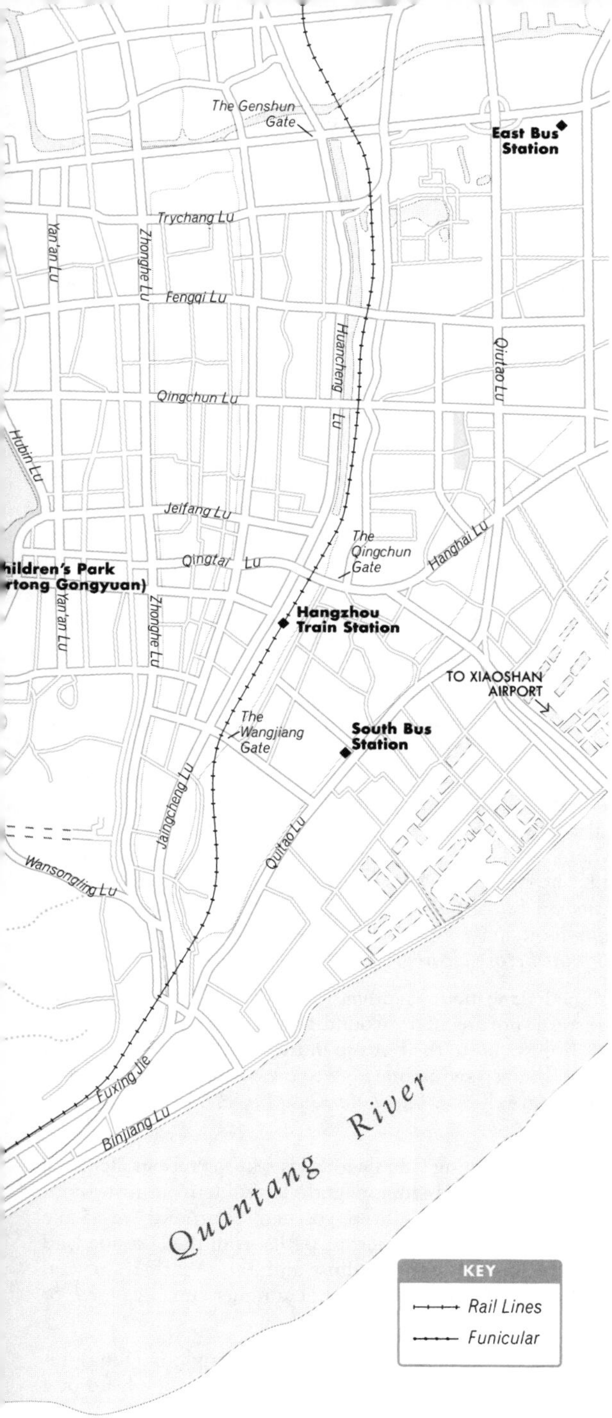

China National Silk Museum (Zhongguo Sichou Bowuguan) . . **10**

China Tea Museum (Zhongguo Chaye Bowuguan) . . **13**

Dragon Well Tea Park (Longjing Wencha) **12**

Evening Sunlight at Thunder Peak Pagoda (Leifeng Xizhao) **7**

Hangzhou Aquarium (Hangzhou Haidi Shijie) **8**

Orioles Singing in the Willow Waves (Liulang Wenying) **9**

Pagoda of Six Harmonies (Liuhe Ta) **11**

Precious Stone Hill (Baoshi Shan) **6**

Solitary Hill Island (Gushan) **2**

Temple of the Soul's Retreat (Lingyin Si) **14**

Three Pools Reflecting the Moon (Santan Yinyue) **3**

West Lake (Xihu) **1**

Yellow Dragon Cave (Huanglong Dong) **5**

Yue Fei Mausoleum (Yue Fei Mu) **4**

design and execute seals. The society's garden has one of the best views of the lake. Solitary Hill Island is home to the **Zhejiang Provincial Museum** (Zhejiang Bowuguan) (☎0571/8797–1177 🌐www.zhejiangmuseum.com 🎫 Free 🕒 Weekdays 8:30–4:30). The museum has a good collection of archaeological finds, as well as bronzes and paintings. ✉ *West Lake* 🎫 *Free* 🕒 *Daily 8–dusk.*

3 On the southern side of the lake is the man-made island of **Three Pools Reflecting the Moon** (Santan Yinyue). Here you'll find walkways surrounding several large ponds, all connected by zigzagging bridges. Off the island's southern shore are three stone Ming Dynasty pagodas. During the Mid-Autumn Moon Festival, held in the middle of September, lanterns are lit in the pagodas, creating the three golden disks that give the island its name. Boats costing between Y35 and Y45 run between here and Solitary Hill Island. ✉ *West Lake* 🎫 *Y20* 🕒 *Daily 7–5:30.*

9 Along the eastern bank of the lake is **Orioles Singing in the Willow Waves** (Liulang Wenying), a nice place to watch boats on the lake. This park comes alive during the Lantern Festival, held in the winter. Paper lanterns are set to float on the river, under the willow bows. ✥ *Near the intersection of Hefang Jie and Nanshan Lu.*

7 Fodor's Choice ★ On the southeastern shore of West Lake is the **Evening Sunlight at Thunder Peak Pagoda** (Leifeng Xizhao). Local legend says that the original Thunder Peak Pagoda was constructed to imprison a snake-turned-human who lost her mortal love on West Lake. The pagoda collapsed in 1924, perhaps finally freeing the White Snake. A new tower, completed in 2002, sits beside the remains of its predecessor. There's a sculpture on each level, including a carving that depicts the tragic story of the White Snake. The foundation dates to AD 976 and is an active archaeological site, where scientists uncovered a miniature silver pagoda containing what is said to be a lock of the Buddha's hair; on display in a separate hall. The view of the lake is breathtaking, particularly at sunset. ✉ *15 Nanshan Lu* ☎ *0571/8796–4515* 🌐 *www.leifengta.com.cn* 🎫 *Y40* 🕒 *Apr.–Nov., daily 8 AM–9 PM; Dec.–Mar., daily 7:30–8:30; last admission 30 mins before closing.*

8 The well-designed **Hangzhou Aquarium** (Hangzhou Haidi Shijie), on West Lake's eastern shore, centers around a walk-through glass tunnel. The main tank brings you to the bottom of the ocean, with sharks and other denizens of the deep swimming above you. There's also a seal pool and several hands-on exhibits. ✉ *49 Nanshan Lu* ☎ *0571/8706–9500* 🎫 *Y60* 🕒 *Daily 8:30–5.*

6 The slender spire of Protecting Chu Pagoda rises atop **Precious Stone Hill** (Baoshi Shan). The brick and stone pagoda is visible from just about anywhere on the lake. From the hilltop, you can see around West Lake and across to Hangzhou City. Numerous paths from the lakeside lead up the hill, which is dotted with Buddhist and Taoist shrines. Several caves provide shade and relief from the hot summer sun. ✉ *North of West Lake.*

5 At the foot of Qixia Hill is **Yellow Dragon Cave** (Huanglong Dong), famous for a never-ending stream of water spurting from the head of a

yellow dragon. Nearby is a garden and a stage for traditional Yue opera performances that are given daily. In a nearby groove you'll see examples of rare "square bamboo." ✉ *Shuguang Lu* ☎ *0571/8798–5860* 🎫 *Y15* 🕒 *Daily 7:30–6.*

Equally celebrated as West Lake is the famous local Dragon Well Tea Park. A short ride southwest of the
12 lake takes you to **Dragon Well Tea Park** (Longjing Wencha), set amid rolling tea plantations. This park is named for an ancient well whose water is considered ideal for brewing the famous local Longjing tea. Opening prices are intentionally high, so be sure to bargain for a good price. ✉ *Longjing Lu, next to Dragon Well Temple.*

★ 13 The fascinating **China Tea Museum** (Zhongguo Chaye Bowuguan) explores all the facets of China's tea culture, such as the utensils used in the traditional ceremony. Galleries contain fascinating information about the varieties and quality of leaves, brewing techniques, and gathering methods, all with good English explanations. A shop also offers a range of tea for sale, without the bargaining you'll encounter at Dragon Well Tea Park. ✉ *Off Longjing Lu, north of Dragon Well Tea Park* 🌐 *www.teamuseum.cn* 🎫 *Free* 🕒 *Daily 8:30 AM–4:30 PM.*

One of the major Zen Buddhist
14 shrines in China, the **Temple of the**
Fodor's Choice ★ **Soul's Retreat** (Lingyin Si) was founded in AD 326 by Hui Li, a Buddhist monk from India. He looked at the surrounding mountains and exclaimed, "This is the place where the souls of immortals retreat," hence the name. This site is especially notable for religious carvings on the nearby **Peak That Flew from Afar** (Feilai Feng). From the 10th to the 14th century, monks and artists sculpted more than 300 iconographical images on the mountain's face and inside caves. Unfortunately, the destruction wrought by the Red Guards during the Cultural Revolution is nowhere more evident than here. The temple and

RENT A BIKE

Shaded by willow trees, West Lake is one of the country's most pleasant places for bicycling. This path, away from car traffic, is also a quick way to move between the area's major sights. There are numerous bike-rental shops around Orioles Singing in the Willow Waves Park. The rental rate is about Y10 per hour. A deposit and some form of identification are usually required.

TOURS

Hotels can set up tours of the city's sights. You can also hire a car, driver, and translator through **CITS**, (✉ 1 Shihan Lu, Hangzhou ☎ 0571/8515–2888), which has an office east of West Lake in the building of the Zhejiang Tourism Board. It's relatively inexpensive, and you'll be privy to discounts you wouldn't be able to negotiate for yourself. Smaller travel services tend to be less reliable and less experienced with the needs of foreign travelers. Taxi drivers at the train station or in front of hotels will often offer tours. Although these can be as good as official ones, your driver's knowledge of English is often minimal.

CLOSE UP

A River Runs Through It

DURING THE AUTUMNAL EQUINOX, when the moon's gravitational pull is at its peak, huge waves crash up the Qiantang River. Every year at this time, crowds gather at a safe distance to watch what begins as a distant line of white waves approaching. As it nears, it becomes a towering, thundering wall of water.

The phenomenon, known as a tidal bore occurs when strong tides surge against the current of the river. The Qiantang Tidal bore is the largest in the world, with speeds recorded up to 25 mi an hour, and heights of 30 feet. The Qiantang has the best conditions in the world to produce these tidal waves. Incoming tides are funneled into the shallow river bed from the Gulf of Hangzhou. The bell shape narrows and concentrates the wave. People have been swept away in the past, so police now enforce a strict viewing distance.

carvings are among the most popular spots in Hangzhou. To avoid the crowds, try to visit during the week. The temple is about 3 km (2 mi) southwest of West Lake. ✉ *End of Lingyin Si Lu* ☎ *0571/8796–9691* *Park Y25, temple Y20* ⏲ *Park daily 6:30 AM–6 PM, temple daily 7–5.*

10 From worm to weave, the **China National Silk Museum** (Zhongguo Sichou Bowuguan) explores traditional silk production, illustrating every step of the way. On display are looms, brocades, and a rotating exhibit of historical robes from different Chinese dynasties. The 1st-floor shop has the city's largest selection of silk, and sells it by the meter. The museum is south of West Lake, on the road to Jade Emperor Hill. ✉ *73-1 Yuhuangshan Lu* ☎ *0571/8706–2129* 🌐 *www.chinasilkmuseum.com* *Free* ⏲ *Daily 8–6.*

11 Atop **Moon Mountain** (Yuelin Shan) stands the impressive **Pagoda of Six Harmonies** (Liuhe Ta). Those who climb to the top of the seven-story pagoda are rewarded with great views across the Qiantang River. Originally lanterns were lit in its windows, and the pagoda served as a lighthouse for ships navigating the river. On the 18th day of the 8th lunar month, the pagoda is packed with people wanting the best seat for Qiantang Reversal. On this day the flow of the river reverses itself, creating large waves that for centuries have delighted observers. Behind the pagoda in an extensive park is an exhibit of 100 or so miniature pagodas, representing every Chinese style. The pagoda is 2½ km (1½ mi) south of West Lake. ✉ *Fuxing Jie, on the Qiantang River* *Y15* ⏲ *Daily 6 AM–6:30 PM.*

Where to Stay & Eat

$$–$$$$ Fodor's Choice ★ ✕ **Louwailou Restaurant.** Back in 1848, this place opened as a fish shack on West Lake. Business boomed and it became the most famous restaurant in the province. Specializing in Zhejiang cuisine, Louwailou makes special use of lake perch, which is steamed and served with vinegar sauce. Another highlight is the classic *su dongpo* pork, slow cooked in yellow-

rice wine and tender enough to cut with chopsticks. Hangzhou's most famous dish, Beggar's Chicken, is wrapped in lotus leaves and baked in a clay shell. It's as good as it sounds. ✉ *30 Gushan Lu, southern tip of Solitary Hill Island* ☎ *0571/8796–9682* ▭ *AE, MC, V.*

$$ ✕ **Haveli.** A sign of the city's cosmopolitan atmosphere, Nanshan Road is home to several good international restaurants. The best of these is this authentic Indian restaurant, with a solid menu of dishes ranging from lamb vindaloo to chicken tandoor cooked in a traditional oven. End your meal with a fantastic mango-flavored yogurt drink. Choose between the dining room with a high peaked ceiling and exposed wood beams or the large patio. A belly dancer performs nightly. ✉ *77 Nanshan Lu, south of Orioles Singing in the Willow Waves* ☎ *0571/8707–9177* *Reservations essential* ▭ *AE, DC, MC, V.*

¢–$$ ✕ **Zhiweiguan Restaurant.** In business for nearly a century, this restaurant's bustling 1st floor is a pay-as-you-go dim-sum counter. No menu necessary: you point to order a bamboo steamer filled with their famous dumplings or a bowl of wonton soup. The 2nd floor is for proper dinner, where the menu is full of well-prepared fish dishes. ✉ *83 Renhe Lu, east side of West Lake* ☎ *0571/8701–8638* ▭ *No credit cards.*

¢–$ ✕ **Lingyin Si Vegetarian Restaurant.** Inside the Temple of the Soul's Retreat, this restaurant has turned the Buddhist restriction against eating meat into an opportunity to invent a range of delicious vegetarian dishes. Soy replaces chicken and beef, meaning your meal is as benevolent to your health as to the animal world. ✉ *End of Lingyin Si Lu western shore of West Lake* ☎ *0571/8796–9691* ▭ *No credit cards* ⊙ *No dinner.*

7

$$$–$$$$ **Hyatt Regency Hangzhou.** Hangzhou's newest luxury hotel, the Hyatt Regency combines careful service, comfortable rooms, and a great location. A large pool with a fountain water show overlooks West Lake. Inside there's a day spa, as well as excellent Chinese and Western restaurants. About two blocks north is Hubing Yi Park Boat Dock, where you can catch boats that ply the lake. The rooms are sleekly furnished, and unlike many hotels in China, the beds here are truly soft. Ask for a room on an upper floor for an unobstructed view. ✉ *28 Hu Bin Lu, 310006* ☎ *0571/8779–1234* 🖷 *0571/8779–1818* 🌐 *www.hyatt.com* *390 rooms, 23 suites* *3 restaurants, room service, in-room safes, minibars, in-room broadband, golf privileges, tennis court, indoor pool, gym, sauna, spa, squash, steam room, 2 bars, shops, children's programs (ages 1–12), dry cleaning, laundry service, concierge, business services, convention center, no-smoking rooms* ▭ *AE, DC, MC, V.*

Fodor's Choice ★

$$–$$$$ **Shangri-La Hotel Hangzhou.** Set on the site of an ancient temple, the Shangri-La is itself a scenic and historic landmark. The hotel's 40 hillside acres of camphor and bamboo trees merge seamlessly into the nearby gardens and walkways surrounding West Lake. Spread through two wings, the large rooms have a formal feel, with high ceilings and heavy damask fabrics. Request a room overlooking the lake. The gym and restaurants are all top caliber. A 1st-floor garden bar is an elegant spot to relax with a drink. ✉ *78 Beishan Lu, 310007* ☎ *0571/8797–7951* 🖷 *0571/8707–3545* 🌐 *www.shangri-la.com* *355 rooms, 37 suites* *3 restaurants, room service, in-room safes, minibars, in-room data*

Fodor's Choice ★

CLOSE UP

Art for Art's Sake

THE CONTEMPORARY ARTS SCENE in Hangzhou grows by the year, with a mix of national and international artists calling Hangzhou home. For current art exhibits, grab a copy of ***In Touch*** (☎ 0571/8763-0035 🌐 www.intouchzj.com), an English-language magazine available in many hotels and coffee shops.

Some of the country's hottest artists show their work at **Contrasts** (✉ No. 20-2b Hubin Lu ☎ 0571/8717-2519 🌐 www.contrastsgallery.com).

At **Loft 49** (✉ 49 Hangyin Lu ☎ 0571/8823-8782 🌐 www.loft49.cn), industrial spaces have been transformed into studios for the cutting-edge artists, sculptors, and architects. This former printing factory has free galleries and a café.

Frequent exhibits of painting and sculpture are on display at **Red Star** (✉ 280 Jianguo Nan Lu ☎ 0571/8770-3888 🌐 www.redstarhotel.com).

ports, tennis court, indoor pool, gym, hair salon, hot tub, massage, sauna, steam room, bicycles, billiards, bar, lobby lounge, shops, babysitting, dry cleaning, laundry service, concierge, bike rentals, concierge floor, Internet, business services, convention center, airport shuttle, travel services, no-smoking rooms ▭ *AE, DC, MC, V.*

¢ **Dong Po Hotel.** This budget business hotel is clean and comfortable. The smaller rooms are rather utilitarian, but the location in the center of town—two blocks from the lake and two blocks from the night market—makes this a good choice. ✉ *52 Renhe Lu, 310000* ☎ *0571/8706–9769* *99 rooms, 3 suites* *Restaurant, business services* ▭ *MC, V.*

Shopping

The best souvenirs to buy in Hangzhou are green tea and silk, but all sorts of wooden crafts, silk fans and umbrellas, and antiques are available in small shops sprinkled around town. For the best Longjing tea, head to Dragon Well Tea Park or the China Tea Museum. Around town, especially along Yanan Lu, you can spot the small tea shops by the woklike tea roasters by the entrances.

China Silk City (Zhongguo Sichou Cheng; ✉ 253 Xinhua Lu, between Fengqi Lu and Tiyuchang Lu ☎ 0571/8510–0192) sells silk ties, pajamas, and shirts, plus silk straight off the bolt. A combination health-food store and apothecary, **Fulintang** (✉ 147 Nanshan Lu ☎ 0571/ 8702–6639) sells herbs and other health-enhancing products. About three blocks north of the China Tea Museum, the **Xihu Longjing Tea Company** (✉ 15 Longjing Lu ☎ 0571/ 8796–2219) has a nice selection of Longjing tea.

Hangzhou's **Night Market** (✉ Renhe Lu, east of Huansha Lu) is thriving. In addition to Hangzhou's best selection of late-night snacks, you'll find accessories of every kind—ties, scarves, pillow covers—as well as knockoff designer goods and fake antiques. It's open nightly 6 PM–10:30 PM.

BOAT TRIPS

You can travel overnight by ferry between Hangzhou and Suzhou on the Grand Canal. Tickets are available through CITS or at the dock. It's a slow trip compared to buses and trains, and it's at night, so there's little to see.

One of the best ways to experience the charm of West Lake is on one of the many boats that ply the waters. Ferries charge Y35 for trips to the main islands. They depart when there are enough passengers, usually about every 20 minutes. Small private boats charge Y80 for up to four people, but you can choose your own route. You can head out on your own boat for Y20, but you can't dock at the islands.

Contact: CITS (✉ Huancheng Bei Lu, Hangzhou ☎ 0571/8515-3360).

To & from Hangzhou

2 hrs by train from Shanghai; 3–4 hrs by train from Suzhou.

Hangzhou is most accessible by train. Travel between Shanghai and Hangzhou is quick and convenient: regular trains take about three hours; newer express trains take only two. The train station is crowded and difficult to manage, but hotel travel desks can often book advance tickets for a small fee. Trains also run to Suzhou (3 hours), Nanjing (5½ hours), and most cities in Fujian.

7

The bus hub for the province is Hangzhou, where you'll find four stations. ■ TIP→ **Make sure you check with your hotel or travel agent which bus station you need to use.** There are buses that will get you to Shanghai in 2 hours or Suzhou in 2½ hours. Hangzhou has several stations spread around the city serving different destinations—buses to Shanghai use the East Bus Station, whereas those to Suzhou use the North Bus Station. Be careful to check that you are headed to the correct terminal.

Hangzhou Xiaoshan International Airport, about 27 km (17 mi) southeast of the city, has frequent domestic flights. Taxis to the airport cost around Y120. A bus leaves from the CAAC office on Tiyuchang Lu every 30 minutes between 5:30 AM and 8:30 PM. It costs Y15 per person.

GETTING AROUND HANGZHOU

In addition to regular city buses, Hangzhou has a series of modern, air-conditioned buses that connect most major tourist sights. They are an easy way to get to more isolated sights. Bus Y1 connects Baidi Causeway, Solitary Hill Island, Yue Fei Mausoleum, the Temple of the Soul's Retreat, and Orioles Singing in the Willow Waves. Bus Y3 runs to Precious Stone Hill, the China National Silk Museum, and the China Tea Museum.

Hangzhou's taxi fleet is among the most modern and comfortable in China, and makes it easy to get from West Lake to far-flung sights like the Temple of the Soul's Retreat and the China Tea Museum (Y30 to Y45).

Shaoxing

★ Shaoxing is alive in the Chinese imagination thanks to the famous writer Lu Xun, who set many of his classic works in this sleepy southern town. A literary revolutionary, Lu Xun broke tradition by writing in the vernacular of everyday Chinese, instead of the stiff, scholarly prose previously held as the only appropriate language for literature.

> **GETTING AROUND**
>
> Although Shaoxing is small enough that walking is the best way to get between many sights, the city's small red taxis are relatively inexpensive. Most trips are Y15.

Today, much of the city's charm is in exploring its narrow cobbled streets. The older sections of the city are made of low stone houses, connected by canals and crisscrossed by arched bridges. East Lake is no match for the grandeur of Hangzhou's West Lake, but its bizarre rock formations and caves make for interesting tours. Shaoxing is also famous for its celebrated yellow-rice wine, used by cooks everywhere.

Exploring

The **Lu Xun Family Home** (Lu Xun Gu Ju) was once the stomping grounds of literary giant and social critic Lu Xun. The extended Lu family lived around a series of courtyards. Nearby is the local school where Lu honed his writing skills. This is a great place to explore a traditional Shaoxing home and see some beautiful antique furniture. ✉ *398 Lu Xun Zhong Lu, 1 block east of Xianhen Hotel* ☎ *0575/513–2080* 🎟 *Y60* ⏲ *Daily 8:30–4:30.*

In a city of bridges, **Figure 8 Bridge** (Bazi Qiao Bridge) is the city's finest and best known. Its long, sloping sides rise to a flat crest that looks like the character for eight, an auspicious number. The current bridge is over 800 years old, and is draped with a thick beard of ivy and vines. It sits in a quiet area of old stone houses with canal-side terraces where people wash clothes and chat with neighbors. ✉ *Bazi Qiao Zhi Jie, off Renmin Zhong Lu.*

The **Zhou Enlai Family Home** (✉ 369 Laodong Lu ☎ 0575/513–3368 🎟 Y18 ⏲ Daily 8–5) belonged to the first premier of Communist China, who came from a family of prosperous Shaoxing merchants. Zhou is credited with saving some of China's most important historical monuments from destruction at the hands of the Red Guards during the Cultural Revolution. The compound, a showcase of traditional architecture, has been preserved and houses exhibits on Zhou's life, ranging from his high-school essays to vacation snapshots with his wife.

The narrow **East Lake** (Dong Hu) runs along the base of a rocky bluff rising up from the rice paddies of Zhejiang. The crazily shaped cliffs were used as a rock quarry over the centuries, and today their sheer gray faces jut out in sheets of rock. You can hire a local boatman to take you along the base of the cliffs in a traditional black awning boat for Y40. ✉ *Yundong Lu, 3 km (2 mi) east of the city center* 🎟 *Y25* ⏲ *Daily 7:30–5:30.*

CLOSE UP

What's Cooking

SHAOXING SECURED ITS PLACE in the Chinese culinary pantheon with Shaoxing wine, the best yellow-rice wine in the country. Although cooks around the world know the nutty-flavored wine as a marinade and seasoning, in Shaoxing the fermented brew of glutinous rice is put to a variety of uses, from drinking straight up (as early as breakfast) to sipping as a medicine (infused with traditional herbs and remedies). Like grape wines, Shaoxing mellows and improves with age, as its color deepens to a reddish brown. It is local custom to bury a cask when a daughter is born and serve it when she marries.

The wine is excellent accompaniment to Shaoxing snacks such as pickled greens, and the city's most popular street food *chou doufu*, which means "stinking tofu." The golden-fried squares of tender tofu taste great, if you can get past the pungent odor. Also, look for dishes made with another Shaoxing product, fermented bean curd. With a flavor not unlike an aged cheese, it's rarely eaten by itself, but complements fish and sharpens the flavor of meat dishes.

7

Where to Stay & Eat

¢–$ ✕ **Sanwei Jiulou.** This restaurant serves up local specialties, including warm rice wine served in Shaoxing's distinctive tin kettles. Relaxed and distinctive, it's located in a restored old building and appointed with traditional wood furniture. The second story looks out over the street below. ✉ *2 Lu Xun Lu* ☎ *0575/893–5578* ▭ *No credit cards.*

¢ ✕ **Xianheng Winehouse** (Xianheng Jiudian). Shaoxing's most famous fictional character, the small-town scholar Kong Yiji, would sit on a bench here, dining on wine and boiled beans. Forgo the beans, but the fermented bean curd is good, especially with a bowl of local wine. ✉ *179 Lu Xun Zhong Lu, 1 block east of the Sanwei Jiulou* ☎ *0575/511–6666* ▭ *No credit cards.*

$–$$ **Shaoxing International Hotel** (Shaoxing Guoji Dajiudian). Surrounded by pleasant gardens, this hotel offers bright, well-appointed rooms and a range of facilities. It's located outside the west gate, near the West Bus Station. ✉ *100 Fushan Xi Lu, 312000* ☎ *0575/516–6788* *302 rooms* *2 restaurants, minibars, pool, tennis court, gym, sauna, business services* ▭ *AE, DC, MC, V.*

$–$$ **Shaoxing Xianheng Hotel.** Conveniently located near many of the city's restaurants, the Shaoxing Xianheng offers modern, comfortable rooms and good service. ✉ *680 Jiefang Nan Lu, 312000* ☎ *0575/806–8688* *221 rooms, 8 suites* *2 restaurants, pool, tennis court, gym, sauna, bar, business services* ▭ *AE, MC, V.*

Shopping

Shaoxing has some interesting local crafts, mainly related to calligraphy and rice wine. The most convenient place to buy souvenirs is the shopping street called **Lu Xun Zhong Lu.** In addition to calligraphy brushes, and fans, scrolls, and other items decorated with calligraphy, look for

Continued on page 218

SPIRITUALITY IN CHINA

Even though it's officially an atheist nation, China has a vibrant religious life. But what are the differences between China's big three faiths of Buddhism, Taoism, and Confucianism? Like much else in the Middle Kingdom, the lines are often blurred.

Walking around the streets of any city in China in the early 21st century, it's hard to believe that only three decades ago the bulk of the Middle Kingdom's centuries-old religious culture was destroyed by revolutionary zealots, and that the few temples, mosques, monasteries, and churches that escaped outright destruction were desecrated and turned into warehouses and factories, or put to other ignoble uses. Those days are long over, and religious life in China has sprung back to life. Even though the official line of the Chinese Communist Party is that the nation is atheist, China is rife with religious diversity.

Perhaps the faith most commonly associated with China is Confucianism, an ethical and philosophical system developed from the teachings of the sage Confucius. Confucianism stresses the importance of relationships in society and of maintaining proper etiquette. These aspects of Confucian thought are associated not merely with China (where its modern-day influence is dubious at best, especially in a crowded subway car), but also with East Asian culture as a whole. Confucianism also places great emphasis on filial piety, the respect that a child should show an elder (or subjects to their ruler). This may account for

(left) Offering up joss sticks.
(below) The Yong he Gong Lama temple in Beijing.

7

Confucianism's status as the most officially tolerated of modern China's faiths.

Taoism is based on the teachings of the *Tao Te Ching*, a treatise written in the 6th century BC, and blends an emphasis on spiritual harmony with that of the individual's duty to society. Taoism and Confucianism are complementary, though to the outsider, the former might seem more steeped in ritual and mysticism. Think of it this way: Taoism is to Confucianism as Catholicism is to Protestantism. Taoism's mystic quality may be why so many Westerners come to China to study "the way," as Taoism is sometimes called.

Buddhism came to China from India in the first century AD and quickly became a major force in the Middle Kingdom. The faith is so ingrained here that many Chinese openly scoff at the idea that the Buddha wasn't Chinese. In a nutshell, Buddhism teaches that attachment leads to suffering, and that the best way to alleviate the world's suffering is to purify one's mind, to abstain from evil, and to cultivate good. In China, there are three major schools: the Chinese school, embraced mainly by Han Chinese; the Tibetan school (or Lamaism) as practiced by Tibetans and Mongolians; and Theravada, practiced by the Dai and other ethnic minority groups in the southwest of the country.

Tian Tan, The Temple of Heaven in Beijing.

TEMPLE FAUX PAS

Chinese worshippers are easygoing. Even at the smallest temple or shrine, they understand that some people will be visitors and not devotees. Temples in China have relaxed dress codes, but you should follow certain rules of decorum.

- You're welcome to burn incense, but it's not required. If you do decide to burn a few joss sticks, take them from the communal pile and be sure to make a small donation. This usually goes to temple upkeep or local charities.

The Buddha

- When burning incense, two sticks signify marriage, and four signify death.
- Respect signs reading NO PHOTO in front of altars and statues. Taoist temples seem particularly sensitive about photo taking. When in doubt, ask.
- Avoid stepping in front of a worshipper at an altar or censer (where incense is burned).
- Speak quietly and silence mobile phones inside of temple grounds.
- Don't touch Buddhist monks of the opposite sex.
- Avoid entering a temple during a ceremony.

TEMPLE OBJECTS

For many, temple visits are among the most culturally edifying parts of a China trip. Large or small, Chinese temples incorporate a variety of objects significant to religious practice.

INCENSE

Incense is the most common item in any Chinese temple. In antiquity, Chinese people burned sacrifices both as an offering and as a way of communicating with spirits through the smoke. This later evolved into a way of showing respect for one's ancestors by burning fragrances that the dearly departed might find particularly pleasing.

BAGUA

Taoist temples will have a bagua: an octagonal diagram pointing toward the eight cardinal directions, each representing different points on the compass, elements in nature, family members, and more esoteric meanings. The bagua is often used in conjunction with a compass to make placement decisions in architectural design and in fortune-telling.

"GHOST MONEY"

Sometimes the spirits need more than sweet-smelling smoke, and this is why many Taoists burn "ghost money" (also known as "hell money"), a scented paper resembling cash. Though once more popular in Taiwan and Hong Kong (and looked upon as a particularly capitalist superstition on the mainland), the burning of ghost money is now gaining ground throughout the country.

CENSER

Every Chinese temple will have a censer in which to place joss sticks, either inside the hall or out front. Larger temples often have a number of them. These large stone or bronze bowls are filled with incense ash from hundreds of joss sticks placed by worshippers. Some incense censers are ornate, with sculpted bronze rising above the bowls.

STATUES

Chinese temples are known for being flexible, and statues of various deities, mythical figures, and multiple interpretations of the Buddha abound. Confucius is usually rendered as a wizened man with a long beard, and Taoist temples have an array of demons and deities.

PRAYER WHEEL

Used primarily by Tibetan Buddhists, the prayer wheel is a beautifully embossed hollow metal cylinder mounted on a wooden handle. Inside the cylinder is a tightly wound scroll printed with a mantra. Devotees believe that the spinning of a prayer wheel is a form of prayer that's just as effective as reciting the sacred texts aloud.

CHINESE ASTROLOGY

According to legend, the King of Jade invited 12 animals to visit him in heaven. As the animals rushed to be the first to arrive, the rat snuck a ride on the ox's back. Just as the ox was about to cross the threshold, the rat jumped past him and arrived first. This is why the rat was given first place in the astrological chart. Find the year you were born to determine what your astrological animal is.

RAT

1924 • 1936 • 1948 • 1960 • 1972 • 1984 • 1996 • 2008

Charming and hardworking, Rats are goal setters and perfectionists. Rats are quick to anger, ambitious, and lovers of gossip.

OX

1925 • 1937 • 1949 • 1961 • 1973 • 1985 • 1997 • 2009

Patient and soft-spoken, Oxen inspire confidence in others. Generally easygoing, they can be remarkably stubborn, and they hate to fail or be opposed.

TIGER

1926 • 1938 • 1950 • 1962 • 1974 • 1986 • 1998 • 2010

Sensitive, and thoughtful, Tigers are capable of great sympathy. Tigers can be short-tempered, and are prone to conflict and indecisiveness.

RABBIT

1927 • 1939 • 1951 • 1963 • 1975 • 1987 • 1999 • 2011

Talented and articulate, Rabbits are virtuous, reserved, and have excellent taste. Though fond of gossip, Rabbits tend to be generally kind and even-tempered.

DRAGON

1928 • 1940 • 1952 • 1964 • 1976 • 1988 • 2000 • 2012

Energetic and excitable, short-tempered and stubborn, Dragons are known for their honesty, bravery, and ability to inspire confidence and trust.

SNAKE

1929 • 1941 • 1953 • 1965 • 1977 • 1989 • 2001 • 2013

Snakes are deep, possessing great wisdom and saying little. Snakes can often be vain and selfish while retaining sympathy for those less fortunate.

HORSE

1930 • 1942 • 1954 • 1966 • 1978 • 1990 • 2002 • 2014

Horses are thought to be cheerful and perceptive, impatient and hot-blooded. Horses are independent and rarely listen to advice.

GOAT

1931 • 1943 • 1955 • 1967 • 1979 • 1991 • 2003 • 2015

Wise, gentle, and compassionate, Goats are elegant and highly accomplished in the arts. Goats can also be shy and pessimistic, and often tend toward timidity.

MONKEY

1932 • 1944 • 1956 • 1968 • 1980 • 1992 • 2004 • 2016

Clever, skillful, and flexible, Monkeys are thought to be erratic geniuses, able to solve problems with ease. Monkeys are also thought of as impatient and easily discouraged.

ROOSTER

1933 • 1945 • 1957 • 1969 • 1981 • 1993 • 2005 • 2017

Roosters are capable and talented, and tend to like to keep busy. Roosters are known as overachievers, and are frequently loners.

DOG

1934 • 1946 • 1958 • 1970 • 1982 • 1994 • 2006 • 2018

Dogs are loyal and honest and know how to keep secrets. They can also be selfish and stubborn.

PIG

1935 • 1947 • 1959 • 1971 • 1983 • 1995 • 2007 • 2019

Gallant and energetic, Pigs have a tendency to be single-minded and determined. Pigs have great fortitude and honesty, and tend to make friends for life.

shops selling the local tin wine pots. The traditional way of serving yellow-rice wine, the pots are placed on the stove to heat up wine for a cold winter night. Also popular are traditional boatmen's hats, made of thick waterproof black felt.

To & from Shaoxing

1 hr (68 km [42 mi]) by bus or train east from Hangzhou.

Hangzhou's East Bus Station has dozens of buses each day to Shaoxing. In Shaoxing, buses to Hangzhou leave from the main bus station in the north of town, at the intersection of Jiefang Bei Lu and Huan Cheng Bei Lu. Trains between Hangzhou and Shaoxing take about 1 hour, but do not leave as frequently as buses. The Shaoxing Train Station is 2½ km (1½ mi) north of the city, near the main bus station.

Xiamen

By Chinese standards, Xiamen is a new city: its history only dates to the late 12th century. Xiamen was a stronghold for Ming loyalist Zheng Chenggong (better known as Koxinga), who later fled to Taiwan after China was overrun by the Qing. Xiamen's place as a dynasty-straddling city continues to this day due to its proximity to Taiwan. Some see Xiamen as a natural meeting point between the two sides in the decades-long separation. Only a few miles out to sea are islands that still technically belong to "The Republic of China," as Taiwan is still officially known.

A prosperous city due to its importance as a trading port, Xiamen suffered because of China's anxieties over Taiwan. But as one of the first cities opened to foreign trade, Xiamen saw the money come rolling in again. It is today one of the most prosperous cities in China, with beautiful parks, amazing temples, and waterfront promenades that neatly complement the port city's historic architecture. Xiamen has a number of wonderful parks and temples well worth visiting.

Exploring Xiamen

❷ **Nanputuo Temple** (Nanputuo Si) dates from the Tang Dynasty. It has been restored many times, most recently in the 1980s, following the Cultural Revolution. Built in the exuberant style that visitors to Taiwan will find familiar, it has roofs that are decorated with brightly painted flourishes of clustered flowers, sinewy serpents, and mythical beasts. Pavilions on either side of the main hall contain tablets commemorating the suppression of secret societies by the Qing emperors. As the most important of Xiamen's temples, it is nearly always the center of a great deal of activity as monks and worshippers mix with tour groups. Attached to the tem-

> **FUJIAN**
>
> One of China's most beautiful provinces, Fujian has escaped the notice of most visitors because of its proximity to more glamorous destinations like Hong Kong and Shanghai. Xiamen is clean and beautiful, and the surrounding area has some of the best beaches north of Hainan. And Gulangyu is a rarity in modern China: a tree-filled island with undisturbed colonial architecture and absolutely no cars.

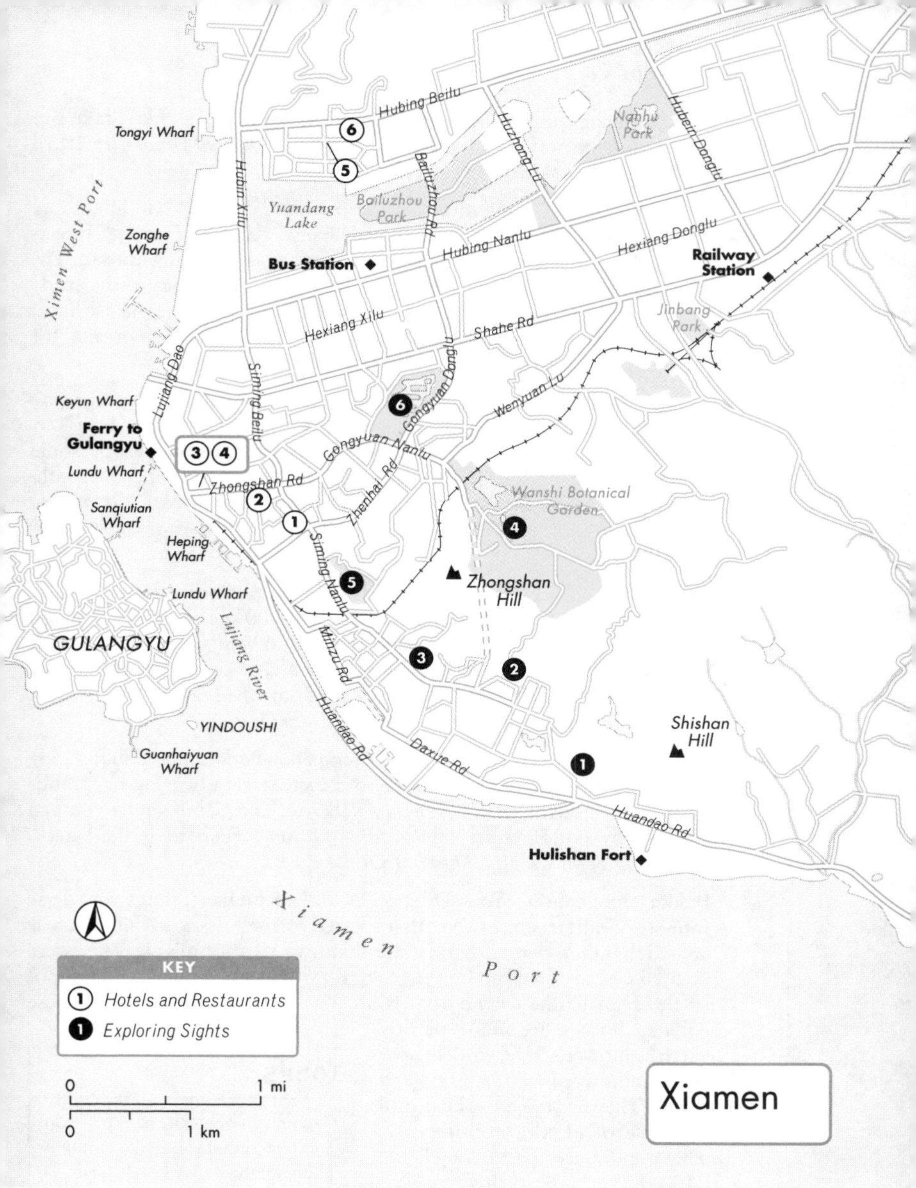

Exploring

Hong Shan Park 5
Nanputuo Temple 2
Overseas Chinese Museum 3
Wanshi Botanical Garden . 4
Xiamen University & Museum of Anthropology 1
Zhong Shan Park 6

Hotels & Restaurants

Guan Hai Canting 3
Holiday Inn Crowne Plaza Harbourview 1
Huangzehe Peanut Soup Shop 2
Lujiang Hotel 4
Marco Polo Xiamen 5
Shuyou Seafood Restaurant 6

ple complex is an excellent vegetarian restaurant. To get here, take Bus 1 or 2 from the port. ✉ *Siming Nan Lu, next to Xiamen University* 🎫 *Y3* ⏲ *Daily 7:30 AM–6:30 PM.*

❶ Housed in a fascinating mix of traditional and colonial buildings close to Nanputuo Temple is **Xiamen University** (Xiamen Daxue). It was founded in the 1920s with the help of Chinese people living abroad. The **Museum of Anthropology** (Renlei Bowuguan), dedicated to the study of the Neolithic era, is one of the most popular destinations. It has a very good collection of fossils, ceramics, paintings, and ornaments. It's open daily 8:30 to 11 and 3 to 5. ✉ *End of Siming Nan Lu.*

❸ In the southern part of the city, the **Overseas Chinese Museum** (Huaqiao Bowuguan) was founded by the wealthy industrialist Tan Kah-kee. Three halls illustrate, with the help of pictures and documents, personal items, and relics associated with the great waves of emigration from southeastern China during the 19th century. ✉ *Off Siming Nan Lu, at foot of Fengzhao Shan* ☎ *0592/208–5345* 🎫 *Y10* ⏲ *Tues.–Sun. 8:30–11:30 and 2–5:30.*

❹ Surrounding a pretty lake, the **Wanshi Botanical Garden** (Wanshi Zhiwuyuan) has a fine collection of more than 4,000 species of tropical and subtropical flora, ranging from eucalyptus and bamboo trees to orchids and ferns. There are several pavilions, of which the most interesting are those forming the **Temple of the Kingdom of Heaven** (Tianjie Si). ✉ *Huyuan Lu, off Wenyuan Lu* 🎫 *Y10* ⏲ *Daily 8–6.*

❻ Commemorating Dr. Sun Yat-sen, **Zhong Shan Park** (Zhong Shan Gong Yuan) is centered around a statue to the great man bearing his granddaughter's inscription. There is a small zoo, lakes and canals you can explore by paddleboat. The annual Lantern Festival is held here. ✉ *Zhong Shan Lu and Zhenhai Lu* 🎫 *Free.*

Hakka Roundhouses (Yong Ding Tu Lou). Legend has it that when these four-story-tall structures were first spotted by the American military, fear spread that they were silos for some unknown gigantic missile. They were created centuries before by the Hakka, or "Guest People," an offshoot of the Han Chinese who settled all over southeastern China. These earthen homes are made of raw earth, glutinous rice, and brown sugar, reinforced with bamboo and wood. They are the most beautiful example of Hakka architecture. The roundhouses are in Yong Ding, 210 km (130 mi) northwest of Xiamen. To get here, take a bus from Xiamen to Longyan, then transfer to a minibus headed to Yong Ding. ✉ *Yong Ding* 🎫 *Y20.*

TOURS

Xiamen is a great city to explore on your own, but if you'd like to hire a guide, all the major hotels have English-speaking guides. Tours can also be arranged through any China Travel Service office.

Where to Stay & Eat

★ $–$$$$ ✕ **Shuyou Seafood Restaurant.** Shuyou means "close friend," and that's how you're treated at this upscale establishment. Considered one of the best seafood restaurants in China (and certainly in Xiamen), Shuyou serves fresh seafood in an opulent setting. Downstairs, the tanks are filled with lobster, prawns, and crabs, and upstairs diners feast on seafood dishes cooked in Cantonese and Fujian styles. If you're in the mood for other fare, the restaurant is also known for its excellent Peking duck and goose liver. ✉ *Hubin Bei Lu, between Marco Polo and Sofitel hotels* ☎ *0592/509–8888* ▭ *AE, MC, V.*

$–$$ ✕ **Guan Hai Canting.** On the rooftop of the waterfront Lujiang Hotel, this terrace restaurant has beautiful views over the bay. The Cantonese chef prepares delicious seafood dishes and dim-sum specialties like sweet pork buns and shrimp dumplings. ✉ *54 Lujiang Lu, across from ferry terminal* ☎ *0592/202–2922* ▭ *AE, MC, V.*

¢ ✕ **Huangzehe Peanut Soup Shop.** Peanuts get the star treatment at this popular restaurant near the waterfront. Tasty peanut soups, peanut sweets, and even peanut dumplings show off the culinary potential of the humble goober. ✉ *24 Zhongshan Lu* ☎ *0592/212–5825* ▭ *No credit cards.*

★ $$–$$$$ **Holiday Inn Crowne Plaza Harbourview.** With an excellent location overlooking the harbor, this hotel is among the best in the city. Rooms are spacious and comfortable, as you'd expect from the chain, and the staff is friendly and attentive. The hotel's restaurants are particularly good, and the 1st-floor coffee shop is the only place in Xiamen to get a good New York–style deli sandwich. Golfers will want to have a drink at the 1st-floor bar, which has a small putting green. ✉ *12 Zhenhai Lu, 361001* ☎ *0592/202–3333* 🖷 *0592/203–6666* 🌐 *www.holiday-inn.com* *334 rooms, 7 suites* *4 restaurants, in-room safes, in-room broadband, pool, fitness room, sauna, bar, business services, no-smoking floors* ▭ *AE, MC, V.*

$$$ **Marco Polo Xiamen.** Situated between the historic sights and the commercial district, the Marco Polo has an excellent location. The hotel's glass-roof atrium makes the lobby bar a particularly nice place to relax after a day's sightseeing. Nightly entertainment includes a dance band from the Philippines. The guest rooms are comfortable and well appointed. ✉ *8 Jianye Lu, 361004* ☎ *0592/509–1888* 🖷 *0592/509–2888* 🌐 *www.marcopolohotels.com* *246 rooms, 38 suites* *3 restaurants, in-room safes, in-room broadband, pool, gym, sauna, bar, business services, no-smoking rooms* ▭ *AE, MC, V.*

$–$$ **Lujiang Hotel.** In a refurbished colonial building, this hotel has an ideal location opposite the ferry pier and the waterfront boulevard. A rooftop-terrace restaurant looks over the straits. Many of the rooms have ocean views. ✉ *54 Lujiang Lu, 361001* ☎ *0592/202–2922* 🖷 *0592/202–4644* *153 rooms,*

THE SCENE

Although Xiamen is known for its excellent seafood (this is a port city, after all), the city's Buddhist population means it has excellent vegetarian cuisine. Xiamen is probably the best place outside of Taiwan to experience Taiwanese cuisine, and many restaurants advertise their *Taiwan Wei Kou* and *Taiwan Xiao Chi*, meaning "Taiwanese flavor" and "Taiwanese snacks."

18 suites ♿ *4 restaurants, in-room safes, in-room broadband, bar, business services* ▭ *AE, MC, V.*

Outdoor Activities

Xiamen offers some excellent hiking opportunities. Most notable of these are the hills behind the Nanputuo Temple, where winding paths and stone steps carved into the sheer rock face make for a fairly strenuous climb. For a real challenge, hike from Nanputuo Temple to Wanshi Botanical-Garden. If you're still in the mood for a climb after spending a few hours enjoying the garden's beautiful landscape, another more serpentine trail (a relic of the Japanese occupation) leads to Xiamen University. The hike takes the better part of an afternoon, and is well worth it.

The area around Xiamen is filled with fine public beaches. On nice days, sunbathers abound nearly anywhere along Huandao Lu, the road that circles the island.

To & From Xiamen

3 hrs (200 km [124 mi]) by bus southwest of Fuzhou; (500 km [310 mi]) by bus northeast of Hong Kong.

Xiamen has service to all the main cities along the coast as far as Guangzhou and Shanghai. Xiamen Airport, one of the largest and busiest in China, lies about 12 km (7 mi) northeast of the city. A taxi from downtown should cost no more than Y60.

Rail travel to and from Xiamen isn't as convenient as in many other cities. Many journeys involve changing trains at least once. There is, however, direct service to Shanghai, which takes 27 hours. The railway station is about 3 km (2 mi) northeast of the port; bus service between the station and port is frequent.

GETTING AROUND In Xiamen, taxis can be found around hotels or on the streets; they're a convenient way to visit the sights on the edge of town. As most taxi drivers do not speak English, make sure that all your addresses are written in Chinese. Any hotel representative will be happy to do this for you.

Gulangyu

The best way to experience Gulangyu's charm is to explore its meandering streets, stumbling across a particularly distinctive old mansion or the weathered graves of missionaries and merchants. These quiet back alleys are fascinating to wander, with the atmosphere of a quiet Mediterranean city, punctuated by touches of calligraphy or the click of mahjongg tiles to remind you where you really are. And unlike in most Chinese communities, you won't take your life in your hands when crossing the street, as cars are banned on Gulangyu. This island is easy to reach by ferry from Xiamen.

Gulangyu holds a special place in the country's musical history, thanks to the large number of Christian missionaries who called the island home in the late 19th and early 20th centuries. Gulangyu has more pianos per capita than anyplace else in China, with one home in five having one. "Chopsticks" to Chopin—and everything in between—can be heard being played by the next generation's prodigies. The **Piano Museum** (Island of

Drumming Waves) is a must for any music lover. ✉ *45 Huangyan Lu* ☎ *0592/206–0238* 🎫 *Y30* ⏲ *Daily 8:15–5:15.*

From the ferry terminal, turn left and follow oceanfront Tianwei Lu until you come to **Bright Moon Garden** (Haoyue Yuan). The garden is a fitting seaside memorial to Koxinga, and a massive stone statue of the Ming general stares eastward from a perch hanging over the sea. ✉ *Tianwei Lu* ☎ *No phone* 🎫 *Y15* ⏲ *Daily 8–7.*

Continuing along Tianwei Lu, you'll come to **Shuzhuang Garden** (Shuzhuang Huayuan). The garden is immaculately kept and dotted with pavilions and bridges, some extending out to rocks just off shore. ✉ *Tianwei Lu* ☎ *No phone* 🎫 *Y40* ⏲ *Daily 8–7.*

Skillfully mixing history and oddities, **Zhen Qi Shi Jie** is one of the country's odder museums. Part of the museum displays the usual historical information about Fujian and Taiwan and another offers pickled genetic mutations like two-headed snakes, conjoined twin sheep, a few live exhibits like gigantic tortoises, and a room of ancient Chinese sex toys. ✉ *Long Tou Lu, 2 blocks from ferry terminal* ☎ *0592/206–9933* 🎫 *Y35* ⏲ *Daily 8–6:30.*

To & from Gulangyu

5 minutes by boat from Xiamen.

7

Nanjing

The name Nanjing means Southern Capital, and for six dynastic periods the city was the administrative capital of China. Never as successful a capital as Beijing, the locals chalk up the failures of several dynasties here to bad timing, but it could be that the laidback atmosphere of the Yangtze Delta just isn't as suited to political intrigue as the north.

Nanjing offers travelers significantly more sites of historical importance than the economic powerhouse of nearby Shanghai. One of the most impressive is the massive Ming Dynasty sections of the city wall, built to surround and protect the city in the 14th century. There are also a number of traditional monuments, tombs, and gates that reflect the glory of Nanjing's capital days.

The city lies on the Yangtze, and the colossal Second Bridge or the more subdued park at Sparrow Rock are great places for viewing the river. The sheer amount of activity is testimony to its continued importance as a corridor for shipping and trade. Downtown, the streets are choked with traffic, but the chaotic scene is easily avoided with a visit to any of the large parks. You can also take a short ride to ZiJin Mountain. Quiet trails lead between Ming Tombs and the grand mausoleum of Sun Yat-sen.

Exploring Nanjing

❻ **Confucian Temple** (Fuzimiao). The traditional-style temple overlooks the Qinhuai, a tributary of the Yangtze. The surrounding area is the city's busiest shopping and entertainment district and lit with neon at night. The back alleys behind the temple, once home to China's most famous

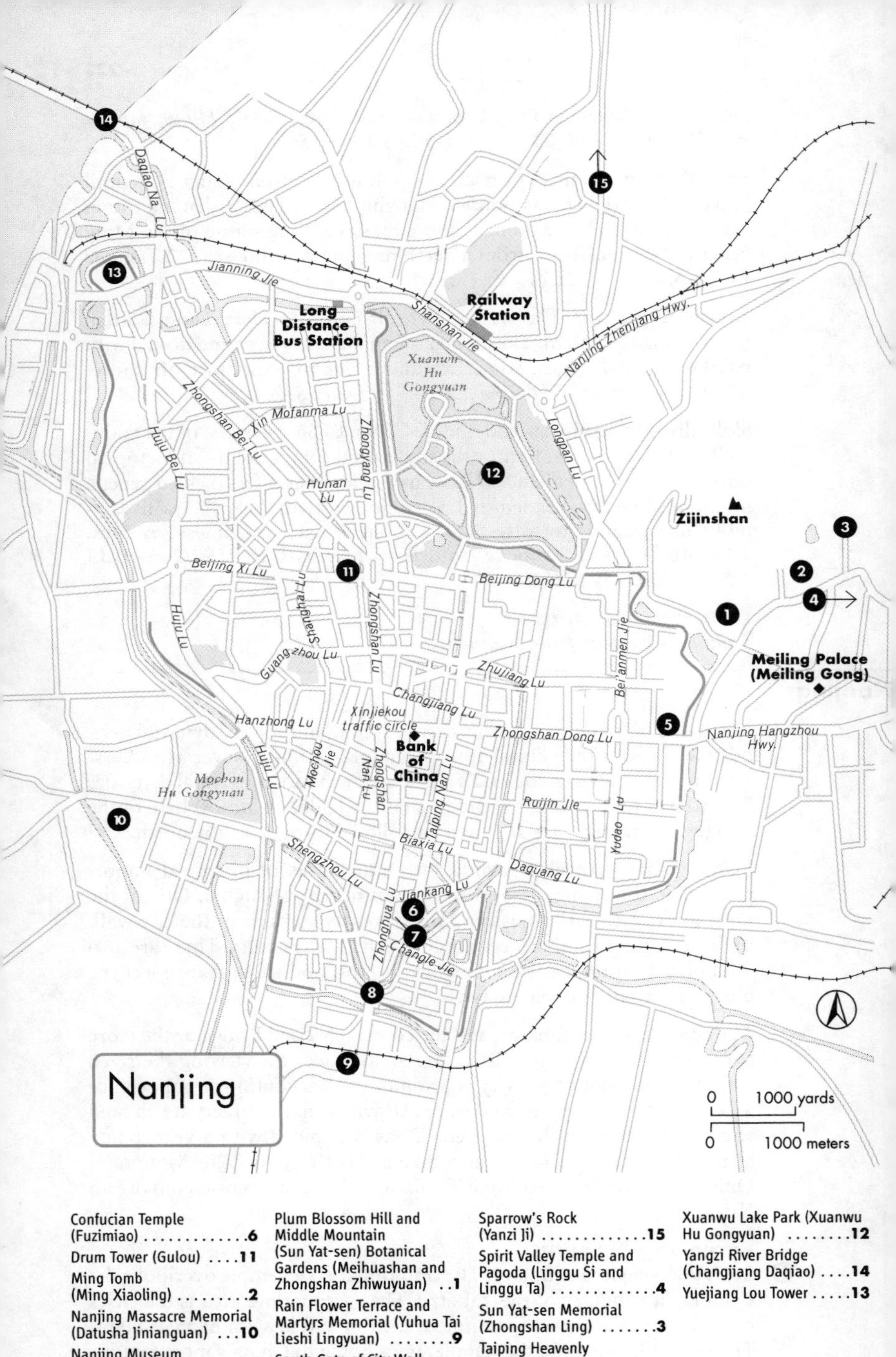

Confucian Temple (Fuzimiao) 6
Drum Tower (Gulou) 11
Ming Tomb (Ming Xiaoling) 2
Nanjing Massacre Memorial (Datusha Jinianguan) . . .10
Nanjing Museum (Nanjing Bowuyuan) 5
Plum Blossom Hill and Middle Mountain (Sun Yat-sen) Botanical Gardens (Meihuashan and Zhongshan Zhiwuyuan) . .1
Rain Flower Terrace and Martyrs Memorial (Yuhua Tai Lieshi Lingyuan) 9
South Gate of City Wall (Zhonghua Men) 8
Sparrow's Rock (Yanzi Ji) 15
Spirit Valley Temple and Pagoda (Linggu Si and Linggu Ta) 4
Sun Yat-sen Memorial (Zhongshan Ling) 3
Taiping Heavenly Kingdom Museum 7
Xuanwu Lake Park (Xuanwu Hu Gongyuan) 12
Yangzi River Bridge (Changjiang Daqiao) 14
Yuejiang Lou Tower 13

district of courtesans, now house a toy market and excellent curio shops. This area has the best bazaars for souvenirs and crafts. Evening tours of the Qinghuai River leave in front of the temple. The cost is Y40 per person ✉ *Zhongshan Lu and Jiankang Lu, On the Qinhuai River* 🎫 *Y15* 🌐 *www.njfzm.com* ⏲ *Daily 8:30–5:30.*

⓫ **Drum Tower** (Gulou). The traditional center of ancient Chinese cities, the 1382 Drum Tower housed the drums used to signal important events, from the changing of the guard to an enemy attack or a fire. Today it holds only one drum. If you're in the area, you can duck inside to see the first-floor art exhibition. ✉ *1 Dafang Xiang, Beside Gulou People's Square* ☎ *025/8663–1059* 🎫 *Y5* ⏲ *Daily 8:30–5:30.*

Fodor's Choice ★

❷ **Ming Tomb** (Ming Xiaoling). The ancient tomb of the founder of the Ming Dynasty, called Tomb of Filial Piety, is one of the largest burial mounds in China. The emperor Hong Wu was born a peasant and orphaned early on. He became a monk and eventually led the army that overthrew the Yuan dynasty. He chose Nanjing for the capital of the Ming Dynasty, but his son returned the capital to Beijing. Visitors approach the tomb through a grand entrance of stone animals. The lions, elephants, camels, and mythical creatures kneel in tribute to the emperor and stand as guardians to the tomb. Winding paths behind make the Ming Tomb area a rewarding place to explore, but as in all Chinese tombs the entrance is hidden to foil looters. For a detailed history, buy a book at the entrance shop; English signage is sparse. ✉ *Mingling Lu, On Purple Mountain* 🎫 *Y50* ⏲ *Daily 8:30–5.*

❿ **Nanjing Massacre Memorial** (Datusha Jinianguan). In the winter of 1937, Japanese forces occupied Nanjing. In the space of a few days, thousands of Chinese were killed in the chaos, which became commonly known as the "Rape of Nanjing." This monument commemorates the victims, many of whom were buried in a mass grave. Be advised, however: this is not for the squeamish. Skeletons have been exhumed from the "Grave of Ten Thousand" and are displayed with gruesomely detailed explanations as to how each lost his or her life. The memorial also displays artifacts from the Sino-Japanese reconciliation after World War II, which ended the conflict between the two countries on a less strident, more hopeful note. To get here, take Bus 7 and 37 from Xinjiekou. ✉ *418 Shui Ximen Da Jie, West of Mouchou Lake Park* ☎ *025/8650–1033* 🌐 *www.nj1937.org* 🎫 *Free* ⏲ *Tues.–Sun. 8:30–4:30.*

❺ **Nanjing Museum** (Nanjing Bowuyuan). With one of the largest and most impressive collections in China, the Nanjing Museum has excellent displays that set objects in historical context. For instance, beside the shelves of ancient pottery there is a re-created kiln to illustrate how traditional objects were formed. The permanent collection includes excellent works in jade,

TOURING TIPS

Once on Purple Mountain, the best way to get around is Bus Y3, a tourist bus that runs from the train station to Ming Tomb, Sun Yat-sen Botanical Gardens, Sun Yat-sen Mausoleum, and Spirit Valley Pagoda.

silk, and bronzes. There's also a treasure room with some eye-popping displays. In a modern hall the museum's curators have pushed the envelope—and pushed some buttons—with some controversial temporary exhibits. ✉ *Zhongshan Dong Lu, inside Zhongshan Gate, East of the city center* ☎ *025/8480–2119* 🌐 *www.njmuseum.com/english* 🎫 *Y20* ⏲ *Daily 9–4:30.*

7 **Plum Blossom Hill and Sun Yat-sen Botanical Gardens** (Meihuashan and Zhongshan Zhiwuyuan). This hillside explodes with plum blossoms in early spring. The garden is a nice place for a picnic, but is only worth a special trip when the flowers are in bloom. The exhibits at the botanical gardens, on the other hand, are a rewarding experience for anyone interested in the flora of China. ✉ *1 Shixiang Lu, Northeast of Nanjing Museum* 🎫 *Y50* ⏲ *Daily 6:30–6:30.*

9 **Rain Flower Terrace and Martyrs Memorial** (Yuhua Tai Lieshi Lingyuan). The terrace gets its name from the legend of Yunzhang, a 15th-century Buddhist monk who supposedly pleased the gods so much with his recitation of a sutra that they showered flowers on this spot. The site was used for a more grim purpose in the 1930s, when the Nationalists used it to execute their left-wing political enemies. The site was transformed into a memorial park with massive statues of heroic martyrs, soaring obelisks, flower arrangements of the hammer and sickle, and a moving museum that uses personal objects to convey the lives of some of those executed here. ✉ *215 Yuhua Lu, , Outside Zhonghua Gate* 🎫 *Y35* ⏲ *Park daily 7 AM–10 PM, memorial daily 8–5:30.*

8 **South Gate of City Wall** (Zhonghua Men). Built as the linchpin of the city's defenses, this is less of a gate than a complete fortress, with multiple courtyards and tunnels where several thousands soldiers could withstand a siege. It was even attacked; armies wisely avoided it in favor of the less heavily fortified areas to the north. Today bonsai enthusiasts have displays in several of the courtyards. ✉ *Southern end of Zhonghua Lu, South side of city wall* 🎫 *Y15* ⏲ *Daily 8–6.*

15 **Sparrow's Rock** (Yanzi Ji). North of the city, this small park overlooking the Yangzi is worth the trip. Paths wind up the hill to several lookout points for what may be Nanjing's best view of this great river. The park's name comes from the massive boulder over the water that supposedly resembles a bird. To get here, take Bus 8 to the last stop. ✉ *Northeast of Mount Mufu, on the Yangtze* 🎫 *Y6* ⏲ *Daily 7:30–6.*

4 **Spirit Valley Temple and Pagoda** (Linggu Si and Linggu Ta). The

THAT'S THE TICKET

If you'll be seeing a number of sights in Nanjing, a yearly ticket is a bargain. There are two different cards. The Garden Card (Y120) provides admission to Sparrow's Rock, South Gate of the City Wall, the Taiping Heavenly Kingdom Museum, and the Sun Yat-sen Botanical Gardens. The Purple Mountain Card (Y100) covers admission to Ming Tomb, Sun Yat-sen Mausoleum, and the Spirit Valley Temple and Pagoda. The cards can be bought at any of these spots. All you need is a passport and an ID-sized photo.

temple commemorates Xuan Zang, the monk who brought Buddhist scriptures back from India. Farther up the hill is a 9-story granite pagoda with a staircase that spirals up the central pillar. (The top is dizzyingly high.) This pagoda was built as a solemn memorial to those killed by the Nationalists in 1929; today, vendors sell plastic balloons to throw off the top balcony. On the grounds is the brick Beamless Hall. The magnificent 14th-century architecture is now given over to propagandistic "historical" reenactments. Although the temple and pagoda may not be worth a special trip, they are close to Ming Tomb and other attractions around Purple Mountain. ✉ *Ta Lu, Southeast of Sun Yats-en Memorial* ☎ *025/8444–6111* 🎫 *Pagoda Y15, temple Y2* ⏲ *Sept.–May 8:30–5, June–Aug. daily 6:30–6:20.*

3 **Sun Yat-sen Memorial** (Zhongshan Ling). Acknowledged by the Nationalist and Communist government alike, the father of modern China lies buried in a delicately carved marble sarcophagus. His resting place is the quiet center of a solemn and imposing monument to the ideas that overthrew the imperial system. On the mountain are steep trails up the pine-covered slopes that feel worlds away from the bustle of Nanjing. A popular destination for Chinese tourists, the mausoleum can get crowded on weekends; try to visit on a weekday. ✉ *Lingyuan Lu, East of the Ming Tomb* 🎫 *Y40* ⏲ *Sept.–May 8:30–5, June–Aug. daily 6:30–6:20.*

7 **Taiping Heavenly Kingdom Museum** (Taiping Tianguo Lishi Bowuguan). Commemorating a particularly fascinating period of Chinese history, this museum follows the life of Hong Xiuquan, a Christian who led a peasant revolt in 1859. He ultimately captured Nanjing and ruled for 11 years. Hong, who set himself up as emperor, claimed to be the younger brother of Jesus. On display are artifacts from the period. After browsing the museum, you can walk around the grounds of the Ming Dynasty garden compound that houses the museum. During the day, it is the calmest spot in Nanjing. In the evening from 6 to 11 there are performances of opera and storytelling. Reasonably priced English-speaking guides make up for the poor English signage. ✉ *128 Zhanyuan Lu, Beside the Confucian Temple* ☎ *025/5223–8687* 🎫 *Y50* ⏲ *Daily 8–4:30.*

12 **Xuanwu Lake Park** (Xuanwu Hu Gongyuan). More lake than park, this pleasant garden is bounded by one of the longer sections of the monumental city wall, which you can climb for a good view of the water. Purple Mountain rises in the east, and the glittering skyscrapers of modern Nanjing are reflected in the calm water. Causeways lined with trees and benches connect several large islands in the lake. ✉ *Off Hunan Lu, In the northeast corner of the city, outside the city wall* 🎫 *Y20* ⏲ *Daily 8–8.*

14 **Yangzi River Bridge** (Changjiang Daqiao). Completed in 1968 at the height of the Cultural Revolution, the bridge is decorated in stirring Socialist Realist style. Huge stylized flags made of red glass rise from the bridge's piers, and groups of giant-sized peasants, workers, and soldiers stride forward heroically. Look closely and you'll even see one African—a reminder of Mao's support for revolutionaries around the world. The

7

Great Bridge Park lies on the south side. From here you can take an elevator from the park up to a small museum. ✉ *End of Daqiao Nan, Northwest section of the city* 🎫 *Free* ⏲ *Daily 9–5.*

13 **Yuejiang Lou Tower.** This massive tower complex, built in the new millennium in Ming Dynasty style, looks out over a broad sweep of the Yangtze River. The founding emperor of the Ming Dynasty wrote a poem describing his plans to have a tower built here where he could view the river. Other imperial business got in the way, and for several centuries the building remained on paper. The grand tower and its surrounding buildings were built in 2001 in a historically accurate style, but it somehow seems too sterile. ✉ *202 Jianning Lu, Northwest corner of the city* ☎ *025/5880–3977* 🌐 *www.yuejiangtower.com* 🎫 *Y30* ⏲ *Daily 8–6.*

Tours

Major hotels will often arrange a tour guide for a group. Nanjing China Travel Service can arrange almost any type of tour of the city.

TOUR GUIDES **Nanjing China Travel Service** (✉ 12 Baizi Ting, South of the Drum Tower ☎ 025/8336–6227 🌐 www.njcts.com).

Where to Stay & Eat

★ $$–$$$ ✕ **Dingshan Meishi Cheng.** One of Nanjing's finest restaurants, Dingshan Meishi Cheng serves local cuisine in a traditional setting. The food here is not as hot as that from Sichuan, nor as sweet as that from Shanghai. There's a set price menu that includes 4 cold dishes, 4 hot dishes, and a whopping 18 small dessert dishes, all for Y60. ✉ *5 Zhanyuan Lu, Near Confucian Temple* ☎ *025/5220–9217* ▭ *AE, MC, V.*

$–$$ Fodor's Choice ★ ✕ **Baguo Buyi.** Nanjing cuisine is generally mild, but if you are craving something spicy, Baguo Buyi is one of the best places to try authentic Sichuan cuisine. The food is searingly hot, in sharp contrast to the sweeter flavors of Eastern Chinese cuisine. The stew of beef and yellow tofu is delicious, as is the steamed river fish served in a caldron of peppercorns. The dining room is decorated with traditional wood carvings and antique furniture. ✉ *211 Longpan Zhong Lu, at Yixian Qiao* ☎ *025/8460–8801* ▭ *No credit cards.*

★ $–$$ ✕ **Shizi Lou.** Anchoring the strip of restaurants of Shizi Qiao, near the Shanzi Road Market, Shizi Lou is a great introduction to Huaiyang fare. Resembling an indoor market, you can walk between stands and point to the dishes you want to sample. The "stinky tofu" is very good and not as malodorous as it's billed. The place is famous for local meatballs, with a dozen types from which to choose. ✉ *29 Hunan Lu, Near Shizi Bridge* ☎ *025/8360–7888* ▭ *No credit cards.*

$$$–$$$$ 🏨 **Jinling Hotel.** Nanjing's best-known hotel has a great location in the center of the city. It's a huge modern building connected to a shopping center. The travel agency on the first floor provides friendly

KEEPING CURRENT

For more information on bars and restaurants in Nanjing, pick up a copy of the local bilingual *Map Magazine* at your hotel. It has listings and reviews of many popular spots in the city, as well as upcoming cultural events.

and efficient service. On the second floor is the most authentic Japanese food in town. The guest rooms have every comfort. ✉ *2 Xinjiekou, 210005* ☎ *025/8471–1888 or 025/8471–1999* 📠 *025/8471–1666* *570 rooms, 30 suites* *7 restaurants, 2 cafés, gym, hair salon, bar, business services, meeting room* 💳 *AE, MC, V.*

$ **Central Hotel.** This lodging caters to travelers by arranging day tours in and around Nanjing. The 24-hour travel desk also sets up tours to more distant destinations. The modern rooms are stylish and reasonably priced. The sleek sauna and beautiful star-shape courtyard pool are inviting after a long day of sightseeing. ✉ *75 Zhongshan Lu, 210005* ☎ *025/8473–3888* 📠 *025/441–4194* *354 rooms, 22 suites* *2 restaurants, coffee shop, pool, gym, sauna, bar, dance club, shops, business services, meeting room* 💳 *AE, MC, V.*

¢ **Nanjing Hotel.** Built in 1936, the old-fashioned hotel surrounded by lawns and trees seems pleasantly out of place in such a busy area of town. The staff is well trained and friendly. A separate section has simpler rooms that are less attractive, but are also half the standard rate. Rooms have different amenities, so ask to see a few before you decide. ✉ *259 Zhongshan Bei Lu, 210003* ☎ *025/8682–6666* 📠 *025/342–2261* *307 rooms, 14 suites* *3 restaurants, gym, hair salon, massage, sauna, business services, meeting room* 💳 *AE, MC, V.*

Shopping

The best place to buy traditional crafts, art, and souvenirs is the warren of small shops in the center of the city. The lavish embroidered robes once worn by the emperors were traditionally produced in Nanjing, and the gift shop at the **Brocade Research Institute** (✉ 240 Chating Dong Jie, behind Nanjing Massacre Memorial ☎ 025/8651–8580) sells beautiful examples of traditional brocade.

Nanjing is a convenient place to pick up many of the traditional crafts of Jiangsu—purple sand teapots, flowing silks, interesting carvings, and folk paper cuttings. The **Nanjing Arts & Crafts Company** (✉ 31 Beijing Dong Lu ☎ 025/5771–1189) has a range of items, from jade and lacquerware to tapestries. In the courtyard of the Confucian Temple, the **Chaotian Gong Antique Market** (✉ Zhongshan Lu and Jiankang Lu ☎ No phone) has an array of curios, ranging from genuine antiques to fakes of varying quality. The market is open every day, but is liveliest on weekend mornings.

Bargaining is necessary and the prices are reasonable at the **Fabric Market** (✉ 215 Zhongshan Bei Lu ☎ No phone Northwest of the Drum Tower). The vendors can also arrange tailoring.

To & From Nanjing

2½ hrs (309 km [192 mi]) by fast train west of Shanghai; 4½ hrs by normal train.

Buses for Shanghai leave from the Zhong Shan Nan Road Bus Station. The trip takes between 3 and 4 hours. Buses bound for Suzhou depart from the Zhongshan Nan Road Station, and can be as quick as 2 hours.

Buses bound for Yangzhou leave frequently from the Long Distance Bus Station and take 1 hour.

Trains to Shanghai leave every half hour or so. There are several different kinds of trains, depending on the number of stops. For a speedier journey, request a K or T coded ticket. Fast trains take about 3 hours, while the slower ones can be as long as 4½ hours. One train each day makes the trip in 2½ hours. Trains to Suzhou are on the Shanghai line, and all stop there with the exception of the direct train. Travel time is 2–3 hours.

Suzhou

Suzhou has long been renowned as a place of culture, beauty, and sophistication. It produced scores of artists, writers, and politicians over the centuries, and it developed a local culture based on refinement and taste. Famous around the world for its carefully designed classical gardens, Suzhou's elegance extends even to its local dialect—Chinese often say that two people arguing in the Suzhou dialect sounds more pleasant than lovers talking in standard Chinese.

Unlike in other cities in Eastern China, glass-and-steel office parks have been barred from old city center, and this preservation makes Suzhou a pleasant place to explore. There is excellent English signage on the roads, and the local tourism board has even set up a convenient information center to get you on the right track.

Only an hour outside of Shanghai, the tourist trail here is well-worn however, and during the high season you will find yourself sharing these gardens with packs of foreign and domestic tour groups. It is worth strategizing and getting up early to hit the most popular places before the crowds descend.

Exploring Suzhou

Suzhou is threaded by a network of narrow waterways. The canals that now seem quaint were once choked with countless small boats ferrying goods between the city's merchants. All of these small channels lead eventually to Imperial China's main conduit of trade and travel, the **Grand Canal** (Da Yunhe), which passes through the outskirts of town. The **Precious Belt Bridge** (Baodai Qiao), is an ancient bridge of 53 arches that bound over Tantai Lake where it meets the Grand Canal. ✉ *Beyond Pingmen Gate, north on Renmin Lu.*

9 **Blue Wave Pavilion** (Canglang Ting). The Blue Wave Pavilion is the oldest existing garden in Suzhou, dating back more than 900 years to the Song Dynasty. With a simple design, the garden grounds feel a little wilder than the relative newcomers. The central pond is an expansive stretch of water that reflects the upturned eaves of the surrounding buildings. Over 100 different lattice designs shading the windows provide visual variety as you saunter the long

> **WATER WHEELS**
>
> The old city is circled by a moat, and you can take an "aquatic bus" that leaves from the bus station. The cost is Y15 per person.

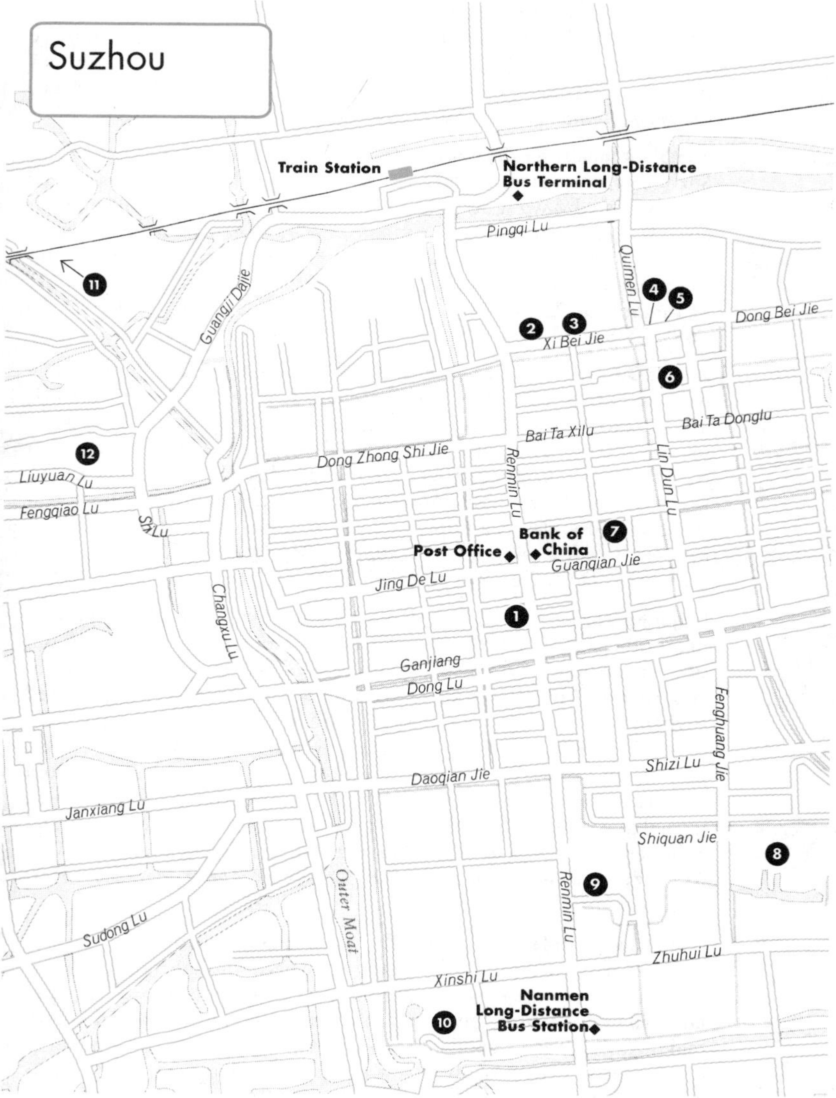

Blue Wave Pavilion (Canglang Ting) **9**
Humble Administrator's Garden (Zhuo Zheng Yuan) **5**
Joyous Garden (Yi Yuan) **1**
Lingering Garden (Liu Yuan) **12**
Lion's Grove Garden (Shizi Lin) **6**
Master of the Nets Garden (Wangshi Yuan) . . **8**
North Temple Pagoda (Beisi Ta) **2**
Pan Gate (Panmen) **10**
Suzhou Arts & Crafts Museum **4**
Suzhou Museum of Arts & Crafts (Gongyi Meishu Bowuguan) **3**
Temple of Mystery (Xuanmiao Guan) **7**
Tiger Hill (Huqiu) **11**

corridor over the water. A rocky hill rises in the center of the pond, atop which stands the square Blue Wave Pavilion itself. The **Pure Fragrance Pavilion** showcases Qing Dynasty furniture at its most extreme; the entire suite is created from gnarled banyan root. ✉ *East of Renmin Lu, between Shiquan Jie and Xinshi Lu* 🎫 *Y30* ⏲ *Daily 7:30–5:30.*

Fodor'sChoice ★ **Humble Administrator's Garden** (Zhuo Zheng Yuan). More than half of Suzhou's largest garden is taken up by ponds and lakes. The garden was built in 1509 by Wang Xianjun, an official dismissed from the imperial court. He chose the garden's name from a Tang Dynasty line of poetry reading "humble people govern," perhaps a bit of sarcasm considering the grand scale of his private residence. ✉ *178 Dongbei Jie, 1 block east of Lindun Lu* ☎ *0512/6751–0286* 🌐 *www.szzzy.cn* 🎫 *Y70* ⏲ *Daily 7:30–5:30.*

Joyous Garden (Yi Yuan). The youngest garden in Suzhou, Joyous Garden was built in 1874. It borrows elements from Suzhou's other famous garden: rooms from the Humble Administrator's, a pond from the Master of the Nets. The most unusual original feature in the garden is an oversize mirror, inspired by a tale of the founder of Zen Buddhism, who stared at a wall for years to find enlightenment. From April to October, the garden doubles as a popular teahouse in the evening. ✉ *343 Renmin Lu, 1 block south of the Temple of Mystery* ☎ *0512/6524–9317* 🎫 *Y15* ⏲ *Daily 7:30 AM–midnight.*

Lingering Garden (Liu Yuan). Windows frame other windows, undulating rooflines recall waves, and a closed corridor transforms into a room open to the pond at this interesting garden. The compound provides an endless array of architectural surprises: in a corner an unexpected skylight illuminates a planted nook; windows are placed to frame bamboo as perfectly as if they were painted. The **Mandarin Duck Hall** is particularly impressive, with a lovely moon gate engraved with vines and flowers. In the back of the garden stands a 70-foot-tall rock moved here from Lake Taihu. Ongoing solo musical performances on erhu and zither enliven the halls. ✉ *79 Liuyuan Lu, west of the moat* ☎ *0512/6533–7903* 🌐 *www.gardenly.com* 🎫 *Y40* ⏲ *Daily 7:30–5:30 (last ticket sold at 5).*

★ 22 **Lion's Grove Garden** (Shizi Lin). This garden uses countless gnarled formations from nearby Lake Taihu to create a surreal moonscape. A labyrinth of man-made caves surrounds a small lake. There's a popular local saying that if you talk to rocks, you won't need a psychologist, making this garden a good place to spend a 50-minute hour. A tearoom on the second floor of the main pavilion overlooks the lake. ✉ *23 Yuanlin Lu, 3 blocks south of the Humble Administrator's Garden* ☎ *0512/6727–8316* 🌐 *www.szszl.com* 🎫 *Y30* ⏲ *7:30–5:30.*

★ 17 **Master of the Nets Garden** (Wangshi Yuan). All elements of Suzhou style are here in precise balance: rock hills, layered planting, and charming pavilions overlooking a central pond. The garden is a favorite spot on tour group itineraries. To avoid the crowds, visit in the evening, when you can saunter from room to room enjoying traditional opera, flute, and dulcimer performances—as the master himself might have enjoyed.

Performances are held from mid-March to mid-November. ✉ *11 Kuo Jia Tou Gang, west of Shiquan Lu* ☎ *0512/6529–3190* 🌐 *www.szwsy.com* 🎫 *Y30* ⏲ *Daily 7:30–5 (last ticket sold at 4:30).*

19 **North Temple Pagoda** (Beisi Ta). One of the symbols of ancient Suzhou, this temple towers over the old city. This complex has a 1,700-year history, dating to the Three Kingdoms Period. The wooden pagoda has nine levels; you can climb as high as the eighth level for what might be the best view of Suzhou. Within the grounds are the Copper Buddha Hall and Plum Garden. ✉ *Xibei Jie and Renmin Lu, 2 blocks west of Humble Administrator's Garden* ☎ *0512/6753–1197* 🎫 *Y15, Y10 more to climb pagoda* ⏲ *Mar.–Oct., daily 7:45–6.*

18 **Pan Gate** (Pan Men). Traffic into old Suzhou came both by road and canals, so the city's gates were designed to control access by both land and water. This gate—more of a small fortress, actually—is the only one that remains. In addition to the imposing wooden gates on land, a double sluice gate can be used to seal off the canal and prevent boats from entering. A park is filled with colorful flowers, in contrast to the subdued traditional gardens elsewhere in the city. A small platform extends over a pond where voracious carp turn the water into a thrashing sheet of orange and yellow as they compete for food that tourists throw down. You can climb the **Ruiguang Pagoda,** a tall, slender spire originally built more than 1,000 years ago. ✉ *1 Dong Dajie, southwest corner of the old city* ☎ *0512/6530-0827* 🌐 *www.szpmjq.com* 🎫 *Y25* ⏲ *Daily 8–4:45.*

7

20 **Suzhou Arts and Crafts Museum.** The highlight here is watching artists in action. They carve jade, cut latticework fans from thin sheets of sandalwood, and fashion traditional calligraphy brushes. Perhaps most amazing is the careful attention to detail of the women embroidering silk. The attached shop is a good place to pick up quality crafts. ✉ *58 Xibei Lu., between Humble Administratoor's Garden and the North Pagoda* ☎ *0512/6753–4874* 🎫 *Y15* ⏲ *Daily 9–5.*

Suzhou Museum. This is the most modern building to emerge amidst a neighborhood of traditional architecture. The glass and steel structure is the valedictory work for 90 year-old modernist master I. M. Pei and will house historical objects from Suzhou's ancient past. ✉ *Dongbei Jie, Next to Humble Administrator's Garden* ☎ *0512/6754–1534.*

23 **Temple of Mystery** (Xuanmiao Guan). One of the best-preserved Taoist compounds, the Temple of Mystery backs a large square that is now a lively market. Founded in the 3rd century, the temple is a rare example of a wooden structure that has lasted centuries, still retaining parts from the 12th century. Fortunately, it suffered very little damage in the Cultural Revolution and retains a splendid ceiling of carefully arranged beams and braces painted in their original colors. Taoist music is performed throughout the day. ✉ *Guanqian Jie* ☎ *0512-67276616* 🌐 *www.szxmg.com* 🎫 *Y10* ⏲ *Daily 8:30–5.*

25 **Tiger Hill** (Huqiu). This hill is the burial place of the King of the State of Wu, who founded the city in BC 514. At the top of the approach is a huge sheet of stone called **Thousand Man Rock,** where legend has it that

CLOSE UP

Exploring the Water Villages

CENTURIES-OLD VILLAGES, preserved almost in their original state, are scattered around Suzhou. Bowed bridges span narrow canals, as traditional oared boats paddle by, creating an almost perfect picture of a way of life long past. A trip to one of these villages will probably be a highlight of your trip to Eastern China.

Be careful which village you choose, though. The tourist dollars that flow in may have saved these villages from the wrecking ball, but they have also changed their character to differing degrees. Those closest to the larger cities can be the most swamped by tour groups. Trekking to an out-of-the-way destination can pay off by letting you find a village that you will have all to yourself.

The most famous of the water villages is undoubtedly **Zhouzhuang.** Its fame is partly due to its proximity, just 45 minutes from Suzhou and an hour away from Shanghai. As a result, more than 2.5 million visitors head to the water village of Zhouzhuang each year to catch a glimpse of the China that was. Its charm is reduced by the sheer numbers of tourists who elbow their way through the streets. And there's something artificial about the whole experience. By the "ancient memorial archway," which isn't ancient at all, is a ticket window. The steep entrance fee of Y100 gets you into water village-turned-gift shop.

Crowds aside, Zhouzhuang is fun for families. Several residences, some 500 years old, let you see what life was like in the Ming and Qing dynasties. There are several storefronts where you can see brick making, bamboo carving, and basket weaving—traditional crafts that up until recently were in widespread use throughout the countryside. The food is typical country fare, making it a nice break from the fancier cuisine of Suzhou and Shanghai. The most famous dish, a fatty cut of pork leg, is a bit oily for most Western palates. But there are also pickled vegetables and wild greens to sample. For crafts, skip the snuff bottles and teapots, which are of low quality. Opt for something you probably won't find elsewhere: homemade rice wine, rough-hewn ox-horn combs, and bamboo rice baskets.

Buses to Zhouzhuang leave from Suzhou's North Bus station every half hour between 7 AM and 5 PM. The 1½-hour trip is Y15 to Y25.

The pick of the water villages is **Tongli,** 30 minutes from Zhouzhuang and 1½ hours from Suzhou. There's a more reasonable entrance fee of Y60. A number of locals still live and work here, making this village seem more authentic than Zhouzhuang. The streets are cobbled, and the complete absence of cars make Tongli feel like it's from a different era. You can still find yourself wandering on quaint side streets or creeping down impossibly narrow alleyways that open onto canals and bridges. Tongli is the largest of the water villages, imminently photographable, and a pleasure to explore. Near the entrance gate are several private homes offering beds, and throughout the village are tea shops and small tables set out in front of the canals. Hiring a boat (Y60 for up to 6 people) to float down the canals gives you a different perspective on the town.

A favorite spot in Tongli is Tuisi Garden, a slightly smaller version of the private courtyard parks found in Suzhou. Tongli is also home to the **Ancient Chinese Sexual Culture Museum** (✉ Entrance to town ☎ 0512/6332-2973), housed in a former girls' school. The controversial exhibition of ancient erotic toys and art is the project of a retired university professor.

Buses to Tongli leave from the square in front of Suzhou Train Station every 20 to 30 minutes between 7 AM and 5 PM. The journey is Y6 to Y10.

Even farther off the beaten path is **Luzhi,** about a half hour from Suzhou and Zhouzhuang. It has been described as a "museum of bridges." There are over 40 here, in all different shapes and sizes. Many of the older women in the village preserve traditional customs, wearing traditional headdresses and skirts.

Luzhi is also notable for the spectacular **Baosheng Temple** (✉ Luzhi ☎ 0512/6501-0067), a yellow-walled compound that is famous for its breathtaking collection of Buddhist arhats. Arranged on a wall of stone, these clay sculptures are the work of Yang Huizhi, a famous Tang Dynasty sculptor. They depict Buddhist disciples who have gained enlightenment, works from over 1,000 years ago that still show the character and artistic vision of their creator. The temple also features a well-preserved temple bell from the end of the Ming Dynasty.

Luzhi-bound buses leave from the square in front of Suzhou Train Station every 30 minutes between 6:30 AM and 6:30 PM. The 40-minute drive is Y10.

7

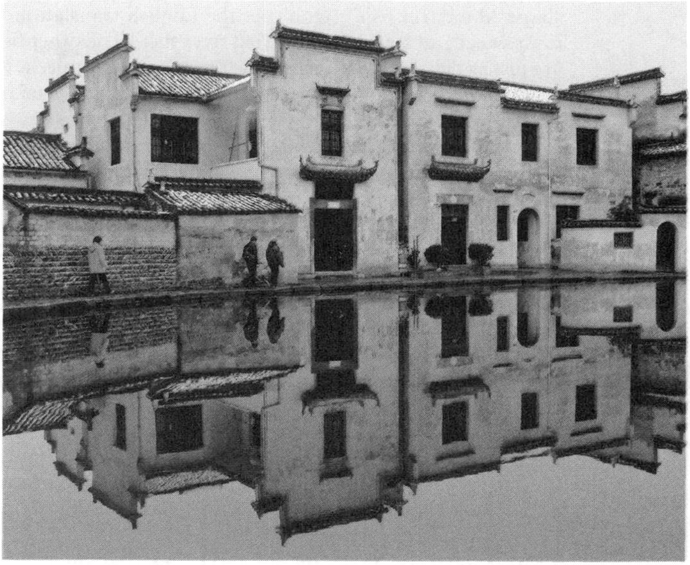

the workers who built the tomb were thanked for their work with an elaborate banquet. The wine, alas, was drugged, so they died to keep the secret of the tomb's entrance. Modern archaeologists think they have discovered it hidden under the artificial lake. The secret may be out, but the king's wish to rest in peace is ensured by the fact that excavating the tomb would bring down the fragile Song Dynasty pagoda that stands above. The **Leaning Pagoda** is one of the most impressive monuments in Suzhou, with Persian influence evident in the arches and other architectural elements. A helpful audio guide explains many of the park's legends. ✉ *Huqiu Lu, northwest of the city* ☎ *0512/6532–3488* 🎫 *Y60* ⏲ *Daily 7:30–5.*

Where to Stay & Eat

In addition to the restaurants below, Shiquan Jie is quickly becoming one of the city's restaurant hubs, with both Suzhou-style restaurants and Chinese regional cuisine from Xinjiang to Yunnan. Many offer English menus, and are popular with both locals and guests at nearby hotels.

★ $–$$$ ✕ **Deyuelou.** This restaurant has served Suzhou-style food for more than 400 years. The menu boasts a wide array of fish dishes as well as a particularly tasty *deyue tongji* (braised chicken). It also specializes in an attractive type of food presentation, the ancient art of "garden foods"—an assortment of small dishes arranged to resemble various sorts of gardens, with foods portraying flowers, trees, and rocks. You can also try the local-style dim sum. ✉ *27 Taijian Nong, south of the Temple of Mystery* ☎ *0512/6523–8940* ▭ *AE, MC, V.*

★ $–$$ ✕ **Pine and Crane** (Songhelou). The food here is the type once served on riverboats during banquet cruises—hence the popular designation "boat food." A particularly good dish here is the *songshu guiyu,* or "squirrel-shape Mandarin fish" (Don't let the English translation turn you off: it's a sweet and sour boneless fried river fish.) The other fish dishes here are just as delicious. The venerable restaurant has a sleek, tasteful decor. ✉ *18 Taijian Nong, south of the Temple of Mystery* ☎ *0512/6523–3270* ▭ *AE, MC, V.*

¢ ✕ **Huangtianyuan.** Here the specialty is the local favorite of *gaotuan* (rice gluten), made by pounding rice to a fine paste. In business since 1821, the eatery's menu changes with the seasons. A year-round house specialty is *babao fan* (syrupy rice with various sweets, nuts, and fruit bits). The sweets here come in all sizes and colors, including green rice balls and red bean-filled dumplings. All the desserts are subtly sweet, not the sugary concoctions that Westerners are used to. ✉ *86 Guanqian Jie* ☎ *0512/6727–7033* ▭ *No credit cards.*

$$$–$$$$ Fodor's Choice ★ 🏨 **Sheraton Suzhou Hotel & Towers.** Suzhou's most luxurious hotel has a two-story stone entrance topped by a pagoda lobby that is modeled after the Pan Gate. (If you want to compare, it sits behind the hotel.) The garden views from the courtyard-facing rooms are stunning. Guests have access to a fitness center and a striking Roman-style pool. However, the accommodations are not huge, Internet access is only available in the most expensive rooms, and the location is less than central. The Garden Brasserie presents an Asian-style buffet. ✉ *259 Xinshi Lu, 215007* ☎ *0512/6510–3388* 📠 *0512/6510–0888* 🌐 *www.sheraton-*

suzhou.com ⇨ 370 rooms, 30 suites ♁ 3 restaurants, room service, cable TV, some in-room data ports, pool, gym, hot tub, massage, sauna, steam room, bar, shop, babysitting, dry cleaning, laundry service, concierge, concierge floor, Internet room, business services, no-smoking rooms, no-smoking floors ▭ AE, DC, MC, V.

★ **$–$$$** **Gloria Plaza Hotel Suzhou.** From the watercolor paintings lining the halls to the cascading waterfall windows of its Sampan Restaurant, the Gloria Plaza Hotel stands out as an inviting property. The large standard rooms dwarf the furniture inside; rooms on the executive floor fill the space better by adding a pullout couch. The hotel is a five-minute walk from Guanqian Jie's restaurants and nightclubs. The business facilities are useful not just for those on a business trip, but for anyone who wants to stay connected. ✉ *535 Ganjiang Dong Lu, 215006* ☎ *0512/6521–8855* 📠 *0512/6521–8533* 🌐 *www.gphsuzhou.com* ⇨ *281 rooms, 13 suites* ♁ *2 restaurants, room service, in-room safes, minibars, cable TV, in-room data ports, gym, massage, sauna, steam room, bar, babysitting, laundry service, concierge, Internet room, business services, no-smoking rooms* ▭ *AE, DC, MC, V.*

¢–$ Fodor's Choice ★ **Suzhou Hotel.** This hotel is a short walk from the Master of the Nets Garden and a stretch of restaurants, bars, and clubs. In the Chinese-style suites, lovely moon gates separate the bedrooms from the sitting areas. The guest rooms are tastefully appointed. The inner-facing rooms overlook a garden. Even with the window open, the only noise is the croaking of frogs in a pond. ✉ *115 Shiquan Jie, 215006* ☎ *0512/6520–4646* 📠 *0512/6520–4015* 🌐 *www.suzhou-hotel.com* ⇨ *283 rooms, 23 suites* ♁ *2 restaurants, room service, minibars, cable TV, gym, hair salon, massage, sauna, bar, dry cleaning, laundry service, business services, no-smoking floors* ▭ *AE, MC, V.*

Shopping

The city's long history has encouraged a tradition of elegant and finely worked craft objects. One of the best known is double-sided embroidery, where two separate designs are carefully stitched on both sides of a sheet of silk. The city is also famous for its finely latticed sandalwood fans. Both are available at the Suzhou Arts and Crafts Museum. The area outside the gate of the Master of the Nets Garden has dozens of small stalls selling curios and inexpensive but interesting souvenirs.

You can get jewelry and carvings at the **Suzhou Jade Carving Factory** (✉ 33 Baita Xi Lu ☎ 0512/6727–1224). Near the North Pagoda, the **Suzhou Silk Museum Shop** (✉ 661 Renmin Lu ☎ 0512/6753–4941) is really the reason to come to the Silk Museum.

To & From Suzhou

1 hr (84 km [52 mi]) by train west of Shanghai.

Buses to Shanghai take about an hour. Trains, which depart about every 20 minutes, take anywhere from 40 minutes to 1½ hours.

At a Glance

ENGLISH	PINYIN	CHINESE CHARACTERS
POINTS OF INTEREST		
HANGZHOU	Hángzhōu	杭州
EXPLORING		
Baidi	Báidī	白堤
China National Silk Museum	Zhōngguó Sīchóu Bówùguǎn	中国丝绸博物馆
China Tea Museum	Zhōngguócháyèbówùguǎn	中国茶叶博物馆
Dragon Well Tea Park	Lóngjǐngwénchá	龙井闻茶
Evening Sunlight at Thunder Peak Pagoda	Léifēngxīzhào	雷锋夕照
Hangzhou Aquarium	Hángzhōuhǎidǐshìjiè	杭州海底世界
Moon Mountain	Yùelúnshān	月轮山
Orioles Singing in the Willow Waves	Liǔlàngwényíng	柳浪闻莺
Precious Stone Hill	Bǎoshíshān	宝石山
Running Tiger Spring	Hǔpǎomèngquán	虎跑梦泉
Solitary Hill Island	Gūshāndǎo	孤山岛
Temple of the Soul's Retreat	Língyǐnsì	灵隐寺
Three Pools Reflecting the Moon	Sāntányìnyuè	三潭印月
WEST LAKE		
Yellow Dragon Cave	Huánglóngdòng	黄龙洞
Yue Fei Mausoleum	Yuèfēimù	岳飞墓
WHERE TO STAY & EAT		
Dong Po Hotel	Dōngpōbīnguǎn	东坡宾馆
Hyatt Regency Hangzhou	Hángzhōukǎiyuèjiǔdiàn	杭州凯悦酒店
Lingyin Si Vegetarian Restaurant	Língyǐnsìsùzhāi	灵隐寺素斋
Louwailou Restaurant	Lóuwàilóu	楼外楼
Shangri-La Hotel Hangzhou	Hángzhōuxiānggélǐlāfàndiàn	杭州香格里拉饭店
Sofitel Westlake Hangzhou	Hángzhōusuǒfēitèxīhúdàjiǔdiàn	杭州索菲特西湖大酒店
Zhiweiguan Restaurant	Zhīwèiguān	知味观

SHAOXING	Shàoxìng	绍兴
EXPLORING		
Bazi Qiao Bridge	Bāzìqiáo	八字桥
Cai Yuanpei's House	Càiyuánpéi gùjū	蔡元培故居
Catholic Church of St. Joseph	Tiānzhǔjiàotáng	天主教堂
East Lake	Dōnghú	东湖
Lu Xun Family Home	Lǔxùn gùjū	鲁迅故居
Zhou Enlai Family Home	Zhōu ēnlái gùjū	周恩来故居
WHERE TO STAY & EAT		
Sanwei Jiulou	Sānwèijiǔlóu	三味酒楼
Shaoxing International Hotel	Shàoxīng guójì dàjiǔdiàn	绍兴国际大酒店
Shaoxing Xianheng Hotel	Shàoxìng xiánhēng dàjiǔdiàn	绍兴咸亨大酒店
Xianheng Winehouse	Xiánhēng jiǔdiàn	咸亨酒店
XIAMEN	xià mén shì	厦门市
EXPLORING		
Hakka Roundhouses	kè jiā tǔ lóu	客家土楼
Hong Shan Park	huáng shān gōng yuán	黄山公园
Jinmen	jīn mén	金门
Nanputuo Temple	nán pǔ tuó sì	南普陀寺
Overseas Chinese Museum	huá qiáo bó wù guǎn	华侨博物馆
Wanshi Botanical Garden	wàn shí zhí wù yuán	万石植物园
Xiamen University	xià mén dà xué	厦门大学
Zhong Shan Park	zhōng shān gōng yuán	中山公园
WHERE TO STAY & EAT		
Dafang Vegetarian Restaurant	dà fāng sù shí guǎn	大方素食馆
Guan Hai Canting	guān hǎi cān tīng	观海餐厅
Holiday Inn Crowne Plaza Harbourview	hǎi jǐng huáng guān jià rì jiǔ diàn	海景皇冠假日酒店
Huangzehe Peanut Soup Shop	huáng zé hé huā shēng tāng diàn	黄则和花生汤店
Lujiang Hotel	lù jiāng bīn guǎn	鹭江宾馆
Marco Polo Xiamen	mǎ kě bō luó dà jiǔ diàn	马可波罗大酒店
Shuyou Seafood Restaurant	shū yǒu hǎi xiān dà jiǔ lóu	舒友海鲜大酒楼

7

GULANGYU	gǔ làng yǔ	鼓浪屿
EXPLORING		
Bright Moon Garden	hào yuè yuán	皓月园
Piano Museum	gāng qín bó wù guǎn	钢琴博物馆
Shuzhuang Garden	shū zhuāng huā yuán	菽庄花园
Zhen Qi Shi Jie	zhēn qí shì jiè	珍奇世界
NANJING	Nán jīng	南京
EXPLORING		
Confucian Temple	FūzǐMiào	夫子庙
Drum Tower	Gǔ lóu	鼓楼
Ming Tomb	Míng Xiào líng	明孝陵
Nanjing Massacre Memorial	Nánjīng dàtúshā jìniànguǎn	南京大屠杀纪念馆
Nanjing Museum	Nánjīng bówùyuàn	南京博物院
Plum Blossom Hill and Sun Yat-sen Botanical Gardens	Méihuāshān hé zhōngshān zhíwùyuán	梅花山和中山（孙中山）植物园
Rain Flower Terrace and Martyrs Memorial	Yǔhuātái hé lièshìjìniànguǎn	雨花台和烈士纪念馆
South Gate of City Wall	Zhōnghuá mén	中华门
Sparrow's Rock	Yànzǐjī	燕子矶
Spirit Valley Temple and Pagoda	Línggǔsì hé línggǔtǎ	灵谷寺和灵谷塔
Sun Yat-sen Memorial	Sūnzhōngshān jìniànguǎn	孙中山纪念馆
Taiping Heavenly Kingdom Museum	Tàiopíng Tiānguó Bówùguǎn	太平天国博物馆
Xuanwu Lake Park	Xuánwǔhú gōngyuán	玄武湖公园
Yangzi River Bridge	Nánjīng chángjiāng dàqiáo	南京长江大桥
Yuejiang Lou Tower	Yuèjiāng lóu	阅江楼
WHERE TO STAY & EAT		
Baguo Buyi	Bāguó bùyī	巴国布衣
Central Hotel	Zhōngxīn dàjiǔdiàn	中心大酒店
Dingshan Meishi Cheng	Dīngshān měishíchéng	丁山美食城
Jimingsi Vegetarian Restaurant	Jīmíngsìsùzhāi	鸡鸣寺素斋
Jinling Hotel	Jīnlíng fàndiàn	金陵饭店
Nanjing Hotel	Nánjīng fàndiàn	南京饭店

SUZHOU	Sū zhōu	苏州
EXPLORING		
Blue Wave Pavilion	Cānglàng tíng	沧浪亭
Grand Canal	Dà yùnhé	大运河
Hanshan Temple	Hánshān sì	寒山寺
Humble Administrator's Garden	Zhuōzhèng yuán	拙政园
Joyous Garden	Yí yuán	怡园
Lingering Garden	Liú yuán	留园
Lion's Grove Garden	Shīzī lín	狮子林
Master of the Nets Garden	Wǎngshī yuán	网师园
North Temple Pagoda	Běisì tǎ	北寺塔
Pan Gate	Pán mén	盘门
Suzhou Arts and Crafts Museum	Sūzhōu gōngyìměishù bówùguǎn	苏州工艺美术博物馆
Suzhou Museum	Sūzhōu bówùguǎn	苏州博物馆
Temple of Mystery	Xuánmiào guàn	玄妙观
Tiger Hill	Hǔ qiū	虎丘
West Garden Temple	Xīyuán sì	西园寺
WHERE TO STAY & EAT		
Bamboo Grove Hotel	Sūzhōu zhúhuī fàndiàn	苏州竹辉饭店
Deyuelou	Déyuè lóu	得月楼
Gloria Plaza Hotel Suzhou	Sūzhōu kǎilái dàjiǔdiàn	苏州凯莱大酒店
Huangtianyuan	Huángtiān yuán	黄天园
Pine and Crane	Sōnghè lóu	松鹤楼
Sheraton Suzhou Hotel & Towers	Xǐláidēng dàjiǔdiàn	喜来登大酒店
Suzhou Hotel	Sūzhōu fàndiàn	苏州饭店

7

VOCABULARY GUIDE

PRONUNCIATION & VOCABULARY

PRONUNCIATION & VOCABULARY

	Chinese	English Equivalent	Chinese	English Equivalent
Consonants				
	b	boat	p	pass
	m	mouse	f	flag
	d	dock	t	tongue
	n	nest	l	life
	g	goat	k	keep
	h	house	j	and yet
	q	chicken	x	short
	zh	judge	ch	church
	sh	sheep	r*	read
	z	seeds	c	dots
	s	seed		
Vowels				
	ü	you	ia	yard
	üe	you + e	ian	yen
	a	father	iang	young
	ai	kite	ie	yet
	ao	now	o	all
	e	earn	ou	go
	ei	day	u	wood
	er	curve	ua	waft
	i	yield	uo	wall
	i (after z, c, s, zh, ch, sh)	thunder		

Word Order

The basic Chinese sentence structure is the same as in English, following the pattern of subject-verb-object:

He took my pen.	Tā ná le wǒ de bǐ.
s v o	s v o

Nouns

There are no articles in Chinese, although there are many "counters," which are used when a certain number of a given noun is specified. Various attributes of a noun—such as size, shape, or use—determine which counter is used with that noun. Chinese does not distinguish between singular and plural.

a pen	yìzhī bǐ
a book	yìběn shū

Verbs

Chinese verbs are not conjugated, and they do not have tenses. Instead, a system of word order, word repetition, and the addition of a number of adverbs serves to indicate the tense of a verb, whether the verb is a suggestion or an order, or even whether the verb is part of a question. *Tāzaì ná wǒ de bǐ.* (He is taking my pen.) *Tā ná le wǒ de bǐ.* (He took my pen.) *Tā you méi you ná wǒ de bǐ?* (Did he take my pen?) *Tā yào ná wǒ de bǐ.* (He will take my pen.)

Tones

In English, intonation patterns can indicate whether a sentence is a statement (He's hungry.), a question (He's hungry?), or an exclamation (He's hungry!). In Chinese, words have a particular tone value, and these tones are important in determining the meaning of a word. Observe the meanings of the following examples, each said with one of the four tones found in standard Chinese: *mā* (high, steady tone): mother; *má* (rising tone, like a question): fiber; *mǎ* (dipping tone): horse; and *mà* (dropping tone): swear.

Phrases

You don't need to master the entire Chinese language to spend a week in China, but taking charge of a few key phrases in the language can aid you in just getting by.

Common Greetings

Hello/Good morning.	Nǐ hǎo/Zǎoshàng hǎo.
Good evening.	Wǎnshàng hǎo.
Good-bye.	Zàijiàn.
Title for a married woman or an older unmarried woman	Tàitai/Fūrén
Title for a young and unmarried woman	Xiǎojiě
Title for a man	Xiānshēng
How are you?	Nǐ hǎo ma?
Fine, thanks. And you?	Hěn hǎo. Xièxie. Nǐ ne?
What is your name?	Nǐ jiào shénme míngzi?
My name is . . .	Wǒ jiào . . .

Shanghai Essentials

PLANNING TOOLS, EXPERT INSIGHT, GREAT CONTACTS

There are planners, and there are those who fly by the seat of their pants. We happily place ourselves among the planners. Our writers and editors try to anticipate all the issues you may face before and during any journey, and then they do their research. This section is the product of their efforts. Use it to get excited about your trip to Shanghai, to inform your travel planning, or to guide you on the road should the seat of your pants start to feel threadbare.

www.fodors.com/forums

GETTING STARTED

We're really proud of our Web site: Fodors.com is a great place to begin any journey. Scan "Travel Wire" for suggested itineraries, travel deals, restaurant and hotel openings, and other up-to-the-minute info. Check out "Booking" to research prices and book plane tickets, hotel rooms, rental cars, and vacation packages. Head to "Talk" for on-the-ground pointers from travelers who frequent our message boards. You can also link to loads of other travel-related resources.

RESOURCES

ONLINE TRAVEL TOOLS

All the Web sites listed below are in English. If you want to read Chinese-only Web sites in English, try using Google's "Translate this page" tool. It might not read like Shakespeare, but you'll get the gist of the information.

All About Shanghai **China Digital Times** 🌐 http://chinadigitaltimes.net is an excellent Berkeley-run site tracking China-related news and culture in serious depth. **China National Tourism Office** 🌐 www.cnto.org gives a general overview of traveling in China. **China Travel Services (U.S. site)** 🌐 www.chinatravelservice.com, the state-run travel agency, is a helpful starting place. **Chinese Government Portal** 🌐 http://english.gov.cn. **Live in Shanghai** 🌐 http://shanghaidaily.com/live is the most up-to-date, down-to-earth information on life in Shanghai; the transportation section is excellent. **Shanghai City Weekend** 🌐 www.cityweekend.com.cn is an online version of the local magazine with top-notch searchable listings on just about everything in Shanghai. **Shanghai Municipality** 🌐 www.shanghai.gov.cn is the comprehensive (if slightly dry) government guide to the city. **Shanghai Tour** 🌐 http://lyw.sh.gov.cn/en/ is the official government tourism Web site, with advice on sightseeing, hotels, and restaurants.

Business **American Chamber of Commerce in Shanghai** 🌐 www.amcham-shanghai.org has a Web site packed with useful business information and links to other resources. ***China Business Weekly*** 🌐 www.chinadaily.com.cn/bw/bwtop.html is a weekly magazine from the *China Daily* newspaper. **Chinese Government Business Site** 🌐 http://english.gov.cn/business.htm has news, links, and information on business-related legal issues from the Chinese government.

Culture **China Vista** 🌐 www.chinavista.com/experience has incredibly detailed information on all aspects of Chinese arts and culture. **Chinese Culture** 🌐 www.chinaculture.org is a detailed, searchable database with information on Chinese art, literature, film, history, and more.

Currency Conversion **Google** 🌐 www.google.com does currency conversion. Just type in the amount you want to convert and an explanation of how you want it converted (e.g., "14 Swiss francs in dollars"), and then voilà. **Oanda.com** 🌐 www.oanda.com also allows you to print out a handy table with the current day's conversion rates. **XE.com** 🌐 www.xe.com is a good currency conversion Web site.

Local Insight **Enjoy Shanghai** 🌐 www.enjoyshanghai.com has searchable listings for eating out, shopping, and finding Wi-Fi spots. **Shanghai Expat** 🌐 http://shanghai.asiaxpat.com has advice and listings from foreigners living in Shanghai. **Shanghai-ed** 🌐 www.shanghai-ed.com provides expat expertise on the city. **Shanghaiist** 🌐 www.shanghaiist.com is the city's best blog, run by the same people as NYC's Gothamist; it gives a different take on what's going down in town. ***SH Magazine*** 🌐 www.asia-city.com is a quirky weekly rag whose online version gives the lowdown on just about everything happening in town. **Shanghai Eats** 🌐 www.shanghai-eats.com lists hundreds of local restaurants, bars, and clubs, all authoritatively reviewed. ***That's Shanghai*** 🌐 www.thatssh.com is a glossy local monthly that's also available online.

Newspapers ***China Daily*** 🌐 www.chinadaily.com.cn is the country's leading English-language daily. ***People's Daily*** http://english.peopledaily.com.cn is an English edition of China's most popular—and most propagandistic—local daily. ***Shanghai Daily*** http://english.eastday.com is the city's English-language newspaper.

Safety **Transportation Security Administration** (TSA) www.tsa.gov

Time Zones **Timeanddate.com** www.timeanddate.com/worldclock can help you figure out the correct time anywhere in the world.

Weather **Accuweather.com** www.accuweather.com is an independent weather-forecasting service with especially good coverage of hurricanes. **Shanghai Weather** http://weather.china.org.cn. **Weather.com** www.weather.com is the Web site for the Weather Channel.

Other Resources **CIA World Factbook** www.odci.gov/cia/publications/factbook/index.html has profiles of every country in the world. It's a good source if you need some quick facts and figures.

INSPIRATION

Get yourself into a Shanghainese mood with some great reads. **Shanghai Chick-Lit:** Wei Hu's *Shanghai Baby,* banned in China. **Memoirs of Mao:** *Life and Death in Shanghai,* by Nien Cheng. **The City Under Siege:** J.G. Ballard's *Empire of the Sun* and Kazuo Ishiguro's *When We Were Orphans,* both set in WWII Shanghai. **Classic Fiction:** seminal writer Lu Xun's *Diary of a Madman.*

There are plenty of great books that lend insight into Chinese culture. **Big Name Fiction:** Gao Xinjiang's *Soul Mountain,* Ha Jin's *Waiting,* and Dai Sijie's *Mr. Muo's Traveling Couch.* **China 101:** *The China Reader: The Reform Era,* edited by Orville Schell and David Shambaugh, and *The Search for Modern China* by Jonathan Spence. **How about Mao?:** Dr. Li Zhisui's *The Private Life of Chairman Mao.*

Before your trip, settle in for an evening of cinema that was set, or made, in Shanghai. **Old Shanghai:** Zhang Yimou's *Shanghai Triad* (1995), Josef von Sternberg's *Shanghai Express* (1935), and Merchant-Ivory's *The White Countess* (2005). **Shanghai Today:** Wang Xiaoshuai's *Shanghai Dreams* (2005). **Censored in China:** Lou Ye's *Suzhou River* (2000).

WORD OF MOUTH

After your trip, be sure to rate the places you visited and share your experiences and travel tips with us and other Fodorites in "Travel Ratings" and "Talk" on www.fodors.com.

VISITOR INFORMATION

For general information before you go, including information about tours, insurance, and safety, call or visit the Web site of the China National Tourist Office.

Shanghai Tour, the government tourism Web site, is a good planning resource. It runs the official Shanghai Tourist Information and Service Centers, which have branches all over town, usually identifiable by big aquamarine signs. Reasonably informed staff dole out free maps and leaflets, and can also book hotels, restaurants, and flights. Compare prices with other travel agencies, as Shanghai Tour is often not the cheapest. The Web site lists branch details.

The two best-known Chinese travel agencies are China International Travel Service (CITS) and China Travel Service (CTS), both under the same government ministry. Although they have some tourist information, they are businesses, so don't expect endless resources if you're not buying a tour or flight through them.

China National Tourist Office New York: ☎ 888/760-8218 ✉ Los Angeles: ☎ 800/670-2228 www.cnto.org. **China International Travel Service** (CITS) Shanghai: ☎ 021/6289-8899 or 021/6289-4510 www.scits.com ✉ U.S.: ☎ 626/568-8993 www.citsusa.com. **China Travel Service** (CTS) Shanghai: ☎ 021/6247-8888 ✉ New York: ☎ 800/899-8618 www.chinatravelservice.com. **Shanghai Tour** ☎ 021/6252-0000 http://lyw.sh.gov.cn/en/.

THINGS TO CONSIDER

GOVERNMENT ADVISORIES

■ TIP→ **If you're a U.S. citizen traveling abroad, consider registering online with the State Department (https://travelregistration.state.gov/ibrs/), so the government will know to look for you should a crisis occur in the country you're visiting.**

General Information & Warnings **Australian Department of Foreign Affairs & Trade** 🌐 www.smartraveller.gov.au. **Consular Affairs Bureau of Canada** 🌐 www.voyage.gc.ca. **U.K. Foreign & Commonwealth Office** 🌐 www.fco.gov.uk/travel. **U.S. Department of State** 🌐 www.travel.state.gov.

GEAR

Forget Paris, New York, and Milan—the new center of the fashion universe is Shanghai. People in the rest of China dress for comfort, but the Shanghainese dress to kill. This is a city where suits are still *de rigueur* for meetings and business functions. Slop around in flip-flops and worn denims and you will feel like there's a neon "tourist" sign over your head. Pack your nicer pairs of jeans or capri pants for sightseeing—there are plenty of fake handbags around with which to dress them up come dinner.

From May through September it's seriously hot and sticky, but air-conditioning in hotels, restaurants, and museums can be arctic—keep a wrinkle-proof sweater or shawl in your day pack. In October and April, a jacket or sweater should suffice. Temperatures plunge into the 30s and 40s Fahrenheit (0–10°C) in November and stay low until mid-March so you'll need a heavy-duty jacket or overcoat. No self-respecting Shanghai resident leaves home each morning without a folding umbrella, nor should you.

That said, in Shanghai you can prepare to be unprepared: the city is a clothing-shopper's paradise. If a bulky jacket's going to put you over the airline limit, buy one for next to nothing in China and leave it behind when you go.

Keep packets of Kleenex and antibacterial hand wipes in your day pack—paper isn't a feature of Chinese restrooms. Watson's is a pharmacy chain with various branches around town; they stock international toiletry brands and tampons, which are otherwise hard to find in Shanghai.

> **WORD OF MOUTH**
>
> "For Tokyo, Shanghai, and Hong Kong, you need to bring your best clothes. Like you would going to New York, London, and Paris." –rkkwan

PASSPORTS & VISAS

All U.S. citizens, even infants, need a valid passport with a tourist visa stamped in it to enter China (except for Hong Kong, where you only need a valid passport). It's always best to have at least six months' validity on your passport before traveling to Asia.

Children traveling with only one parent do not need a notarized letter of permission to enter China. However, as these kinds of policies can change, being over-prepared isn't a bad idea.

The cost to apply for a new passport is $97 for adults, $82 for children under 16; renewals are $67. Allow six weeks for processing, both for first-time passports and renewals. For an expediting fee of $60 you can reduce this time to about two weeks. If your trip is less than two weeks away, you can get a passport even more rapidly by going to a passport office with the necessary documentation. Private expediters can get things done in as little as 48 hours, but charge hefty fees for their services.

VISAS

Getting a tourist visa (known as an "L" visa) in the United States is straightforward. Standard visas are for single-entry stays of up to 30 days, and are valid for 90 days from the date of issue (*not* the date of entry), so don't get your visa too far in advance. Costs range from $50 for a tourist visa issued within two to three working days to $80 for a same-day service.

Note: The visa application will ask your occupation. The Chinese don't look favorably upon those who work in publishing or the media. People in these professions routinely state "teacher" under "occupation." Before you go, contact the embassy or consulate of the People's Republic of China to gauge the current mood.

China officially denies visas (and thus entry) to anyone suffering from infectious diseases, including leprosy, AIDS, venereal diseases, and contagious tuberculosis. You must complete information regarding these on applications and on entering the country. However, this information is almost never checked for tourist visas; medical tests are required for longer visas.

Under no circumstances should you overstay your visa. To extend your visa, stop by the Entry and Exit Administration Office of the Shanghai Public Security Bureau a week before your visa expires. The office is known as the PSB or the Foreigner's Police, and is open weekdays 9 to 11:30 and 1:30 to 4:30. It's extremely bureaucratic, but it's usually no problem to get a month's extension on a tourist visa. You need to bring your passport and a registration of temporary residency from your hotel. You generally need to leave your passport for 5 to 7 days, so do any transactions requiring it (and make copies!) beforehand. If you are trying to extend a business visa, you'll need the above items as well as a letter, from the business that originally invited you to China, stating it would like to extend your stay for work reasons. Rules are always changing (Visa to Asia has up-to-date information), so you will probably need to go to the office at least twice to get all your papers in order.

Passport & Visa Information **Chinese Consulate** New York: ☎ 212/244-9456 🌐 www.nyconsulate.prchina.org. **U.S. Department of State** ☎ 877/487-2778 🌐 http://travel.state.gov/passport. **Visa to Asia** 🌐 www.visatoasia.com/china.html. **Visa Office of Chinese Embassy, Washington** ☎ 202/338-6688 🌐 www.china-embassy.org.

U.S. Passport & Visa Expediters **A. Briggs Passport & Visa Expeditors** ☎ 800/806-0581 or 202/464-3000 🌐 www.abriggs.com. **American Passport Express** ☎ 800/455-5166 or 603/559-9888 🌐 www.americanpassport.com. **Passport Express** ☎ 800/362-8196 or 401/272-4612 🌐 www.passportexpress.com. **Travel Document Systems** ☎ 800/874-5100 or 202/638-3800 🌐 www.traveldocs.com. **Travel the World Visas** ☎ 866/886-8472 or 301/495-7700 🌐 www.world-visa.com.

Visa Extensions **Entry and Exit Administration Office, Shanghai Public Security Bureau** ✉ 333 Wusong Lu, Huangpu District ☎ 021/6357-7925 🌐 www.shanghai.gov.cn.

GENERAL REQUIREMENTS FOR SHANGHAI	
Passport	Must be valid for 6 months after date of arrival.
Visa	Required for U.S. citizens ($25-$80)
Required Vaccinations	None
Recommended Vaccinations	Hepatitis A and B, typhoid, influenza, booster for tetanus-diptheria
Driving	Chinese driver's license required
International Departure Tax	Y90 ($11)
Domestic Departure Tax	Y50 ($6)

SHOTS & MEDICATIONS

No immunizations are required for entry into China, but it's a good idea to be immunized against typhoid and Hepatitis A and B before traveling to Shanghai, as well as routine tetanus-diphtheria and measles boosters. In winter, a flu vaccination is also smart, especially if you're infection-prone or are a senior citizen. For

Trip Insurance Resources

INSURANCE COMPARISON SITES		
Insure My Trip.com		www.insuremytrip.com.
Square Mouth.com		www.quotetravelinsurance.com.
COMPREHENSIVE TRAVEL INSURERS		
Access America	866/807-3982	www.accessamerica.com.
CSA Travel Protection	800/873-9855	www.csatravelprotection.com.
HTH Worldwide	610/254-8700 or 888/243-2358	www.hthworldwide.com.
Travelex Insurance	888/457-4602	www.travelex-insurance.com.
Travel Guard International	715/345-0505 or 800/826-4919	www.travelguard.com.
Travel Insured International	800/243-3174	www.travelinsured.com.
MEDICAL-ONLY INSURERS		
International Medical Group	800/628-4664	www.imglobal.com.
International SOS	215/942-8000 or 713/521-7611	www.internationalsos.com.
Wallach & Company	800/237-6615 or 504/687-3166	www.wallach.com.

more information *see* Health *under* On the Ground in Shanghai, *below.*

TRIP INSURANCE

Comprehensive trip insurance is especially valuable if you're booking a very expensive or complicated trip (particularly to an isolated region) or if you're booking far in advance. Who knows what could happen six months down the road? But whether or not you get insurance has more to do with how comfortable you are assuming all that risk yourself.

Comprehensive travel policies typically cover trip-cancellation and interruption, letting you cancel or cut your trip short because of a personal emergency, illness, or, in some cases, acts of terrorism in your destination. Such policies also cover evacuation and medical care. Another type of coverage to look for is financial default—that is, when your trip is disrupted because a tour operator, airline, or cruise line goes out of business.

Consider buying medical-only coverage at the very least. Neither Medicare nor some private insurers cover medical expenses anywhere outside of the United States besides Mexico and Canada (including time aboard a cruise ship, even if it leaves from a U.S. port). Medical-only policies typically reimburse you for medical care (excluding that related to pre-existing conditions) and hospitalization abroad, and provide for evacuation. You still have to pay the bills and await reimbursement from the insurer, though.

■ TIP→ Even at Shanghai's public hospitals foreigners need to pay fees to register, to see a doctor, and then for all tests and medication. Prices are cheap compared to the city's fancy foreigner clinics, where you pay $100 to $150 just for a consultation, but most doctors don't speak English and hygiene standards are low even at better public hospitals.

Expect comprehensive travel insurance policies to cost about 4% to 7% of the total price of your trip (it's more like 12% if you're over age 70). A medical-only policy may or may not be cheaper than a comprehensive policy. Always read the fine print of your policy to make sure that you are covered for the risks that are of most concern to you. Compare several policies to make sure you're getting the best price and range of coverage available.

BOOKING YOUR TRIP

Jnless your cousin is a travel agent, you're probably among the millions of people who make most of their travel arrangements online. But have you ever wondered just what the differences are between an online travel agent (a Web site through which you make reservations instead of going directly to the airline, hotel, or car-rental company), a discounter (a firm that does a high volume of business with a hotel chain or airline and accordingly gets good prices), a wholesaler (one that makes cheap reservations in bulk and then re-sells them to people like you), and an aggregator (one that compares all the offerings so you don't have to)? Is it truly better to book directly on an airline or hotel Web site? And when does a real live travel agent come in handy?

ONLINE

The current hotel glut in Shanghai means finding accommodation is rarely a problem. However, the predominance of high-end establishments means prices can be steep. Although it's always worth a quick look at online accommodation sites, sometimes dropping an e-mail directly to the hotel can get you similar, if not better, rates.

For flight prices within China, eLong is a useful resource—it lists most major domestic airlines at reasonable rates.

■ TIP→ **To be absolutely sure everything was processed correctly, confirm reservations made through online travel agents, discounters, and wholesalers directly with your hotel before leaving home.**

WITH A TRAVEL AGENT

If you use an agent—brick-and-mortar or virtual—you'll pay a fee for the service. And know that the service you get from some online agents isn't comprehensive. For example Expedia and Travelocity don't search for prices on budget airlines like jetBlue, Southwest, or small foreign carriers. That said, some agents (online or not) *do* have access to fares that are difficult to find otherwise, and the savings can more than make up for any surcharge.

A knowledgeable brick-and-mortar travel agent can be a godsend if you're booking a package trip that's not available to you directly, an air pass, or a complicated itinerary including several overseas flights. What's more, travel agents that specialize in a destination may have exclusive access to certain deals and insider information on things such as charter flights. Agents who specialize in types of travelers (senior citizens, gays and lesbians, naturists) or types of trips (cruises, luxury travel, safaris) can also be invaluable.

A top-notch agent planning your trip to China will make sure you get the correct visa application and complete it on time; the one booking your cruise may get you a cabin upgrade or arrange to have a bottle of champagne chilling in your cabin when you embark. Complain about the surcharges all you like, but when things don't work out the way you'd hoped, it's nice to have an agent to put things right.

■ TIP→ **Remember that Expedia, Travelocity, and Orbitz are travel agents, not just booking engines. To resolve any problems with a reservation made through these companies, contact them first.**

Booking hotels and flights for Shanghai is easy to do without a travel agent, though you may get preferable rates (or room upgrades) if you use one. If you're planning to visit other places in China, a travel agent can save time and hassle, especially with internal flights, as schedules can change without warning. An agent can track this and adjust your tickets accordingly. Be careful booking with Internet-based Chinese agencies from abroad, as not all are legal travel agencies. Stick with those we list here, or at least be sure to get recommendations from a reputable source before handing over your credit card information.

Online Booking Resources

AGGREGATORS		
Kayak	www.kayak.com	looks at cruises and vacation packages.
Mobissimo	www.mobissimo.com.	
Qixo	www.qixo.com	compares cruises, vacation packages, and even travel insurance.
Sidestep	www.sidestep.com	compares vacation packages and lists travel deals.
Travelgrove	www.travelgrove.com	compares cruises and vacation packages.
BOOKING ENGINES		
Cheap Tickets	www.cheaptickets.com	discounter.
Expedia	www.expedia.com	large online agency that charges a booking fee for airline tickets.
Hotwire	www.hotwire.com	discounter.
lastminute.com	www.lastminute.com	specializes in last-minute travel; the main site is for the U.K., but it has a link to a U.S. site.
Luxury Link	www.luxurylink.com	has auctions (surprisingly good deals) as well as offers on the high-end side of travel.
Onetravel.com	www.onetravel.com	discounter for hotels, car rentals, airfares, and packages.
Orbitz	www.orbitz.com	charges a booking fee for airline tickets, but gives a clear breakdown of fees and taxes before you book.
Priceline.com	www.priceline.com	discounter that also allows bidding.
Travel.com	www.travel.com	allows you to compare its rates with those of other booking engines.
Travelocity	www.travelocity.com	charges a booking fee for airline tickets, but promises good problem resolution.
ONLINE ACCOMMODATIONS		
Asia Hotels	www.asia-hotels.com	good selection of mid- to top-end hotels.
Asia Travel	www.asiatravel.com	popular place to get hotel deals.
CTrip	www.ctrip.com	China-based site, and one of the best places to start looking for hotels.
China Hotel Guide	http://china-hotelguide.com	sometimes has good discounts for better hotels.
China.org.cn	http://hotel.china.org.cn	government-authorized portal with a huge number of listings.
Hotelbook.com	www.hotelbook.com	focuses on independent hotels worldwide.
Hotel Club	www.hotelclub.net	good for major cities worldwide.
Hotels.com	www.hotels.com	big Expedia-owned wholesaler that offers rooms in hotels all over the world.
Quikbook	www.quikbook.com	offers "pay when you stay" reservations that allow you to settle your bill when you check out, not when you book.
Sino Hotel	www.sinohotel.com	has a good range of the pricier hotels in Shanghai.
OTHER RESOURCES		
Bidding For Travel	www.biddingfortravel.com	good place to figure out what you can get and for how much before you start bidding on, say, Priceline.

The agencies below are accustomed to dealing with expatriates and English-speaking visitors; they can arrange both domestic and international travel. For additional agents, check out the travel section of *That's Shanghai*.

Agent Resources **American Society of Travel Agents** ☎ 703/739–2782 🌐 www.travelsense.org. **American Express** ✉ Shanghai Centre, 1376 Nanjing Xi Lu, Jing'an District ☎ 021/6279–8082 🌐 www.americanexpress.com. **China International Travel Service** (CITS) ✉ 1277 Beijing Xi Lu, Jing'an District ☎ 021/6289–6925 🌐 www.cits.com.cn. **Great West Travel** ✉ Suite 563, Shanghai Centre, 1376 Nanjing Xi Lu, Jing'an District ☎ 021/6279–8489 🌐 www.great-west-travel.com. **Passeport Chine** ✉ Room D, 14th fl., 336 Jian Ning Lu, Jing'an District ☎ 021/6215–3815 🌐 www.passeport-chine.com. **STA Travel** ✉ Suite 305, 158 Han Zhong Lu, Zhabei District ☎ 021/6353–2683 🌐 www.statravel.com.cn.

ACCOMMODATIONS

Opening a hotel seems quite the "in" thing to do in Shanghai these days. The choice of accommodation is wide, and takes in most tastes and budgets. However, that's not to say choosing a hotel is always easy: the Chinese star system is a little unpredictable, and Web sites are often misleading for all but the biggest names. For lesser establishments, try to get recent personal recommendations: the forums on Fodors.com are a great place to start.

Location is the first thing you should consider. This is a **big** city: there's no point shlepping halfway across town for one particular hotel when a similar option is available more conveniently. Most of the big international hotels are in the newer Pudong District, which is ideal for business travelers. If you're planning to sightsee, you're better off over the river in Puxi. Most of the city's budget accommodations are close to the Bund. Consider where you'll be going, then pick your bed.

Many of Shanghai's 4- or 5-star hotels belong to familiar international chains, and are usually a safe—if pricey—bet. You can expect swimming pools, a concierge, and business services here. Locally owned hotels with 4 stars or less have erratic standards, as bribery plays a big part in star acquisition. However, air-conditioning, color TVs, and private Western-style bathrooms are the norm for 3 to 4 stars; even lone-star hotels have private bathrooms, albeit with a squatter toilet. Extra-firm beds are a trademark of Chinese hoteliers even in luxury chains.

CATEGORY	COST
$$$$	over Y1,800
$$$	Y1,401–Y1,800
$$	Y1,101–Y1,400
$	Y700–Y1,100
¢	under Y700

All prices are in yuan for two people in a standard double room in high season, excluding 10%–15% service charges.

Most hotels and other lodgings require you to give your credit-card details before they will confirm your reservation. If you don't feel comfortable e-mailing this information, ask if you can fax it (some places even prefer faxes). However you book, get confirmation in writing and have a copy of it handy when you check-in.

Be sure you understand the hotel's cancellation policy. Some places allow you to cancel without any kind of penalty—even if you prepaid to secure a discounted rate—if you cancel at least 24 hours in advance. Others require you to cancel a week in advance or penalize you the cost of one night. Small inns and B&Bs are most likely to require you to cancel far in advance. Most hotels allow children under a certain age to stay in their parents' room at no extra charge, but others charge for them as extra adults; find out the cutoff age for discounts.

TIP→ **Assume that hotels operate on the European Plan (EP, no meals) unless we specify**

that they use the Breakfast Plan (BP, with full breakfast), Continental Plan (CP, continental breakfast), Full American Plan (FAP, all meals), Modified American Plan (MAP, breakfast and dinner), or are all-inclusive (AI, all meals and most activities).

APARTMENT & HOUSE RENTALS

There's an abundance of furnished rental properties for short- and long-term lets in Shanghai. Prices vary wildly. At the top end are luxury apartments and villas, usually far from the city center and best accessible by (chauffeur-driven) car. Usually described as "serviced apartments" or "villas," these often include gyms and pools, and rents are usually well over $2,000 a month.

There are a lot of well-located midrange properties in new apartment blocks. They're usually clean, with new furnishings, with rents starting at $500. Finally, for longer, cheaper stays, there are normal local apartments. These are firmly off the tourist circuit and often cost only a third of the price of the midrange properties. Expect mismatched furniture, erratic amenities, and varying insect populations. What you get for your money fluctuates so be prepared to shop around.

Property sites like Move and Stay, Sublet, and Pacific Properties have hundreds of apartments all over town. The online classifieds pages in local English-language magazines like *SH* or *Shanghai-ed* are good places to start looking for cheaper properties.

Online Booking Resources

Move and Stay 🌐 www.moveandstay.com/shanghai. **Pacific Properties** 🌐 www.worthenpacific.com. ***Shanghai-ed*** 🌐 www.shanghai-ed.com. ***SH* magazine** 🌐 www.asia-city.com. **Sublet.com** 🌐 www.sublet.com.

HOMESTAYS

Single travelers can arrange homestays (often in combination with language courses) through the China Homestay Club. Generally these are in upper-middle-class homes that work out to be at least as expensive as a cheap hotel—prices start at $150 to $180 a week. Nine times out of 10, the family has a small child in need of daily English conversation classes. ChinaHomestay.org is a different organization, which charges a single placement fee of $300 for a stay of three months or less.

Organizations **China Homestay Club** 🌐 www.homestay.com.cn. **ChinaHomestay.org** 🌐 www.chinahomestay.org.

HOSTELS

Membership in any HI association, open to travelers of all ages, allows you to stay in HI–affiliated hostels at member rates. One-year membership is about $28 for adults; hostels charge about $10 to $30 per night. Members have priority if the hostel is full; they're also eligible for discounts around the world, even on rail and bus travel in some countries.

Budget-accommodation options are improving in Shanghai; most are near the Bund. However, the term "hostel" is still used vaguely—the only thing guaranteed is shared dorm rooms; other facilities vary. There are several clean youth hostels in Huangpu, including three HI affiliates, but flea-ridden dumps are also common, so always ask to see your room before paying. Try to pick somewhere close to a subway. A private room in a low-end hotel is often just as cheap as these so-called hostels; some guesthouses and hotels also have cheaper dorm beds in addition to regular rooms. Backpackers and young travelers account for most of the guests.

Hostelling International–USA ☎ 301/495-1240 🌐 www.hiusa.org.

Youth Hostel Association of China ☎ 020/8734-5080 🌐 www.yhachina.com.

AIRLINE TICKETS

Most domestic airline tickets are electronic; international tickets may be either electronic or paper. With an e-ticket the only thing you receive is an e-mailed receipt citing your itinerary and reservation and ticket numbers. The greatest advantage of an e-ticket is that if you lose your receipt, you can simply print out another copy or ask the airline to do it for you at check-in. You usually pay a surcharge (up to $50) to get a paper ticket, if you can get one at all. The sole advantage of a paper ticket is that it may be easier to endorse over to another airline if your flight is canceled and the airline with which you booked can't accommodate you on another flight.

TIP→ Discount air passes that let you travel economically in a country or region must often be purchased before you leave home. In some cases you can only get them through a travel agent.

If you are flying into Asia on a SkyTeam airline (Delta or Continental, for example) you're eligible to purchase their Asia Pass. It includes more than 10 Chinese cities (including Shanghai, Beijing, Xian, and Hong Kong) as well as destinations in 20 other Asian and Australasian countries. The pass works on a coupon basis; the minimum (three coupons) costs $750, whereas six come to $1,410.

China Southern Airlines's China Air Pass is excellent value if you're planning to fly to several destinations within the country: the minimum 3-coupon pass comes to $329, whereas 10 cost $909. The catch? You have to be flying in from abroad on one of their flights. Hong Kong isn't included in the pass, but Shenzhen, just over the border, gets you close enough. Bear in mind that Chinese domestic-flight schedules can be very flexible—flights may be changed or canceled at a moment's notice.

Air-Pass Info **Asia Pass** SkyTeam ☎ 800/523-3273 Continental, 800/221-1212 Delta 🌐 www.skyteam.com. **China Air Pass** China Southern Airlines ☎ 888/338-8988 🌐 www.cs-air.com.

RENTAL CARS

Driving yourself is not a possibility when vacationing in Shanghai, as the only valid driver's licenses are Chinese ones. Neither U.S. licenses nor IDPs are recognized in China. However, this restriction should be cause for relief, as the city traffic is terrible, its drivers manic, and getting lost practically inevitable for first-timers.

A far better idea, if you want to get around by car, is to put yourself in the experienced hands of a local driver and sit back and watch them negotiate the traffic jams. All the same, consider your itinerary carefully before doing so—the subway is far quicker for central areas. Save car travel for excursions farther afield.

The quickest way to hire a car and driver is to flag down a taxi and hire it for the day—if you're happy with a driver you've used for a trip around town, ask them. After some negotiating, expect to pay between Y350 and Y600, depending on the type of car. Most hotels can make arrangements for you, though they often charge you double their rate—no prizes for guessing whose pocket the difference goes into. As most drivers do not speak English, it's a good idea to have your destination and hotel names written down in Chinese.

Another alternative is American car-rental agency Avis, which includes mandatory chauffeurs as part of all rental packages. A car and driver usually cost Y740 to Y850 ($93 to $110) per day for an economy vehicle. Collision insurance (CDW) is compulsory and included automatically in the rental rate.

If your heart is set on driving, it is possible for foreigners to get a Chinese license, but you need to have a temporary residence permit. Then it takes a week or two and a whole load of paper-pushing.

Major Agencies **Avis** ☎ 800/331-1084 🌐 www.avis.com.

VACATION PACKAGES

Packages *are not* guided excursions. Packages combine airfare, accommodations, and perhaps a rental car or other extras (theater tickets, guided excursions, boat trips, reserved entry to popular museums, transit passes), but they let you do your own thing. During busy periods packages may be your only option, as flights and rooms may be sold out otherwise. Packages will definitely save you time. They can also save you money, particularly in peak seasons, but—and this is a really big "but"—you should price each part of the package separately to be sure. And be aware that prices advertised on Web sites and in newspapers rarely include service charges or taxes, which can up your costs by hundreds of dollars.

TIP→ Some packages and cruises are sold only through travel agents. Don't always assume that you can get the best deal by booking everything yourself.

Each year consumers are stranded or lose their money when packagers—even large ones with excellent reputations—go out of business. How can you protect yourself? First, always pay with a credit card; if you have a problem, your credit-card company may help you resolve it. Second, buy trip insurance that covers default. Third, choose a company that belongs to the United States Tour Operators Association, whose members must set aside funds to cover defaults. Finally, choose a company that also participates in the Tour Operator Program of the American Society of Travel Agents (ASTA), which will act as mediator in any disputes. You can also check on the tour operator's reputation among travelers by posting an inquiry on one of the Fodors.com forums.

A vacation package to Shanghai is unlikely to save you much money over booking things yourself, though it might make things quicker and easier. One of the services the company will provide is arranging your Chinese visa. If you're only staying in Shanghai, it's easy to book your hotel and you really don't need a package for other activities. It's cheaper to book excursions through one of Shanghai's many local tour companies. You can do this before your trip to be sure of a place on the day you want.

Organizations **American Society of Travel Agents** (ASTA) ☎ 703/739-2782 or 800/965-2782 🌐 www.astanet.com. **United States Tour Operators Association** (USTOA) ☎ 212/599-6599 🌐 www.ustoa.com.

TIP→ Local tourism boards can provide information about lesser-known and small-niche operators that sell packages to only a few destinations.

GUIDED TOURS

Guided tours are a good option when you don't want to do it all yourself. You travel along with a group (sometimes large, sometimes small), stay in prebooked hotels, eat with your fellow travelers (the cost of meals is sometimes included in the price of your tour, sometimes not), and follow a schedule. But not all guided tours are an if-it's-Tuesday-this-must-be-Belgium experience. A knowledgeable guide can take you places that you might never discover on your own, and you may be pushed to see more than you would have otherwise. Tours aren't for everyone, but they can be just the thing for trips to places where making travel arrangements is difficult or time-consuming (particularly when you don't speak the language). Whenever you book a guided tour, find out what's included and what isn't. A "land-only" tour includes all your travel (by bus, in most cases) in the destination, but not necessarily your flights to and from or even within it. Also, in most cases prices in tour brochures don't include fees and taxes. And remember that you'll be expected to tip your guide (in cash) at the end of the tour.

Few companies organize package trips only to Shanghai. It's usually part of a bigger China or Asia multidestination package. You get a day or two in Shanghai, with the same sights featured in most tours. If you want to explore the city in any kind of depth, you're better doing it by yourself or getting a private guide.

Shopping stops plague China tours, so inquire before booking as to when, where, and how many to expect. Although you're never obliged to buy anything, they can take up big chunks of your valuable travel time, and the products offered are always ridiculously overpriced. Even on the best tours, you can count on having to sit through at least one or two.

Small groups and excellent guides are what Overseas Adventure Travel takes pride in. Two of their China tours include Shanghai. Adventure Center has a huge variety of China packages, including trekking, cycling, and family tours. China Focus Travel has 10 different China tours—they squeeze in a lot for your money. Ritz Tours is a midrange agency specializing in East Asian tours. R. Crusoe & Sons is an offbeat company that organizes small group or tailor-made private tours. For something more mainstream, try Pacific Delight; for serious luxury, head to Artisans of Leisure.

Recommended Companies **Adventure Center** ☎ 800/228-8747 ⊕ www.adventurecenter.com. **Artisans of Leisure** ☎ 800/214-8144 ⊕ www.artisansofleisure.com. **China Focus Travel** ☎ 800/868-7244 ⊕ www.chinafocustravel.com. **Overseas Adventure Travel** ☎ 800/493-6824 ⊕ www.oattravel.com. **Pacific Delight** ☎ 800/221-7179 ⊕ www.pacificdelighttours.com. **R. Crusoe & Sons** ☎ 800/585-8555 ⊕ www.rcrusoe.com. **Ritz Tours** ☎ 626/289-7777 ⊕ www.ritztours.com.

SPECIAL-INTEREST TOURS

BIKING

Bike China Adventures organizes trips of varying length and difficulty all over China—their 17-day tour includes Shanghai. Tours don't include flights.

■ TIP→ **Most airlines accommodate bikes as luggage, provided they're dismantled and boxed.**

Bike China Adventures ☎ 800/818-1778 ⊕ www.bikechina.com.

CULTURE

Local guides are often "creative" when it comes to history and culture, so having an expert with you can make a big difference. Learning is the focus of Smithsonian Journeys' small group tours, which are led by university professors. China experts also lead National Geographic Expeditions's trips, though all that knowledge doesn't come cheap. Wild China is a local company with some of the most unusual trips around. For example, one of their cultural trips explores China's little-known Jewish history.

National Geographic Expeditions ☎ 888/966-8687 ⊕ www.nationalgeographicexpeditions.com. **Smithsonian Journeys** ☎ 877/338-8687 ⊕ www.smithsonianjourneys.org. **Wild China** ☎ 010/6465-6602 ⊕ www.wildchina.com.

CULINARY

Artisans of Leisure's culinary tour takes in Shanghai and Beijing from the cities' choicest establishments, with prices to match. Intrepid Travel is an Australian company specializing in budget, independent travel. Their China Gourmet Traveller tour includes market visits, cooking demonstrations, and lots of eating at down-to-earth restaurants. Imperial Tours' Culinary Tour combines sightseeing with cooking lectures and demonstrations, and lots of five-star dining. Only Artisans of Leisure's tours include airfare.

Artisans of Leisure ☎ 800/214-8144 ⊕ www.artisansofleisure.com. **Imperial Tours** ☎ 888/888-1970 ⊕ www.imperialtours.net. **Intrepid Travel** ☎ 613/9473-2626 ⊕ www.intrepidtravel.com.

GOLF

China Highlights organizes golf packages that combine Shanghai sightseeing with golfing at the Binhai Golf Club.

China Highlights ☎ 800/268-2918 ⊕ www.chinahighlights.com.

HIKING

The Adventure Center's Yangtse River Explorer combines hiking in the Three Gorges area with time in Shanghai.

Adventure Center ☎ 800/228-8747 ⊕ www.adventurecenter.com.

TRANSPORTATION

Central Shanghai is cut in two by the Huangpu River. To the east is the city's new financial district, glitzy modern Pudong, where the iconic Pearl TV Tower sits. On the west lies Puxi, the old city, home to most of Shanghai's tourist attractions. Pudong and Puxi are linked by three bridges, two tunnels, three subway crossings, and various ferries.

The focus of Puxi is Huangpu District, Shanghai's downtown. It contains the linchpin of Shanghai's tourist scene, the Bund, a good place to get your bearings. Nanjing Lu (Shanghai's anwer to Fifth Avenue) connects the Bund to Renmin (People's) Square. Also in Puxi are traditional Nanshi, the Former (sometimes called Old French Concession) French Concession, ultratrendy Xintiandi, and Xuhui and Jing'an.

A rough grid system governs the streets of central Shanghai. East–west streets take their names from Chinese cities (Beijing Lu or Yan'an Lu, for example); provinces or regions give their names to north–south streets (such as Heinan Lu or Sichuan Lu). As in many U.S. cities, Shanghai's street names change slightly along their length with the addition of a compass point. Thus Beijing Xi Lu and Beijing Dong Lu are Beijing Road East and Beijing Road West, respectively.

For the uninitiated, Shanghai's street-numbering system can be cryptic—numbers can refer to buildings or to lanes intersecting major thoroughfares. Most people navigate by proximity to landmarks and subway stations instead.

Shanghai has two concentric ring roads. The Inner Ring Road roughly contains the downtown area, the French Concession, and Pudong; whereas the Outer Ring Road connects the city's two airports. Several elevated expressways cross through town.

There are various public-transportation options in Shanghai and all are good. Look into the Shanghai Public Transportation Card, known as the **Jiaotong card.** It's a stored-value card that can be used on all forms of public transport: you just swipe it over the ticket-gate sensor to deduct your fare. You can buy a Jiaotong card in subway stations and in some convenience stores, such as Alldays. You'll pay a refundable deposit of Y30 for the card, then add as much money to it as you think you'll use. It works on the subway and the MagLev (the high-speed train to the airport), as well as in buses, ferries, and even in taxis.

■ TIP→ Ask the local tourist board about hotel and local transportation packages that include tickets to major museum exhibits or other special events.

BY AIR

Shanghai is one of China's three major international hubs, along with Beijing and Hong Kong. You can catch a nonstop flight there from Chicago (14 ½ hours), San Francisco (17 hours), Los Angeles (16 hours), Sydney (13 hours), and London (12 hours). Note that China Eastern is the only operator that runs nonstop LA and London flights. Flights from New York generally have a stopover in Beijing, Hong Kong, or a U.S. city, and take between 17 and 25 hours.

Though most airlines say that reconfirming your return flight is unnecessary, some local airlines cancel your seat if you don't reconfirm. Play it safe, and check with your airline carefully.

Airlines & Airports **Airline and Airport Links.com** 🌐 www.airlineandairportlinks.com has links to many of the world's airlines and airports.

Airline-Security Issues **Transportation Security Administration** 🌐 www.tsa.gov has answers for almost every question that might come up.

AIRPORTS

Shanghai has two major airports: most international flights go through ultramodern Pudong International Airport (PVG), 45 km (30 mi) east of the city, wheras domestic routes operate out of the older Hongqiao International Airport (SHA), 15 km (9 mi) west of the city center.

Both Pudong and Hongqiao have a departure tax of Y90 for international flights and Y50 for domestic. You pay before check-in by purchasing a coupon from booths (near the check-in counters at Pudong, or just inside the terminal at Hongqiao); this coupon is collected at the entrance to the main departure hall.

Clearing customs and immigration can take a while, especially at overcrowded Pudong, so make sure you arrive at least two hours before your scheduled flight time. Check-in desks at Pudong are not always clearly signed, so bank on hunting around a little. Likewise, prepare for some exercise between immigration and the gate: this is one big airport, and there are few people movers. Hongqiao may look worn and tattered in comparison, but fewer passengers and smaller distances make both departure and arrival processes smoother and quicker. Indeed, many business travelers prefer to fly to Hongqiao.

At Pudong, both Chinese and Western-style fast-food outlets abound—Starbucks and KFC are two names you'll recognize—but quality is generally poor. Most are open from around 7 AM to 11 PM. Be warned that prices for even a soft drink vary wildly from place to place. Take ample distractions in case of delays: the shopping in both airports is poor, and even airline business-class lounges have limited Internet access and little entertainment.

While wandering either airport, someone may approach you offering to carry your luggage, or even just give you directions. This "helpful" stranger will almost certainly expect payment. Many of the X-ray machines used for large luggage items aren't film-safe, so keep film in your carry-on luggage.

NAVIGATING SHANGHAI

True, Shanghai is a *big* place that's heaving with people. Don't be daunted: once you understand the logic behind its layout and its street names, getting your bearings is fairly straightforward.

- Buy the newest street and subway maps you can—be sure they have Chinese characters *and* Pinyin, so you can compare street names. Mark your hotel on your map clearly, and ask the hotel desk clerk to note the name and address in Chinese for you, too.
- Keep your eye out for central landmarks like Huangpu River, Renmin Square, the Bund, and the Pearl TV Tower.
- Nanshi, the old Chinese city, is full of mazelike lanes that can be confusing. If you get lost, don't be shy—show someone your map and they're sure to help you out.
- Five crucial words of Chinese can help unravel Shanghai's seemingly confusing street names: the compass points *bei* (north), *dong* (east), *nan* (south), *xi* (west), and *zhong* (middle). These distinguish different sections of long streets.
- Shanghai's public transport system is very efficient, and a combination of subway, buses, taxis, and walking can easily get you to all the places you're likely to be visiting.

Airport Information **Hongqiao International Airport** ☎ 021/6268-8918 🌐 www.shanghaiairport.com. **Pudong International Airport** ☎ 021/9608-1388 🌐 www.shanghaiairport.com.

GROUND TRANSPORTATION

Taking a taxi is the most comfortable way into town from Pudong International Airport. Expect to pay around Y150 to Y160 for the hourlong trip to Puxi; getting to the closer Pudong area takes 40 minutes and costs Y120. Note that at rush hour, journey times can easily double.

From Hongqiao, a taxi to Puxi starts at Y60 and takes 30 to 40 minutes; expect an hour for the costlier trip to Pudong hotels. A taxi from one airport to the other takes about an hour and costs Y200 to Y240.

When you arrive, head for the clearly labeled taxi stand just outside each terminal. The (usually long) line moves quickly. Ignore offers from touts trying to coax you away from the official taxi line—they're privateers looking to rip you off. Insist that drivers use their meters, and do not negotiate a fare. If the driver is unwilling to comply, feel free to change taxis.

If you're feeling sci-fi, consider taking the flashy MagLev (magnetic levitation) train, which floats above its tracks at 430 kph (267 mph), whipping you to the Longyang Lu subway station in just eight minutes. Though exciting, the trip isn't very practical. Unless you're staying in eastern Pudong, you need to transfer to the subway to get downtown. This involves walking and suitcase-hauling *and* a ride of at least another half hour. The MagLev runs between 7 AM and 9 PM and costs Y50 one-way, so if there's more than two of you it makes economic sense to take a cab and save the ride for another day.

Many hotels offer free airport transfers to their guests—ask when you book. Otherwise, shuttle buses link Pudong Airport with a number of hotels (routes starting with a letter) and transport hubs (routes starting with a number) in the city center. Timetables vary, but most services run every 10 to 20 minutes between roughly 7 AM and the last flight arrival (usually around midnight). Trips to Puxi take about 1½ hours and cost between Y19 and Y30. From Hongqiao, Bus 925 runs to People's Square, but there's little room for luggage. It costs Y4.

Dazhong Taxi Company ☎ 021/96822. **Jinjiang Taxi** ☎ 021/96961. **MagLev Train** ☎ 021/2890-7777 🌐 www.smtdc.com. **Pudong Airport Shuttle Buses** ☎ 021/6834-6612. **Qiangsheng Taxi** ☎ 021/6258-0000.

To and From Pudon Airport

MODE OF TRANSPORT, DURATION, AND PRICE TO PUXI/PUDONG AREAS		
Taxi	60 min./40 min.	Y160/Y120
MagLev	8 min. (plus 30 min. on subway)/ 8 min.	Y50 (and Y3 for subway)/ Y50
Bus	90 min./60 min.	Y19-30/Y20

FLIGHTS

Air China is China's flagship carrier. It operates nonstop flights from Shanghai to various North American and European cities. Although it once had a slightly sketchy safety record, the situation has improved dramatically, and it is now part of Star Alliance. China Southern is the major carrier for domestic routes, and connects Shanghai to cities all over the country, and is operating more and more international routes, as is China Eastern.

The service on most Chinese airlines is more on par with low-cost American airlines than with big international carriers—be prepared for limited legroom, iffy food, and possibly no personal TV. More importantly, always arrive at least two hours before departure, as chronic overbooking means latecomers just don't get on.

You can make reservations and buy tickets in the United States directly through airline Web sites or with travel agencies. It's worth contacting a Chinese travel agency like China International Travel Service (CITS) (⇨ Visitor Information, *below*) to compare prices, as these can vary substantially.

Airline Contacts **Air Canada** ☎ 021/6279-2999 🌐 www.aircanada.com. **Air China** ☎ 021/5239-7227 or 021/6269-2999 🌐 www.fly-airchina.com. **Asiana** ☎ 021/6219-4000 🌐 www.us.flyasiana.com. **British Airways** ☎ 800/810-8012 🌐 www.ba.com. **China Eastern** ☎ 021/6268-8899 🌐 www.ce-air.com. **China Southern Airlines** ☎ 021/6226-2299 🌐 www.cs-air.com/en. **Japan Airlines** ☎ 021/6288-3000 🌐 www.jal.com. **Northwest Airlines** ☎ 800/225-2525, 021/

6884-6884 in Shanghai 🌐 www.nwa.com. **Shanghai Airlines** ☎ 021/6255-8888 🌐 www.shanghai-air.com. **Singapore Airlines** ☎ 021/6289-1000 🌐 www.singaporeair.com. **Thai Airways** ☎ 021/5298-5555 🌐 www.thaiair.com. **United Airlines** ☎ 800/864-8331 for U.S. reservations, 800/538-2929 for international reservations, 021/3311-4567 in Shanghai 🌐 www.united.com. **Virgin Atlantic Airways** ☎ 021/5353-4600 🌐 www.virgin-atlantic.com.

BY BIKE

Cycling is still the primary form of transportation for many Shanghai residents, despite the government's best efforts to discourage it by banning bikes on main roads. Shanghai's frenzied traffic is not for the faint of heart, though fortunately most secondary streets have wide, well-defined bike lanes. The pancake-flat city landscape means that gears just aren't necessary—take your cue from locals and roll along at a leisurely pace. For relaxed riding, head to the beautiful lanes of the Old French Concession. Pudong roads have far less traffic but also less scenery. If a flat tire or sudden brake failure strikes, seek out the nearest street-side mechanic (they're everywhere), easily identified by their bike parts and pumps.

Few hotels rent bikes (hostels are usually the exception), but you can inquire at bike shops or even corner stores, where the going rate is around Y30 a day, plus a refundable deposit, which is often high enough to cover the cost of the bike itself. Check the seat and wheels carefully prior to accepting the rental, or else you'll be stopping to fix flats all day.

Bicycle lights are nonexistent, so cycle with caution at night. Most rental bikes come with a lock or two, but they're usually pretty low quality. Instead, leave your wheels at an attended bike park—peace of mind costs a mere Y0.50. Helmets are just about unheard of in Shanghai, though upmarket rental companies like Bodhi Bikes rent them. They charge Y150 or more for their bikes, but they're mountain bikes in great condition. They also organize mountain-biking tours.

If you're planning a lot of cycling, note that for about Y200 you can buy your own basic bike; expect to pay three or four times that for a mountain bike with all the bells and whistles. Supermarkets like Carrefour or the sports shop Decathlon are good places to buy them.

Bike China Adventures has a 17-day bike trip that includes Shanghai, along with other destinations in China.

Bike Rentals **Bohdi Bikes** ☎ 021/5266-9013 🌐 www.bohdi.com.cn.

Bike Tours **Bike China Adventures** ☎ 800/818-1778 🌐 www.bikechina.com.

Shops With Bikes **Carrefour** ✉ 2671 Gaoqing Lu Pudong ☎ 021/5065-7391 🌐 www.carrefour.com.cn. **Decathlon** ✉ 393 Yinxiao Lu Pudong ☎ 021/5045-2479 🌐 www.decathlon.com.cn.

BY FERRY

WITHIN SHANGHAI

More than 20 ferry lines cross the Huangpu River between Pudong and Puxi. The most convenient ferry for tourists runs daily between the Bund in Puxi and Pudong's terminal just south of the Riverside Promenade. There are no seats, merely an empty lower deck that welcomes the masses with their bikes and scooters. The per-person fare is Y2 each way. The ferries leave the dock every 10 minutes, 24 hours a day.

TO & FROM SHANGHAI

Boats leave from Shanghai's Wusong Passenger Terminal for destinations along the Yangzi River such as Wuhan and Chongqing; coastal cities such as Nantong, Dalian, and Ningbo; and the outlying island of Putuoshan. First-class cabins have comfortable beds and their own washbasin.

The Shanghai Ferry Company and the China-Japan International Ferry Company both operate services to Osaka,

Japan, from the International Passenger Terminal at Waihongqiao. Boats leave at midday on Tuesday and Saturday, respectively; the trip takes around two days. There are restaurants, a game room, and even karaoke on board.

You can purchase tickets for both international and domestic services (in Chinese) at each terminal, or through China International Travel Service (CITS) for a small surcharge.

China-Japan International Ferry Company ✉ 908 Dongdaming Lu, Hongkou District ☎ 021/6595-7988. **China International Travel Service** (CITS) ☎ 021/6289-8899 🌐 www.cits.com.cn. **Pudong-Puxi ferry** ✉ Puxi dock, the Bund at Jinling Lu, Huangpu District ✉ Pudong dock, 1 Dongchang Lu, south of Binjiang Da Dao, Pudong. **Shanghai Ferry Company** ☎ 021/6537-5111 🌐 www.shanghai-ferry.co.jp.

BY BUS

TO SHANGHAI

China has some fabulous luxury long-distance buses with air-conditioning and movies. Many intercity services depart more regularly than trains. However, buying tickets for them can be complicated if you don't speak Chinese—you may end up on one of the cramped old-style affairs, much like an old-fashioned school bus. Drivers don't usually speak English, either. Taking a train or an internal flight is often much easier.

> **LUCKY NUMBER**
>
> Sichuan Airlines bought the number +86-28-8888-8888 for 2.33 million yuan ($280,723) during an auction of more than 100 telephone numbers in 2003, making it the most expensive telephone number in the world. The number eight, (*ba* in Chinese) is considered lucky in China, as it is similar to the Cantonese word for "getting rich."

Most of Shanghai's long-distance services leave from the Shanghai Long Distance bus station, across the square from the Shanghai Railway Station in Zhabei. You buy tickets in the massive circular ticket lobby; allow time for the walk to the departure gate.

Bus Information **Shanghai Long Distance Bus Station** ✉ North Square, Shanghai Railway Station, 1662 Zhongxing Lu, Zhabei District ☎ 021/6605-0000.

WITHIN SHANGHAI

Shanghai claims to have more bus lines than any other city on earth—around 1,000—though so much choice probably hinders rather than helps. In fact, unless you know Shanghai well, public buses aren't the best choice for getting around. Although there are more and more air-conditioned services, most buses are hot and crowded in summer and cold and crowded in winter. Just getting on and off can be, quite literally, a fight. Pickpocketing is rife so watch your belongings very carefully. Fares on regular services cost Y1; air-conditioned routes cost Y2; longer routes can cost up to Y4. To buy a ticket you drop the right change into the box next to the driver as you get on, or swipe your Jiatong card (*see* Transportation, *above*). If you do decide to take city buses, Micah Sittig's encyclopedic Web site has English translations of all of Shanghai's routes.

There are some exceptions to the no-bus rule. Bus route 911 runs down Huaihai Lu through the Old French Concession, with great views over the compound walls of the beautiful old Shanghai buildings that line the thoroughfare. Route 936 runs between Pudong and Puxi, passing the Shanghai Zoo, and number 20 passes by the Bund, Jing'an Temple, Nanjing Road, and Renmin Square.

Local Bus Information **Micah Sittig's Shanghai Bus Route Translations** 🌐 http://msittig.wubi.org/bus/talk/. **Passenger Hotline** Chinese only ☎ 021/1608-8160.

BY CAR

Highways connect Shanghai to neighboring cities such as Suzhou and Nanjing in the west, and Hangzhou in the south. However, due to government restrictions, it's virtually impossible for nonresidents of China to drive. You can, however, hire a car and driver through your hotel's transportation service or through Hertz or Avis, both of which have several locations throughout the city.

Car travel in China, even when you're in the passenger seat, can be frightening. Cars speed to pass one another on one-lane roads, constantly blaring their horns. Taxis and pedicabs pass within inches of each other at intersections. Lanes and traffic rules seem ambiguous to those not accustomed to the Chinese style of driving.

Taxi driver–identification numbers can be used to report bad behavior or bad driving, and thus tend to inspire more care. Many taxi drivers are also held liable for the condition of their vehicles, so they are less likely to take dangerous risks.

BY SUBWAY

Shanghai's quick and efficient subway system—called the Shanghai Metro—is an excellent way to get around town, and the network is growing exponentially.

Line 1 runs north–south, crossing the Former French Concession, with a stop at the Shanghai Railway Station. It intersects with Line 2 at People's Square, a labyrinth of a station with 2 levels, 20 exits, and *lots* of people. Line 2, which will eventually link Hongqiao International Airport with Pudong International Airport, is an east–west line that runs under Nanjing Lu along part of its length, and crosses to Pudong close to the Bund. You can transfer from it to the MagLev at Longyang Station in Pudong. Line 3 (formerly known as the Pearl Line) starts in north Shanghai and loops around the west of the city center; useful stops include Shanghai South Railway Station. Line 4 is a circle line that goes around Puxi and through Pudong, crossing the Huangpu River at two places—at this writing, its southwest segment was yet to open. Line 5 is a commuter spur line connecting southwest Shanghai to Line 1.

WORD OF MOUTH

"We took many taxis in China and found them efficient, cheap and honest–one spent 10 minutes hunting us down after my daughter left her bag on the backseat and wouldn't accept the money I offered him in thanks. Apart from one extended sightseeing drive we never found any reason to agree a price beforehand. No drivers we found spoke any English, but you're OK as long as you have your destination written (unambiguously) in Chinese, or get the hotel staff to direct the driver." –Neil Oz

Subway stations are marked by signs with a jagged red "M" for Metro. Signs are not always obvious, so be prepared to hunt around for entrances or ask directions.

Stations are usually sparklingly clean and safe, as are trains. Navigating the subway is very straightforward: station names are clearly displayed in Chinese and Pinyin. There are maps in each station, although not all exit signs list their corresponding streets. Once on board, each stop is clearly announced in Chinese and English. Trains get very crowded at rush hour, when pickpocketing can be a problem.

Fares depend on how far you travel: most trips within the city center cost Y3 to Y5, with the maximum fare at Y8. Ticket machines have instructions in English; press the button for the fare you want then insert your coins. Alternatively, go to the ticket booth where sellers sometimes speak some English. Keep your ticket handy; you'll need to insert it into a second turnstile as you exit at your destination. If you're going to do more than one or two trips on the subway (or on any other form of transportation), get yourself a rechargeable Jiaotong card. It saves you time waiting on line for tickets.

Trains run regularly, with three to six minutes between trains on average. Generally speaking, you can change lines without having to buy a new ticket; changes marked TRANSFER are the exception. The best online guide to the Shanghai Metro is at the *Shanghai Daily* "Live in Shanghai" site.

Live in Shanghai 🌐 http://shanghaidaily.com/live. **Shanghai Metro Passenger Information** ☎ 021/6318-9000 🌐 www.shmetro.com.

BY TAXI

Taxis are plentiful, easy to spot, and by far the most comfortable way to get around Shanghai, though increasing traffic means they're not always the fastest. Almost all are Volkswagen Santanas or Passats, and they come in a rainbow of colors, which reflect the company they work for. These include teal (Dazhong; most locals' first choice), green (Bashi), yellow (Qiangsheng), red (Premium cab), dark blue (Blue Union), and white (Jinjiang). All are metered.

There's a base fee of Y11 for the first 3 km (2 mi), then Y2 per km for the first 10 km (6 mi), then Y3 per kilometer thereafter. After 10 PM the base fee goes up to Y14, and there's a 20% surcharge per kilometer. You also pay for waiting time in traffic. Tipping is unheard of—indeed most taxi drivers return even the smallest change. In compact central Shanghai, outrageous traffic drags out otherwise short cab rides.

WORD OF MOUTH

"I find the taxis to be among the best in the world . . . very honest, cheap, efficient and know the cities with an amazing amount of detail. Meters are always used in legitimate taxis and you will 99% of the time get a much better deal than if you try to pre-negotiate a fix priced 'deal.'"
–walkinaround

Drivers usually know the terrain well, but as most don't speak English, having your destination written in Chinese is a good idea. (Keep a card with the name of your hotel on it handy for the return trip.) Hotel doormen can also help you tell the driver where you're going. It's a good idea to study a map and have some idea where you are, as some drivers will take you for a ride—a much longer one—if they think they can get away with it.

Taxi Companies **Centralized Taxi Reservations** Chinese only ☎ 021/96965. **Dazhong Taxi Company** ☎ 021/96222. **Jinjiang Taxi** Chinese only ☎ 021/96961. **Qiangsheng Taxi** Chinese only ☎ 021/6258-0000. **Shanghai Taxi Authority** ☎ 021/6323-2150.

BY TRAIN

China's enormous rail network is one of the world's busiest. Trains are usually safe and run strictly to schedule. Buying tickets can be complicated, but trips are generally hassle-free.

Shanghai is connected to many destinations in China by direct train. Trains to southern China, including Hong Kong, will eventually leave from the gleaming Shanghai South Railway Station in Xuihui. Billed as the world's biggest circular station, it looks more like an airport inside than a train station. It opened in mid-2006 with limited services, but more routes will eventually transfer here. The huge ticketing hall is on the ground floor; the upstairs waiting room can accommodate over 16,000 people. Trains to northern and western China leave from the older Shanghai Railway Station. Both stations have easy transfers to the subway. The best train to catch to Beijing is the overnight express that leaves around 6 PM and arrives in Beijing the next morning. The express train for Hong Kong departs around noon and arrives at the Kowloon station 24 hours later.

The train system has four classes, but instead of first class and second class, in China you talk about hard and soft. Hard seats (*yingzuo*) are often rigid benchlike seats guaranteed to numb the buttocks within seconds; soft seats (*ruanzuo*) are more like the seats in long-distance American trains. For overnight journeys, the cheapest option is the hard sleeper (*yingwo*), open bays of six bunks, in two tiers of three. They're cramped, but not uncomfortable; however, you take your own bedding and share the toilet with everyone in the car. Soft sleepers (*ruanwo*) are more comfortable: their closed compartments have four beds and include bedding. Trains to Shanghai, Hong Kong, and Xian have a deluxe class, with only two berths per compartment and private bathrooms. The nonstop Z-series trains are even more luxurious. Train types are identifiable by the letter preceding the route number: Z is for nonstop, T is for a normal express.

Train fares are more expensive for foreigners than for the Chinese, and vary drastically depending on where you buy them. You can buy most tickets 10 days in advance; 2 to 3 days ahead is usually enough time, except during the three national holidays—Chinese New Year (two days in mid-January to February), Labor Day (May 1), and National Day (October 1). If you can, avoid traveling then: tickets are sold out weeks in advance.

The cheapest rates are at the train station itself, where they only accept cash. Most travel agents, including China International Travel Service (CITS), can book you tickets for a small surcharge (Y20 to Y50), and save you the hassle of going to the station. You can also buy tickets through online retailers like China Train Ticket. They deliver the tickets to your hotel but you often end up paying much more than the station rate.

Overpriced dining cars serve meals that are often inedible, so you'd do better to make use of the massive thermoses of boiled water in each compartment and take along your own noodles or instant soup, like locals do. Trains are always crowded, but you are guaranteed your designated seat, though not always the overhead luggage rack. Note that theft on trains is increasing; on overnight trains, sleep with your valuables or else keep them on the inside of the bunk.

TAXI TRAVEL

- Hailing a cab on the street is usually the best (and safest) way to go. However, taxis can't stop within 30 meters (100 feet) of an intersection.
- *Never* accept offers of rides from cabbies touting their services outside tourist sights: you're walking into a rip-off. Taxis arranged by your hotel doorman may also have some hidden surcharges. When in doubt, walk out and hail one.
- Unless you're looking to book a cab all day, the metered rate is always better than negotiating a fixed fare.
- Avoid taxis during rush hour (7:30 AM–9:30 AM and 4 PM–7 PM); walk or take the subway instead.
- Be meter-conscious: check that the cabbie starts the meter *after* you get in, that it's not in an unusual place (near the floor, for example) and that there's nothing obstructing your view of it.

You can find out just about everything about Chinese train travel at Seat 61's fabulous Web site. China Highlights has a searchable online timetable for major train routes. The tour operator Travel China Guide has an English-language Web site that can help you figure out train schedules and fares.

Note that the operators at train station information numbers don't usually speak English.

China Highlights 🌐 www.chinahighlights.com/china-trains/index.htm. **Seat 61** 🌐 www.seat61.com/China.htm. **Shanghai Railway Station** ✉ 303 Moling Lu, Zhabei District ☎ 021/6317–9090. **Shanghai South Railway Station** ✉ Between Liuzhou Lu and Humin Lu, Xuhui District ☎ 021/6317–6060. **Travel China Guide** 🌐 www.travelchinaguide.com/china-trains/index.htm.

ON THE GROUND

BUSINESS SERVICES & FACILITIES

Your hotel (or another nearby mid- to top-end one) is the best place to start looking for business services, including translation. Most are very up-to-speed on businesspeople's needs and can put you in touch with other companies if necessary. Regus and the Executive Centre are international business-services companies with several office locations in Shanghai. They provide secretarial services, meeting and conference facilities, and office rentals. Talking China is a reputable translation and interpretation service.

The Executive Centre ☎ 021/5252-4618 🌐 www.executivecentre.com. **Regus** ☎ 800/819-0091 🌐 www.regus.cn. **Talking China** ☎ 021/6279-3688 🌐 www.talkingchina.com.

COMMUNICATIONS

INTERNET

Shanghai is a very Internet-friendly place for those bearing laptops. Most mid- to high-end hotels have in-room Internet access; if the hotel doesn't have a server but you have a room phone you can usually access a government-provided ISP, which only charges you for the phone call. Wi-Fi is growing exponentially—many hotels and even cafés provide it free.

If you're traveling technology-light, your hotel usually has a computer with Internet access that you can use. Internet cafés are also ubiquitous, but it's an unstable business and new ones open and close all the time. Known as *wang ba* in Chinese, they're not usually signposted in English, so ask your hotel to recommend one nearby. Prices (and cleanliness) vary considerably, but generally range from Y3 to Y10 per hour.

Remember that there is strict government control of the Internet in China. There's usually no problem with Web-based mail, but you may be unable to access news and even blogging sites.

Cybercafes 🌐 www.cybercafes.com lists over 4,000 Internet cafés worldwide.

PHONES

The good news is that you can now make a direct-dial call from virtually any point on earth. The bad news? You can't always do so cheaply. Calling from a hotel is almost always the most expensive option; hotels usually add huge surcharges to all calls, particularly international ones. In some countries you can phone from call centers or even the post office. Calling cards usually keep costs to a minimum, but only if you purchase them locally. And then there are cell phones (⇨ *below*), which are sometimes more prevalent—particularly in the developing world—than landlines; as expensive as cell-phone calls can be, they are still usually a much cheaper option than calling from your hotel.

The country code for China is 86; the city code for Shanghai is 21, and 10 for Beijing. To call Shanghai from the United States or Canada, dial the international-access code (011), followed by the country code (86), the city code (21), and the eight-digit phone number.

Numbers beginning with 800 within China are toll-free. Note that a call from China to a toll-free number in the United States or Hong Kong is a full-tariff international call.

CALLING WITHIN CHINA

The Chinese phone system is cheap and efficient. You can make local and long-distance calls from your hotel or any public phone on the street. Shanghai's public phones are usually bright red cabins. Some accept coins, but it's easier to buy an IC (integreated circuit) calling card, available at convenience stores and newsstands (⇨ Calling Cards, *below*). Local calls are generally free from landlines, though your hotel might charge a nominal rate. Long-distance rates in China are very low. For once, calling from your hotel room is a viable option, as hotels can only add a 15% service charge.

Shanghai's city code is 021, and Shanghai phone numbers have eight digits—you only need to dial these when calling within the city. In general, city codes appear written with a 0 in front of them; if not, you need to add this when calling another city within China.

For directory assistance, dial 114. If you want information for other cities, dial the city code followed by 114 (note that this is considered a long-distance call). For example, if you're in Shanghai and need directory assistance for a Beijing number, dial 020–114. The operators do not speak English, so if you don't speak Chinese you're best off asking your hotel for help.

To make long-distance calls from a public phone you need an IC card (⇨ Calling Cards, *below*). To place a long-distance call, dial 0, the city code, and the eight-digit phone number.

Local directory assistance ☎ 114. **Time** ☎ 117. **Weather** ☎ 121.

CALLING OUTSIDE CHINA

To make an international call from within China, dial 00 (the international access code within China) and then the country code, area or city code, and phone number. The country code for the United States is 1.

IDD (international direct dialing) service is available at all hotels, post offices, major shopping centers, and airports. By international standards prices aren't unreasonable, but it's vastly cheaper to use a long-distance calling card, known as an IP (Internet protocol) card (*See* Calling Cards, *below*). These cards' rates also beat AT&T, MCI, and Sprint hands-down. If you do need to use these services, dial 108 (the local operator) and the local access codes from China: 11 for AT&T, 12 for MCI, and 13 for Sprint. Dialing instructions in English will follow.

Access Codes **AT&T Direct** ☎ 800/874-4000,108-11 from China. **MCI WorldPhone** ☎ 800/444-4444, 108-12 from China. **Sprint International Access** ☎ 800/793-1153, 108-13 from China.

CALLING CARDS

Calling cards are a key part of the Chinese phone system. There are two kinds: the IC card (integrated circuit; *àicei ka*), for local and domestic long-distance calls on pay phones; and the IP card (Internet protocol; *aipi ka*) for international calls from any phone. You can buy both at post offices, convenience stores, and from street vendors.

IC cards come in denominations of Y20, Y50, and Y100, and can be used in any pay phone with a card slot—most Shanghai pay phones have them. Local calls using them cost around Y0.30 a minute, and less on weekends and after 6 PM.

To use IP cards, you first dial a local access number. This is often free from hotels, while at public phones you need an IC card to do so. You then enter a card number and PIN, and finally the phone number, complete with international dial codes. When calling from a pay phone, both cards' minutes are deducted at the same time, one for local access (IC card) and one for the long-distance call you placed (IP card). There are countless different card brands; China Unicom is one that's usually reliable. IP cards come with face values of Y20, Y30, Y50, and Y100. However, the going rate for them is up to half that, so bargain vendors down. Y50 gets you around 20 minutes' talking time.

CELL PHONES

If you have a multiband phone (some countries use different frequencies than what's used in the United States) and your service provider uses the world-standard GSM network (as do T-Mobile, Cingular, and Verizon), you can probably use your phone abroad. Roaming fees can be steep,

LOCAL DOS & TABOOS

CUSTOMS OF THE COUNTRY

"Face" is the all-important issue in China. A cross between pride and social status, it's all about appearances yet its cultural roots run deep. Shame someone publicly, and you may lose their friendship for life; make them look good, and you'll go far. What makes people lose and gain face is complicated, but respect is the key issue. Don't lose your cool if things go wrong, especially when reserving tickets and hotel rooms. Instead, be stern but friendly—raising your voice and threatening will get you nowhere. Keep facial expressions and hand gestures to a minimum; when pointing, use your whole hand, not a finger.

Locals often seem less than forthcoming when giving information. Be patient, they're not trying to mislead you, but rather keep you happy by telling you what they think you want to hear. Keep asking questions until you find out what you want.

Shanghai is a very cosmopolitan city by Chinese standards, and its residents are used to seeing foreigners. However, you may still be stared at, especially if you're not white. Get used to the cry of *laowai* (a not-very-complimentary word for "foreigner") everywhere you go, too. Simply smile back or treat it all humorously.

For guidelines on dining etiquette, *see* Eating Out, *below*.

GREETINGS

Chinese people aren't very touchy-feely with one another, even less so with strangers. Save bear-hugs and cheek-kissing for your next European trip, and stick to handshakes and low-key greetings when you are first meeting local people. Eye contact is often avoided the first time you meet someone. Always use a person's title and surname until they invite you to do otherwise.

SIGHTSEEING

By and large, the Chinese are a rule-abiding bunch. Follow their lead and avoid doing anything street signs advise against. Although you won't be banned from entering any sightseeing spots on grounds of dress, you'd do well to avoid overly skimpy or casual clothes.

Shanghai is a crowded city; pushing, nudging, and line-jumping are commonplace. It may be hard to accept, but it's not considered rude, so avoid reacting (even verbally) if you're accidentally shoved.

OUT ON THE TOWN

It's a great honor to be invited to someone's house, so explain at length if you can't go. Arrive punctually with a small gift for the hosts; remove your shoes outside if you see other guests doing so. Eating lots is the biggest compliment you can pay the food (and the cook).

Tea, served free in all Chinese restaurants, is a common drink at mealtimes, though many locals only accompany their food with soup. It's quite normal to order other drinks, though, especially beer.

Smoking is one of China's greatest vices. No-smoking sections in restaurants are nonexistent, and people light up anywhere they think they can get away with it—including on public transport, at times.

Holding hands in public is OK, but keep passionate embraces to the hotel room.

DOING BUSINESS

Time is of the essence when doing business in Shanghai. Make appointments well in advance and be extremely punctual, as this shows respect. Chinese people have a keen sense of hierarchy in the office: if you're visiting in a group, the senior member should lead proceedings.

Suits are still the norm in China, regardless of the outside temperature. Women should avoid plunging necklines, heavy makeup, overly short skirts, or high heels. Pants are completely acceptable. Women can expect to be treated as equals by local businessmen.

Face is ever-important. Never say anything that will make people look bad, especially in front of superiors. Avoid being pushy or overly buddylike when negotiating: address people as Mr. or Ms. until they invite you to do otherwise, respect silences in conversation and don't hurry things or interrupt. When entertaining, local businesspeople may insist on paying: after a slight protest, accept, as this lets them gain face.

Business cards are a big deal: not having one is like not having a personality. If possible, have yours printed in English on one side and Chinese on the other (your hotel can usually arrange this in a matter of hours). Proffer your card with both hands and receive the other person's in the same way, then read it carefully and make an admiring comment about the person's job title or the card design.

Many gifts, like clocks and cutting implements, are considered unlucky in China. Food—especially presented in a showy basket—is always a good gift choice, as are imported spirits. Avoid giving four of anything, as the number is associated with death. Offer gifts with both hands, and don't expect people to open them in your presence.

LANGUAGE

One of the best ways to avoid being an "ugly" American is to learn a little of the local language. You need not strive for fluency; even just mastering a few basic words and terms is bound to make chatting with the locals more rewarding. Everyone in Shanghai speaks Putonghua (*pǔtōnghuà*, the "common language") as the national language of China is known. It's written using ideograms, or characters. In 1949 the government also introduced a phonetic writing system that uses the Roman alphabet. Known as Pinyin, it's widely used to label public buildings and station names, so even if you don't speak or read Chinese, you can easily compare Pinyin names with a map.

Many Shanghai residents also speak the local Chinese dialect, Shanghainese. It uses the same characters as Putonghua for writing, but the pronunciation is so different as to be unintelligible to a Putonghua speaker. The city government actively discourages the use of Shanghainese in front of visitors.

Chinese grammar is simple, but a complex tonal system of pronunciation means it usually takes a long time for foreigners to learn Chinese. Making yourself understood can be tricky, however, the Chinese will appreciate your making the effort to speak a few phrases understood almost everywhere. Try "Hello"—"*Ní hǎo*" (nee **how**); "Thank you"—"*Xiè xiè*" (shee-**yeh,** shee-**yeh**); and "Good-bye"—"*Zai jian*" (dzai **djan**). When pronouncing words written in Pinyin, remember that "q" and "x" are pronounced like "ch" and "sh," respectively; "zh" is pronounced like the "j" in "just"; "c" is pronounced like "ts."

Not many Shanghainese speak English, though travel agents and the staff in most hotels and upscale restaurants are usually exceptions. If you're lost and need help, look first to someone under 30, who may have studied some English in school. In shops, calculators and hand gestures do most of the talking.

however: 99¢ a minute is considered reasonable. And overseas you normally pay the toll charges for incoming calls. It's almost always cheaper to send a text message than to make a call, since text messages have a very low set fee (often less than 5¢).

If you just want to make local calls, consider buying a new SIM card (note that your provider may have to unlock your phone for you to use a different SIM card) and a prepaid service plan in the destination. You'll then have a local number and can make local calls at local rates. If your trip is extensive, you could also simply buy a new cell phone in your destination, as the initial cost will be offset over time.

TIP→ If you travel internationally frequently, save one of your old cell phones or buy a cheap one on the Internet; ask your cell-phone company to unlock it for you, and take it with you as a travel phone, buying a new SIM card with pay-as-you-go service in each destination.

If you have a tri-band GSM or a CDMA phone, pick up a local SIM card (*sim ka*) from any branch of China Mobile or China Unicom, such as the ones in the arrivals hall at Pudong Airport. You'll be presented with a list of possible phone numbers, with varying prices—an "unlucky" phone number (one with lots of 4s) could be as cheap as Y50, whereas an auspicious one (full of 8s) could fetch Y300 or more. You then buy prepaid cards to charge minutes onto your SIM—do this straight away as you need credit to receive calls. Local calls to landlines cost Y0.25 a minute, and to cell phones Y0.60. International calls from cell phones are very expensive. Remember to bring an adapter for your phone charger. You can also buy cheap handsets from China Mobile. If you're planning to stay even a couple of days this is probably cheaper than renting a phone.

China Mobile Phones and PandaPhone rent cell phones, which they can deliver to your hotel or the airport. Renting a basic Nokia handset costs US$10 for the first two days, then US$1 a day thereafter. You then pay the same local or international call rates as any other cell-phone user.

Cellular Abroad ☎ 800/287-5072 🌐 www.cellularabroad.com rents and sells GSM phones and sells SIM cards that work in many countries. **China Mobile Phones** ☎ 021/5109-7153 🌐 www.china-mobile-phones.com. **China Mobile** ☎ 1860 English language assistance 🌐 www.chinamobile.com is China's main mobile-service provider. **China Unicom** ☎ English-language assistance 1001 is China's second-largest main cell-phone company. **Mobal** ☎ 888/888-9162 🌐 www.mobalrental.com rents mobiles and sells GSM phones (starting at $49) that will operate in 140 countries. Per-call rates vary throughout the world. **PandaPhone** ☎ 800/820-0293 🌐 www.pandaphone.com. **Planet Fone** ☎ 888/988-4777 🌐 www.planetfone.com rents cell phones, but the per-minute rates can be as much as $4.

CUSTOMS & DUTIES

You're always allowed to bring goods of a certain value back home without having to pay any duty or import tax. But there's a limit on the amount of tobacco and liquor you can bring back duty-free, and some countries have separate limits for perfumes; for exact figures, check with your customs department. The values of so-called "duty-free" goods are included in these amounts. When you shop abroad, save all your receipts, as customs inspectors may ask to see them as well as the items you purchased. If the total value of your goods is more than the duty-free limit, you'll have to pay a tax (most often a flat percentage) on the value of everything beyond that limit.

Except for the usual prohibitions against narcotics, explosives, plant and animal material, firearms, and ammunition you can take anything into China that you plan to take away with you. Cameras, video recorders, GPS equipment, laptops, and the like should pose no problems.

However, China is very sensitive about printed matter deemed seditious, such as religious, pornographic, and political items, especially articles, books, and pictures on Tibet. All the same, small amounts of English-language reading materials aren't generally a problem. Customs officials are for the most part easygoing, and visitors are rarely searched. It's not necessary to fill in customs-declaration forms, but if you carry in a large amount of cash, say several thousand dollars, you should declare it upon arrival.

You're not allowed to remove any antiquities dating from before 1795. Antiques from between 1795 and 1949 must have an official red seal attached—quality antique shops know this and arrange it.

Information in Shanghai U.S. Information

U.S. Customs and Border Protection
🌐 www.cbp.gov.

DAY TOURS & GUIDES

You can't turn a corner in Shanghai these days without tripping over tour companies or a guide desperate for your patronage. *Never* accept unsolicited offers of tours—these are common around popular sights, but lead to scams most of the time.

Although it's true that sightseeing tours often pack a lot in, think carefully before signing up for one, because most Shanghai tours are vastly more expensive than visiting the same sights alone, even if you hire your own car and driver. Well, you're paying for the guide, you say. True, but years of censorship and a limited education system means that guides often aren't as clued in on places as, say, your guidebook (though they tell charming stories packed with interesting "facts"). Many companies see you as a handy cash cow to be milked all day long—they make substantial cuts at the inevitable shopping stop-offs (mostly rip-offs), restaurant visits, and through tips, normally not a part of Chinese culture.

Independent sightseeing in Shanghai may seem a daunting prospect, but with a little research it's actually fairly straightforward. Downtown areas like the Bund, the Old French Concession, and Nanshi are easy to reach and you can see them at your own pace, and you can make out-of-town trips by hiring a car and driver, or taking an air-conditioned bus. If you do decide to go on an organized tour, shop around. The forums on Fodors.com are a great place to see what companies fellow travelers have used recently, how much they paid, and what they thought of them.

The state-run agencies, China Travel Service (CTS) and China International Travel Service (CITS), are usually reliable, though their prices aren't always the cheapest around. At CITS you can arrange private or group tours. China Highlights has a range of Shanghai group-tour packages, some of which include hotels. The shorter tours are reasonably priced (for a tour, that is).

Recommended Tours/Guides **China Highlights** China: ☎ 773/283-1999 ✉ U.S.: ☎ 800/268-2918 🌐 www.chinahighlights.com. **China International Travel Service** Shanghai: ☎ 021/6289-8899 or 6289-4510 🌐 www.scits.com ✉ U.S.: ☎ 626/568-8993 🌐 www.citsusa.com.

China Travel Service Shanghai: ☎ 021/6247-8888 ✉ U.S.: ☎ 800/899-8618 🌐 www.chinatravelservice.com.

EATING OUT

In China, meals are really communal events, so food in a Chinese home or restaurant is always shared—you usually have a small bowl or plate into which you transfer food from the center platters. Although cutlery is available in many restaurants, chopsticks are the utensil of choice.

The standard eating procedure is to hold the bowl close to your mouth and shovel in the contents without any qualms. Noisily slurping up soup and noodles is also the norm, as is belching when you're done. Covering the tablecloth in crumbs, drips, and even spat-out bones is a sign you've enjoyed your meal. It's considered bad manners to point with or play with your chopsticks, or to place them on top of your rice bowl when you're finished eating (place the chopsticks horizontally on the table or plate). Avoid, too, leaving your chopsticks standing up in a bowl of rice—they look like the two incense sticks burned at funerals.

If you're invited to a formal Chinese meal, be prepared for great ceremony, endless toasts and speeches, and a grand variety of elaborate dishes. Your host will be seated at the "head" of the round table, which is the seat that faces the door. Wait to be instructed where to sit. Don't start eating until the host takes the first bite, and then simply help yourself as the food comes around, but don't take the last piece on a platter. Always let the food touch your plate before bringing it up to your mouth; eating directly from the serving dish is bad form.

Shanghai dishes tend to be sweeter and oilier than other regional Chinese food. Shanghai's trademark dishes include Beggar's Chicken (a whole chicken baked in clay or an inedible dough, which is then cracked open), drunken chicken (braised in rice wine), stinky tofu (fermented bean curd—the name says it all), and mouth-watering pork dumplings known as *xiaolongbao*.

MEALS & MEALTIMES

Food is a central part of Chinese culture, and so eating should be a major activity on any trip to Shanghai. Breakfast is not a big deal in China—congee, or rice porridge (*zhou*) is the standard dish. Early-morning food stalls also sell glutinous rice balls (*ci fan tuan*) and savory donuts (*youtiao*). Most mid- and upper-end hotels do big buffet spreads, while Shanghai's blooming café chains provide lattes and croissants all over town.

Snacks are a food group in themselves. There's no shortage of small shops selling grilled meat or chicken, bowls of noodle soup, and the ubiquitous *xiaolongbao* (steamed dumplings). Many visitors seem loath to eat from stalls—you'd be missing out on some of the best nibbles around, though. Pick a place where lots of locals are eating to be on the safe side.

The food in hotel restaurants is usually acceptable, but vastly overpriced. Restaurants frequented by locals always serve tastier fare at better prices. Don't shy from trying establishments without an English menu—a good phrasebook and lots of pointing can usually get you what you want.

Lunch and dinner dishes are more or less interchangeable. Meat (especially pork) or poultry tends to form the base of most Shanghai dishes. Seafood is also very popular. Vegetables—especially warming winter cabbage and onions—and tofu play a big role in meals. As in all Chinese food, dairy products are scarce. Chinese meals usually involve a variety of dishes, which are always ordered communally in restaurants. Eat alone or order your own dishes and you're seriously limiting your food experience.

If you're craving Western food (or sushi or a curry), rest assured that Shanghai has plenty of world-class international restaurants, many complete with celebrity chefs. American fast-food chains also abound. Most higher-end Chinese restaurants have a Western menu, but you're usually safer sticking to the Chinese food.

Meals in China are served early: breakfast until 9 AM, lunch between 11 and 2, and dinner from 5 to 9. Restaurants and bars catering to foreigners may stay open longer

WORD OF MOUTH

"If you're familiar with eating Chinese-style (shared dishes, chopsticks) you can seek out local restaurants with English-translation menus or illustrations of dishes—a good meal for two will cost no more than Y100 (US$12). Hotel restaurants may be convenient but are very poor value." —Neil Oz

hours. Unless otherwise noted, the restaurants listed in this guide are open daily for lunch and dinner.

PAYING

At most restaurants you ask for the bill at the end of the meal, like you do back home. At cheap noodle bars and street stands you often pay up front. Only very upmarket restaurants accept payment by credit card. For guidelines on tipping *see* ⇨Tipping *below.*

CATEGORY	COST
$$$$	over Y300
$$$	Y151–Y300
$$	Y81–Y150
$	Y40–Y80
¢	under Y40

All prices are per person in yuan for a main course at dinner.

RESERVATIONS & DRESS

Regardless of where you are, it's a good idea to make a reservation if you can. In some places (Hong Kong, for example), it's expected. We only mention them specifically when reservations are essential (there's no other way you'll ever get a table) or when they are not accepted. For popular restaurants, book as far ahead as you can (often 30 days), and reconfirm as soon as you arrive. (Large parties should always call ahead to check the reservations policy.) We mention dress only when men are required to wear a jacket or a jacket and tie.

WINES, BEER & SPIRITS

Forget tea; today the people's drink of choice is beer. Massively popular amongst Chinese men, it's still a bit of a no-no for Chinese women, however. Tsingtao, China's most popular brew, is a 4%-proof lager that comes in liter bottles and is usually cheaper than water. Many other regional beers are available in Shanghai, as are international brews.

WORD OF MOUTH

Was the service stellar or not up to snuff? Did the food give you shivers of delight or leave you cold? Did the prices and portions make you happy or sad? Rate restaurants and write your own reviews in "Travel Ratings" or start a discussion about your favorite places in "Travel Talk" on www.fodors.com. Your comments might even appear in our books. Yes, you, too, can be a correspondent!

When you see "wine" on the menu, it's usually referring to sweet fruit wines or distilled rice wine. The most famous brand of Chinese liquor is Maotai, a distilled liquor ranging in strength from 35 to 53% proof. Like most firewaters, it's an acquired taste.

There are basically no licensing laws in China, so you can drink anywhere, and at any time, provided you can find somewhere open to serve you.

ELECTRICITY

The electrical current in China is 220 volts, 50 cycles alternating current (AC) so most American appliances can't be used without a transformer. A universal adapter is especially useful in China as wall outlets come in a bewildering variety of configurations: two- and three-pronged round plugs, as well as two-pronged flat sockets.

Consider making a small investment in a universal adapter, which has several types of plugs in one lightweight, compact unit. Most laptops and cell-phone chargers are dual voltage (i.e., they operate equally well on 110 and 220 volts), so require only an adapter. These days the same is true of small appliances such as hair dryers. Always check labels and manufacturer instructions to be sure. Don't use 110-volt outlets marked FOR SHAVERS ONLY for high-wattage appliances such as hair dryers.

Steve Kropla's Help for World Travelers 🌐 www.kropla.com has information on electrical and telephone plugs around the world. **Walkabout Travel Gear** 🌐 www.walkabouttravelgear.com has a good coverage of electricity under "adapters."

EMERGENCIES

If you lose your passport, contact your embassy immediately.

In a medical emergency don't call for an ambulance. The Shanghai Ambulance Service is merely a transport system that takes you to the closest hospital, not the hospital of your choice. If possible, take a taxi to the hospital; you'll get there faster. The best place to head in a medical emergency is the Shanghai United Family Hospital or the World Link Medical Center, which have 24-hour emergency services (including dental) and pharmacy assistance. The Shanghai East International Medical Center has similar services but no dentistry. SOS is an international medical service that arranges Medivac. Huashan and Huadong hospitals are both local hospitals with foreigners' clinics. Although cheaper than the international clinics, their hygiene standards aren't as high.

Shanghai has different numbers for each emergency service, but staff often don't speak English. If in doubt, call the U.S. embassy first: staff members are available 24 hours a day to help handle emergencies and facilitate communication with local agencies.

Lifeline, a nonprofit support group for expatriates, operates a counseling hotline daily noon to 8 PM. The clinics and hospitals listed below have a number of English-speaking doctors on hand. At most hospitals, few staff members will speak English.

Medical Services **Huadong Hospital** ✉ Foreigners' Clinic, 2F, 221 Yanan Xi Lu, Jing'an District ☎ 021/6248-3180 Ext. 30106. **Huashan Hospital** ✉ Foreigners' Clinic, 15F, 12 Wulumuqi Zhong Lu, Jing'an District ☎ 021/6248-3986, 021/6248-9999 Ext. 2531 for 24-hour hotline. **Shanghai East International Medical Center** ✉ 551 Pudong Nan Lu., Pudong District ☎ 021/5879-9999 🌐 www.seimc.com.cn.

Shanghai United Family Health Center private ✉ 1139 Xian Zia Lu, Changning District ☎ 021/5133-1900, 021/5133-1999 emergencies 🌐 www.unitedfamilyhospitals.com. **SOS International Shanghai Office** ✉ Sun Tong Infoport Plaza, 22nd fl., Unit D-G, 55 Huaihai Xi Lu, Xuhui District ☎ 021/5298-9538 general inquiries, 021/6295-0099 emergencies 🌐 www.internationalsos.com.

World Link Medical Center ✉ Room 203, West Tower, Shanghai Center, 1376 Nanjing Xi Lu, Jing'an District 🖂 Hongqiao Clinic ✉ Mandarin City, 1F, Unit 30, 788 Hongxu Lu, Minhang District 🖂 Jian Qiao Clinic ✉ 51 Hongfeng Lu, Jian Qao, Pudong ☎ 021/6445-5999 🌐 www.worldlink-shanghai.com.

Foreign Consulates **United States Consulate** ✉ 1469 Huaihai Zhong Lu, Xuhui District ☎ 021/6433-6880, 021/6433-3936 after-hours emergencies 🖂 Citizen Services Section, Westgate Mall, 8th fl., 1038 Nanjing Xi Lu, Jing'an District ☎ 021/3217-4650 🌐 http://shanghai.usconsulate.gov.

General Emergency Contacts **Fire** ☎ 119. **International SOS Medical Services 24-hour Alarm Center** ☎ 021/6295-0099. **Police** ☎ 110, 021/6357-6666 (English). **Shanghai Ambulance Service** ☎ 120.

Hotline **Lifeline** ☎ 021/6279-8990.

Pharmacies The most reliable places to buy prescription medication is at the 24-hour pharmacy at the World Link Medical Center and the Shanghai United Family Health Center (⇨ Medical Services, *above.*). During the day, the Watson's chain is good for over-the-counter medication; there are several branches all over town.

Watson's Pharmacy ✉ Westgate Mall, 1038 Nanjing Xi Lu, Jiang'an District.

HEALTH

The most common types of illnesses are caused by contaminated food and water. Especially in developing countries, drink only bottled, boiled, or purified water and drinks; don't drink from public fountains or use ice. Tap water in Shanghai is safe for brushing teeth, but you should buy bottled water to drink. Make sure food has been thoroughly cooked and is served to you fresh and hot; avoid vegetables and fruits that you haven't washed (in bottled or purified water) or peeled yourself. If you have problems, mild cases of traveler's diarrhea may respond to Imodium (known generically as loperamide) or Pepto-Bismol. Be sure to drink plenty of fluids; if you can't keep fluids down, seek medical help immediately.

Infectious diseases can be airborne or passed via mosquitoes and ticks and through direct or indirect physical contact with animals or people. Some, including Norwalk-like viruses that affect your digestive tract, can be passed along through contaminated food. If you are traveling in an area where malaria is prevalent, use a repellant containing DEET and take malaria-prevention medication before, during, and after your trip as directed by your physician. Condoms can help prevent most sexually transmitted diseases, but they aren't absolutely reliable and their quality varies from country to country. Speak with your physician and/or check the CDC or World Health Organization Web sites for health alerts, particularly if you're pregnant, traveling with children, or have a chronic illness.

For information on travel insurance, shots and medications, and medical-assistance companies *see* Shots & Medications *under* Things to Consider *in* Before You Go, *above*.

SPECIFIC ISSUES IN SHANGHAI

Pneumonia and influenza are common among travelers returning from China—talk to your doctor about inoculations before you leave. If you need to buy prescription drugs, try to go to the pharmacies of reputable private hospitals like the World Link Medical Center. Do *not* buy them in street-side pharmacies as the quality control is unreliable. Staff at the hospitals listed here (⇨ Emergencies, *above*) speak English; indeed many doctors are expats.

OVER-THE-COUNTER REMEDIES

Most pharmacies carry over-the-counter Western medicines and traditional Chinese medicines. By and large, you need to ask for the generic name of the drug you're looking for, not a brand name. Oral contraceptives are also available without prescription, but quality in regular pharmacies varies.

HOURS OF OPERATION

Most offices are open between 9 and 6 on weekdays; most museums keep roughly the same hours but 6 or 7 days a week. Everything in China grinds to a halt for the first two or three days of Chinese New Year (sometime in mid-January through February), and opening hours are often reduced for the rest of that season.

Banks and government offices are open weekdays 9 to 5, although some close for lunch (sometime between noon and 2). Bank branches and China Travel Service (CTS) tour desks in hotels often keep longer hours and are usually open Saturday (and occasionally even Sunday) mornings. Many hotel currency-exchange desks stay open 24 hours.

Pharmacies are open daily from 8:30 or 9 AM to 6 or 7 PM. Some large pharmacies stay open until 9 PM or even later.

Shops and department stores are generally open daily 8 to 8; some stores stay open even later in summer, in popular tourist areas, or during peak tourist season.

HOLIDAYS

National holidays include New Year's Day (January 1); Spring Festival, aka Chinese New Year (late January/early February); Qingming Jie (April 4); International Labor Day (May 1); Dragon Boat Festival (late May/early June); anniversary of the founding of the Communist Party of China (July 1); anniversary of the founding of the Chinese People's Liberation Army (August 1); and National Day—founding of the Peoples Republic of China in 1949 (October 1); Chongyang Jie or Double Ninth Festival (9th day of 9th lunar month).

MAIL

Sending international mail from China is extremely reliable. Airmail letters to any place in the world should take 5 to 14 days. Express Mail Service (EMS) is available to many international destinations. Letters within Shanghai arrive the next day, and mail to the rest of China takes a day or two longer. Domestic mail can be subject to search so don't send sensitive materials, such as religious or political literature, as you might cause the recipient trouble.

Service is more reliable if you mail letters from post offices rather than mailboxes. Buy envelopes here too, as there are standardized sizes in China. You need to glue stamps onto envelopes as they're not self-adhesive. Most post offices are open daily 8 to 7; many keep even longer hours. Your hotel can usually send letters for you, too.

You can use the Roman alphabet to write an address. Do not use red ink, which has a negative connotation. You must also include a six-digit zip code for mail within China. The Shanghai municipality's postal code is 200000, and each of the city's districts differs in the fifth and sixth digits; for example, Xuhui district is 200030.

Sending airmail postcards costs Y4.50 and letters Y5–Y7.

> **WORD OF MOUTH**
>
> "I had a horrible experience with travellers cheques when I took a trip to Shanghai 2 years ago. Spare yourself the trouble and use an ATM card or credit card at an ATM machine. There are ATM machines everywhere in Shanghai, literally a bank on every corner. Just be sure not to lose the card." -gotekix

Forest green signs identify the many branches of China Post in Shanghai. The main post office is at 276 Suzhou Bei Lu, and there are also English-speaking staff at the Shanghai Center and Xuhui branches.

Main Branches Post Office ✉ 276 Suzhou Bei Lu, Hongkou District ✉ Shanghai Center, 1376 Nanjing Xi Lu, Jing'an District ✉ 133 Huaihai Lu, Xuhui District ☎ 021/6393-6666 Ext. 00.

SHIPPING PACKAGES

It's easy to ship packages home from China. Take what you want to send *unpacked* to the post office—everything will be sewn up officially into satisfying linen-bound packages, a service which costs a few yuan. You have to fill in lengthy forms, and enclosing a photocopy of receipts for the goods inside isn't a bad idea, as they may be opened by customs along the line. Large antiques stores often offer reliable shipping services that take care of customs in China. Large international couriers operating in Shanghai include DHL, Federal Express, and UPS. Your hotel can also arrange shipping parcels, but there's usually a hefty mark up on postal rates.

Express Services DHL ☎ 800/810-8000 🌐 www.cn.dhl.com. **FedEx** ☎ 800/988-1888 🌐 www.fedex.com. **UPS** ☎ 800/820-8388 🌐 www.ups.com.

MONEY

The easiest way to obtain Chinese currency in Shanghai is at an ATM. HSBC's machines are the most reliable. Otherwise, the best places to convert your dollars into yuan are at your hotel's front desk or a branch of a major bank, such as Bank of China, CITIC, or HSBC. All these operate with standardized government rates—anything cheaper is illegal, and thus risky. You need to present your passport to change money.

Although credit cards are gaining ground in China, for day-to-day transactions cash is definitely king. Getting change for big notes can be a problem, so try to stock up on tens and twenties when you change money.

ITEM	AVERAGE COST
Cup of coffee at Starbucks	Y25
Glass of local beer	Y30
Cheapest Metro ticket	Y3
1 km (1//2) mi taxi ride in Shanghai	Y11
Hourlong foot massage	Y50
Fake Chloé purse	Y200

Prices throughout this guide are given for adults. Substantially reduced fees are almost always available for children, students, and senior citizens.

■ TIP→ **Banks never have every foreign currency on hand, and it may take as long as a week to order. If you're planning to exchange funds before leaving home, don't wait until the last minute.**

ATMS & BANKS

Your own bank will probably charge a fee for using ATMs abroad; the foreign bank you use may also charge a fee. Nevertheless, you'll usually get a better rate of exchange at an ATM than you will at a currency-exchange office or even when changing money in a bank. And extracting funds as you need them is a safer option than carrying around a large amount of cash.

■ TIP→ **PIN numbers with more than four digits are not recognized at ATMs in many countries. If yours has five or more, remember to change it before you leave.**

ATMs are widespread in Shanghai and rates are as good, if not better, than at exchange desks. The most reliable ATMs are HSBC's. They also have the highest withdrawal limit, which offsets the transaction charge. Of the Chinese banks, your best bet for ATMs is the Bank of China, which accepts most foreign cards. That said, machines frequently refuse to give cash for mysterious reasons. Move on and try another. On-screen instructions appear automatically in English.

CREDIT CARDS

In Shanghai, American Express, MasterCard, and Visa are accepted at most major hotels and a growing number of upmarket stores and restaurants. Diners Club is accepted at many hotels and some restaurants.

Throughout this guide, the following abbreviations are used: **AE,** American Express; **DC,** Diners Club; **MC,** MasterCard; and **V,** Visa.

It's a good idea to inform your credit-card company before you travel, especially if you're going abroad and don't travel internationally very often. Otherwise, the credit-card company might put a hold on your card owing to unusual activity—not a good thing halfway through your trip. Record all your credit-card numbers—as well as the phone numbers to call if your cards are lost or stolen—in a safe place, so you're prepared should something go wrong. Both MasterCard and Visa have general numbers you can call (collect if you're abroad) if your card is lost, but you're better off calling the number of your issuing bank, since MasterCard and Visa usually just transfer you to your bank; your bank's number is usually printed on your card.

If you plan to use your credit card for cash advances, you'll need to apply for a PIN at least two weeks before your trip. Although it's usually cheaper (and safer) to use a credit card abroad for large purchases (so you can cancel payments or be reimbursed if there's a problem), note that some credit-card companies *and* the banks that issue them add substantial percentages to all foreign transactions, whether they're in a foreign currency or not. Check on these fees before leaving home, so there won't be any surprises when you get the bill.

■ TIP→ **Before you charge something, ask the merchant whether or not he or she plans to do a dynamic currency conversion (DCC). In such a transaction the credit-card *processor***

WORST-CASE SCENARIO

All your money and credit cards have just been stolen. In these days of real-time transactions, this isn't a predicament that should destroy your vacation. First, report the theft of the credit cards. Then get any traveler's checks you were carrying replaced. This can usually be done almost immediately, provided that you kept a record of the serial numbers separate from the checks themselves. If you bank at a large international bank like Citibank or HSBC, go to the closest branch; if you know your account number, chances are you can get a new ATM card and withdraw money right away. **Western Union** (☎ 800/325-6000 🌐 www.westernunion.com) sends money almost anywhere. Have someone back home order a transfer online, over the phone, or at one of the company's offices, which is the cheapest option. The U.S. State Department's **Overseas Citizens Services** (☎ 202/647-5225) can wire money to any U.S. consulate or embassy abroad for a fee of $30. Just have someone back home wire money or send a money order or cashier's check to the United States Department of State, which will then disburse the funds as soon as the next working day after it receives them.

(shop, restaurant, or hotel, not Visa or MasterCard) converts the currency and charges you in dollars. In most cases you'll pay the merchant a 3% fee for this service in addition to any credit-card company and issuing-bank foreign-transaction surcharges.

Dynamic currency conversion programs are becoming increasingly widespread. Merchants who participate in them are supposed to ask whether you want to be charged in dollars or the local currency, but they don't always do so. And even if they do offer you a choice, they may well avoid mentioning the additional surcharges. The good news is that you *do* have a choice. And if this practice really gets your goat, you can avoid it entirely thanks to American Express; with its cards, DCC simply isn't an option.

Reporting Lost Cards **American Express** ☎ 800/992-3404 in the U.S. or 336/393-1111 collect from abroad 🌐 www.americanexpress.com. **Diners Club** ☎ 800/234-6377 in the U.S. or 303/799-1504 collect from abroad 🌐 www.dinersclub.com. **MasterCard** ☎ 800/622-7747 in the U.S., 636/722-7111 collect from abroad or 010/800-110-7309 in China. 🌐 www.mastercard.com. **Visa** ☎ 800/847-2911 in the U.S. or 410/581-9994 collect from abroad, 010/800-711-2911 in China 🌐 www.visa.com.

CURRENCY & EXCHANGE

The Chinese currency is officially called the yuan (Y), and is also known as *renminbi* (RMB), or "People's Money." You may also hear it called *kuai,* an informal expression like "buck." It's pegged to the dollar at around Y8.

Both old and new styles of bills circulate simultaneously in China, and many denominations have both coins and bills. The Bank of China issues bills in denominations of 1 (burgundy), 2 (green), 5 (brown or purple), 10 (turquoise), 20 (brown), 50 (blue or occasionally yellow), and 100 (red). There are 1-yuan coins, too. The yuan subdivides into 10-cent units called *jiao*or *mao*; these come in bills and coins of 1, 2, and 5. The smallest denomination is the *fen,* which comes in coins (and occasionally tiny notes) of 1, 2, and 5. Counterfeiting is rife in China, and even small stores inspect notes with ultraviolet lamps. Change can be a problem—don't expect much success paying for a Y13 purchase with a Y100 note, for example.

Exchange rates in China are fixed by the government daily, so it's equally good at branches of the Bank of China, at big department stores, or at your hotel's exchange desk, which have the added advantage of often being open 24 hours a day. Any lower rates are illegal, so you're exposing yourself to scams. A passport is required to change money.

Hold on to your exchange receipt, which you need to convert your extra yuan back into dollars.

TIP→ Even if a currency-exchange booth has a sign promising no commission, rest assured that there's some kind of huge, hidden fee. (Oh . . . that's right. The sign didn't say no *fee*.) And as for rates, you're almost always better off getting foreign currency at an ATM or exchanging money at a bank.

TRAVELER'S CHECKS & CARDS

Most hotels don't accept traveler's checks as payment, and only some branches of the Bank of China exchange them, usually at a worse rate than cash.

If you must get traveler's checks, AmEx is better known and more widely accepted; you can also avoid hefty surcharges by cashing AmEx checks at AmEx offices. Whatever you do, keep track of all the serial numbers in case the checks are lost or stolen.

American Express now offers a stored-value card called a Travelers Cheque Card, which you can use wherever American Express credit cards are accepted, including ATMs. The card can carry a minimum of $300 and a maximum of $2,700, and it's a very safe way to carry your funds. Although you can get replacement funds in 24 hours if your card is lost or stolen, it doesn't really strike us as a very good deal. In addition to a high initial cost ($14.95 to set up the card, plus $5 each time you "reload"), you still have to pay a 2% fee for each purchase in a foreign currency (similar to that of any credit card). Further, each time you use the card in an ATM you pay a transaction fee of $2.50 on top of the 2% transaction fee for the conversion—add it all up and it can be considerably more than you would pay when simply using your own ATM card. Regular traveler's checks are just as secure and cost less.

American Express ☎ 888/412-6945 in the U.S., 801/945-9450 collect outside of the U.S. to add value or speak to customer service 🌐 www.americanexpress.com.

RESTROOMS

Public restrooms abound in Shanghai—the street, parks, restaurants, department stores, and major tourist attractions are all likely locations. Most charge a small fee (usually less than Y1), but seldom provide Western-style facilities or private booths. Instead, expect squat toilets, open troughs, and rusty spigots; WC signs at intersections point the way to these facilities. Toilet paper or tissues and antibacterial hand wipes are good things to have in your day pack. The restrooms in the newest shopping plazas, fast-food outlets, and deluxe restaurants catering to foreigners are generally on par with American restrooms.

Find a Loo The Bathroom Diaries 🌐 www.thebathroomdiaries.com is flush with unsanitized info on restrooms the world over—each one located, reviewed, and rated.

SAFETY

There is little violent crime against tourists in China, partly because the penalties are severe for those who are caught—China's yearly death-sentence tolls run into the thousands. Single women can move about Shanghai without too much hassle. Handbag-snatching and pickpocketing do happen in markets and on crowded buses or trains—keep an eye open and your money safe and you should have no problems. Use the safe in your hotel room to store any valuables, but always carry your passport with you for identification purposes.

Shanghai is full of people looking to make a quick buck. The most common scam involves people persuading you to go with them for a tea ceremony, which is often so pleasant that you don't smell a rat until several hundred dollars appear on your credit-card bill. "Art students" who pressure you into buying work is another common scam. The same rules that apply to hostess bars worldwide are also true in Shanghai. Avoiding such scams is as easy as refusing *all* unsolicited services—be it from taxi or pedicab drivers, tour guides, or potential "friends."

Shanghai traffic is as manic as it looks, and survival of the fittest (or the biggest) is the main rule. Crossing streets can be an extreme sport. Drivers rarely give pedestrians the right-of-way and don't even look for pedestrians when making a right turn on a red light. Cyclists have less power but are just as aggressive.

Shanghai's severely polluted air can bring on, or aggravate, respiratory problems. If you're a sufferer, take the cue from locals, who wear surgical masks, or a scarf or bandana as protection.

■ TIP→ **Distribute your cash, credit cards, I.D.s, and other valuables between a deep front pocket, an inside jacket or vest pocket, and a hidden money pouch. Don't reach for the money pouch once you're in public.**

TAXES

There is no sales tax in China. Hotels charge a 5% tax; bigger, joint-venture hotels also add a 10% to 15% service fee. Some restaurants charge a 10% service fee.

A departure tax of Y50 (about $6) for domestic flights and Y90 (about $11) for international flights (including flights to Hong Kong and Macau) must be paid in cash, in dollars or yuan, at the airport. People holding diplomatic passports, passengers in transit who stop over for less than 24 hours, and children under 12 are exempt from the departure tax.

TIME

Shanghai is 8 hours ahead of GMT, 13 hours ahead of New York, 14 hours ahead of Chicago, and 16 hours ahead of Los Angeles. There's no daylight saving time, so subtract an hour in summer.

TIPPING

Tipping is a tricky issue in China. It's officially forbidden by the government, and locals simply don't do it. In general, follow their lead without qualms. Nevertheless, the practice is beginning to catch on, especially amongst tour guides, who often expect Y10 a day. Official China Travel Service representatives aren't allowed to accept tips, but you can give them candy, T-shirts, and other small gifts. You don't need to tip in restaurants or in taxis—many drivers insist on handing over your change, however small.

INDEX

PHOTO CREDITS

Cover Photo (Nanjing Street): *Alex Mares-Manton/Asia Images/Getty Images*. 5, *Peter Adams/age fotostock*. **Chapter 1: Experience Shanghai:** 9, *Justin Guariglia/age fotostock*. 12 (left), *Wolfgang Kaehler/Alamy*. 12 (top right), *JLImages/Alamy*. 12 (bottom center), *China National Tourist Office*. 12 (bottom right), *Cui Youli/age fotostock*. 13 (top left), *Sylvain Grandadam/age fotostock*. 13 (bottom left), *Dennix Cox/Alamy*. 13 (top center), *Ulana Switucha/Alamy*. 13 (right), *Sylvain Grandadam/age fotostock*. 14-15, *ImagineChina*. 16, *Pat Behnke/Alamy*. 17, *Ulana Switucha/Alamy*. 18, *Peter Adams/age fotostock*. 19, *ImagineChina*. 20-21, *ImagineChina*. 22 (top), *Mary Evans Picture Library/Alamy*. 22 (bottom), *ImagineChina*. 23 (top), *José Fuste Raga/age fotostock*. 23 (bottom), *P. Narayan/age fotostock*. 24, *Robert Harding Picture Library Ltd/Alamy*. 25, *ImagineChina*. 26-27, *SuperStock/age fotostock*. 28-29, *ImagineChina*. 30 (left and top right), ImagineChina. 30 (bottom right), *Bruno Perousse/age fotostock*. **Chapter 2: Neighborhoods:** 35, *Rafael Macia/age fotostock*. 39, *Michele Falzone/Alamy*. 41, *Elyse Singleton*. 44-47, *ImagineChina*. 50, *SuperStock/age fotostock*. 53, *Martin Norris/Alamy*. 56, *ImagineChina*. 59, *Martyn Vickery/Alamy*. 61, *Mehdi Chebil/Alamy*. 63, *ImagineChina*. 65, *SuperStock/age fotostock*. 66 (top right), *José Fuste Raga/age fotostock*. 66 (bottom right), *Mary Evans Picture Library/Alamy*. 67 (top left), *China National Tourist Office*. 67 (bottom left), *Visual Arts Library (London)/Alamy*. 67 (right), *Panorama Media (Beijing) Ltd./Alamy*. 68 (left), *Popperfoto/Alamy*. 68 (top right), *Eddie Gerald/Alamy*. 68 (bottom right), *North Wind Picture Archives/Alamy*. 69 (left), *Beaconstox/Alamy*. 69 (top right), *Bruno Perousse/age fotostock*. 70 (left), *Kevin O'Hara/age fotostock*. 70 (bottom right), *A.H.C./age fotostock*. 71 (top left), *Tramonto/age fotostock*. 71 (bottom left), *ImagineChina*. 71 (right), *Iain Masterton/Alamy*. 72, *AM Corporation/Alamy*. 75, *ImagineChina*. 78, *Tibor Bognar/Alamy*. 81, *ImagineChina*. 84, *Giles Robberts/Alamy*. 87, *ImagineChina*. **Chapter 3: Shopping:** 89-90, *ImagineChina*. 91 (top), *Sylvain Grandadam/age fotostock*. 91 (bottom), *ImagineChina*. 92, *ImagineChina*. 103, *ImagineChina*. 104 (top and center), *Elyse Singleton*. 104 (bottom), *Pat Behnke/Alamy*. 105 (top left), *Elyse Singleton*. 105 (top right), *ImagineChina*. 105 (bottom left), *ImagineChina*. 105 (bottom right), *Elyse Singleton*. 106 (top), *Kevin O'Hara/age fotostock*. 106 (bottom), *Pixonnet.com/Alamy*. 107 (left), *ImagineChina*. 107 (right), *Ulana Switucha/Alamy*. 108, *Elyse Singleton*. **Chapter 4: Arts & Nightlife:** 117-19, *ImagineChina*. **Chapter 5: Where to Eat:** 135-36, ImagineChina. 137, *Tina Manley/Alamy*. 138, *ImagineChina*. 145, *Peter Adams/age fotostock*. 146 (both), *ImagineChina*. 147 (left), *ImagineChina*. 147 (top right), *JTB Photo/Alamy*. 147 (bottom right), *Iain Masterton/Alamy*. 148 (top), *ImagineChina*. 148 (bottom), *Profimedia. CZ S.r.o./Alamy*. 149 (top left), *Iain Masterton/Alamy*. 149 (center left), *Tim Graham/Alamy*. 149 (bottom left), *Craig Lovell/Eagle Visions Photography/Alamy*. 149 (right), *Cephas Picture Library/Alamy*. 150 (top and bottom left), *ImagineChina*. 150 (top right), *Doug Scott/age fotostock*. 150 (bottom right), *ImagineChina*. **Chapter 6: Where to Stay:** 171, *Starwood Hotels & Resorts*. 173, *Regent Hotels & Resorts*. **Chapter 7: Side Trips:** 197, *Dennis Cox/Alamy*. 200, *Hemis/Alamy*. 212, *La Belle Aurore/Alamy*. 213, *Wojtek Buss/age fotostock*. 214 (top), *Wojtek Buss/age fotostock*. 214 (bottom), *blaneyphoto/iStockphoto*. 215 (top and center), *ImagineChina*. 215 (bottom), *Serge Kozak/age fotostock*. 216-17, *helloyiying/iStockphoto*. 235, *Juan Carlos Muñoz/age fotostock*.

ABOUT OUR WRITERS

Having lived and traveled throughout China for the past five years, **David Taylor** has spent the last three working as a writer and editor, mostly in the fields of travel, hospitality, and food and beverage. Although Shanghai has developed a superb fine-dining scene, he is still more often to be found hunched over *gou bao rou* and *jiaozi* at his favorite Dongbei restaurant than sipping champagne over the Bund. David updated the dining chapter of this guide.

Victoria Patience grew up in Hong Kong, and she's never stopped calling Asia home. Her first solo trip was through China, at age 16, and she's been fascinated with the country ever since. A train ride from Hong Kong took her all the way to London, where she studied Spanish and Latin American literature. She now lives in Buenos Aires but returns to Asia regularly. Victoria updated the Essentials chapter.

A resident of Shanghai since 1998, **Lisa Movius** has written extensively about China's contemporary art, culture, society, and economy. She contributes regularly to the *Asian Wall Street Journal*, *Art in America*, and *Women's Wear Daily*, as well as *The New Republic*, *The Guardian*, and *Salon.com*. Lisa is originally from San Diego and graduated from Brown University. She updated the Arts & Nightlife chapter.

Elyse Singleton has been living in Shanghai since 2001. Her work has appeared in the *Shanghai Star*, the *Sydney Morning Herald*, and Shanghai's leading English language magazine *that's Shanghai*. She has traveled extensively through China as a writer and photographer. Elyse wrote the Experience, Neighborhoods, and Shopping chapters, as well as the Markets piece.

Rachel King Berlin has danced with the Shanghai Theatre Academy and the Zhuheniao Dance Collective, managed the largest contemporary art gallery in China, and traveled by train in hard sleeper all over China. As a resident of Shanghai, Rachel tuned up her Mandarin skills, learned the fine art of haggling, and completed her quest to find the perfect dumpling. Rachel wrote the lodging chapter for this guide.